MONSTER! ISSUE 31

MONSTER! CONTAINS PHOTOS, DRAWINGS, AND ILLUSTRATIONS INCLUDED FOR THE PURPOSE OF CRITICISM AND DOCUMENTATION. ALL PICTURES COPYRIGHTED BY RESPECTIVE AUTHORS, PRODUCTION COMPANIES AND/OR COPYRIGHT HOLDERS.

EDITORIALIZING

Andy Ross

VICTORIAN VALUES
& VIDEO NASTIES

THE BEYOND

Here in the UK, we're about to wave goodbye the oh-so-fleeting British summertime and are all set to enter the crisp, golden depths of Autumn once more. Thankfully, before Christmas once again thrusts its fiscal excess upon us, we still have the one-stop hiatus of Halloween to look forward to. A seasonal celebration of all things grotesque and macabre, the long-established stateside tradition of "Trick or Treat" is still a relatively new one on this side of the Atlantic. Back in the day—well, back in *my* day, anyway (by which I mean the mid-1970s)—as a yearly fixture, Halloween was to pass by almost unnoticed. Whilst we regularly crafted costumes for ourselves (largely out of plastic bin-bags!) and set out on a door-to-door pilgrimage, the most we ever got out of Halloween was maybe an apple, a couple of ten-pence pieces and a whole *LOT* of verbal abuse. Suffice to say, times were very different back then. In the days before the PC/Mac, the digital disc and the cell-phone, the methods by which we kept ourselves amused may well seem archaic by contemporary standards.

Whilst most kids possessed some form of push-bike (and latterly, a skateboard) those that didn't at the very least owned a football. *[That's a so-called "soccer" ball to our American readers! – SF.]* For the normal everyday kids of the time, games of tag, playing "armies" (wherein some smartarse always had "just one last grenade" to lob) and "jumpers for goalposts" footie *[a.k.a "soccer" in N. America! – SF]* were to prove amusement enough (at least until puberty kicked in).

On the *other* side of the coin—largely outcast from juvenile society and, as such, invariably entombed within the confines of their own bedroom—there existed the *weird* kids like me. In what was an exclusively working-class environment, "weird" was a label widely reserved for those who pursued far-less-physical activities. In my case, it was used to describe a socially awkward child who, besides being terrible at sports, knew far too much than was healthy about horror films. A fascination kindled by the BBC2 "Horror Double

Bill" *[I remember those!* ☺ – SF], fueled by Forry Ackerman's *Famous Monsters of Filmland*, and finally set ablaze by the small-screen adaptation of Stephen King's *Salem's Lot* (1979, USA, D: Tobe Hooper), by the 1980s, the widespread availability of the Video Cassette Recorder (VCR)—first Betamax, then VHS—was to turn a passing interest into something of a bizarre obsession. Prior to the advent of the VCR, British monster kids could only access material that programmers and parents considered appropriate and, as such, it deigned to put us way behind everyone else. Whilst the monstrous stable of Universal, Hammer, AIP, and Amicus were frequently featured in the Saturday night double-headers, the more "risqué" European offerings—those of Rollin, Franco and Bava *et al*—never once saw the light of day. Even the Toho productions that featured the king of the monsters himself, Godzilla, were something of a rarity on British television screens.

By this observance alone, one is drawn to presume that foreign films (particularly those hailing from France and Italy) were widely regarded as unsuitable for UK audiences. Desperately observing an outmoded belief in Victorian values, censorship in the British Isles was among the most archaic in Western society. Forged from an opinion that the lower classes were inherently unable to differentiate between fact and fiction, this bloody-minded attitude was to provide the foundation for Mary Whitehouse's moral rights campaign. Perhaps more so in England, the increasing popularity of the VCR coupled with unregulated access to allegedly "unsuitable" film material was to mirror the moralistic backlash that Bill Gaines' EC Comics had endured some three decades earlier. Keenly supported by Margaret Thatcher's Conservative Government, in 1984 the controversial Video Recordings Act was summarily brought into being. Swiftly adopted by the sensationalist media and labeled the "video nasties", of the many titles that were deemed illegal either to own or disseminate were **ZOMBIE FLESH EATERS** (*Zombi 2*, a.k.a. **ZOMBIE**, 1979, Italy, D: Lucio Fulci), **CANNIBAL APOCALYPSE** (*Apocalypse domani*, 1980, Italy, D: Antonio Margheriti), **THE LAST HOUSE ON THE LEFT** (1972, USA, D: Wes Craven), **TENEBRAE** (1982, Italy, D: Dario Argento) and **I SPIT ON YOUR GRAVE** (1978, USA, D: Meir Zarchi).

As with Gaine's lurid comic books, in the British Board of Film Censors (BBFC)'s eyes, the video nasty was virtually entirely responsible for all the ills in contemporaneous society. Stranger still were the number of "mainstream" horror films (many of which are widely considered as modern-day

If you've never seen Fulci's 1979 horror classic, this mock lobby card by Silver Ferox Design gives you some idea what all the fuss was about!

3

IF ONLY THEY WOULD DIE...
HELL OF THE LIVING DEAD
Regie di VINCENT DAWN

Ditto for this one by the same designer for Bruno Mattei's 1980 zombie gut-cruncher, which was released as **ZOMBIE CREEPING FLESH** in guest editorializer Andy R's neck of the world

classics) that were either removed from circulation or hacked to pieces by the censors. Among this secondary batch of "distasteful" movies were listed **THE BEYOND** (*...E tu vivrai nel terrore! L'aldilà*, 1981, Italy, D: Lucio Fulci), **DEAD AND BURIED** (1981, USA, D: Gary Sherman), **THE EVIL DEAD** (1981, USA, D: Sam Raimi), **THE EXORCIST** (1973, USA, D: William Friedkin) and **POSSESSION** (1981, France/West Germany, D: Andrej Zulawski). Turning a blind eye to industrial decay, mass unemployment and inner city social tensions, insofar as the tabloid media of the day was concerned, it was the video nasty that embodied the root of all evil. In retrospect (given the rather ruthless nature of Thatcher's government) one can't help but suggest that the furor whipped-up by the video nasties outrage was a genuine godsend for the so-called "Iron Maiden". Whilst her government continued to pummel the trade unions and sell out the country's public services through privatization, the argument over the video nasty was to proffer a timely and somewhat convenient distraction.

As the 1980s drew to a close, titles that had been withdrawn from the domestic marketplace were steadily awarded a new lease of life on the big screen. Upon watching the film for the first time as a 23-year-old, whilst I might have arrived late to **THE EXORCIST**'s party, the film's effect was to prove nonetheless absorbing. Truth be told, it wasn't until the dawn of the new millennium that British horror fans were given the opportunity to

make up for lost time, and a major player in the relaxation of UK censorship laws was to come by means of the home computer. With previously banned or censored films now readily available from overseas markets, the emergence of the internet was to severely undermine the authority of the BBFC. With the relaxation of censorship laws following in 1999 (a move which also made hardcore pornography legally available for the first time ever on British shores), the BBFC were to revisit films that had suffered immeasurably under their previous incarnation. With Gaspar Noé's **IRREVERSIBLE** (2002, France), Lars Von Trier's **ANTICHRIST** (2009, Denmark/France/Germany/Italy/Poland/Sweden) and Tom Six's **THE HUMAN CENTIPEDE (FIRST SEQUENCE)** (2009, Netherlands) released uncut in UK cinemas, the heavy veil that once hung over contentious film had finally been lifted. A culturally significant event, and one that was to witness such titles as **THE WITCH WHO CAME FROM THE SEA** (1976, USA, D: Matt Cimber) and **ZOMBIE CREEPING FLESH** (*Virus: L'inferno dei morti viventi*, a.k.a. **HELL OF THE LIVING DEAD**, 1980, Italy/Spain, D: Bruno Mattei) occupying shelf space in the high street DVD store, the only real dilemma that now faced British genre fans was finding the time to catch up with them all!

Placing my love of horror cinema to one side for a moment (and trust me, we are going somewhere with this), a secondary escape for my younger self was drawing silly pictures. Heavily influenced by the larger-than-life adventures of Marvel's canon of spandex-clad avengers, almost as soon as I could grasp a pencil, every spare minute I had was dedicated towards honing my skills as an artist. Essentially self-taught, whilst my secondary (read: high) school art teachers frowned upon my increasingly macabre renderings (I had absolutely no interest in painting trees or bowls of fruit!), I carried on with a bloody-minded disregard. Loaning my rudimentary skills to such varied projects as theatrical backdrops, local advertising and tee-shirt design, in 2003 I allied myself to the growing indie comics scene based in Newcastle-upon-Tyne. Invited to submit a series of short strips by (the now) US-based graphic artist Leonie O'Moore (*Heavy Metal*), if there was one thing my tenure on *There Goes Tokyo* taught me, it was that fans made for the most enthusiastic of creators.

Which, in a roundabout way, brings me to my current involvement in *Monster!* Returning to the big bad world following a 22-year stint in the British Armed Forces, what struck me more than anything was the fact that I no longer felt part of a wider family. Kicking my heels and drifting from one job to another (before curiously settling into a phlebotomy role), an invitation from Dawn Dabell to submit some artwork for issue 2 of *Multitude of Movies* was to reignite that sense of camaraderie. With this issue marking my tenth involvement as artist/contributor, I feel rather honored to be in a position to pen this month's (this *bi*-month's?) editorial. As someone who believed themselves to be in possession of an intimate knowledge of the horror genre, *Monster!* has proved time and time again just how delusional I am! What never ceases to amaze me about *Monster!* is the vibrancy and diversity that comes free with every issue. From Tim Paxton's ongoing romance with the colorful world of Indian and Pakistani cinema through to periodic contributor Troy Howarth's boundless enthusiasm for mainland Euro-horror, *Monster!* remains one of the few genre titles that regularly brings a little bit of everything for everyone. Duly observing that mantra, this month's double-sized issue features a veritable smorgasbord of monstrous articles and reviews. Besides Stephen Bissette exploring the realms of the TV phenomenon *Stranger Things* and providing an insightful interview with comics artist Jason Shiga, there's also Tim Paxton observing the Hindi horror **VEERANA** (1988, India, D: The Ramsay Brothers) and Steve Fenton's retrospective of the Mexican Neutron saga, while Grand Poobah Brian Harris dares to flip the lid on that heinous beastie otherwise known as **BASKET CASE** (1982, USA, D: Frank Henenlotter) to review its pair of so-so sequels, plus much more besides.

Add to this the customary review section, a wealth of illustrative titillation, and the ever-invaluable monstrous movie check-list (with bonus "hot off the presses" video availability info), and what could possibly compliment your selection of DVD/Blu-ray Halloween horrors than this gloriously gargantuan issue of *Monster!*?

Yes indeed, folks, Halloween is once again upon us. As one of the few times of the year wherein the young at heart get to dress up and be equally as mischievous as their little darlings, in the UK we're now every bit as sold on Halloween as our American and Canadian cousins long have been. With hastily-adapted "bin-bag" costumes resigned to the rubbish heap where they belong, today's tiny terrors have no end of festive wardrobe to choose from. From classical witches and demons through to superheroes, science fiction baddies and outer space aliens, that the chain-stores these days prepare themselves well in advance for the excitable onslaught proves just how far we've evolved in the last 40 years. Whilst I may not be donning suitable attire and joining in with the "trick or treat" brigade, as a 50-year-old who vividly recalls his own fruitless childhood endeavors by way of stocking the cupboards with sugary goodness, I'm already prepared for this year's festivities. So with Halloween already taken care of, I'm left with the age-old dilemma in respect to my film viewing choices for the night in question. And out of the myriad fright features currently occupying my "must-see" list, the eternal quandary remains: *what in the holy hell should I watch now?!*

WANTED! More Readers Like John L. Vellutini's domesticated *bakeneko*, Olie

THE HOUSE OF RAMSAY

by Tim Paxton & Kinshuk Gaur

SAI OM PRODUCTIONS

F.U. RAMSAY PRESENTS

TULSI RAMSAY & SHYAM RAMSAY'S

VEERANA

वीराना

DIRECTED BY
TULSI RAMSAY & SHYAM RAMSAY • MUSIC **BAPPI LAHIRI** • PRODUCED BY **KANTA RAMSAY** AND **ANJALI RAMSAY**

Promotional pressbook artwork

"The public comes to see ghosts in the movie... and we had our first 15 minutes in public once, showing the ghost"
~ *Tulsi Ramsay*

The story of this film is based on fiction. This is a fictitious story influenced by old folklores. In this film, evil powers like ghosts, spirits, witches and black magic have been mentioned that have no connection with today's reality. Viewers should watch this film only for entertainment. This film has no connection with reality.
– From **VEERANA**'s pre-credits disclaimer c/o the Censor Board, which puts the kibosh on any superstitious beliefs which the film might encourage

By now regular readers of *Monster!* have no doubt found themselves familiarized with India's self-proclaimed "Kings of Horror Cinema", a.k.a. the Ramsay Family. Over the course of this mag's run thus far, all of the Ramsays' creature features (even the unreleased 1982 **MAUT KA SAYA**) have variously been covered to some degree in one manner or another, by way of numerous reviews and articles. With this entry from "The House of Ramsay", we have saved what is the brothers' most accomplished work for last: **VEERANA**, which was made in 1985 but was held up for three years due to censorship problems (more about that later).

Now, before I give away any details about it, I'll let my collaborator Kinshuk share his own personal views on the film:

"*VEERANA was the only Ramsay movie that I ever got a chance to watch in a cinema hall. Although I never got to see it on its original 1988 release, I remember when I was in school it was rescreened at one of the cinemas in the town around 1997 (now that town has developed into a city and converted to a state capital). At the time, this particular cinema hall was a sleazy one, which* used to repeat popular old B and C grade movies from years past; and, to add, it was the period of single-screen cinema. Times have changed, and this theatre has been renovated and now screens new movies. It is comforting to perceive a single screen-theatre holding itself against multiscreen cinema. I still remember the audience reaction for the two key scenes. The first was Sameer (Vijayendra Ghatge)'s initial ploy to find and hunt down the witch Nakita, which also showcases a steamy scene between Vijayendra and the witch Kamal Roy. This scene opened with loud whistles and shouts in the cinema hall. The second beging when Vijay Arora being seduced by Jasmin and then getting killed. This was one of the most sizzling and erotic scenes in the movie. When viewed by the audience in the cinema hall it was with a pin-drop silence*".

VEERANA is by far one of the best-produced horror films ever helmed by the Ramsays.[1] Some consider that it is also the very pinnacle of Hindi

---

1   They also made non-horror films—more simple thrillers than all-out chillers—some of which which are very good; my favorite of them being **GHUNGROO KI AWAAZ** (1981), which stars Rekha and was "inspired" by Alfred Hitchcock's **VERTIGO** (1958, USA).

SAI OM PRODUCTIONS F.U. RAMSAY PRESENTS

TULSI RAMSAY & SHYAM RAMSAY'S

VEERANA

DIRECTED BY TULSI RAMSAY & SHYAM RAMSAY ● MUSIC BAPPI LAHIRI ● LYRICS INDIVAR ● ANJAAN ● PHOTOGRAPHY GANGU RAMSAY ● KANTA RAMSAY AND PRODUCED BY ANJALI RAMSAY

Business As Usual: India's crazy mixed-up cut-and-paste lobby cards often rival those of the Japanese brand, which scaled the heights of zaniness in the 1960s and '70s with their promotional materials for *Godzilla* films, etc.

horror cinema, although critics are divided on this matter, as we do also have Ram Gopal Varma's 1992 **RAAT** in stiff competition with it for the top spot. Then there are the best of the country's numerous film industries to consider; but for simplicity's sake we will stay on the Bollywood path (i.e., in the Hindi industry) and not stray off into the cinematic output shot in any of the many other languages indigenous to the subcontinent, each of which have their own separate industries. Although parts of **VEERANA** are highly derivative of other horror films, such as **THE EXORCIST** (1973, USA) and any number of Italian "rip-off" possession flicks from the '70s besides, Ramsay movies are more the filmic cousins of England's fog-thick Hammer Studios and Italian Mario Bava's generally low-budget-but-essential fare. Yes, the Ramsays did so love recreating/replicating their inspiration sources, sometimes at a scene-to-scene level.[2]

The film features a group of cloaked magicians with giant, prune-like heads who sit around a table in an underground dungeon silently rocking back and forth; a manic *tantrik* who dabbles in the black arts; a ghost-witch of the type that is commonly called a *chudail* (a.k.a. *churel* or *cudel*); as well as a half-dozen other derivatives

acquired from all across the subcontinent, from down at its southernmost tip to way up in the North, where **VEERANA** was made. In the past, *Monster!* has reviewed an assortment of Indian films in which such undead zombie witches have made their presences known. Shyam and Tulsi took a cue from folklore and spiced-up their film by having the sinful witch's legs do a 180-degree rotation before she offs the tourist who offered her lift (such a feet [sic; pun intended!] also features briefly in Ram Gopal Varma's **DEYYAM** [1996]), and such a "foot-reversing" phenomenon is often reported with "actual" sightings of *chudail*. We can also see the filmmakers' attraction to giant statues, as depicted in Ramsay earlier horror movies. Here we witness a massive stone statue of Shaitan—which is where the name "Satan" comes from, by the way—seated atop a throne that shoots fire from his upturned palms; a prop readymade for a heavy metal album cover or "live" onstage during their tour.

There is no fooling around in this film, and what little fat that *could* be trimmed from the story are two popular elements which audiences really enjoy: those being the comedy—which is unusually tolerable, in this case—and the musical numbers, which are quite good. But is **VEERANA** the very *best* of the best...? Right from the start,

2   http://timesofindia.indiatimes.com/Ramsay-international/
articleshow/21659332.cms

the film is nothing but non-stop drama, action, sexiness and gore galore. Most importantly, as I already mentioned above, **VEERANA**, their only movie to feature a female monster, was held up for a year or more, with censors insisting on no less than *46* cuts in total, trimming out everything from the expected (i.e., shots of stripping for a bath, suggestive dialogue) to the unexpected (i.e., the brutality of the villagers needed to be toned-down some during the creature's execution scene, and the censors also ordered the removal of a shot showing a man being booted in the nuts, too).[3] Despite all this censorial reediting, the brothers just rerouted their weird sexuality even further, in the process making **VEERANA** just about as perfect as any Ramsay horror film is ever going to get.

Now that we have hopefully whetted your appetite, let's get on to our review...

VEERANA
(a.k.a. VENGEANCE OF THE VAMPIRE or CREEPY FOREST)
India, 1988

This movie was released during what at the time was the absolute aesthetic apex of Bollywood

3 http://www.filmcomment.com/blog/kaiju-shake-down-the-ramsays-of-bollywood

horror cinema. It was 1988, and **VEERANA** was sandwiched between four other classic monster movies from the Ramsays: **PURANA MANDIR** (1984), **3D SAAMRI** (1985), **TAHKHANA** (1986) and **PURANI HAVELI** (1989); yet for some reason it doesn't shine quite so brightly as the others.

After a brief introduction to the chief baddies in the film, **VEERANA** then promptly dives right into the action. A struggling, naked young man is seen chained to the floor of a dank temple, and this is where the vampiric high-priestess Nakita (Kamal Roy) first makes her appearance. And what a grand one it is! Simply by removing her fancy bat-pendant from around her neck, the gorgeous witch Nakita transforms herself into a hideous creature. This monster then wastes no time in plunging a huge blade into the justifiably terrified male captive' chest. "Today, Nakita will quench her thirst by drinking your warm blood!" cackles the coven's evil *tantrik* priest (Rajesh Vivek).

Cut to the home of local landowner Thakur Mahender Pratap Singh (Kulbhushan Kharbanda), who receives the news that the body of the murdered young man has been found hanging from a tree just outside the village; the fourth victim to be slaughtered in such a horrid matter of late. Superstitious local peasants blame a mysterious woman they have seen prowling around the village

Business Unusual: The Ramsays had a runaway hit on their hands with **VEERANA** in 1987, and it was spectacular lobby cards like this one which helped pack movie-houses to the rafters!

after nightfall. One man declares that she is a witch, and goes on to relate some tale of how she can even turn into a bat. Although Pratap Singh's brother Sameer (Vijayendra Ghatge) doesn't believe in such nonsensical superstitions, he is determined to put a stop to the mysterious killings. Pratap Singh gifts his brother with a powerful "*Om*" wand to ward off evil (just in case), and wishes him well as Sameer speeds off in his roadster.

It's not long before he discovers the enchanting Nakita wandering the forest road alone, and he pulls up beside her to offer her a ride home. They travel in silence and soon arrive at a huge mansion, where, once inside all and cozy, they decide to take a bubble bath together. While Sameer gets comfy in the tub, Nakita enters with a large towel wrapped around her. They exchange all the usual "sexy" Bollywood banter. "Free your body from these clothes," a breathless Sameer growls, "I want to understand your youth closely". She drops the towel and snuggles up to the man in the tub. "You're clinging to me the way a snake clings to a sandalwood tree." While nuzzling Nikita, Sameer notices the bat pendant around her neck. "Your skin is just like a serpent's skin. A *poisonous* serpent," he says; to which she relies playfully, "Be alert. The serpent might bite you!"

Just then Sameer snatches Nakita's bat pendant and jerks it violently from around her neck. Nakita transforms into her hideous *chudail* form, then advances to kill Sameer. Luckily, he is able to subdue her with the handy Om wand which his uncle had so fortuitously "just happened" to give him. The snarling monster is then dragged off bodily to the village square, where she is to be executed as a witch, screeching and growling all the while; they put first a hood, then a noose around her neck. Then, with little fanfare, she is hanged by the neck until dead (which makes a change from the usual burning-at-the-stake scene common to these witch's curse scenarios). Later that night after everyone is gone and while the corpse of Nakita is still hanging from the gallows, the *tantrik* and his hooded minions steal into the courtyard to cut the body down. They then spirit the deceased beastess away back to the old temple shrine, where the wizard seals it in a sarcophagus, all the while promising to provide Nakita with a new body...that of Thakur Mahendra Pratap's wholesome daughter, Jasmine!

Later that next day, Sameer offers to drop his little niece, Jasmine (played by juvie actress Baby Swati), at her

The Many Faces Of Evil: (...Well, *two* at least!) Four images of the vampiric high-priestess Nakita in her ugly phase; her normal human form was played by Kamal Roy. There has been a hotbed of discussion on a few Ramsay-related Facebook sites whether that actress herself portrayed the fully-transformed *chudail*, or if a stunt stand-in was actually under all the latex. Bottom photo is of the evil *tantrik*, played by brooding actor Rajesh Vivek

boarding school on the other side of the *veerana* ("spooky woods"; hence the title). As they enter the forest, the engine of his car overheats and dies (a popular trope in countless horror films, Indian or otherwise). Sameer then leaves the young girl alone in the car as he goes off in search of water for the radiator. It is then that Jasmine is put under a spell by the *tantrik* (who was hiding behind a tree spying on them the entire time—the scoundrel!), who then snips off a lock of her hair. Having done this, up to no good, the wily wizard scuttles back to the evil temple with it. He wraps the hair around a voodoo doll, which he then promptly pops into a bottle sealed with a lemon. Following this, he places the hex into the recently deceased Nakita's open tomb, whereupon the young girl is supernaturally drawn to the cursed temple. When Sameer discovers she has gone missing, in best hero fashion he immediately rushes to her rescue. At the temple he witnesses the demoness drawing Jasmine into her sarcophagus, at which the witch possesses the girl. Upon being surrounded by the coneheads, they beat him and drag him off. The possessed child is then returned to her family by the *tantrik*, who concocts a cover story of having discovered the young girl wandering lost. But when questioned about the child's uncle, the sneaky *baba* can only shake his head, and craftily proceeds to relate a fictitious tale of woe involving

a thunderstorm and a car crash, as a result of which Sameer's body was swept away downriver. This ruse proves successful, and the tricky *tantrik* is welcomed in Thakur Mahendra's home, where he is asked to be the young girl's spiritual guide, no less. Now all the evil wizard has to do is wait until she is old enough for his evil mistress to possess her body, thus returning to a semblance of life in her fleshly vessel.

But, as Thakur's wife (Rama Vij) notices, the child who was returned has been changed by her supernatural brush with death. The woman is worried about how oddly the girl is acting, even more so when she witnesses Jasmine killing fish using some kind of inexplicable telekinetic power (the tank explodes under her gaze!). Amongst other things, she also witnesses the kid psychically causing blood to manifest and drip from her dead uncle's photo. Hence, it's no small wonder that her suitably concerned auntie demands that the child should receive some sort of spiritual counseling for her strange behavior. Jasmine overhears this plan, following which her auntie pays the ultimate price: she is found hanging by her neck from a ceiling fan (which, for some odd reason is a highly popular method of death in Indian horror films). Thakur is horrified by this incident and sends his other niece Sahila out of harm's way

Ramsay Rival: It may not have been the first *chudail* film, but **VEERANA** was without a doubt the most influential. **HATYARIN** is an equally-cool 1991 witch film from director Vinod Talwar, the final fifteen minutes of which are some of the weirdest to be found in *all* of Indian cinema! Highly imaginative SFX and makeup create a hyperactive horror that rivals even those in some of the most insane HK and Taiwanese black magic films from the 1980s

The seductive evil of the sultry Jasmine

to Mumbai, leaving him and the baba to raise the little devil child all by themselves.

Years pass and the action jumps ahead, as it does in many Indian films, without any technical gimmicks such as a dissolve or anything else to indicate to us that time has rolled onward for its characters. In **VEERANA**, we know that has happened simply because both Thakur Mahendra and the *tantrik* both now "suddenly" have grey hair. (Not that such matters as logical time progression and pacing have ever been of much import in a Ramsay horror film anyway, as it's the monster which matters most.)

It's around this point that we are introduced to the now-grown Jasmine while she is taking a sexy bubble bath as the creepy manservant Raghu (Gulshan Grover, veteran film star of over 400 movies) tries to sneak a peek while she sings away obliviously in the bathroom. Rather than a child actress as before, Jasmine is now played by an actress known only as Jasmin, who is without a doubt one of the most mysterious and least-known actresses in all of Indian cinema. Brunette, sexy, with a piecing stare and shapely figure, the actress really captures your attention and draws you into her world; one filled with erotic desires, possession, and death. Jasmin[4]—her mononym (something

which many, *many* Indian actors, directors and singers use)—is still as much of a mystery today as she was when **VEERANA** was originally released some three years after it was in the can (something we will go into more later). Though this was not her first movie, as mentioned by *India Today* in a 1988 article, Jasmin—her name notwithstanding—is as fresh as a daisy; or so the sexy young thing, 36-26-36 and 5' 5", would have us believe. Her first films were made by director N.D. Kothari: the 1979 drama **SARKARI MEHMAAN**, a cop thriller co-starring Vinod Khanna and Amjad Kahn; and **DIVORCE**, a 1984 romantic drama in which she appeared as a second-tier player. **SARKARI MEHMAAN** was not well received, so Jasmin went back to her college studies and then tried modeling for a spell before returning to film with a vengeance.

"If the leading man is able to excite me, I don't mind kissing him", purred Jasmin, who has already bagged a film with handsome leading actor Dharmendra. "I'm even willing to shed my clothes if I get a director like Raj Kapoor."[5]

---

4   This habit of using a single moniker as name-branding (think Prince, Madonna, etc.) is wonderful if you happen to hit the big time and strike it rich in the world of entertainment. If not, then a mononymous name makes gathering any kind of information about more obscure personalities

most difficult indeed. This especially holds true for someone like Jasmin, who made only three known films before vanishing. To make matters worse, there is a new rising star in the word of Southern Cinema who also goes by the name of Jasmin. Promotional images of her charms have flooded Google to the point that digging up any information on **VEERANA**'s Jasmin is nigh-on impossible.

5   http://indiatoday.intoday.in/story/india-in-1987-major-events-and-happenings/1/192386.html

Now, just *what* makes **VEERANA** a cult classic of Indian horror is a topic for debate, although it is clear that the film does explore local folklore and features a sensuous witch named Nakita. For the 1980s horror movie scene, this latter aspect was pretty erotic stuff, but it was as classy as any filmmaker could make it (despite the cuts). It wasn't just the monster and the magic, but the gorgeous leading lady Jasmin. **VEERANA** made Jasmin an overnight star, but at a price. She oozed sexiness and animal magnetism, and **VEERANA** was to be her breakout film. But after the film was released and became a hit she abruptly vanished from the limelight.

There are all sorts of theories as to her disappearance, and the most popular one is that she was approached by the shady underworld of filmmaking and asked to perform all sorts of sexual favors. This is not that uncommon in any film industry around the world, but from reports I have read, the '80s and '90s was rife will all sorts of seedy and slimy goings-on.[6] Apparently, she asked for—but was refused assistance from—the local Maharashtra police force, and left India for the United States before she ended up being raped or worse.[7] Rumors, innuendo, hearsay and just plain false reports of her have been popping up on Indian cinema blogs for the past few years, but there has never been any real verification as to what she is us up to nowadays...if anything.

(But, back to the film at hand...) Jasmin is now full-grown, a startlingly striking raven-haired beauty. She lives with her uncle and his servants, but she is very moody and stays shut up in her bedroom most of the time. She also has a bad habit of vandalizing her room's contents, taking long baths, and wandering around in the nearby *veerana*. Worried about Jasmin's sanity, the Thakur sends for her cousin to come and visit. The two girls were close as youngsters, so maybe Sahila visiting might have a calming effect on her troubled cousin. She agrees to the visit, taking time off from her studies at college to do so. On the way to her uncle's *haveli* ("house"), Sahila runs into trouble when Zimbaru (played by an actor with the unfortunate mononym of Gorilla!), a hulking servant of the evil *baba*, attempts to kidnap her after she pulls her car over to the side of the road for a break. Luckily for her, she is rescued by the

film's male hero Hemant (played by hunky he-man Hemant Birje, fresh off his popular stint as Tarzan in Babbar Sudhash's 1985 beefcake *junglee* classic **ADVENTURES OF TARZAN**), who rightfully takes Zimbaru to task.[8]

At this point we are also introduced to **VEERANA**'s comedy relief. As one director told me a few years ago, these brief "funny" bits that are ordinarily inserted into Indian films (be they from Bollywood, Kollywood, Sandalwood, etc.) are intended to give audiences a brief respite from all the "horror tension" (hopefully) generated elsewhere. I have never been a fan of these silly moments, which are typically full of nonsensical banter, bad puns, slapstick, or/and song. The worst offenders in any Ramsay film have to be either the insufferable Johnny Lever or Jagdeep, with all their manic mugging for the camera, supposedly funny voices and puerile physical comedy. In **VEERANA** we have the chubby wannabe film director who calls himself "Hitcock" *[sic!]* played by Satish Shah, an actor who must go down in film history as the least-offensive "comedian" ever hired by the Ramsays. He must've made quite an

---

8   Gorilla was a popular henchman/villain in a number of Bollywood action/horror/crime films; he also got a beatdown by his **VEERANA** co-star Hemant Birje in **ADVENTURES OF TARZAN**.

The Servants Of Evil: One of the mysterious "coneheads" *[top]* that assist the *tantrik* with his rituals; and then there's Zimbaru *[above]*, who's more of an all-purpose goon, and does all the "heavy lifting"

---

6   The film **MISS LOVELY** (2012, D: Ashim Ahluwalia) portrays the raunchy underbelly of grade-Z grindhouse film industry skullduggery with its horror films and sexual abuse that some of its female stars reportedly endured.

7   Southern "erotic" actress Silk Smitha mysteriously died ("suicide") after a much-publicized account of rape and forced work by various producers.

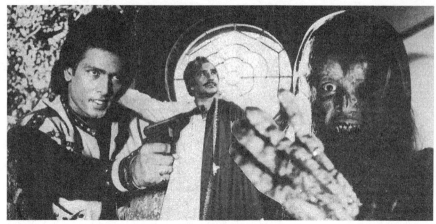

Promotional pressbook art for **VEERANA**, giving us a rare glimpse at the monster's "normal" eye; something which is typically covered up by the hanging locks of a shaggy fright-wig in the film itself

impression on them, as he later got parts in both **PURANI HAVELI** (1989 [see *Monster!* #4, p.11]) and **SHAITANI ILAAKA** (1990 [see *M!* #8, p.5]). In **VEERANA** his shtick is kept restrained to a tolerable level as he acts-out scenes he's read about in two books on "Horror" he carries with him wherever he goes, deriving pleasure from the horrendous things happening around him—as if he is actually enacting a part in one of his own imaginary productions.

Unfortunately, Rajendra Nath is also in the film, acting—like *one* wasn't enough—as the "backup" comedian who supports Satish Shah's much milder Hitcock. Playing Thakela, the "wacky hotel manager" character, the late Nath, who had been seen in previous Ramsay films,[9] here comes complete with goofy voice, silly hat and an oddball sidekick in the form of an exceedingly mini midget with a mustache (little people are always guaranteed comic gold, don't you know!). Luckily for us, Nath's and his sidekick's parts are small—pun intended— so we don't have too much to suffer through.

Now that all the principal players have been assembled, the film really begins to roll (as if all the monsters and magic of the first 45 minutes weren't enough for you!). The spirit of Nakita takes possession of Jasmin/Jasmine and, dressed to kill (*um*...literally) she chats-up a gas station manager who is examining her car as well as admiring her gams. "You're a great mechanic", she flatters him, looking him up and down. He

gulps, "I've repaired many good cars, ma'am". Jasmin licks her lips. "*Really?*" she replies. "Then come to the lake behind the old mansion tonight. I want you to repair *this* car" (i.e., the sassy lassie's classy chassis). Later that night, she returns to the service station to pick up the mechanic and take him out to the old mansion for some—*er*—"after-hours auto repairs", so to speak. First she gets him drunk on some high-quality liquor then, after bedding the man, Jasmin's eyes turn from brown to green (a sure sign of spiritual possession in any Indian film) before next proceeding to transform into the grotesquely grotty creature known as the witch Nakita. The murderous *chudail* grabs ahold of a large, dangerous-looking blade, returns to her sleeping lover, nuzzles his belly, then plunges the knife into the surprised man's guts.

The vengeful spirit of Nakita continues her slaughter when she yet again possesses Jasmin the following night. The young woman wanders in the *veerana*, where she is picked-up by an intoxicated driver. Lonely for female company, the motorist believes his luck has changed and that Jasmin will be his ticket to heaven. Sadly, this is not to be the case, for, while admiring her form sitting next to him in the passenger seat of the auto, his eyes slyly caressing her shapely exposed ankles, to his horror, he notices her feet slowly begin turning 180° so that they are now pointing backwards instead. *Danger!! Chudail Alert!!!!* Jasmin then transforms into the corpse-like witch and rips the poor gibbering man's throat out. (Serves ya right for being D.U.I. and getting fresh, bub!)

Enough being enough, the suspicious and worried Thakur contacts an old friend, a noted psychiatrist,

---

9 **DAK BANGLA** (1987), **TAHKHANA** (1986), **TELE-PHONE** and **HAVELI** (both 1985), **PURANA MANDIR** (1984), **HOTEL** (1981), **GUEST HOUSE** and **SABOOT** (both 1980).

requesting that a psychological evaluation be performed on his daughter. Of course, that means our professor will put her under hypnosis for medical reasons. This technique is a well-worn trope in devil-possession films, having shown up in numerous Italian **EXORCIST** rip-offs and other such movies. While under his hypnotic power, Jasmin begins to recall a horrible past full for unspeakable events. Then her voice changes into a snarl and her eyes once again change to green, and she vows to kill the entire cast of the film!

The Ramsays' hits just kept right on coming, and **VEERANA** is arguably the pinnacle in their many-splendored roster. The film manages the near-impossible balancing act which other Indian horror productions are hard-pressed to achieve. While the comedic moments are annoying, they aren't too off-putting, and Bappi Lahiri's musical numbers are among the best of his career (most notable being "Sathi Tu Kaha Hai", wherein we are introduced to the sultrily exotic/erotic beauty of Jasmin), it's the pacing which saves **VEERANA** from being a dud. There are a few dead spots (mostly when Hitcock is babbling about making horror films, or when the continuity is off), but Shyam's editing skills keeps those moments to a minimum. One wonders if this is because the film was delayed for so long while it was repeatedly (re-)submitted to India's notoriously horror-shy CBFC (Central Board of Film Certification), and thus the director had plenty of time in the interim to review and revise the film with additional tweaks?

Later that evening, our college-educated professor is understandably unnerved at seeing Jasmin transform into the monster, and he promptly flees the mansion. As he roars away from the horror in his sports car, the witch flies after him, causing him to veer off the road and crash. He mistakenly believes he is now safe—that is until Nakita smashes through his windshield, causing the poor man's eyeballs to explode before he dies! The witch-bitch's murder spree doesn't end there, as the creepy groundskeeper also winds up dead after a supernatural buzzsaw "accident" at the Thakur's sawmill.

Meantime, Hemant and Sahila become ever closer and more amorously inclined towards one another, and their fear that Jasmin is indeed demonically possessed is justified when they follow the evil *tantrik* back to the dank temple of doom he and the monstress call home. Once there, the two young lovers are quickly captured by the evildoers and tossed into his dungeon—where they discover that the believed-dead Sameer Pratap is actually alive. He had been held prisoner for the past twelve years by the *tantrik*. (The why of it is never really

explained.) Luckily for them, Hitcock the director wannabe discovers them while wandering the *veerana* in hopes of deriving inspiration for his proposed movie project. He, Sameer, and Hemant succeed in subduing hulking henchman Zimbaru, then all flee back to the family mansion.

Meanwhile, during all of this, Jasmin is called back to the temple where she will be sacrificed on the *amavasya* (night of the full moon) so that the witch can possess her firm young body for keeps (intentionally or not shades of the title vengeful hag's plans for Barbara Steele's character in

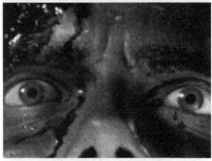
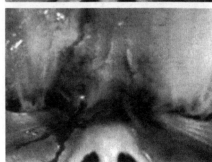

The Eyes Have It...And Then They *Don't*: The spooky-eyed Jasmine *[top]* drops a triple-whammy on some poor soul *[center]*, causing his eyeballs to explode *[above]*; one of the more gruesome effects to surprisingly survive the strict Indian censor's scissor-snips

Meeting Her Maker--*Sort Of*: As in numerous Indian horror films, the monster is unstoppable by normal human means until it runs up against a god-like Shiva *[top]*. Then, as the love flows forth from the "living statue", the witch Nakita first slowly succumbs to the deity's charms *[above]*, then she begins to dissolve into a gooey skeleton

Michael Reeves' **THE SHE BEAST** [*La sorella di Satana*, 1966, UK/Italy]). Jasmin is prepared to meet her doom, as she stands in a trance before the huge idol of the *shaitan* dressed in a fine gown with a *gajra* (garland of flowers) placed around her neck. The *baba* cackles, brandishing his ceremonial *trishul* as the circle of coneheads softly chant a horrid mantra. Just in the nick of time (as if on cue), Jasmin's family arrives on the scene, and all chaos ensues. A pitched battle breaks out as swords flash, fists pummel, and stones and even animal skulls are used to beat back the villains. During the mad melee, Jasmin's uncle manages to reach the witch's sarcophagus and destroys the bottle containing the voodoo doll. In so doing he is fatally wounded by the *baba*. With the hex destroyed, the witch's essence leaves Jasmin and returns to the corrupt form of the corpse-like *chudail*. The she-monster rises from her tomb, but the *tantrik* is killed when he is run through by a pike that is attached to a holy Om. In all this confusion of death and destruction—the coneheads explode as well (that part was really *weird*!)—the monster is forced back into her coffin and it is sealed shut...

But **VEERANA** does not end there, by any means. Oh no. First we have the cataclysmic climactic conflict of Good vs. Evil coming up! Hemant and Sameer, with the help of some local torch-wielding villagers (gotta have them; sort of like in **DARWAZA** and **TAHKHANA**'s climax, they just appear out of nowhere), our heroes transport the witch's sarcophagus to the local temple to Lord Shiva. There the monster is released from her prison, only to come face-to-face with a statue of the most powerful deity in all the Hindu pantheon of gods. To no avail, Nakita hisses and screams up a storm, only to have her exit barred by the villagers. Within seconds her evil is neutralized by the goodness and love of Shiva, at which she falls to the ground and her body rapidly disintegrates. Hemant and Sahila are by now deeply in love, and, for the bittersweet conclusion, the film's final few seconds show us the despairing and emotionally-alienated Jasmin standing alone on a clifftop overlooking the sea; making for what is truly the most poignant ending to be found in any Ramsay horror film.

****

Although she wasn't the first, the witch in **VEERANA** was without a doubt the most majorly badass of any female monster that had ever graced Indian cinema to that point. Kiran Ramsay's aforementioned and much-maligned **SHAITANI ILAAKA** (from '90) has a similar set-up, with that film's major villain being a *chudail* named

Bride Of The Monster: All dolled-up in her bridal finery, the gorgeous Jasmine is about to have her soul sacrificed so that the witch Nakita can possess her completely

Lalbai (Neelam Mehra), although the furry demon that plagued people in that film was an entirely separate entity from the witch herself. **SHAITANI ILAAKA** suffered from some very uneven production and is considered a minor film, although Yours Truly did give it a more than favorable review in *Monster!* #8 (p.5). Puja Jatinder Bedi's much more recent **GHOST** (2012) runs **VEERANA** a close second, albeit the appearance of the former's title ethereal being was more derivative of those typically seen in Japanese *onryō* (怨霊 / "vengeful spirit") and Korean *gwisin* (귀신) ghost films. The makeup effects for **VEERANA**'s Nakita, while simple, are nonetheless effective for it. In monster form, Nakita's face and hands are gnarled and bumpy, she had long jagged, rotten teeth, and a single bloated red eye dominated her visage. An unkempt fright-wig topped it off, keeping much of Srinivasa Roy's prosthetic appliqué obscured, which helped things for the simple fact that at times the rubber and greasepaint *did* tend to begin peeling off during the various action sequences. The same makeup artist's work on this film's fearful female tops my list of the Ramsays' creature creations quality-wise, along with the weird mummy in **DAK BANGLA**, the furry demon from **SHAITANI ILAAKA**, the resurrected killer from **AAKHRI CHEEKH**, the colossal but goofy yeti from **THE MAGNIFICENT GUARDIAN** (*Ajooba kudrat ka*, 1991 [see *M!* #3, p.51]), and the sinister Saamri

from **PURANA MANDIR** (1984; see *M!* #4, p.9]). Roy would later vanish from the movie scene, but not before also fabricating a few non-Ramsay monsters for such low-budget films as K. Chandra's **KHOONI KI PYASI** (1990, see *M!* #22, p.92).

What eventually sets **VEERANA** apart from all the others is the deep and delicious footprint of Indian folklore which is stomped into the plot. This is the only Ramsay movie wherein the villain is a true *chudail*. These creatures are among the most popular types of supernatural protagonists in Indian cinema and, along with the siren-like *mohini*

A Flower Wilted: Her soul torn to shreds, Jasmine is left alone and despondent in the film's closing seconds

17

Trade ad for the Ramsays' successful TV series, *The Zee Horror Show*

(another female ghost which is sometimes depicted with inverted feet like the *chudail*), they have also appeared in the Ramsays' iconic TV anthology series *Zee Horror Show* (1993-97), which then became renamed and continued as *Anhonee* (1997-2000). These two important and influential Indian teleseries unsurprisingly never aired in the USA, not even on subscription-based, program-hungry satellite feeds. Luckily, my pal Kinshuk saw them on their initial airings and recalls the episodes

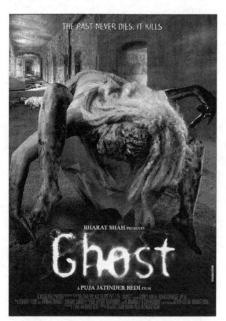

THE PAST NEVER DIES. IT KILLS

BHARAT SHAH PRESENTS

Ghost

A PUJA JATINDER BEDI FILM

Puja Jatinder Bedi's **GHOST** (2012) is an extreme example of a later date *chudail*-themed film being heavily influenced by Japanese films such as Hideo Nakata's **THE RING** (ロング / *Ringu*, 1998)

"Dehshat", "Daayan", "Pyaas", "Khauff", "Mukti", "Tadap", "Dastak", "Aatma", "Kabar", "Fatal Love", "Aafat", "Gehrayee", "Cheekh", "Veerana" and "Invitation", to name only a handful; around 80% of these episodes featured their lead female characters playing *chudail*s. As Shyam Ramsay was quoted, "We made over 700 episodes of *The Zee Horror Show*. The Ramsays became a household name with this show" *[many of whose episodes, if by no means all, are currently up for view in some form or other on that modern media miracle/resource whose initials are "YT" – ed]*. Every brother, other than Keshu, was involved, and Tulsi's son Deepak directed some 200 episodes. Speaking of their TV show, *Monster!* (i.e., myself, with a little help from my friends) is currently working on a future episode guide to both the *Zee Horror Show* and its subsequent "reincarnation" *Anhonee*. Kinshuk is the expert when it comes to the two series. Once the original run of the series was over, they were never aired again comprehensively. The Zee network—hence the horror show's original title—are one of India's largest suppliers of satellite broadcasters, and have a whole bouquet of channels which replay programming from "yesteryear". Zee Smile is one of these channels, and it delighted its viewers when they re-aired certain episodes of *Anhonee* in 2015. Regrettably, Zee has taken that particular channel off-the-air for some months now. Luckily, the good news is that some *ZHS* and *Anhonee* followers did record these episodes in decent quality and uploaded them to YouTube for others' continued enjoyment. *[I've even spotted an odd episode or two on there that came complete with English subs, which is a real bonus! – SF.]* As per sources, the Pakistani-based Apna Channel is currently airing original episodes of *Anhonee* duly retitled as the *Apna Horror Show* on Friday nights. The irony is that no actual *Indian* telechannel has the rights for the shows, and—surprisingly enough considering the vast horror boom that's been going on worldwide for some years straight now—Zee seemingly isn't showing either any interest or willingness to rebroadcast these amazing series yet again. Moreover, complicating matters still further, none of the Ramsays apparently own the rights to their own shows, which is quite an ill-fated state of affairs indeed.

The lure of the *chudail* hasn't gone away either, although the trend in Indian horror has been more towards spiritual possession. Although **VEERANA** does deal with the possession of a young woman by an evil spirit, that ghost also has a physical form when it commits its all-important acts of murder and mayhem. This oddball dichotomy—the ethereal which is also able to become corporeal—is nothing new in Asian cinema, and can be seen in many a Hong Kong or Japanese (or Filipino, etc.) horror film, and has not surprisingly shown up in other Indian horror films like Vinod Talwar's 1991 **KHOONI PANJA** for example (see *M!* #10 [p.5]). More often than not, the two types of monstrous creatures are interchangeable, and it all merely depends on the plot of a film or the whims of its makers.

Puja Jatinder Bedi's above-cited 2012 spooker **GHOST** is an extreme example of a later date *chudail*-themed film being heavily influenced by Japanese films such as Hideo Nakata's **THE RING** (リング / *Ringu*, 1998) and its teeming ilk. In Bedi's film, the ghost of a murdered woman enacts revenge through various bloody methods. The *chudail*-like creature can appear as a beautiful woman of flesh but also scuttles about like a spider, and can also reach for people out of mirrors and launch other supernatural attacks from the non-physical plane. **GHOST** was heavily criticized for its excessive use of blood, although there was no actual "meaty" gore involved other than for some scenes of animals being slaughtered at a butcher's shop. Director Bedi also ran afoul of India's "Freedom of Religion" censorship laws when the film's protagonist, a white Christian (played by Russian model-turned-part-time actress Julian Bliss), was raped and then crucified by hateful Hindu villains. The hideous monster in **GHOST** was probably the closest any Indian horror film has come to a **VEERANA**-like creature that wasn't a cheap knockoff pumped-out by the likes of Kanti Shah and his cronies. Speaking of which, in 2001 Krishan Shah, Kanti's brother, directed (to put the term loosely) a film called **TAHKHANA**. However, despite the title, this is *not* a remake of the 1984 Ramsay monster movie **TAHKHANA**, but rather a scene-per-scene copy of **VEERANA**. Also, in 2006, Krishan Shah's brother Kanti directed a horror movie called **VIRANA** *[sic]*. Go figure! As per usual for any Shah production, Krishan's **TAHKHANA** is a shabby yet nonetheless fascinating budgetless horror film. The visuals attempt to ape Gangu's Bavaeqsue cinematography, with red and blue gels dominating much of the production. There is even a "hideous" *chudail* creature, even if the makeup job on the actress is less-than-convincing, as it simply looks as if a bunch of cooked oatmeal was smeared on her face. But that was just how Shah & Co. rolled back in the day! More successfully executed *chudail*-like examples appear in Vinod Talwar's classic **HATYARIN** (1991), Ram Gopal Varma's **DEYYAM** (1996), and P. Chandrakumar's **CHUDAIL: THE WITCH** (1998). The latest addition to the roster of such films is **CHUDAIL STORY** (2016), which also has a seductress witch played by Preeti Soni, and which will be covered by me in our next issue.

Let's talk about the movie's *acting*... The show-

The Kanti Krew's Wannabe Ramsay Horrors: Despite what the cover of the VCD claims *[top]*, this is *not* the 1986 Ramsay film **TAHKHANA**. Rather, it is the 2001 micro-budget Kishan Shah opus which rips-off **VEERANA** scene-per-scene (it stars Satnam Kaur, Amit Pachori, Anil Nagrath, Ramesh Goyal, and Joginder). Not to be outdone by his brother, Kanti Shah's 2006 **VIRANA** (wacky poster art seen above) features the usual gaggle of acting stand-ins: Sapna, Vinod Tripathi, Anil Nagrath, and Amit Pachori. Despite the title similarity, this **VIRANA** *[sic!]* has nothing whatsoever to do with the Ramsay film, and is just your run-of-the-mill rubber-masked monster movie

stealer is undeniably Jasmin, who looks stunningly opulent as the sinister witch, which we discussed earlier. Seasoned actor Kulbhushan Kharbanda dials-down his past villainous roles to play that of the kindly Thakur, while popular minor character actor Vijeyandra is very good as Sameer, Thakur's younger brother. Both actors are still active on the Bollywood scene. Sahila Chaddha, who plays Sahila,[10] overacts shamelessly to the point of delivering her dialogue in a very irritating manner. Gulshan Grover, a veteran of over 400 films, is a delight as the creepy servant who loses his head, and Satish Shah is natural as Hitcock the wannabe horror director. Beetle-browed Rajesh Vivek is the evil *tantrik*, a role which would typecast him for much of his career, as he later filled similar parts in such films as **KHOONI MURDAA** (1989, D: Mohan Bhakri), **KAFAN** (1990, D: Dhirendra Bohra), **KHATRA** ([1991, D: H.N. Singh] as a Frankenstein Monster-type of villain; see *M!* #23), Vinod Talwar's **TERI TALASH MEIN** (1990) and **HATYARIN** (1991), **BHAYAANAK** (1998, D: R. Mittal), **CHUDAIL NO. 1** (1999, D: R. Kumar), **MALIK EK** (2010, D: Deepak Balraj Vij), as well as a handful of Kanti Shah/Sapna titles when he must've really needed the money.

The Ramsays have often saved "washed-up" actors from fading into obscurity by casting them in their movies, thus rejuvenating their careers. Consider, for instance, Anil Dhawan from **DARWAZA** (1978 [see *M!* #30, p.108]). He had been a popular star who fell from favor, only to land a part in an obscure monster movie production. When **DARWAZA** became a hit, so his career was saved, along with his bacon. Meatheaded actor Hemant Birje didn't see it that way when he was chosen to star as the handsome lead in **VEERANA**, however. Birje, who was in many Ramsay films after launching his career with the B-movie **ADVENTURES OF TARZAN**, refuses an interview. Instead he sent out this cryptic SMS, reprinted here verbatim: "Bcoz ramsay film i loss my cariyr." *[sic!]*[11]

The film's *filmi* bits were conducted by Bappi Lahri, who has been referred to by many as the R.D. Burman of B-grade filmmakers. Lahri was the musical director who collaborated the most with the family of filmmakers, scoring **AUR KAUN** (1979), **GUEST HOUSE** (1980), **SABOOT** (1980), **DAHSHAT** (1981), **HAVELI** (1985), **SAAMRI 3D** (1985), and **DAK BANGLA** (1987), as well as **VEERANA**. The music of **VEERANA** is haunting, with "Saathi Rae Mere Saathi" being played in background most of the

---

10 Having the main characters of a film possessing the actual same names of the actors portraying them is something not that unusual for Indian films.

11 Translation: "Because of the Ramsays' film, I have lost my career." *http://www.motherlandmagazine.com/ramsay-international/*

Almost every Indian film has some dreadful moments of drollery intended to "lighten the mood" for the audience. Pictured above are two of the least-offensive characters from **VEERANA**. Wannabe filmmaker Hitcock *[sic!]* (Satish Shah) is seen on the right lugging around his precious books on horror, while his companion Sahila (Sahila Chaddha) contemplates whether she should mug some more for the camera or not

time. Another track, "Turu Baba" is peppy, but the pathetic dance moves by Hemant Birje and Sahila Chaddha spoil much of its fun. Kiran Kumar was the film's choreographer (who should not be confused with the actor of the same name), and although he has managed better dance numbers, "Turu Baba" was not one of them. It was as if Kumar went out for a sandwich and the actors went into some free-jazz dance routine, to put it charitably. The background soundtrack is good, although its inspiration was most definitely Lalo Schifrin's score for Stuart Rosenburg's 1979 horror hit **THE AMITYVILLE HORROR**. Despite that "slight" bit of plagiarism, the mock-Schifrin background score actually sounds better than the original. Indeed, the Ramsays must have loved it so much that they reused it for a few more of their films (typically as stingers and mood enhancers), as well as in the *Zee Horror Show*.

Speaking of unauthorized use, there is one scene where a snippet of the infamous human-faced dog from Philip Kaufman's **INVASION OF THE BODY SNATCHERS** (1978, USA) is shown for a split-second. For comic relief, the filmmaker wannabe Hitchcock laments on making the perfect horror film. He brandishes a pair of "how-to" books, which he is seen carrying throughout **VEERANA**,[12] and dreams of coming up with the perfect horror film—which he will do, of course, by plagiarizing/pillaging existing tried-and-trusted sources from elsewhere.

Ramsay had all the ingredients to make a blockbuster. Though they had tasted success in movies like **DO GAZ ZAMEEN KE NEECHE** (a.k.a. **TWO YARDS UNDER THE GROUND**, 1972), **PURANA MANDIR** (1984) and loads of other movies that were released in '70s and '80s, it was **VEERANA** that really gave them a cult success. This movie had everything in the right proportions: horror, gore, sexiness without stooping to vulgarity (although bold enough for audiences of the day), and comedy (thank God that Rajendra Nath's presence was only very limited!). The 1980s and '90s were a golden age for Indian horror, and **VEERANA** is its iconic high-watermark. This was also a time when Hollywood was churning-out some of its classics of the genre thick and fast, although the cable TV industry in India had then not yet boomed. What little of foreign horror fare

that the Indian audience was able to catch was via videotape (VCDs would later supplant tapes, and have remained popular despite their low resolution and the advent of DVD/Blu-ray along with countless streaming video services). So, **VEERANA** was something out-of-the-mold for an Indian audience. For much of Indian cinema to follow, the following scenes from the film became iconic, and with time turned into vital tropes for the genre as a whole:

1. *Sameer's (Vijayendra Ghatge) initial ploy to find and hunt down the witch Nakita, which also showcases a steamy scene between Vijayendra and the witch Kamal Roy;*
2. *Possession of Jasmin by Nikita when she was accompanied by Sameer to her hostel;*
3. *Rama Vij killed by the possessed young Jasmin. This scene was shot through a fish tank, which at first seems like a purely visual flourish, but then a talented young girl named Vaishnavi playing young Jasmin (possessed by a dead witch) uses her freaky, staring eyes to make the tank explode in front of her concerned aunt;*
4. *Nikita becoming a witch in a traveling car and turning her legs 180 degrees before killing the lift-giver;*
5. *Vijay Arora being seduced by Jasmin and then getting killed. One of the most sizzling and erotic scenes in the movie (viewed by the audience in the cinema hall with a pin-drop silence);*
6. *Psychiatrist Narendra Nath inquiring into Jasmin's past by hypnotizing her;*
7. *TV static screen and the psychiatrist Narendra Nath getting the first view of the witch;*
8. *Psychiatrist getting killed by a flying Nakita. Prior to this, lots of gore involved (like the bursting of the psychiatrist's eyes);*
9. *Gulshan Grover getting killed in the wood factory (one of the best scenes in the movie, and the final horror scene before going into the climax). This can be considered a gore sequence, as showcasing such brutal murder during the late '80s was not as visually delightful for the Indian audience.*

The sad thing about the above list is that all of the mentioned sequences will be missed by any Indian born after the late 1990s, as **VEERANA**, when aired on Indian satellite channels nowadays, is heavily censored. Almost all of the horror scenes have been excised, and the eroticism has been substantially dialed back. Considering the scope of what can be seen nowadays on cable and YouTube, this unnecessary cutting rather boggles the mind. Your best option to watch this and any Ramsay film "unedited" (which means the theatrical print that was eventually okayed by the CBFC) and with English subtitles is to get your hands on the

---

12 One is a horror anthology called *The Best Horror Stories* (1979, edited by Lynn Picknett) and the other is a history of the genre called *The Encyclopedia of Horror* (1981, Richard Davis). Ironically, although the Davis book is an "encyclopedia" on the subject of horror films, it mentions nary a single Indian production (something that even editor Phil Hardy's essential *The Encyclopedia of Horror Movies: The Complete Film Reference* likewise fails to do, although it gleefully catalogues films from Hong Kong, Japan, Indonesia, as well as other non-Western productions).

Indian pre-release poster art of sexy siren Preeti Soni as the titular spook from Surya Lakkoju's 2016 film **CHUDAIL STORY**

three original Mondo Macabro DVDs which are now long-out-of-print (and fetching insane prices on eBay, etc). MM released six Ramsay movies in total, and licensed the exclusive rights for a limited time. After those rights expired, Deepak sold the rights to the Mondo Macabro titles and most of their back catalogue to a company for broadcast on YouTube (including **SAAMRI 3D** and **HOTEL**, both of which you can find on YT with subtitles).

Four decades after they started making movies, the Ramsay Brothers are now being rediscovered by a whole new generation of horror fans, even if the films are typically viewed as being "camp". They are now shown weekly on various Indian satellite channels, as are the two groundbreaking TV shows which the family began in 1991 and ran for eight fruitful seasons. Cherishing this old style of horror may be fine for the YouTube generation or those old-timers who want to be thrilled like they did as teenagers, but the interest in the Ramsay style has yet to translate into anything profitable for the remaining members of the family. Shyam Ramsay's woefully inept **NEIGHBOURS: THEY ARE VAMPIRES** (2014, see *M!* #12, p.35) tried and failed rather dismally to reignite the old black magic. The film was merely a tired rehashing of the ever-popular, *über*-plagiarized '80s vampire film **FRIGHT NIGHT** (1985, USA, D: Tom Holland) that, in places, had brilliant touches of Gangu Ramsay's cinematography which was smothered in a lumbering plot and free-for-all direction. Deepak Ramsay's **AATMA** (2006 [see *M!* #9, p.61]), while

not a financial success, was certainly head-and-shoulders above **NEIGHBOURS** artistically.

So, as *Monster!* comes to a close in reviewing every Ramsay monster film we could find, leaving out the non-monster thrillers and pseudo-*gialli* like **ANDHERA** (1975), **AUR KAUN** (1979), **GUEST HOUSE** (1981) and **TELEPHONE** (1985). But what of the future? In a 2013 interview with *dnaindia.com*, Deepak Ramsay, son of Tulsi, who has been the second unit director and assistant director on films like **INSPECTOR DHANUSH** (1991; a cop drama), **BANDH DARWAZA** (1990), and **VEERANA** (of which he was also a co-author) was quoted in saying, "Yes, the Ramsay brothers are planning to remake **VEERANA** in 3D. We are still in the initial planning and scripting stages. It's too early to say whether the script will be the same as the original **VEERANA** or will have some changes, as we don't want to reveal the plot now. All I can say is that we are going to do it in a big way and not the usual small budget horror flicks that we used to do earlier. We plan to announce the film in the next couple of months. Apart from being in 3D, the **VEERANA** remake will have lots of visual effects. I can't talk beyond that as everything is under wraps. All I will say is that it's going to be a comeback for the Ramsays in a big way!"[13] Shyam Ramsay's daughter Saasha was also marked to be the possible director of the film.

A source close to the family of filmmakers has remarked: "With the genre of thriller-horrors reigning nowadays, the Ramsays have decided to revisit one of their well known films Veerana. Of late several filmmakers are making scary films, they feel as they were the pioneers of the genre in the Hindi film industry they need to get back to it. Their productions always had an old mansion, a door full of blood or an evil being in search of power. Now they want to recreate the yesteryear film with the latest in technology."[14]

However, after a recent lengthy (yet unquotable) discussion with Tulsi Ramsay, I learned that **VEERANA 2** (be it sequel or remake) has since gone unmade, possibly permanently. Shyam's daughter Saasha (co-director of **NEIGHBOURS**) was recently attached to yet another project, but that too seems to have dissipated like so much phony mist pumped-out by the dry ice machine on set of an atmospheric horror film. Which is sad. However, as any horror film fan knows, the real monsters come out after the fog has lifted and... then the thrills begin!

13 *http://www.dnaindia.com/entertainment/report-veerana-to-haunt-again-this-time-in-3d-1853167*

14 Froma 2012 article; *http://www.mid-day.com/articles/ram-say-brothers-back-in-action/180939*

DEMON
WITH THE INKY HAND

Jason Shiga's *Demon* Pushes
Possession Beyond the Breaking Point!

Jason Shiga interviewed by Stephen R. Bissette

Since I had a hand in plenty of horror comics as a creator (writer, penciler, artist), packager, editor, publisher, and co-publisher back in the day, I'm often asked by folks what my favorite horror comic is these days.

Most folks presume I'll name one of the most obvious titles among the current 21st Century horror comics boom—say, The Walking Dead *(which I do continue to read and enjoy), or Alan Moore's and Jacen Burrows'* Providence, *or maybe Joe Hill and Gabriel Rodriguez's* Locke and Key *or Terry Moore's* Rachel Rising. *Yes, I dig all those; most ask about the recent Archie Comics experiments with the genre (which I'm not too thrilled by, but maybe it's because I harbor a long-standing grudge against the old Archie Comics regime, and how they actively crushed horror comics when it was opportune to do so). But no, no, those aren't the current favorite for me.*

I tend to get blank looks when I say, without hesitation, that my current favorite horror comic is without a doubt Jason Shiga's Demon.

*I tend to get the same screwy look when I mention how Michael DeForge's comix (*Lose, Ant Colony, *etc.) are terrific horror comics, or how Chris Ware is probably the era's most disturbing horror comics creator (Ware's work really hammers my soul in ways comics rarely ever have), and, yes, I'm a Charles Burns junkie and a Junji Ito addict as well; but citing Shiga's* Demon *as my current favorite of the genre just leaves folks cold.*

Say what?! *You've never heard of* Demon? *Time to change that void in your experience, Bunky, and catch up!*

And take a breath, while you can, because whatever you think a comic book titled Demon *might be, I'm here to promise you you've never, ever read a comic or graphic novel like Jason's* Demon *before.*

Demon *doesn't* look *like a horror comic. It doesn't* read *like a horror comic. It doesn't* play *like a horror comic.*

But, oh, man—is it ever *a horror comic!*

****

24

Hang 'Em High: Jason Shiga's *Demon* begins where most comic book stories end! *[All Demon artwork ©2016 Jason Shiga, all rights reserved; used with permission]*

So, what is *Demon*? And why am I writing about it here, in this zine?

Jason Shiga's *Demon* draws from numerous branches of the pop cultural possession family tree. Demonic possession has been a staple of multiple (almost all) religious belief systems for centuries. For Western pop culture, the most common early reference points remain the Old Testament's accounts of Saul's possession (1 Samuel 16:23)

and Sarah's possession (Tobit 3:8) and multiple references to possession in the New Testament (i.e., Matthew 8:28-34, in which Jesus exorcised two men suffering from demonic possession by driving the demons into a herd of pigs; also see Mark 5:1-20 and Luke 8:26-39). In Judaism, belief in the *dybbuk*—a spirit capable of possessing a human host—emerged in the 16th Century, codified in the 20th via Shloyme Zanvi Rappoport (a.k.a. "S. Ansky")'s play *The Dybbuk, or Between Two*

Worlds (*Tzvishn Zwey Weltn der Dibukor*, 1913-1916), which debuted on stage in 1920 and was first filmed in 1937.

The contemporary magical body-swapping genre was arguably initiated by Thomas Anstey Guthrie's *Vice Versa: A Lesson to Fathers* (1882, writing as "F. Anstey"), adapted in the 20th Century to radio (1947), television (1981), and cinema (including Peter Ustinov's 1948 British adaptation starring Roger Livesey and Anthony Newley, and the 1988 uncredited-to-Guthrie/Anstey feature film version starring Judge Reinhold and Fred Savage). Many variations and variants followed, including Thorne Smith's novel *Turnabout* (1931) on through to musical composer Mary Rodgers' children's book *Freaky Friday* (1972), which arguably launched the modern-day kids-switch-bodies-with-parents genre. Rodgers herself penned a *Freaky Friday* book series, including *A Billion for Boris* (1974), *Summer Switch* (1982), and Rodgers' and Heather Hach's *Freaky Monday* (2009), but it was the Disney feature film versions entitled **FREAKY FRIDAY** (1976, remade in 1995 and 2003) that launched a thousand spinoffs, rip-offs, remakes, and revamps. Television ran with the popular science fiction spin *Quantum Leap* (aired March 26, 1989 to May 5, 1993), while American movie

theaters drew audiences with variations on the theme like **BIG** (1988), **18 AGAIN!** (1988), **17 AGAIN** (2009), and so on.

In the meantime, there have been plenty of darker spins on the tried-and-true trope. Body-swapping as a means of prolonging life was essential to horror films like **THE MEPHISTO WALTZ** (1971), **THE BROTHERHOOD OF SATAN** (1971), **NOTHING BUT THE NIGHT** (1973), **ALISON'S BIRTHDAY** (1981), et cetera. Closer to the *The Dybbuk* in spirit (pun intended)—wherein love was the force bonding a departed spirit to the body of a lost betrothed—were the body-hopping sprites, ghosts, and angels of the friendlier film fantasies of the 'Forties. In cinema, the "body switch/possession" genre arguably began with **ONE GLORIOUS DAY** (1922), in which Johnny Fox played the pie-eyed disembodied spirit "Ek", seeking a human body to occupy. Body-hopping ghosts became a staple once **HERE COMES MR JORDAN** (1941, remade by Warren Beatty and Buck Henry in 1978 as **HEAVEN CAN WAIT**) scored at the boxoffice, followed by its sequel **DOWN TO EARTH** (1947) and the many benevolent-ghost-and/or-angels occupying various mortal coils thereafter, on into the present day (i.e., **ALL OF ME** [1984], **GHOST** [1990], etc.).

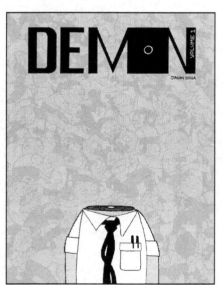

Going Topless: Cover art by Jason Shiga for the First/Second US mainstream market book edition of *Demon: Volume 1* (2016); three more volumes will follow in 2017. Incredibly, nothing has been trimmed or censored from Jason's original online and self-published print version; read at your own risk!

But, hey, this is *Monster!*, so it's the *demonic* versions of the body-hoppers we're all about here, and Jason Shiga's *Demon* is tuned-into that malevolent vibe in spades. As I've discussed in the pages of *Weng's Chop* (see my two-part article in *WC* #8 and #8.5), the body-hopping-demon subgenre in cinema owes its roots to Guy de Maupassant's "Le Horla/The Horla" (1886/1887). We can trace its successors along multiple paths, including Barry Pain's "An Exchange of Souls" (1911), H.P. Lovecraft's "The Thing on the Doorstep" (written 1933, published in *Weird Tales*, January 1937), Robert Bloch's "Yours Truly, Jack the Ripper" (*Weird Tales*, July 1943), and science-fiction variants including John W. Campbell, Jr.'s (writing as "Don A. Stuart") "Who Goes There?" (*Astounding Science-Fiction*, August 1938), Philip K. Dick's "Human Is" (*Startling Stories*, Winter 1955), Rod Serling's "The Trade-Ins" episode of *The Twilight Zone* (April 13th, 1962), et cetera.

Horror comics have borrowed endlessly from these stories, as evidenced by the Pre-Code EC Comics story "Judy, You're Not Yourself Tonight" (*Tales from the Crypt* #25 [August 1951]; adapted to the TV series as "Judy, You're Not Yourself Today" [June 12th, 1990]) and the later Archie Goodwin/ Steve Ditko gem "The Spirit of the Thing" (*Creepy* #9, June 1966)—two vivid, gruesome variations on

Lovecraft's body-swapper horror tale "The Thing on the Doorstep." Another Pre-Code wandering-souls-possessing-various-bodies gem was the Avon one-shot *The Dead Who Walk* (1952, writer unknown, art attributed to Tex Blaisdell [*"Out of the Unknown Came the Evil Spirits of the Dead!"*]); as one of the shuddering skeletal dead haunting the terrified woman on the cover exclaimed, "I want a body so that I can *LIVE* again!" If we were going to continue listing horror comics stories and series involving body-hoppers, we'd be filling pages and pages of this issue; superhero comics, too, had their share of body-hopping heroes, moving from host body to host body. Prominent among them was the Tower Comics *T.H.U.N.D.E.R. Agents* character NoMan—the agent name for deceased scientist Anthony Dunn, whose "power" involved transferring his surviving mind/being into surrogate android bodies he'd constructed for that task prior to his death (along with other devices Dunn created, such as NoMan's invisibility cloak)—who also briefly enjoyed his own title (1965+). Circus acrobat Boston Brand had to solve his own murder once he became the body-leapfroggin' Deadman in *Strange Adventures* #205 (October 1967), created by Arnold Drake and Carmine Infantino, popularized by their immediate successors Jack Miller and Neal Adams; Deadman remains a staple of the DC Comics (and DC/Vertigo) universe. Chris Claremont and John Byrne's run on *The Uncanny X-Men* (see #125, September 1979) inevitably included its own host-body-possessing mutant Proteus a.k.a. Mutant X (actually Kevin McTaggert, son of Scottish geneticist Moira McTaggert) as the Marvel universe's more destructive variant (possession by Proteus results in body burn-out, quite literally). Yes, rest assured, Jason Shiga is tapping some very potent four-color and black-and-white comics roots with *Demon*!

As Jason happily admits in the following interview, movies and TV shows provided much of the initial inspiration for *Demon*. The first movie adaptation of "The Horla" was the Vincent Price vehicle **DIARY OF A MADMAN** (1963), just two years after *Thriller* adapted Bloch's "Yours Truly, Jack the Ripper" for television (April 11, 1961), initiating the concept of Jack the Ripper as an invisible, murderous demonic entity capable of moving from host-to-host to continue his bloody work; Bloch himself scripted TV's SF spin on that story for *Star Trek*'s classic "Wolf in the Fold" (December 22, 1967). Science fiction television embraced the notion readily, most memorably via the renegade Time Lord from Gallifrey who called himself The Master (originally played by Roger Delgado) on *Dr. Who* (introduced in 1971 in "Terror of the Autons"). More in accord with the *Monster!* mandate, William Peter Blatty's blockbuster

Muzzles, Massacres & Mazes: Cover art by Jason Shiga for the First/Second US mainstream market book edition of *Demon: Volume 2* (February 2017)

bestselling novel *The Exorcist* (1971) spawned **THE EXORCIST** (1973), making demons hopping from human host-to-host coast-to-coast an international phenomenon. David Cronenberg proposed mind-into-body "possession" as a life-saving telekinesis skill in **SCANNERS** (1981),

No Man Is An Island: Wally Wood's Silver Age Tower Comics *T.H.U.N.D.E.R. Agents* character NoMan was the surviving android form of dead scientist Anthony Dunn, who could shift his surviving essence into surrogate android bodies, plus wear and wield an invisibility cloak

So, that's why *Demon* is required reading for all *Monster!* readers—and believe you me, creator Jason Shiga is pretty much into the same weird shit we are, as this exclusive interview reveals. Jason propels this peculiar clutch of subgenres into a mind-blowing procession of explorations, revelations, and its own apocalyptic end-game in his brilliant new serialized graphic novel, *Demon*.

We'll do our best to talk about *Demon* without giving too much away. In the meanwhile, you can always read *Demon* online.[1]

****

INSPIRATION

SRB: Demon kicks off with such a pure concept, dramatized quite effectively. How, or from where, did the idea for Demon come to you?

JS: I guess I'm a believer in that old maxim, "1% inspiration and 99% perspiration", especially when it comes to comics. All my books have just one or two ideas at their core. Most of the work for me is just a very thorough exploration of every nook and cranny of that idea. A book takes 2-5 years to make, so I feel a cartoonist really needs only 2-3 good ideas a decade.

For me it's more about how to take the hundreds of ideas I might have and figure out which ones are fruitful, which ones seem fruitful but lead to dead ends 80% of the way though a story, which ones are fun to tell people about but flail on the page, etc., etc.

To answer your question more directly, the original premise of *Demon* had more to do with the Buddhist notion of reincarnation. The whole theology never made sense to me if my soul passed on to another body but your memories didn't. I feel that next person really wouldn't be you. But what if there was someone who, when they died,

Woodchuck At The Wheel: While we've chosen to focus on *Demon*'s demonic predecessors, the "day-in-the-life-repeated ad infinitum" time loop aspect of Jason Shiga's masterpiece graphic novel owes a vast debt to the plight of TV weatherman Phil Connors (Bill Murray) in Harold Ramis' and Danny Rubin's classic fantasy **GROUNDHOG DAY** (1993, USA)

the same year the demonic possession and body-leapfrogging gore quotient escalated globally thanks to Sam Raimi's **THE EVIL DEAD** (1981) and its sequels.

After de Maupassant and Bloch, though, I'd argue that William Peter Blatty's *Legion* (1983) codified what became *the* template for the demon-leaping-from-body-to-body shtick for the end of the 20th Century and beyond. By the time Blatty later adapted and directed his own film version of *Legion* as **EXORCIST III** (1990), the device was familiar to audiences via multiple body-hopping demonic and/or monstrous variations: **NINJA III: THE DOMINATION** (1984), **THE HIDDEN** (1987), **SHOCKER** (1989), **JASON GOES TO HELL: THE FINAL FRIDAY** (1993), **FALLEN** (1998), et cetera. The wildest cinematic incarnation of the theme arguably remains Charlie Kaufman's and Spike Jonze's **BEING JOHN MALKOVICH** (1999), but in many ways, *Demon* echoes elements of Ben Ripley's and Duncan Jones' recent SF thriller **SOURCE CODE** (2011).

Truth be told, nobody—but *nobody*!—has ever gone where *Demon* goes, though.

1   Demon is readable online at Jason's website (@ *http://www.shigabooks.com/newreaders.php*), or you can buy hard copies of all 21 issues complete, as a special set, or via the *extra*-special set complete with all 21 issues, a handsome handcrafted slipcase, all four Demon posters, *and* a complete set of PDFs (@ *http://www.shigabooks.com/store.php*). It's all there waiting for you, or you can preorder the forthcoming mass-market First/Second graphic novel editions, scheduled for October 2016 and February 2017 release. Volume 1 can be pre-ordered on Amazon (@ *https://www.amazon.com/Demon-1-Jason-Shiga/dp/1626724520/ref=sr_1_1?ie=UTF8&qid=1468810240&sr=8-1&keywords=Jason+Shiga+Demon*); Volume 2 is also at the same site (@ *https://www.amazon.com/Demon-2-Jason-Shiga/dp/1626724539/ref=sr_1_2?ie=UTF8&qid=1468810240&sr=8-2&keywords=Jason+Shiga+Demon*). Whichever edition you read, buy, collect, or gift, *Demon* is highly recommended; as far as I'm concerned, it's an essential genre work, and a real masterwork.

reincarnated to a completely random person on earth and also retained all their memories? Obviously the premise changed a lot from there, but I like to think the story still retains a lot of the original Buddhist flavor.

I'm also a huge pop culture junkie. If I'm being honest, a lot of my ideas are just minor variants on the TV shows, movies, novels or comics I've consumed. I'm a big fan of body-switching comedies from the 1980s, *Quantum Leap*, *Breaking Bad*, *Death Note*, **GROUNDHOG DAY**, *Interview with a Vampire*, Rudy Rucker books and *Memoirs of an Invisible Man* (the novel). All that crap just stirs around in my head, gets filtered through my own autobiography and world view, and I guess once in a while something sticks.

Ah, then, let me push a little more on genre: Possession and the "body-jumping possession" theme have been a staple of horror literature and movies for a long while. Were there any specific texts or films that offered inspiration, or even springboarded aspects of Demon—*and if so, which ones?*

FALLEN is the obvious one, although that's maybe more action than horror. That movie is the main reason I included a scene where Jimmy tries to possess a chimpanzee. The ring Jimmy sees when he dies comes from **THE RING** (I'm one of the maniacs who preferred the American one). **THE EXORCIST** of course is one of my favorites. Jimmy even mentions the movie in issue 4. As an atheist, I'm not quite on board with the message of that movie. I feel they could have tried one more doctor at least. I'll admit it's extremely tricky to remove the supernatural element from horror. **ALIEN** is one of my favorite movies that's done it successfully. Everyone talks about the plot holes in **PROMETHEUS**, but my biggest problem with that movie is that they inserted religious themes into one of the great materialist horror movies.

With *Demon*, I wanted everything to be materialist. The soul is replaced by the flastical *[Google it! – eds.]*, instead of damnation I use the notion of existential dread, even the rapture at the end has a materialist explanation.

Given the pop cultural stew you say fueled Demon—*part of why I loved the ride, and love where you went with it, is that it* is *a horror comic epic, but ignores all the conventional trappings and tropes of the genre. Was that calculated?*

As you may have guessed, I *love* genre and I *love* horror, in particular horror manga. My favorite living cartoonist is Kazuo Umezu, so much so that I named my son Kazuo after him. And for me his masterpiece was *Drifting Classroom*. The ending

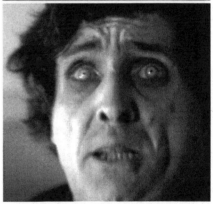

Ready, Set—*Jump*!: *[Top to bottom]* The body-hopping possession horrors of the silver screen that Jason Shiga grew up with included serial killer Edgar Reese (Elias Koteas) in Nicholas Kazan's and Gregory Hoblit's **FALLEN** (1998), Samara (Daveigh Chase) in Ehren Kruger's and Gore Verbinski's 2002 American remake of **THE RING** (makeup by Rick Baker), and of course William Peter Blatty's and William Friedkin's **THE EXORCIST** ([1973] makeup by Dick Smith; Jason Miller as Father Damien Karras, shown here at the very moment of his self-sacrificial possession by the demon Pazuzu)

Manga Mayhem: Kazuo Umezu's seminal horror manga have had a profound influence on a generation or more of international cartoonists, including Jason Shiga

of that book I think of as the greatest ending in any genre or medium.

I *love* tropes too. But one nice thing about tropes is that most readers are trope-literate themselves to the point where as an author you can play with their expectations. For example, one trope that's gotten a lot of criticism recently is the "damsel in distress". I tried to carefully set things up more or less conventionally, with Sweetpea literally being held in a castle by the antagonist. There's familiar elements like a candle, a rope and what looks like a vat of acid, as well as little bits of misdirections, like Sweetpea eyeing a nearby *katana*. This is all in service of getting readers to ask the wrong questions to themselves, like, "How's Jimmy going to save her?" or "How's she gonna get out of this?" But the scene doesn't end the way you think it will.

Were there any images, ideas, or sequences in Demon *(or your earlier works) specifically inspired by Kazuo Umezu's work?*

There's a 70-page sex-fight sequence in Umezu's *14* that was very influential. Also, I love the way he draws the facial expressions on children, especially when they're gasping or realizing something horrific about their situation (it happens a lot in his books).

****

STORYTELLING

There's an amoral clarity to your telling of the story in Demon. *Did that emerge organically from the concept, or did you struggle at all with that?*

From fairly early on, I knew Jimmy was going to be killing a lot of people, so that immediately limits how moral I can make this character. I was worried about readers wanting to follow someone so completely amoral; he never has a "save the cat" moment, as they say. But I feel most of those screenwriting tricks are horseshit. It is true that maybe 95% of genre fiction can be categorized as a conflict between good and evil. And it's easy to see why. It's a powerful theme that strikes some chord deep within the human psyche. It brought us everything from **STAR WARS** to **SCHINDLER'S LIST**. But I tried really hard to avoid that in *Demon* and make it more about behavior. The initial conceit for the characters was that Jimmy is Libertarian and Hunter is Totalitarian.

The opening chapters have an elegant, schematic simplicity to them. You're laying out a mathematical problem. Did that determine the visual style you worked up for Demon?

I think you might be giving me a little more credit than I deserve. I do have friends like Derke Kirk Kim who can draw three different styles for the three different stories in *Eternal Smile*. But that's not me.

One of my biggest breakthroughs as a cartoonist was realizing that I draw the way that I draw. I'm not a natural artist, but I don't have to be embarrassed about my abilities as an artist either. I've always felt I was by far the least-skilled and -talented among my closest cartoonist friends (Derek, Gene Yang, Lark Pien, Jesse Hamm) and, for a long time, I felt like I wasn't a "real" cartoonist because I never had a full grasp of anatomy or perspective. I worked like hell to get my art to communicate clearly and drag it past the boundary between bad and not bad, but even after all these years, it's still a struggle for me.

Maybe this is a bad message for younger developing artists, but for me this realization really allowed me to quit trying to be Otomo and focus on making the comics that I want to read and write.

You wisely work with the skillset you have; clearly, you've worked hard over the years to develop that skillset. Let's go further: Your hero is driven not by malice, but by his own curiosity. In that, I presume he reflects your own curiosity in playing this out to the end, and thus, reflects yourself?

Yes! Jimmy is *me*! I admit it. One of my favorite storytelling techniques is taking a very simple premise and thinking through every possible angle on it. I'd call it science fiction, but I guess that name is already taken.

Wakey-Wakey: Sly echoes of both **RINGU/THE RING** and **GROUNDHOG DAY** resound when Jimmy wakes up in what appears to be the same motel room after committing suicide in Jason Shiga's *Demon*

Were there any points in creating **Demon** *where you flinched from an image, narrative turn, or idea because it went "too far", or it just didn't fit?*

Yeah, there were a few "too far" moments. At one point, I had Jimmy skywriting a message to Gellman and then flying his airplane into the side of the Chrysler building. There's another panel that depicted Jesus, the Pope, Vishnu, Buddha and Moses having sex with a camel. The incest years were thankfully removed as well.

****

PERSPIRATION

Let's get into the meat and potatoes of making comics, in the context of **Demon.** *How did you begin work, and at what point did you settle on your approach to the narrative?*

I know everyone likes to work a little differently, but I need to have everything scripted before I pencil a single panel. And I penciled all 720 pages of *Demon* before I inked a single page as well.

You did it Jimmy! You're free!

But what next? Hunter and his men will come looking for you.

Demon On The Highway: Jimmy makes his way onto the open road—and into further calamities—in Jason Shiga's *Demon* (2016)

Getting back to scripting, once I've got the premise pinned down I generally write backwards. Last scene first, then a few plot points in the middle and then the paths to connect them all together. I know it's not the best method for writing interesting characters. You usually want to let your characters choose the direction the story goes and not push your characters around the board like chess pieces. I'm trying to be better at it, but for me characterization has always been more of a struggle.

That's interesting: when I write fiction (like my short story "Copper" in The New Dead*), I have to hammer down what I think at the time is my opening paragraph, what I think is my last paragraph or full ending, and one sequence in the middle that's vivid to me—and then I work toward completion having those reference points in place. With my comics, it's less schematic, but I did write and draw what I* thought *was the beginning of* Tyrant® *first, which once it was on paper convinced me I needed two entire chapters* beforehand to set up that (false) starting point, but I never would have gotten there without completing pages of that false beginning.

At what point in your writing process did the powerful opening chapter of Demon take shape for you? How did that materialize?

The opening was one of the first parts of *Demon* I came up with. If it looks familiar, it's probably because my favorite movie of all time is **GROUNDHOG DAY**, and my favorite scene in it was Bill Murray's suicide montage.

If I'm being honest, I think we've all had suicidal thoughts. I usually never get too far in those thoughts because I think of all the people that would be devastated by my death. In 2008 my Dad died and my Mom died the next year. My kid wasn't born until 2012. So there was this two-year period for me where I basically felt like I could die and nobody would care. I could finally die in peace without feeling guilty about it. I wouldn't say I was suicidal, but I was extremely reckless. It's a long story, but I ended up wandering deep into the woods in Nepal for three days and getting completely lost. Then I almost got exploded in a terrorist attack in Varanasi. I had continuous diarrhea for three months, I returned home 50 pounds lighter, but I was glad to be alive

Oh, man, Jason—we're all glad you're here, and that you're still here! Going back to your characterizations: When you're writing, do your characters propel the narrative, or does your story structure determine who they are, where they are, what they do?

Usually, my story structure determines who the characters are and what they do. I guess it's the whole Hitchcock thing where the guy stuck behind a rear window all day just happens to be a photographer and has a collection of lenses in his room. Similarly, Jimmy just happens to have a photographic memory and be an actuary, and has processed thousands of causes of death over his career.

I know it's probably not the best way to write characters. I doubt that's how Peter Bagge or Charles Schultz did it. Those two are just complete masters when it comes to characterization. Whenever I see a new issue of *Hate* on the shelf, it's like I get to hang out with some old friends I haven't seen in a couple years. I tried to write a more character-based book with *Empire State*. It didn't come naturally, and I really had to push myself to get characters that felt real to me. My next book is going to be more character-based as well, so we'll see how that goes.

Following directly upon that, do you write as a means of escalating "problem-solving"? Demon plays out like an expansive, elaborate conceptual chess game. In one way, it's quite formalist, almost diagramatic at times, in terms of the narrative—but as in your earlier Meanwhile, it keeps surprising the reader.

Yeah. Most of my books are structured around a series of puzzles. It's the engine that propels the narrative forward. My basic operating principle is that at any point in the story, the reader should be asking themselves, "What's gonna happen next?" or "How's he gonna get out of this one?" But in the end, I do hope my readers get a little more out of

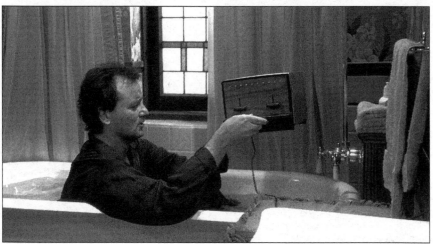

"This Dick Is *Toast!*": Phil Connors (Bill Murray) prepares to add some sizzle to his "easy" exit in Harold Ramis' and Danny Rubin's **GROUNDHOG DAY** (1993)

my books than reading a collection of brainteasers. I like to think I can fill up the structure with themes and whatnot. This might sound a little highfalutin', but with *Demon* I really wanted folks to ponder the meaning of their existence.

****

YA GOTTA HAVE SOUL

Demon indeed prompts often profound philosophical thought. Where has your own meditation on the meaning of existence taken you, Jason?

Well, if you couldn't guess from reading *Demon*, I've got a pretty nihilistic worldview. Basically, Jimmy's monologue in chapter 14 is more or less how I view the world. I love *Quantum Leap* and **GROUNDHOG DAY**, but the aspect I could never really get on board with was the idea of good deeds or *seva* somehow breaking you out of the karmic cycle. I guess I have a dark sense of humor, but I love the idea of Jimmy trying to do some good for once in his life at the very end of the story, but then accidentally killing billions of people and bringing on the Rapture.

How did you consciously pour that into **Demon**? *Where there any surprises in that process for you, philosophically?*

I actually changed the ending slightly from the original. In an earlier draft, Jimmy knowingly brings on the Rapture. It seemed a little truer to his character, but somewhat repetitive to me. But in the end I felt I wanted Jimmy to change. One of the most satisfying things to see in fiction is watching characters change over the course of a long story.

There's another expression of mathematics at work in horror: a cumulative emotional equation, or string of equations, for emotional effect. As a genre, there's also a game played with the reader—it's a game we devotees of the genre know well and love, part of the fascination and fun—the game of setting-up a horror story based on a premise of something terrible or traumatic occurring, then escalating the horror up to (or beyond) a certain threshold for emotional effect. Upping the ante, so to speak: "Here, you think this is bad? Wait until this happens!" It's true of subtle ghost stories and relatively "quiet" weird tales, and more blatantly evident in Grand Guignol and splatter, escalating the "gross-out". Demon plays that game beautifully—on multiple levels.

I feel that's an element of good genre fiction in general. Starting off quiet and then upping the ante. Half an hour into the movie, Luke Skywalker gets knocked-out by a Tusken raider. By the end, we're watching his entire battalion getting decimated by the empire. *Demon* is 720 pages, and one of my favorite things about working in a format that long was being able to set things up very slowly. The premise of the book isn't even revealed until 100 pages in.

You cited the original Buddhist inspiration for **Demon** *right from the beginning of our conversation, and this epic arrives at your*

Dr. Samuel Beckett (Scott Bakula) and the *Quantum Leap* (1989-93) time machine—which could *only* send the time traveler back to the past, and *only* transfer a person's consciousness (i.e., the traveler's mind ends up in an existing person's body, while the mind that was in the "host" person's body ends up in the future, in the time traveler's body)

Moment Of Impact: Jimmy decides to make roadkill out of himself as Jimmy—and Jason Shiga—"up the ante" in *Demon*

dramatization of the Rapture; we've also talked about pop culture artifacts and horror movies as inspiring aspects of Demon. *This begs a few questions, if you're willing to entertain them: first of all, you said you're an atheist, and that* Demon *is inherently a materialist work with a nihilistic bent, but may I ask, what were you raised with or as, and where has that led for you as an adult?*

I was raised atheist. My Dad was into Zen Buddhism. He went to the local temple regularly, and I'd go with him every now and then. It was a huge part of his life. But as you may know, that form of Buddhism is more philosophical and less

supernatural to the point where he might as well have been atheist too.

Given the enormous workload and timeframe Demon *exacted, how did the unabashedly irreverent aspects of* Demon *mesh with your emotional life? Was it hard, or was it inspiring, just pure fun, to play with such abandon with such religious ideas?*

I think the only part of *Demon* I felt might have crossed the line in terms of kicking a religion in the nards was a panel I drew that depicted the Pope, Moses, Jesus, Shiva and Buddha having sex with

Where the hell did he go?

Cop On The Beat: Gellman puzzles over the trail of corpses and the mystery of "Jumpin' Jimmy" that propel *Demon* to greater and greater excess

camels. My wife was so revolted, she couldn't see that it was done with love, and I actually meant it as a compliment to those religions. I ended up changing it so that they're all holding hands on top of a hill, but in a way, I think that's way worse.

I'm curious when the concept of the Rapture first entered your viewscreen, as a person. Does your concept of the Rapture—as satirically depicted in Demon*—emerge from your readings on populist religious beliefs, readings of prophetic scripture,* *or from the many Christian horror movies involving the Rapture (and there are a lot of 'em, going back to the 1940s)?*

Honestly, most of my conception of the Rapture comes from the *Left Behind* series of books and movies by Tim LaHaye. They're all incredibly stupid, but I have to admit the hook is fuckin' dynamite.

Agreed! I have Christian friends and family who get angry when I say the **Left Behind** *books,* spinoffs (the Y/A series), and movies are Christian horror, but—well, they are, clearly, to me, and savagely punitive Christian horror at that. That said, do you see Demon as a retort to such fare?

Not really. I suppose when you've got a hammer the whole world looks like a nail to you. *Demon* utilizes a lot of horror tropes, but if pressed I'd probably describe it as "superhero" or "*shonen*".

I am curious about your friends who are offended by your description of the *Left Behind* series is horror. There doesn't seem to be any judgment in that classification, especially coming from someone like you or me who loves horror. I'm guessing that they feel viewing the book through the lens of genre implies I don't take their theology very seriously and maybe they've got a point. In a sense, I don't really take any theology seriously as literal truth. But that doesn't matter to me as a consumer of art. I'm sure there's some ancient Greek dude who would think the **JASON AND THE ARGONAUTS** movie is a documentary. He's wrong. It didn't literally happen, but it's still one of my all-time favorite movies.

There seems to be a presumption that by citing a genre reference point, I'm trivializing the devotion and faith that some people pour into reading, or seeing, something like the Left Behind *series. Well, especially where it ends up—have you ever read the final two instalments of the* Left Behind *book series?—it's definitely epic horror on a grand scale. There's also, however, an unspoken presumption that by citing genre, I'm pointing out the obvious: these exist to* make money. *That*

mercantile assessment is in itself a "judgment". So, debasing ourselves and our conversation further, "Did you do Demon for the money, Jason?" seems to be an obvious question ripe with similar implicit judgment and presumption.

Well, I'm not gonna lie. Of course I want *Demon* to be a smash. But if I cared about money as my top priority, obviously *Demon* would look a lot different. It would probably be a YA or children's graphic novel. It would be about an angel. Also, it would be a video game or an app.

My favorite comics are usually a skillful synthesis of the commercial and the avant-garde. That goes for movies and books too. I love Cornell Woolrich and Hitchcock, even though I feel there's not any real meaning to **NORTH BY NORTHWEST**. More recently, I felt the new Dan Clowes book, *Patience*, in particular was really good at straddling that line between potboiler and art.

****

TAKING CARE OF BUSINESS

What was the initial process of finding a home beyond self-publishing for Demon? *Was the content itself a hurdle?*

Surprisingly, no. My very first question for *[First/ Second's Senior Editor]* Calista Brill was if she had any reservations about the cum knife. In my mind, it was still something I wasn't willing to compromise on. I'd rather *Demon* never be published at all than remove a single drop of cum from the book

Amy (Fabianne Therese), Dave (Chase Williamson), and John (Rob Mayes) hate to tell ya, but **JOHN DIES AT THE END** (2012, USA) in Don Coscarelli's adaptation of David Wong's webserial novel (launched 2001, completed as manuscript 2004, first published in book form 2007)

(not that you even see that much of it; the whole sequence was very tastefully depicted). Luckily, Calista told me the cum knife was her favorite part.

How did you end up going with First/Second on Demon's *mainstream book edition—and how in hell did you negotiate the landmark (to my eyes) terms (i.e., keeping it online, keeping self-publishing rights, etc.)?*

I wish I could say I had some sort of brilliant negotiating tactic, but the truth of it is First/Second's just really smart and forward thinking when it comes to that sort of stuff. I think a more traditional publisher would see the webcomic or the minis as competition for the book. But I think some recent hits like *The Martian [2011; mass market edition 2014]* or *50 Shades of Grey [2011; mass market edition 2012]* have shown the exact opposite. Releasing a book online for free can actually help to build an audience for it.

Yes; John Dies At the End *(webserial: 2001-2003; edited ms., 2004; first print edition, 2007) demonstrated that some time ago. Good point. Whose decision was it to release* Demon *in four mainstream book editions/volumes, Parts 1 through Part 4, and what were the factors in that decision?*

That was actually my idea. Having the whole thing complete and looking back on it, I felt it sort of naturally cleaved itself into four volumes. But let's be honest, I wanted to have the biggest graphic novel. I designed *Demon* to be *one* page longer than *[Craig Thompson's graphic novel] Habibi [2011].* But I also realize big graphic novels are also a bit of a white elephant. They're annoying to read or hold in bed and impossible to bring around with you. *Demon* was so *shonen*-inspired to begin with, I found it just really lent itself to the manga format, so that's what we went with in the end.

Craig Thompson, you win...for now.

Have you reworked any aspects of Demon *for the First/Second four-volume edition?*

A few minor plot points here and there.

I was initially worried about the cum-farting or camel sex or semen knives being too much for a major publisher like First/Second. But I feel having released *Demon* as a webcomic first helped to lock down some of those story elements in the public imagination. It's like they've become canonized now.

Ah, a "canonized" Demon—*you'll never top that, and a perfect note to end upon. Thanks for your time and for sharing all this, Jason. Here's hoping* Demon *is a smash hit!*

DEMON SIDEBAR #1:

JASON SHIGA BIBLIOGRAPHY

Jason generously provided the following bibliography of his comics creations—minicomics, comics, and graphic novels—to date, citing completion dates first (publication dates, if they differ, follow the year of completion). The bracketed titles are titles Jason didn't list, but which other online sources do. Jason's self-published minicomics are tagged with an asterisk (*), the rest were published in chapbook, book, or graphic novel format. ~SRB

Phillip's Head – 1996 (1997)
The Adventures of Doorknob Bob – 1997
Grave of the Crickets (never finished) – 1997
[*Mortimer Mouse* – 1997]
[*The Family Circus* – 1997]
The Last Supper – 1997
The Bum's Rush – 1998
The Date – 1999
Double Happiness – 1999 (2000; Xeric Award winner, 1999)
Meanwhile... - 2000 (2001)
Bus Stop - 2000 (2004)
Fleep – 2001 (2002, Sparkplug Comics; Eisner

Award winner, Best One-Shot; Ignatz Award winner, Outstanding Story)
Knock Knock – 2002
Bookhunter – 2003 (2007, Sparkplug Comics; Stumptown Comics Award, Best Writer)
Various *Nickelodeon* Strips – 2003-2008
Hello World – 2004
Empire State: A Love Story (Or Not) – 2007 (2011, Abrams)
Meanwhile... (redrawn and colored) – 2009 (2010, Amulet Books)
Demon #1-#21 - 2014-2016 (2014 Ignatz Award winner)

Interview ©2016 Stephen R. Bissette, with thanks to Jason Shiga, Alec Longstreth, and Jon Chad. This interview was conducted via email May-June 2016. *Demon*™ and ©2016 Jason Shiga, artwork included with permission for illustrative purposes only.

Jason Shiga on "Conjuring-up"

DEM◯N

Because my readers have demanded it, today I'll talk about my process for making *Demon*. But first, a little personal journey…

Like a lot of cartoonists, I started out with the cruddiest possible supplies, because I was cheap. I used the crappiest photocopiers, the cheapest paper and I adapted my artwork to try and get the nicest-looking art from those tools. When I started to take comics a little more seriously, I read-up on what the pros use and decided, if I want to be pro myself, I need to use those same tools. I bought a Rapidograph and Strathmore paper. But I also became more conservative both in terms of output and style, because in my mind, every square inch of that paper was costing me money.

Ultimately, I feel expensive tools can defeat the whole purpose of comics. To use a hiphop analogy, oil paints and violins are expensive to the point of being out of the reach to huge swaths of the population. But some kids in the Bronx figured out you can make art with busted-up record players and cans of spray paint. There is no Stradivarius of the cartooning world. Every cartoonist I know just figured out what combination of hacks and shortcuts works best for them. I've been cartooning for 15 years, and I'm back to using the absolute cheapest pens, non-archival paper and whatever garbage I can get my hands on.

Writer/artist Jason Shiga (photo from *https://tkscll.wordpress.com/2010/12/08/jason-shiga-interactive-comic/* which also features a video tutorial "How to Make Your Own Interactive Comic" by Jason!)

WRITING

I write all my scripts and make all my sketches in Daiso notebooks with Papermate ballpoint pens. When it comes time to turn them into thumbnails, I'll take a letter-size piece of copy paper, fold it in half and thumbnail directly onto it. This way, I have some idea what images go where relative to the spread, the edges, the fold and my hands. After I've got enough of these thumbnails, I'll gather them up into an "issue" and flip through it, pretending I'm a reader.

PENCILING

Once the entire project is thumbnailed from beginning to end, I'll start in on the pencil roughs. I used to use pencils but found it hurt my hands, as I gripped the pencil too tight and ended up breaking off the lead anyway. Now, I use Papermate ballpoint pens. If you buy a 60-pack, they're literally 10 cents each. If I make a mistake, I'll redraw it on a separate sheet of paper and tape it back onto the original. With *Demon*, as in the case of all my books, I wanted to pencil the entire project before starting the inks.

INKING AND LETTERING

I use a size 2 Windsor Newton 222 brush and Higgins black ink. When I'm inking, my fingers can get sweaty and the metal ferrule on the brush slips between my fingers, and I end up squeezing tighter and then I get carpal tunnel syndrome. A quick fix I found that works is I wrap a rubber band around the metal ferrule. The thickness of the rubber keeps the ferrule from slipping between my fingers as well. For lettering, I'll type the dialogue up on the computer, fiddle with the kerning in Photoshop and then print it out onto paper. Then I'll lightbox it onto my pages using a Micron 08.

Another gratuitous-but-welcome shot of one of the monsters from **MUTILATIONS**

MUTILATIONS

Reviewed by Dennis Capicik

USA, 1986. D: Lawrence Thomas

In 1979, the FBI were tasked with investigating a series of animal mutilations that took place throughout the American midwest, and although their initial report concluded that much of the mutilations were the result of natural predation, some anomalies did arise. Of course, this led to further discussions among conspiracy theorists about extraterrestrial involvement or satanic cults as possible culprits. At the time, given the ongoing popularity of Steven Spielberg's **CLOSE ENCOUNTERS OF THE THIRD KIND** (1977, USA) and this intriguing new string of events, art-house director and Robert Altman protégé Alan Rudolph opted to helm **ENDANGERED SPECIES** (1982, USA), which revolved around a series of animal mutilations, UFO conspiracies and government cover-ups. Taking a page out of Rudolph's still sadly-underrated conspiracy film, Oklahoma native Lawrence Thomas decided to film his own version of the events, with considerably different results. Shot on 16mm in 1986 outside Tulsa, this barely feature-length film also contains the usual conspiracy theories—and even a few totally off-the-wall ones—but with a '50s monster movie spin, which includes some one-of-a-kind, bargain-basement-but-enthusiastic monster FX work.

During a late-night field trip, astronomy professor Jim McFarland (Al Baker) and a few of his eager-to-please students "just happen" to witness a meteor ("I believe what we have there is some sort of meteor…"), which looks like nothing more than a lighted match superimposed over the night sky. Later that night, three hobos, who "just happen" to be reading about cattle mutilations in *The Daily Tribune*, observe an alien spaceship landing in the

Top: Principal cast members of **MUTILATIONS** *[from left to right]* Al Baker, Katherine Hutson, Richard Taylor and Shelly Creel. **Pic #2:** D.I.Y. friggin' flyin' saucer attack! **Pic #3:** Eugene (William Jerrick)'s SFX "stunt stand-in" goes all screwy in the head. **Above:** Assistant cameraman Brett Reynolds on the set of **MUTILATIONS** in 1986. He and the film's female co-lead Shelly Creel (=Reynolds) were wed in 1988. *[Top and bottom photos courtesy of Shelly Reynolds]*

nearby junkyard ("Always did wanna meet some little green fellers from space!"), but are soon slaughtered by some giant, clawed alien creature. Organizing a trip to Barry Hill to investigate some "strange aerial sightings", Jim and his students are soon perplexed by a number of "slaughtered, mutilated and half-eaten" cows…but that's nothing compared to the (quote) "aliens that look like creatures outta hell!"

Running just over an hour, **MUTILATIONS** never outstays its welcome, and despite the shoestring budget, the enthusiasm on display and resourceful stop-motion FX make a nice change of pace from the usual DIY efforts of the time. In issue #61 of *Fangoria* magazine (circa 1987), Lawrence Thomas talked to John Wooley about the completion of the film: "The picture's live-action portion was shot in 16 days; stop-motion work and other optical FX took several weeks". Most of the FX were courtesy of John Fischner, "a sculptor and Ray Harryhausen devotee", who does the best he can with the severely limited budget allotted him, and, although they are quite crude, they're lively enough to raise an affectionate smile from any self-respecting monster movie fan; it actually resembles an even lower-budgeted Brett Piper film, which isn't necessarily a bad thing at all. In one of the film's first FX scenes, a horribly-mutilated cow is found writhing in obvious agony, which is nicely executed using some effective stop-motion, but what is meant to be a "disturbing" scene is, to some degree, laughable, simply because this disfigured cow looks like it was made out of Play-Doh! The aliens themselves are considerably more impressive, and although they aren't revealed until the film's last act, their large tri-clawed arms—which are featured on many of the film's promotional materials—make plenty of appearances as they rip through torsos and crush skulls.

In spite of the spirited if budget-constrained FX work, most of the "acting" is amateurish across the board, which is to be expected, but at times, it's all so over-the-top that it almost borders on all-out parody. When Jim, driving a minivan full of screaming students, tries to evade a rather aggressive flying saucer as it chases them through the Oklahoma farmlands, he pulls over at a local diner for shelter, where Buck Jensen (Bill Buckner), the diner's owner, seems annoyed at all the "noise" out there. When they reveal their incredible story, he just shrugs it off and takes their order. Exhausted, Jim orders "Hamburgers and fries all round", but one of his students exclaims, "No cows for me, thanks! Just French fries". Some of the other locals, including Harvey (Charley Hill), a farmer who is seen repeatedly patting his trusty firearm, become quite intrigued by their story, but Jim doesn't have much to offer them other than for a barrage of fumbled lines while ominous music plays on the soundtrack, "dramatically" underscoring his each and every line of dialogue. During the climax, in one of the film's funnier—and better-acted—lines, Buck lets fly at the aliens as he hollers, "Eat my biscuits, you bloodsucker!" simply because he used "yesterday's biscuits" as wadding for his shotgun. Back at the diner, Harvey eventually tells them to visit Oliver Matson (John Bliss), who's been "terrorized every night by aliens from outer space", but is apparently "crazy as a loon."

Caught in the middle of a thunderstorm, Oliver begrudgingly admits them into his out-of-the-way shack then proceeds to talk about "spaceships from another world" and his abduction by aliens, which *this* time resemble "demons outta hell" ("They shot at me with some kind of stun-gun! Made me see stars! Hit me in the face!"). But then, in a completely bizarre sidestep, he goes on to outline the parallels of "prophet" Joseph Smith (1805-1844), founder and 1st President of the Church of Jesus Christ of Latter Day Saints, along with his message from God concerning "visions that he had revealed to Moses many millennia ago" about other worlds he had created: apparently then, this is a Christian-themed alien invasion film we've got here! Oliver continues ranting on about alien spaceships that crash-landed in 1947 (an obvious nod to Roswell), as well as governmental cover-ups and threats about getting locked-up in the state asylum. Even though he continues to raise a stink with the authorities about the state of affairs, however, nothing is ever done about it, and the aliens just keep right on returning (quote) "whenever they get hungry".

The film's second half gets considerably more lively, as Jim and his students fend for their lives among a candy-colored landscape of stop-motion FX and cheap-but-welcome prosthetic makeup effects. In one scene, Eugene (William Jerrick), the group's resident geek, is slowly reduced to a bubbling pile of glop, while another student is gutted by one of the creature's umbilical-like clawed appendages. The protagonists eventually discover some tunnels underneath the house and attempt to escape via this route; much like in David Michael Hillman's (a.k.a. Melanie Anne Philips) far more effective and atmospheric **THE STRANGENESS** (1985, USA [see *Monster!* #20, p.16]), the claustrophobic tunnels provide a nice backdrop as they battle a variety of stop-motion monsters resembling goofier versions of Ray Harryhausen's Ymir from Nathan Juran's **20**

MILLION MILES TO EARTH (1957, USA); a resemblance which, even if purely unintentional, makes for a nice touch anyway.

Even though **MUTILATIONS** does muster up some decent energy with its enthusiastic FX work, the uniformly poor performances and amateurish production will most likely turn most viewers away, but fans of '80s direct-to-video or SOV ("shot-on-video") fare will find plenty to enjoy here. And besides, it's a helluva lot better than either Christopher Lewis' **BLOOD CULT** or **THE RIPPER** (both 1985), a pair of Oklahoma-shot SOV snoozers made at around the same time.

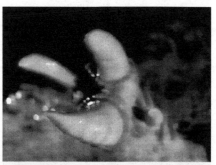

Top: This tri-prong clutching claw from **MUTILATIONS** figured prominently on the film's original Beta/VHS packaging/promo art. **Above:** One of the two "clawcentric" cover options offered by Massacre Video's reversible US DVD jacket (the other is depicted on p.242)

A QUASI/PSEUDO-SPAGHETTI (MONSTER) WESTERN TRIPLE FEATURE

Reviewed by Les Moore

Ready, Aim—*Vampire*! Maxwell Caulfield as the brutal bloodsucker/gunslinger "Shane" aims to displease while fellow fanger/shootist John Ireland stands idly by in **SUNDOWN**

SUNDOWN – THE VAMPIRE IN RETREAT

USA, 1989. D: Anthony Hickox

Daddy: *"How 'bout spaghetti tonight, kids?!"*
Kids: *"Ya-a-a-a-a-ayyyy!!!"*

Unfortunately, due to its ill effect on vampires, no garlic is available in town to season the spaghetti sauce with... and the film could well have used a few more pinches of garlic itself, although it does have just enough in it to keep the average vampire (or maybe even an aswang!) away.

Following the generally fond fan response to what is arguably his most popular monster movie, **WAXWORK**, during pre-production of **SUNDOWN** in '88, as quoted in *Fangoria*, writer-director-actor Hickox boasted, "It's going to be the ultimate vampire movie". Although it most certainly *isn't* (and we've had about a half-gazillion other "ultimate" vampire movies made since which weren't either), it at least made a game try at doing something different. Just preceding the '90s Hollywood western revival,

this was a relatively big-budget (i.e., $3-million) attempt to reinvent and update the shoot-'em-up's stale formula by re-hybridizing it—for the umpteenth time—with the horror genre (horror westerns were certainly nothing new, especially in Mexico, where they had been making them for decades; and prior to the present example, they also periodically appeared even in Hollywood, too). Hoping to inject new blood into the well-tapped (i.e., way-oversucked) blood-drinker movie vein by cross-breeding it with oaters, **SUNDOWN** crams far too many ideas into a single narrative, but is not completely without its entertaining moments...far from it.

Dressed in a snazzy grey suit with silver trim and top hat, David "**KILL BILL**" Carradine appears almost Christopher Lee-like at times as antiheroic head vampire Count Josek Mardulak—alias Count Dracula himself, who else!—who lords it up out in the isolated American desert town of Purgatory. Hero David Harrison (Jim Metzler) is the developer of a "blood substitute" which conscientious vampires who no longer wish to prey on and feed off human cattle can reproduce at their on-site (quote) "Hemotechnics plant". Vampire townspeople

44

(including ever-loveable old timer Dabbs Greer, from Paul Landres' classic **THE VAMPIRE** [1957, USA], as the long-in-the-tooth Otto) all dress in period clothing. Bruce Campbell co-stars as lightning-swift stakeslinger Van Helsing, who knows his way around a vampire just jim-dandy, but is a total sap when it comes to the female sex.

A stop-motion bat-monster—nicely animated by Tony **"RE-ANIMATOR"** Doublin—transforms into hateful pretty-boy bloodsucker Shane (Maxwell Caulfield [also seen in **BACKLASH: OBLIVION II**]). Using "fortified wood" bullets ("Splinters on impact!"), Shane shoots the sheriff ("I'm gonna shoot me a Rasta vampire!"), Quinton Canada (played by African-American actor John Hancock). As chief co-conspirator in vampire elder Ethan Jefferson's plot to revert to the more natural and honorable "old ways" of feeding, Shane opposes both the hero and antihero in town; which, needless to say, is nowhere near big enough for the three of them. Playing the undead Jefferson, John Ireland leads an armed uprising of "old school" (i.e., traditionalist) vampires against their reformed ("domesticated"), synthetic blood-drinking fellows. This culminates in Ireland—dressed in Puritan garb and pasty greyface while giving a surprisingly restrained, dignified reading considering the garish proceedings—facing Carradine for the final showdown. Rather than going at it fang-to-fang, they actually fight a gun duel, hogleg against hogleg, may the best vampire win.

To protect themselves from the deadly effects of direct sunlight, vampires variously use SPF 100-strength sunblock, tote umbrellas or parasols, and hide behind UVA/B-protected tinted glass. As one of the three homicidal hayseed Bisby Bros., bloodthirsty gas station attendant Mort (M. Emmet Walsh) wears a huge *sombrero* to shade himself from harmful solar radiation, and in one scene backhands an assholish customer's entire head clean off! Walsh's work partner/sibling Bailey is played by sometime western player and exploitation movie veteran George "Buck" Flower, and the white trash-talkin' trio make for one of **SUNDOWN**'s more memorable attributes.

Filmed entirely on location in the towns of Moab and Thompson, Utah (in the vicinity of where apple pie western master John Ford directed the great John "Duke" Wayne in **RIO GRANDE** [1950, USA]). Co-executive producer on **SUNDOWN** was Dan Ireland. Music—which at times intentionally evokes a spaghetti western—was composed by Richard Stone, performed by the Graunke Symphony Orchestra (soundtrack recorded at Bavaria Musik Studios, Munich, Germany). Closing theme is Gene

Top: Some of Tony Gardner's slick SFX makeup for **SUNDOWN. Above:** The great M. Emmet Walsh as "shady" vampire gas-jockey Mort Bisby, one of the film's prime selling points

Pitney singing "Town Without Pity" (co-written by Dimitri Tiomkin). This project was dedicated to the memory of the director's father, filmmaker Douglas Hickox (1929-1988).

OBLIVION
USA/Romania, 1994. D: Sam Irvin

Video blurb: *"In the year 3031... it's Cowboys and Aliens".*
Richard Joseph Paul as Zack Stone: *"Vengeance is a hollow pursuit..."*

Co-produced by old hand Albert Band and Castel Films of Bucharest, this pulp "science fiction" (i.e., schlock sci-fi) western was shot in Romania; which possibly helps to explain the perhaps appropriately

Family Resemblance: Can you spot the differences? Andrew Divoff as Redeye in **OBLIVION**, who is the virtual dead-spit of his "identical twin" brother Jaggar (also played by Divoff) in **BACKLASH: OBLIVION 2** (see top right pic, p.49)

synthetic look of the border town back-lot, that is made more disorienting still by weird, would-be "Expressionistic" set design. While seeking a lucrative load of "draconium", a nasty off-worlder outlaw named Redeye ("half-man, half-lizard and *all* mean") murders Marshal Stone in the extraterrestrial border town of Oblivion. The lizardman's effeminately queeny Mexican sidekick refers to his boss as *Rojo-Ojo* (Spanish for "Redeye", natch). The Mexican also makes a "¡We dón' need no steenkeeng batches!" joke at expense of Bogey's classic "gold bug" adventure **THE TREASURE OF THE SIERRA MADRE** (1948, USA, D: John Huston); for which simply by association not only was original "badges" *bandido* Alfonso Bedoya rolling over in his grave, but quite likely Bogart and Huston were too. In **OBLIVION**, another of Redeye's posse is a nymphomaniacal English dominatrix who wields a bullwhip. As well as draconium, lizard-breath also has his sights set on a local damsel-in-distress in the shapely form of Miss Maddy (Jackie Swanson).

With piercing metallic-blue eyes, Meg Foster plays the late marshal's sexy cyborg deputy (who, being part-woman/part-machine is referred to as a "half-breed"). Upon striking a mother lode o' the wuthless yella stuff, prospector hero Zack Stone disappointedly exclaims, "Great. Just what I need... *more* gold!" Ex-*Batman*'s Catwoman Julie Newmar plays a saloon pussy named Miss Kitty

and purrs wa-a-ay too much. And speaking of over-the-hill TV actors, *Star Trek*'s pre-outed George Takei ("Mr. Sulu") overacts horribly as a drunken old doc. Takei makes numerous *'Trek* references, most conspicuously and self-consciously while guzzling from a bottle of Jim Beam ("Jim—beam me up!"). A Winnetou-like Indian brave is staked-out as a snack for giant twin-stingered arachnids called "nightscorps" (depicted via quite passable stop-motion animation). Another of Oblivion's indigenous alien lifeforms is the "Mon-ding" *[sic?]*, an animatronic frog-like varmint used in local Indian vendettas (don't ask!). Former black action star Isaac Hayes plays a draconium appraiser. Lanky Carel Strüycken (better known to millions as "Lurch" from the '90s *Addams Family* movies) plays Mr. Gaunt, a seven-foot-tall undertaker made taller still by a two-foot-high stovepipe hat. There are also Siamese (sorry, I meant to use the more PC term conjoined *[wink]*) twin cowboys, as well as a "no-legs" who nips at the Mexican's kneecaps during the mandatory saloon brawl. Hero Paul kills Redeye using his dead father's "Marshall" *[sic]* badge.

In one scene, the boom-mic is clearly visible at top of frame. The script (by Albert's son, Charles Band) was evidently scribbled in shorthand on the back of a paper napkin. Recalling the efforts of umpteen semi-literate Euro set decorators in umpteen spaghetti westerns, Oblivion's law office is conspicuously misspelled with a proper name,

"Marshall" (as is Paul's tin star). Hanging around the sidelines are some of the absolute *worst*-dressed extras seen since a "Paolo Solvay"/Luigi Batzella western (e.g., **PAID IN BLOOD** [*Quelle sporche anime dannate*, 1971, Italy]). The Bands also collaborated on a similar sci-fi shoot-'em-up, **METALSTORM: THE DESTRUCTION OF JARED-SYN** (USA, 1983), which was originally shot in 3-D. This wasn't. Perhaps that was a good thing, but I shall bitch no more about it. So by all means give this a watch, and get whatever you can out of it.

NOTES: DP on **OBLIVION** was an Italian, Adolfo Bartoli. Its score was composed by Pino Donaggio, conducted by Natale Massara, performed by the Bulgarian Symphony Orchestra (!) and committed to oxide by Marco Streccioni at Sofia's NDK Studios and Rome's CAM Recording Studios (where innumerable Spaghetti soundtracks were cut). 2nd-unit photography was handled by Aldo Antonelli in Romania. An end-card threatens, "To Be Continued..." (It was...)

BACKLASH: OBLIVION 2
USA/Romania, 1995. D: Sam Irvin

Co-produced by Albert Band (along with Yugoslav producers Vlad Paunescu and Oana Paunescu), this was an inglorious throwback to Band's tacky sci-fi pseudo-westerns of the early/mid-'80s, such as his son Charles Band's **METALSTORM: THE DESTRUCTION OF JARED-SYN** (1983, USA), which most readily springs to mind. I was lucky enough to see that in a theater in 3D on its first run over 30 years ago, and for me, while cheesy as they come, it hits far fewer false notes than the *Oblivion* duo do. However, because we really do *want* to *try* awful hard to like them, the more forgiving of us can find at least some entertainment value herein, even while we frequently find ourselves groaning at their contents. Here we get more of the same in this straight-to-video futuristic schlockfest, the immediate sequel to **OBLIVION**, for which principal cast and most major technical credits remain constant.

This follow-up—shot back-to-back—carries on right where its predecessor left off, and includes a prologue flashback montage (*"Once upon a time in OBLIVION..."*) to handily recap #1's events (i.e., the villainous Redeye getting halved by the pincers of two squabbling nightscorps). That said, this might just as well have been entitled "THE RETURN OF REDEYE"; except that the identical green-faced villain who shows up here is actually

Top 2 Pics: **OBLIVION**'s toadishly froggy varmint known as the "Mon-ding" *[sic?]* says *"Riddip!"* Pic #3: Behold the piercingly electricblue gaze of sexy cyborg-woman Stell Barr *[sic!]* (Meg Foster). **Above:** Actor Divoff as Redeye in the first film, who is recognizable by his scarlet eye-patch

Jaggar, Redeye's vengeful bro (albeit played by the same actor in virtually the same makeup and costume. How's that for a lazy and facile way to start a sequel?!).

A character named Crowley owns the map leading to a fortune in draconium ("the most valuable mineral in the galaxy"). Twist is—going a key plot-point of Duccio Tessari's spaghetti western **DON'T TURN THE OTHER CHEEK!** (*Viva la muerte... tua!*, 1971, Italy/Spain/West Germany) one better—rather than on someone's buttock, said map just happens to be tattooed on his *pecker*! (Either it's a real small map or...well, you get the picture.) Hence—strictly out-of-frame, mind you—she known as Lash (Musetta Vander) cuts said male member off; but is at least considerate enough to *kill* the poor guy first. Oh yes, and I should perhaps mention that Lash's wanted poster is obviously a color laser photocopy, although I suppose it isn't really an anachronism when you take the "hi-tech futuristic" setting into account.

As Sweeney, Brit actor Maxwell Caulfield arrives in his intergalactic limousine, playing a foppish, monocle'd, top-hatted English dandy who twirls a vicious walking cane. Caulfield (who had been in Anthony Hickox's **SUNDOWN: THE VAMPIRE IN RETREAT** [1989, USA]) gives the movie's most enjoyable performance, simply because of its sheer over-the-top self-indulgence ("It's amazing how you can manage to take such pleasant words as 'reward' and 'money' and make them sound so distasteful"). Sweeney, "the deadliest bounty hunter in the sector", in the employ of the omnipotent Galaxi-Corp., has pursued the fugitive Lash to Oblivion. His prey subsequently finds himself trapped by a cave-in at the draconium mine. It develops that Sweeney's actual target is Miss Kitty (Julie Newmar—the *Batman* teleseries' "Catwoman"—once again), who is a former industrial spy/saboteur. Even more "surprising" is that lurking behind the dapper limey's polite façade is actually a horned alien monster!

Hero Marshal Stone (Richard Joseph), Sweeney and Jaggar all vie for the privilege of taking Lash in. Under the honor code of the League of Bounty Hunters, Miss Kitty offers Sweeney a challenge: catch me if you can! Accompanied by Stone acting as mediator, Sweeney gets on her spoor. Telegraphed-in all the way from the dark side of Pluto, Miss Kitty's ultimate "death" results in the inevitable return of the Catwoman and a mandatory "cats got nine lives" punchline. Don't all purr at once!

While at least he doesn't say "White man speak with forked tongue!" or, worse yet, "*How!*" the token Amerindian character carries an "all-seeing gem" and mouths too much "philosophical" gobbledygook (rather akin to a stereotypical Hollywood Chinaman

Wacked-Out Alien Arachnid: One of the *Oblivion* two-pack's funky sto-mo-animated "Nightscorps" rears its ugly head and twin stingers, ready to strike!

48

Viewers get a major case of *déjà vu* while watching **BACKLASH: OBLIVION 2! Above:** Four shots from same. **Below:** Its domestic DVD artwork not surprisingly showcased Musetta Vander's dominatrix-like, bullwhip-cracking "Lash" character, who can also wield a pretty mean *cuchillo* too, if needs be (see last still above)!

who constantly punctuates his dialogue with phony Confucianisms ["Confucius say…" even though we know he actually *didn't*]). Lame attempts at comedy (including something really subtle involving brass balls) are even more embarrassing here than in the first film; including some tired *Trinity*-styled fisticuffs as Caulfield effortlessly sidesteps our heroes' punches. Any and all scenes involving a washed-up TV actor are truly an embarrassment to behold. Adding one of the few shreds of class to be had here, a girly painting by Vargas hangs behind the bar in the saloon with quiet dignity, making its surroundings appear all the kitschier by comparison.

Supporting player Jimmie F. Skaggs had played an undead gunman in Richard Governor's direct-to-viddy horror western **GHOST TOWN** (1988, USA); among the final releases of Charles Band's Empire Productions, which was shot at Arizona's Old Tucson Studios.

Although it's all too easy to tear low-budget dreck like this to pieces out of simple vindictiveness, there definitely is some fun to be had here for those with a bent towards schlocky '80s sci-fi and/or tacky '60s teevee. So by all means knock yourselves out!

PRIDE AND PREJUDICE AND ZOMBIES

Reviewed by Andy Ross

UK/USA, 2016. D: Burr Steers

A decidedly tongue-in-cheek costume drama based on the 1813 novel by Jane Austen (albeit awarded an apocalyptic twist courtesy of author Seth Grahame-Smith), **PRIDE AND PREJUDICE AND ZOMBIES**, despite a poor performance at the box-office, remains one of the most vibrant (and curiously charming) zombie offerings of recent years. Proposing that a zombie infestation (like that of the real-life bubonic plague) arrives via the British Empire's lucrative trade routes, by the time we are introduced to the pivotal hero Colonel Darcy (Sam Riley of **MALEFICENT** [2014, USA, D: Robert Stromberg]) the nation is already teetering on the brink of an undead takeover. With a hundred-foot defensive wall encircling the capital and a moat of 30 fathoms providing an additional deterrent, when the area sandwiched within the constructs (i.e., the "In-Between") is breached, all crossings bar one (the Hingham Bridge) are rapidly taken out of commission. A series of events that has led to the infamous madness of the residing monarch, King George, against this backdrop of turbulent uncertainty, the middle classes deem to soldier on in the manner they have best grown accustomed to. Met with cocked muskets by the militia protecting the country residence of Mrs. Featherstone, Colonel Darcy is a man on a mission.

Convinced as to the presence of an infected one in their midst, Darcy's interruption of Featherstone's whist afternoon is not in the slightest bit welcome. Aware that the infected do not become fully manifest until they have partaken of human brains, Darcy possesses the knowledge that they can nevertheless coexist among the living. He utilizes carrion flies to locate the dead flesh within the company, and when the insects alight on a ruddy-faced, rather portly individual, the Colonel dishes out justice in a manner he's readily grown accustomed to. Enter stage-right the imperishably charming Bennet sisters. A group of siblings doted over by their father and yet determined to be married-off by their mother, the Bennets are by far too engaged in the Chinese martial arts to contemplate such feminine ties as dress-making and keeping house. Armed with the knowledge that the eventual death of Mr. Bennet (Charles Dance of *Game of Thrones* [2011-, USA/UK]) will witness the family cast into poverty, the arrival of the dashing—and

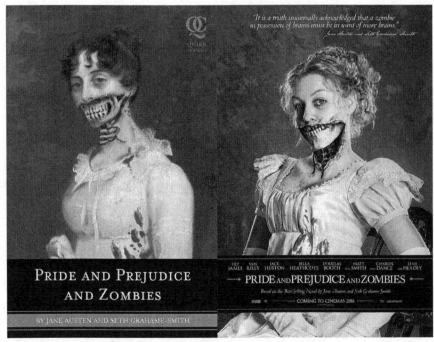

P+P+Z book cover and movie poster comparison

PRIDE+PREJUDICE
+ZOMBIES

COMING SOON

Media mega-conglom Sony/Screen Gems made a major point of hyping this beautifully intricate fine art promo poster for **P+P+Z** all over the internet, but the money-grubbing a-holes apparently never even *thought* of crediting the super-talented artist responsible for creating it, or even allowing them to sign their work, for that matter, otherwise we'd credit the person here

ridiculously wealthy—Mr. Bingley (Douglas Booth of **JUPITER ASCENDING** [2015, USA/Australia, D: The Wachowski Brothers]) piques the canny Mrs. Bennet's curiosity. On the insistence that her reluctant brood should attend a ball to be held in Mr. Bingley's honor, the girls set about attiring themselves accordingly. Whilst Bingley finds himself instantly attracted to the second-eldest, Jane (Bella Heathcote of **DARK SHADOWS** [2012, USA, D: Tim Burton]), Elizabeth's introduction to Colonel Darcy does not go quite so swimmingly. Harboring an early mutual

Sure, as per the title, **PRIDE AND PREJUDICE AND ZOMBIES** has all *that* stuff in it…but equally importantly, it's also got lovely Victorian fillies in frillies, too. (But make no mistake about it, perverts: they can easily make ear-rings out of your gonads, so watch your step!)
[Photo by Jay Maidment]

dislike for one another, when the girls deftly ward off a zombie attack, Darcy's initial assessment of Elizabeth is readily brought into question. When invited over to tea at the Bingley residence (and persuaded by Mrs. Bennet to travel on horseback, as the inclement weather might encourage an overnight invitation), Jane comes under attack after her mount is spooked. Drawing her pistol to down her zombie assailant, Jane fails to notice that the muzzle has become clogged and, as a result, the weapon backfires. After dispatching the revenant by far-less-clinical means, the Bennet girl (now at

This unsettling zombie-mother-with-baby shot from **P+P+Z** immediately reminded us of a similar creepy pair in **THE NIGHT FLIER** (see p.67)

the mercy of the elements) inevitably succumbs to exposure. Upon receiving a message informing her of her sister's condition, Elizabeth rushes to Netherfield and once again finds herself at odds with the narrow-minded Colonel. Steeling himself to "neutralize" Jane should the physician find that the wound on her hand is anything other than powder burns, Darcy's employment of his ever-reliable carrion flies serves to enrage Elizabeth even further. Content that Jane is suffering from no more than a fever and the resultant scarring is the result of a faulty pistol, Elizabeth wastes no time in removing her sister from Darcy's attentions.

Becoming increasingly low on funds and with no male heirs to take command of his estate, Mr. Bennet calls upon his great-nephew, Pastor Collins (Matt *"Doctor Who"* Smith of **TERMINATOR GENYSIS** [2015, USA, D: Alan Taylor]) to court one of his daughters. With his first choice (the fair Jane) already promised to Mr. Bingley, Collins opts to woo the unwilling Elizabeth instead. As they travel to the local village to partake of cake and beverages, the Pastor and the girls happen across an over-turned coach. Drawn to it by cries of help coming from within, when the occupant emerges (and reveals herself to be a zombie) the Pastor absently muses that the undead have retained enough of their human intelligence to orchestrate a rather well-planned ambush. Following this already colorful mix of characters and events, we are inevitably introduced to the deceitful Mr. Wickham (Jack Huston of **AMERICAN HUSTLE** [2013, USA, D: David O. Russell]). Having grown

Long Gams & Long Guns: Three out of the five leggy (and etc.) Bennet Sisters—Mary (Millie Brady), Lydia (Ellie Bamber) and Elizabeth (Lily James)—draw a triple-bead with their lady-sized rifles in **P+P+Z**

up in the same household as Darcy but with the latter acting openly hostile to his childhood friend, Elizabeth finds herself drawn towards Wickham's seeming sincerity. Following a ball wherein he overhears Mrs. Bennet's plans to marry all of her daughters off to well-heeled individuals, Darcy convinces Bingley of the family's monopolist intent towards his fortune. This is an unfortunate decision that allows Wickham to lure Elizabeth into his confidence.

With the first act establishing not only the milieu but also the menace that has come to threaten it, even the casual viewer is left in little doubt as to the direction in which the production is heading. Following Charles Dance's opening credits monologue (effectively bridging the gap between the emergence of the infestation and the "present day") we are swiftly introduced to the pivotal heroine, Elizabeth Bennet. Falling into the same category as, but far more rounded than either Kate Beckinsale's Anna Valerious (from **VAN HELSING** [2004, USA, D: Stephen Sommers) or Gemma Arterton's Gretel (from **HANSEL AND GRETEL** [2013, USA/Germany, D: Tommy Wirkola]), Ms. James' Elizabeth character is a woman very much of the independent breed. Feminine, well-educated and adorable, beneath the genteel façade there beats the heart of a warrior. As with all sisters, the Bennet girls (whilst employing their martial arts training) argue incessantly. However, as a unit (and in particular when faced by a zombie horde!) they present a formidable force to be reckoned with. Unsheathing weapons

(we assume) they habitually secrete in their boots and stocking tops, there is a definite balletic grace about the girls' zombie-slaying antics.

Changing gear somewhat, the second act of **PRIDE AND PREJUDICE AND ZOMBIES** (whilst concentrating more on character interaction) serves to introduce the film's "wolf in the fold". As dashing as Mr. Wickham is, he remains a man with a decidedly chequered past. Darcy despises Wickham, and evidently the feeling is mutual. A master manipulator (albeit in a plan that will sensationally backfire on him), Wickham seeks to exploit the more charitable and caring side of Elizabeth's nature. Last, but by no means least, there is the up-tempo, action-oriented third act of the movie. With one of the Bennet sisters kidnapped by Wickham and held prisoner in the In-Between, both Darcy and Elizabeth charge to the rescue. Alas, with the zombie horde amassing in great numbers and time being of the essence, who will make it across Hingham Bridge before it is ultimately detonated?

When a film of **PRIDE AND PREJUDICE AND ZOMBIES'** undeniable caliber belly-flops at the box-office (reclaiming just $16 million worldwide of its $28 million outlay), one has to wonder what it is that audiences truly crave in this day and age. With an abundance of youthful, handsome cast members, a pacey narrative and a plethora of zombie extras, it's clear that the film was aimed at a predominantly teenage to early-30s demographic. In an area of the horror genre where repetition is beginning to strip the zombie of its natural menace, **PRIDE AND PREJUDICE AND ZOMBIES** offers a rather unique take on the ranks of the walking dead. Establishing early on that zombies remain inert until they eat the brains of human prey, that a community of reanimated cadavers not only exists, but regularly attends Mass to partake of a pig-brain concoction, comes as something of a revelation. Whilst not the stars of the show, the zombies manifest in the film are aesthetically quite brilliant. With mucus oozing through bared nasal passages, and tongues lolling out of emaciated cheeks, the humanity inherent in the film's undead adds an extra layer of creepiness to the proceedings. Add to this the sheer scale of a scene involving the zombie masses swarming towards the last bastion of Hingham Bridge and what you have in **PRIDE AND PREJUDICE AND ZOMBIES** is a film that ticks every box on this particular monster fan's check-list.

Whilst the mash-up concept of Smith's novel may have appeared bizarre, to say the least, its 2009 release was to coincide with a massive rise in the popularity of the zombie archetype. Latterly adapted into the sequential art form by scribe Tony Lee and *Buffy the Vampire Slayer* artist Cliff Richards, whilst both the book and graphic novel were highly entertaining, neither was to loan itself readily to the cinematic medium. With the yarn unraveled and reknit into a working screenplay by director Burr Steers, the film began shooting on September 24th, 2014. It was filmed against some wonderfully evocative backdrops in Buckinghamshire and Hertfordshire, and location work eventually wrapped in Surrey on November 21st. Released by Screen Gems in the USA on February 5th, 2016 and in the UK six days later, the film was met with mixed to below-average reviews from critics. Whilst many chose to criticize the film for not being "scary" enough, of the commentators who appreciated the enthusiasm of the production, most agreed that it was an observant, contemporaneous take on the starchy melodramas of the 19th Century. For monster kids such as myself who recognize the spectacle of the costume drama (but would rather dispense with the foppish romance), **PRIDE AND PREJUDICE AND ZOMBIES** is a quintessential slice of British comedy-horror. A film that refuses to take itself too seriously, and one wherein the actors genuinely appear to be having a great deal of fun, whilst the cast as a whole are magnificent, there are a handful of performances that particularly stand out. First of these (and fresh from playing the title role in Disney's **CINDERELLA** [2015, USA, D: Kenneth Branagh]) is Lily James as Elizabeth. Equally at ease with character-driven dialogue as she is at wielding a sword, James is nowhere near as fragile as her outward appearance might suggest. As the revered Colonel Darcy, Sam Riley delivers a suitably arrogant performance, while Jack Huston is sublimely duplicitous as the villainous Mr. Wickham. The very best of the bunch however, is the marvelous Matt Smith. A relative unknown until he was cast by show-runner Steven Moffat to replace fan favorite David Tennant in the long-running science fiction series *Doctor Who* (BBC TV, 1963-) Smith brings his unique flair for physical comedy to the role of Pastor Collins. With his delivery, timing, and incredible energy influencing every scene he appears in, I found myself sorely lamenting the day he relinquished the keys of the T.A.R.D.I.S.

A sumptuous slice of Austen-inspired melodrama abundant with well-choreographed fight scenes and wittily-scripted exchanges, if **PRIDE AND PREJUDICE AND ZOMBIES** doesn't leave you quietly satisfied, then it could well be you're already infected.

NIGHT OF THE LIVING BABES

Reviewed by Michael Hauss

USA, 1987. D: "Jon Valentine"/Gregory Dark

Magnum Entertainment's Beta/VHS tagline: *"If John Waters Met George Romero You'd Get..."*

This is one of those shot-on-video (SOV) "films" that came from the prolific glut of amateur

It ain't called **PRIDE AND PREJUDICE AND ZOMBIES** for nothing!

production houses pumping-out inferior product straight to home video back in the late '80s. **NOTLB** is cheap as they come, and the actors and actresses are, for the most part, inept in their roles. The plot revolves around two dumb fucks, Chuck (Andy Nichols) and Buck (Louie Bonanno). Chuck's the chatty, outgoing, aggressive one, who is cheating on his wife Sue (Michele Bauer) with any strange woman he can find; while Buck is the weak, passive one who follows meekly along behind him, is madly in love with—*worships*, in fact—his wife Lulu (Connie Woods) and doesn't condone fellow dumb fuck Chuck's cheating ways at all. During a barbecue where Chuck burns the wieners, he shows Buck a newspaper ad for a new place called "Zombie Fantasy Ranch", which Chuck wants to visit, but when asked, Buck refuses to accompany him there. Later that night, Chuck, under the pretense of going bowling, picks up Buck, and when the latter realizes that they are *not* headed in the direction of the bowling alley, Chuck says, "I have a little surprise for you, Buckaroo: we *ain't* going bowling, we're going *balling!*" Buck pleads with Chuck not to go through with it, as he wants no part of it, but Chuck obstinately drives on, talking constantly as they drive. Buck says he's happy with his significant other Lulu, to which Chuck replies, as though it's the only thing that matters, "But will your wife put on garters and pumps and make a braying noise like a donkey in heat?"

They arrive at the Zombie Fantasy Ranch, which turns out to be a home in the suburbs with a cheap-ass sign above its door that says "Mondo Zombie Palace". Buck flatly refuses to go in, but Chuck drags him in against his will. Once inside, they are greeted at the door by a hot woman named Igor (Cynthia Clegg), who leads them to the "lady" of the house, the so-called Madame Mondo (Forest Witt). "She", as it turns out, is an annoyingly unfunny guy in drag, who speaks in that way-overused emasculated falsetto used by

so many female impersonators, which is totally irritating. Mme. Mondo brings out four of her girls, whom she calls the "Mondo Zombie Girls". They have purple, green, pink and blue hair, are all topless, proceed to do some cheers, cheerleader-style, then—in what is an obvious nod to The Mouseketeers on *The Mickey Mouse Club*, of all things!—introduce themselves as Darlene, Doreen, Annette and Cubby. Chuck chooses Doreen, then chooses Darlene for Buck. Former pair then take turns playing cowboy-on-a-horse and Indian-on-a-horse—*clothed*, I might add—while latter pair have slow, passionate "sex" (with their undergarments still on, natch). The movie flashes back and forth to the guys' adventures and Sue and Lulu at home together watching you-know-who's **NIGHT OF THE LIVING DEAD** (1968, USA) on the television. Sue, who knows full-well that Chuck is constantly screwing around on her, says to Lulu, "I had a dream the other night that I killed Chuck with his golf trophy". To which Lulu replies, "That's *horrible*". Sue then shoots back, "No, what's horrible is that he came back to life as a *zombie*, and he wouldn't shut up!"

Meanwhile, back at the (chicken) ranch, when the boys come round after having passed-out following all their "energetic" (read: lethargic)

A quartet of artistically-composed and cerebrally-stimulating images from **NIGHT OF THE LIVING BABES**; that's "Scream Queen" Michelle Bauer—who was billed hereon as Michelle "McClellan"—displaying her amazing acting abilities at bottom left

erotic exploits, they find themselves chained to a wall in the cheap-looking ranch-house interior, wearing pink tutus and tights, no less. You see, Mondo's plan for the duo is to "soften" their brains (which shouldn't be too difficult, considering how soft in the head they are already!) and then, by means of a sex-change raygun device, plans on transforming them into beautiful teenage cheerleaders like the Mondo Zombie Girls. But first they are subjected to the worst tortures ever; which includes a beautiful, big-silicone-breasted stripper who strips down to her G-string and dances non-stop until the boys just can't take it anymore (and neither can we!). Still in need of some more brain-softening, Mme. Mondo then orders, "Turn on the muzak!" If that doesn't do it, then this videotaped atrocity certainly will.

NOTLB has the seedy, sleazy look and feel of a porno flick, and not surprisingly the director hiding behind that "Jon Valentine" alias is none other than the notorious Greg Dark (born Gregory Hippolyte Brown), who, in his adult films such as **NEW WAVE HOOKERS** (1985) and **DEVIL IN MISS JONES: A NEW BEGINNING** (1986, both USA) sent porno films back into the gutter from whence they came by having the subject matter wallow in nasty, nightmarish worlds of sexual excess. His adult films are soul-draining, mind-debasing, degrading experiences to both the films' female participants and the viewers. Dark, a director, producer, screenwriter and music video director, later helmed hundreds of music videos for such wildly varying artists as Linkin Park, Snoop Dogg, Britney Spears, Sublime and the Melvins. There are plenty of online sources that can be referenced about the life and films of the notorious Gregory Dark. Dark also directed a few B-movies along the way, including the crazy Wings Hauser/Brion James sci-fi actioner **DEAD MAN WALKING** (1988) and moonlighting wrestler Kane's stalk-and-slasher **SEE NO EVIL** (2006, both USA), among others.

The main interest in viewing the present production for this reviewer was the inclusion in the cast of the always enjoyable Michelle Bauer, who at this point in her early career was easy on the eyes and had no problem getting naked, as she does in this film (she at least gets topless, anyway), but her acting is over-exaggerated and just plan awful, as are most of her performances. Bauer, who began her acting career in adult films under the name Pia Snow, as of this writing had appeared in more than 130 productions, and is still going strong. She's best-known for **CAFE FLESH** (1982, USA, D: Stephen Sayadian), **HOLLYWOOD CHAINSAW HOOKERS**

(1988, USA, D: Fred Olen Ray), the Jess Franco stinker **LUST FOR FRANKENSTEIN** (1988, Spain/USA) and **GINGERDEAD MAN 2: PASSION OF THE CRUST** (2008, USA, D: Silvia St. Croix). As Chuck herein, Andy Nichols is at least a wee bit amusing with his voice mannerisms and facial distortions. To date he has nine credits to his name, including one in Chuck Vincent's (another director of pornography) R-rated coming-of-age teencom **STUDENT AFFAIRS** (1987, USA), which boasts a cast full of adult performers, including Tracey Adams and Veronica Hart, among others. Buck's portrayer Louis Bonanno has some 13 credits, including a small part in the Vanilla Ice film **COOL AS ICE** (1991, USA, D: David Kellogg) and the lead role in the aforementioned **STUDENT BODIES**. Forest Witt, the actor who plays Mme. Mondo, oddly enough starred in the television series *Fudge* (1995, USA) alongside *The Brady Bunch*'s Eve Plumb, of all people; the series was based on the successful series of Judy Blume books.

Screenwriter Anthony R. Lovett (as "Veronica Cing-mars" [?!]) was also involved in the adult film business as a screenwriter and director. The dialogue in **NOTLB** is stupid, offensive and "totally non-politically correct", as we say these days. The worst, most inane passage comes around 33 minutes into the only roughly hour-long movie, when the chained Chuck asks Igor (who's female, don't forget) what kind of woman Mme. Mondo is, to which Igor replies, "Madame Mondo is a real swell lady. When she first found me, I was out on the streets blowing people's dogs for a quarter, because I was addicted to anti-freeze, just so I could get another half-gallon of coolant." The whole production here is totally amateurish, and everything from top to bottom screams that out loud (at the top of its voice, in fact). The film runs around 58 minutes, and it takes until right near the end before Michelle Bauer finally first loses her top, so all the filler between that time

HISSS had something which most other Indian horror flicks could never afford: really *good* special effects. These largely practical sequences, created by master monster-maker Robert Kurtzman (John Carpenter's IN THE MOUTH OF MADNESS [1995], THE NIGHT FLIER [1997; see p.65], Kevin Smith's TUSK [2014], to mention only a few of his creature creations), transformed actress Mallika Sherawat from hot babe into slithering horror. Some CG was also utilized to complete the sequences

is pure excruciating drivel that could have been written by any pimply-faced teenage male from that timeframe. This is pretty much a total waste of time, in all reality, that might appeal to some '80s sex comedy enthusiasts, but for the rest it's nothing but a time-waster for when you've got a few thousand spare brain-cells to kill.

The "Mondo Zombie Girls" are only called that because they are hypnotized and then used at the ranch to lure and entrap men. They can be brought out of the trance with the clap of the hands. NOTLD plays on a portable B&W TV, but there are no similarities between the two, except for the witless pun in the title. They are not the gut-munching zombies we are so infested with today in our culture, but they more harken back to the Bela Lugosi-hypnotized zombies from WHITE ZOMBIE (1932, USA, D: Victor Halperin). If you've got an hour of your life to waste, go ahead and watch this.

It's stupid, it's offensive, it's at times excruciating to endure, but, along with big hair and mullets, it's also got some of what made the '80s such a great decade for decadence!

The ending does at least boast Michelle Bauer topless. There's even an attempted castration with garden shears, and an eventual sex change is given to one of the characters. *[Hell, those last two things make it sound about as PC-friendly as you can get! – SF.]*

HISSS
(a.k.a. NAGIN: THE SNAKE GODDESS)

Reviewed by Christos Mouroukis

India/USA, 2010.
D: Jennifer Chambers Lynch

Ad-lines: *"She's sexy... venomous... and she'll swallow you whole... Vengeance has a sound."*

Back when there was still an appetite for films (and people still actually had a *job* along with their free time!), straight-to-video productions were a workable solution for producers who couldn't muster sufficient investments to turn out product that would receive actual theatrical distribution. And guess what, in the "mom and pop" video stores, their straight-to-video flicks (or even the shot-on-video ones for that matter) would vie for the same space with the major studios' releases; the winner would be the one with the better box art, and, as was so often the case, the independents would win the game. Similarly, TV movies were a cheap solution for TV channels, because, since you could see them on-the-cheap (meaning you wouldn't have to buy a ticket or a videotape/disc for the privilege) and their running times were equal to those of theatrical features, you would be more likely to accept the bottom-of-the-barrel results without too much complaining. These two formats may not be dead yet (SyFy does well on the TV movie front, and straight-to-DVD releases are a dime a dozen), but their future doesn't exactly look too healthy, mainly because they cost as much as the latest gazillion-dollar Viacom crapfest. It now simply appears that people check on the IMDb, and if a title happens to be straight-to-video, then it automatically becomes stigmatized as inferior. I often find myself biased against straight-to-video titles too, because the rule is that any real effort is only rarely put into them, and no matter how much I'd like to think otherwise, a decent budget guarantees a decent release and what usually comes with it. What is also certainly not extinct is the VHS format (otherwise you wouldn't be reading this column), but sometimes it makes me wonder how many more films I could store in my place if I hadn't have these hundreds of tapes, and had discs instead, not to mention an online "cloud", or whatever they call them. But then again, it fascinates me to have these nice boxes full of colorful art to look at. I'm actually so fascinated by big boxes that even in the DVD era I developed a liking for box sets. I actually want to buy one of these martial arts box-sets one day, and educate myself with it a little, but I never seem to find the time for it, not to mention the cash. But the Blu-ray era is quite peculiar, I think, because it has attracted all sorts of tech-savvy people who seem to care way too much about such technical details as formats, aspect ratios, 4K scans (etc.), whilst in the process forgetting to enjoy *the actual movie itself*. There are reasons why some movies are simply *shit*, and not even "High Definition" is going to change that, least for people like us, who grew up with them. So 2016 is the year I drastically decreased the number of discs I buy and mostly went the V.O.D. route instead (and for that, I am glad for this very magazine's Video Availability Information column in its back pages).

I am absolutely no fan of David Lynch. Even both his **ERASERHEAD** (1977, USA) and **THE ELEPHANT MAN** (1980, USA) bored me to tears, not to mention his experimental shorts that I had to sit through in film school. There appears to be "deep meanings" in his films, but if so I fail to understand them. On the other hand, a few years ago I watched Jennifer Chambers Lynch's **BOXING HELENA** (1993, USA) and I was impressed. Every time I mention to someone that I like Lynch's daughter, they seemingly assume she is a model or an actress, then I have to explain that she is a director in her own right. The few people who know her are mostly aware of her work in high-profile TV

SSSSSexy SSSSSScene: Actress Mallika Sherawat adjusts her rather revealing costume to make sure she stays safely within the limits of strict Indian censorship laws... "nip-slips" are *not* allowed!

series, but I consider her features **SURVEILLANCE** (2008, USA/Germany/Canada) and **CHAINED** (2012, Canada) to be her true masterpieces. **HISSS** is her only film that I hadn't seen prior to this review. It's easy to see why I managed to overlook it.

Set in India, the film has George States (the incredibly overacting TV-actor Jeff Doucette) suffering from brain cancer and wishing to cure himself; so he captures a *nag* (male snake) in order to attract attention from its soulmate *nagin* (female snake). Attention he gets, but the problem is that the she-serpent becomes transformed into a semi-human monstress (Mallika Sherawat, who for the film's screening at Cannes posed for photo ops with a living python for a prop) and next thing you know she's slaughtering people left and right in revenge because virtually every man in the film is a rapist! Now it is up to police officer Vinkram Gupta (Irrfan Khan, in a role that was originally intended for Indian superstar Amitabh Bachchan) to clear up the mystery, despite appearing to be not too much of a believer (the whole scenario is based on Eastern mythology) and find a solution.

This is Jennifer Chambers Lynch's only bad film to date, and it looks pretty much the same as your average (i.e., below-average) SyFy flick. It's not the CGI that's at fault, because that is actually quite decent most of the time (Robert Kurtzman was the creature make-up effects designer); rather it's mostly the whole air of '80s-style naivety that is evident throughout. **HISSS** is not without its merits though, as a lot of "symbolism" is prevalent (chances are someone like Tim Paxton would find more to appreciate here than me), and there is even an effective slow-motion sequence in which some blood-covered extras dance in the rain—a sequence which becomes laughable only when the choreographed gyrations start (western audiences should not worry though, as this is only a minor element and the film doesn't last two-to-three hours, as so many Indian movies do, but is kept to a more tolerable 98 minutes instead). Additional interesting imagery includes the female lead/monster slithering up a streetlight, and a lengthy, elaborate chase sequence which you realize—in student film fashion—was only really included at all in order for a number of interesting locations to be showcased. Jennifer Chambers Lynch went on record by saying that her **HISSS** screenplay was originally a love story, and that it was turned into a horror film in post-production when she no longer had any control over its creative process. She has since disowned it, and her bad experiences on the shoot have been documented in **DESPITE THE GODS** (2012, Australia, D: Penny Vozniak), a documentary which I haven't seen.

Top to Bottom: Three cover variants—the US, Hindi and Telugu DVD editions of **HISSS**

HISSS:

HISSS

Reviewed by Tim Paxton

India/USA, 2010. D: Jennifer Lynch

To understand the complexity of the whole genre of films about human/snake entities, you must first have some knowledge of what these creatures are. My first exposure to the genre came in early 2001, when I bought the Telugu-language Indian film **DEVI** (1999, D: Kodi Ramakrishna). Prior to that, I wasn't aware of sexy Indian snake ladies. I grew up in the 1970s, and our family occasionally went into Cleveland, Ohio for rare nights out together. One restaurant which caught my mother's fancy was a Krishna establishment in Cleveland Heights. Besides offering delicious vegetarian food, the lobby of the place was packed with mythological comics full of blue gods, Ravaska demons, and cobras. Another early memory is Rudyard Kipling's short story "Rikki-Tikki-Tavi" (1893), which was required reading in the fourth grade. I liked the crafty character of Nag the cobra in the short story. I *hated* the mongoose. That bastard killed Nag! I had no idea that Indian cinema was full of cobras, as well. My fascination with India never left me, and decades later I penned a lengthy article for *Weng's Chop* on *Nagin* or "Cobra Lady" Cinema (for wont of a better term, see WC #3). In it, I covered over 50 entries in this funky and fun fantasy/horror/devotional genre from many of the different indigenous Indian film industries—not just the Hindi-language industry, popularly known as "Bollywood". I also included a few other snake lady films just to spice things up.

And Jennifer Lynch's **HISSS** was included in one of those sidebars. The tales of Nagins in Indian cinema covered a period of 50-odd years, and many of them have similar plots. A well-worn and well-known horror trope for Indians involves the vengeful *Icchadhari Naagin*. This is also true for Lynch's film **HISSS**. It was released at a time when *nagin* cinema had—for all intents and purposes—become all-pooped-out (although a TV show on the theme produced by Shyam Ramsay did premiere in 2008, and proved to be highly popular).[1] But why make your *nagin* horror film open pretty much like any other Indian film on the subject? Why not treat the subject in a different manner for a change of pace? As **HISSS** began to unfold, I was left wondering whether director Jennifer Lynch might have believed she was "reinventing" *nagin* cinema or something. But clearly the film doesn't offer up anything new, and its oft-told tale of demi-deicide and the resulting snaky vengeance which springs from it predictably conforms to the genre's strict doctrines.

So why make the film? I haven't read any interviews with the director, nor have I seen the documentary **DESPITE THE GODS** (2012, Australia, D: Penny Vozniak), which chronicles the troubles Lynch had making the film, so I would imagine she began the project simply because she must've been inspired by the idea of the *nagin*, and perhaps she was hoping to make the mythology "hers"... but along the way something went wrong. **HISSS** didn't turn out like I would have expected. I do like the film a great deal, but it's just *nagin* cinema made by a Westerner with a load of cash at her disposal. Unlike all of the *nagin* films that

---

1   http://www.india-forums.com/tellybuzz/starry-takes/1818-the-new-naagin-on-the-block-rubina-sasihuddin.htm

A pretty weird *nagin* movie from Kannada-language director Om Sai Prakash, starring those superstars of Southern Cinema, Prema (of **DEVI** [1999] fame) and Soundarya (from **AMMORU** [1995])

came before it, **HISSS** actually managed to feature a pretty impressive onscreen transformation from snake to woman (and back again), involving both practical and digital effects (Indian SFX are mostly digital—and usually pretty *bad* ones at that). And, while I believe the film was quite successful at accomplishing what it set out to do, others had problems with how Lynch handled the material.

The story is classic: a scientist is keen on obtaining the fabled *naag mani*, a magical jewel or pearl which can be found atop the head of a demigod known as a *nagin* (male) or *nagini* (female). In the case of **HISSS**, the evil scientist is dying of brain cancer and seeks the *naag mani* in hopes of curing his illness. To do this, he capture a male *naag* and uses him to attract the *nagini*. Once he has her in his clutches, he can then demand that she produce the *naag mani* in order to save his skin. The *nagini* transforms into a beautiful woman (Mallika Sherawat) and requests the aid of a police inspector (Irrfan Khan) in an attempt to free her mate.

This is pretty cut-and-dried, by-the-book stuff actually, although the social commentary about the abuse of women in Indian culture was interesting,

and something which I'm sure that Lynch wanted to concentrate on. Interestingly enough, the Hindi press either went bonkers in a positive way over the film, or else openly ridiculed it (e.g., "Truly, when it comes to the quintessential Nagin story, it's got be Sridevi any day. Sorry, lady!"[2] and "I walk out of the theatre and hear popcorn vendors *[and]* ushers go, "Hiss, hisss, hissss, hisssss...." Hilarious! Nag, punch me. Please."[3]) Both critics and audiences had seen it all before.

Many Hindu gods feature snakes in their cosmic makeup, and their tales have provided the basis for many movie plots to be found within Indian Cinema. It is incredibly difficult to separate the two when you make a film about a cobra woman. In fact, I don't think I have seen one Indian *nagin* film which doesn't have elements of the supernatural, be it either overt or subliminal. Genre-wise, these snake films can variously be viewed as mythological, fantasy, and/or horror. Nevertheless, as with William Friedkin's **THE EXORCIST** (1973, USA), the underlying fact is that they are essentially *devotional* movies. Yes, these are religious films, which may come as a surprise for a lot of Westerners who watch them.

"Love, sex, action, drama—HISS has it all. HISS is the first Nagin movie after 24 years, and it's the scariest, sexiest one ever." So says actress Mallika Sherawat, who may not have known that Telugu director A. Kodandarmi's **PUNNAMI NAGU / NAGIN KA INTEQAAM** ("Full Moon of the Snake") had been made just a year previous in 2009, and had a similar plot which involved the sexy snakiness of actress Mumait Khan as the snake woman, Naagraaj.[4] Prior to that, the late visionary director Ram Narayan[5] directed the Oriya-language **NĀGA JYOTI** ("The Shining Cobra"), a 1994 *nagin* film which involves a scientist (we know he's one because he wears glasses and has a goatee—a

2   http://timesofindia.indiatimes.com/entertainment/hindi/movie-reviews/Hisss/movie-review/6793467.cms

3   http://www.hindustantimes.com/movie-reviews/mayank-shekhar-s-review-hisss/story-k9bacox38JF7pq2mkbn-mul.html

4   There have been two TV shows about cobra ladies, one produced by Shyam Ramsay called *Naaginn - Waadon Ki Agniparikshaa* (2007-2009) for Zee TV, and a newer series called *Naagin — Mohabbat Aur Inteqaam Ki Dastaan* for Colors TV (2015-present).

5   Ram Narayan (sometimes credited as Ramnarayan or Rama Narayanan) had made over 120 films in many languages by the time of his death in 2014. His *nagin*-related films include **DAAKSHAYINI** (1993), **NAG DEVTA** ([1994] this has yet to be confirmed), **NAAG LOK** (2003), devotional ones like **RAJA KALI AMMAN** (2006), and, most recently, the incredibly bizarre demon-possession/cyborg/transformers/kid film **KUTTI PISASU** (2010).

sure sign that he's a scholar of some sort!) who uses his sophisticated *nāga*-hunter computer and assorted mechanical gadgets to track down a cobra lady. He wants to capture the *nāginī* and use her *naag mani* to fuel his nefarious studies. In a final showdown—which is vaguely similar to the one in **HISSS**—it comes down to an elemental battle between Religion and Science. The cobra lady is captured by the scientist and subjected to the vicious attacks of robotic vultures (!?). Luckily, however, our victimized *nagini* is able to fashion a holy *lingam* (male symbol of Shiva) and *yoni* (female symbol of the Goddess Shakti) out of sand. She prays to Shiva for help and turns the awful avian automatons on the scientist, who is killed by them. Lynch's film gets nowhere near as wacky as that, but it does manage to satisfy my jones for fantastic thrills when Mallika Sherawat transforms into a half-snake/half-woman monster and takes the scientist to task.

If you warp reality a tad bit, you might even say that Jennifer Lynch's **HISSS** is a *very loose* remake of **NAAG JYOTI**. Seriously, I think it is.

As a point of reference, may I suggest catching up with the classic Hindi film **NAGIN** (1976) by filmmaker Rajkumar Kohli, who was responsible, along with the Ramsays, in "creating" Hindi horror cinema from the ground up. How influential and important this film may be *is* in contention, but I would like to point out that there wouldn't have been half as many *nagin* flicks produced if Rajkumar Kohli hadn't made **NAGIN**. Prior to it (not to be confused with the 1951 film of the same name which dealt with warring tribes in the Indian state of Nagaland), the genre fare overall was primarily devotional or mythological in content, which isn't surprising when you consider the cultural significance of snakes in India. Kohli took the *nāgadevatha* (yet another variation of the *nagin*)

and twisted it into a creature of hate and vengeance. The plot of **NAGIN** will begin to sound very familiar. This is the film that set in motion the "vengeful *nagin*" subgenre. A young man named Vijay (Sunil Dutt) saves the life of a male *nāga* (Jeetendra), and is consequently invited to watch the *ichadhari nāg* and his mate perform their courtship dance. Vijay returns next day with a few disbelieving friends to watch the pair from hiding as the two snakes get down to business. During a particularly sexy dance number, the female *naag* appears in her human form (super-sexy Reen Roy!), while her male partner stays in cobra form. Seeing what they believe is a snake about to bite the woman, one of the ignorant, trigger-happy hunters shoots the male snake dead. Shit hits the fan when, as the *Nagin* cradles her dying lover, she sees "reflected" in his eyes the images of all the men who were there that night. She knows what to do, and with hate in her otherwise kind soul, she sets off after the men…

In case you want to have a **NAGIN** film fessssstival of your own, here's a short list of the best remakes and rip-offs: **DEVATHALARA DEEVINCHANDI** (1977, D: Kommineni Seshagiri Rao; a Telugu rip-off of **NAGIN**), **NEEYĀ** (1979, D: Durai; a Tamil rip-off of **NAGIN**), **NAAGINI** (1991, D: Sripriya; in the Kannada language), **JUNGLE KI NAGIN** (2003, D: Ramesh Lakhiani; in Hindi), **POURNAMI NAAGAM** (2009, D: A. Kodandarami Reddy; in Telugu), and, yes, **HISSS**. So break out some beer, chips or *namak para*, samosas, kachori, or whatever your favorite Indian snack may be. Get comfy on the sofa, but be ready to spend the entire weekend glued there (and to the screen, of course), because each of these films averages-out at around 150 minutes long!

Hisssy Misssy: Reena Roy *[left]* and Jeetendra *[right]* as the sexy she- and he-snakes of Rajkumar Kohli's **NAGIN** (1976); essential viewing for anyone interested in cobra-chick flicks

GARGANTUS
BY CLODE & MARTINEZ

TIRED OF HIS LOCAL BEAT, PLUCKY YOUNG REPORTER KIT EVERHART HAS JOURNEYED TO JAPAN IN SEARCH OF A STORY.

I ALMOST CAN'T BELIEVE THERE MIGHT BE SOLDIERS STILL FIGHTING OLE DUBYA DUBYA TWO. DON'T THEY KNOW IT FINISHED EIGHTEEN YEARS AGO?

EXCUSE ME, BUT CAN YOU TELL ME THE QUICKEST WAY TO OKINAWA? I'M INVESTIGATING A STORY THERE.

OKINAWA? A STORY? THE LAST THING I NEED IS SOME PESKY REPORTER SNOOPING AROUND MY EXPERIMENT. I'M NOT READY YET!

PROFESSOR HAYANO HAS EVERY RIGHT TO BE FEARFUL, BUT NOT OF YOUNG KIT.

IN THE LOST BUNKERS OF OKINAWA WAITS A DREAD MISCREATION.

ロジェクト

ITS NAME IS GARGANTUS, ITS DESTINY IS OUR RUIN.

TO BE CONTINUED

THE NIGHT FLIER

Reviewed by Dennis Capicik

USA, 1997. D: Mark Pavia

Before embarking on **THE NIGHT FLIER**, by this point in his career, producer Richard P. Rubenstein had already produced numerous Stephen King properties, including George A. Romero's **CREEPSHOW** (1982), Mary Lambert's **PET SEMATARY** (1989), Tom Holland's **THINNER** (1996), and, as an executive producer, he also helped bring both King's *The Stand* (1994) and *The Langoliers* (1995, all USA) to television as successful miniseries. Unfortunately, **THE NIGHT FLIER** has never really been given its due, which is a real shame, as it not only maintains a palpable atmosphere of dread throughout but is also highlighted by a terrific central performance from Miguel Ferrer.

Richard Dees (Ferrer) is the senior writer at *"Inside View"*, a trashy (fictitious) *Weekly World News*-type tabloid whose primary mantra, according to Merton Morrison (Dan Monahan), Dees' unscrupulous editor, is to "identify and define the cultural archive of the American mind"; which is to say, delve into the trashiest, most outrageous stories imaginable! Dees is the ultimate cynic, who's seen it all, but hasn't had a cover story for quite some time. Bored and fed-up with his current position, he is assigned to investigate Dwight Renfield (Robert H. Moss), a mysterious man who pilots a black Cessna Skymaster into desolate, small-town airports leaving behind him a trail of bodies, usually drained of blood. Thinking he is just some random serial killer who believes himself to be a vampire, Dees—who wants to (quote) "get back on the front page"—rather resentfully accepts the job after it's initially offered to Katherine Blair (Julie Entwisle), a rookie reporter. However, because he also owns and pilots his own Cessna, the story is eventually given to him instead.

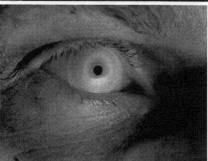

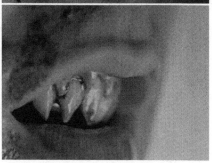

Above: The US poster and two creepy C/U's from **THE NIGHT FLIER**

Like many of Stephen King's stories, **THE NIGHT FLIER** likewise involves ordinary people from small towns who are overcome by some sort of inexplicable supernatural manifestation. In this instance, that uncanny presence is one of King's more fearsome creations, despite the somewhat tired "vampire" premise. At one point, even Ferrer as the jaded Dees skeptically opines, "Vampires are a dime-a-dozen"—which indeed they are—but the idea of the titular creature zooming all across the eastern seaboard in a black, bat-like light airplane (mostly seen in silhouette or from a distance) is certainly a novel one. Much of the narrative is related using flashbacks as Dees doggedly interviews everyone he can in hopes of getting ahead of this so-called serial killer ("You're gettin' under my skin, fella!"), but as he gets closer, he begins to doubt his own sanity, and at one point, when he smears blood on the gravestone of one of the Night Flier's victims to try and get a more sensationalistic pic, he even develops a psychic link with the vampire, much like Renfield's namesake had himself done in Bram Stoker's original novel. Earlier in the film, when confronted by Julie, whom he flippantly refers to as "Jimmy Olsen", he offers his best advice: "Sometimes the story gets to you" and you begin to "believe in the unbelievable", but as Dees gets closer to revealing Renfield's true identity, he himself begins to fall into the very same trap and starts not trusting his own advice.

Naturally, Dees' editor eventually pits one against the other when he also assigns Julie to the case, and even though they form an uneasy alliance, nothing will stop Dees from achieving his goal. When he comes face to face with Renfield at a desolate airport in Wilmington, Virginia, even Renfield is "intrigued" by his figurative "appetite for blood" (this is undoubtedly King's critique of gonzo journalism, which remains just as prescient an issue all these years later *[Perhaps even more so than ever, what with the masses more tabloid garbage that's plastered all over the internet these days! Pardon the intrusion ☺ – SF]*). But in a rather unexpected twist of fate, some of Dees' words ("Never believe what you publish. And never publish what you believe") come back to haunt him even further, and which Julie takes to heart.

Miguel Ferrer, son of late prominent actor José Ferrer ([1912-1992] best-remembered for his roles in Edward Dmytryk's **THE CAINE MUTINY** [1954, USA] and David Lean's **LAWRENCE OF ARABIA** [1962, UK/USA]), has appeared in numerous films and television series over the years, but is still probably best-known for his role as Bob Morton, the cut-throat executive in Paul Verhoeven's **ROBOCOP** (1987, USA). Ferrer always conveys a tough, almost angry edge in many of his performances (which also include Sean S. Cunningham's undersea creature feature **DEEPSTAR SIX** [1989, USA]), and his role here as the washed-up reporter, bored by it all, is some of his best work. Usually relegated to smaller, more often than not villainous roles, Ferrer easily carries the entire film and adds some real believability to the proceedings, playing the seen-it-all skeptic with marvelous aplomb. In one scene, when he comes across a nasty, blood-splattered car accident, he immediately begins snapping pictures, even going so far as to move the bodies around to get a better shot, and right under the eyes of the police, yet. As he follows Renfield's aerial trail in his own Cessna, Dees attempts to interview many of the folks who have seen this mysterious person ("He *ain't* no man!"), scenes which are highlighted by typically hard-nosed dialogue akin to some horror-tinged *film noir*. Early in the narrative, when interviewing Ezra Hannon (John Bennes), one of the mechanics

While **THE NIGHT FLIER** is first-and-foremost a vampire movie, zombies also put in appearances too

working at a small airport, this hardened old-timer quickly sums-up *Inside View* when he mentions using its pages to line his kitty's litter box ("It soaks up that cat-piss real *good*!"), his demeanor quickly changing when he begins describing Renfield's black cloak that (quote) "spread out like a bat", and a bizarre pile of maggot-filled earth underneath his plane. Later, in one of the film's more nerve-wracking moments, Dees enters the cabin of Renfield's plane, to find it caked in blood and with a strange pile of dirt in the cargo hold.

Upon closer inspection, **THE NIGHT FLIER** bears a distinct resemblance to John Llewellyn Moxey's ABC-TV film **THE NIGHT STALKER** (1972, USA, D: Dan Curtis). Adapted by Richard Matheson from Jeff Rice's then-still-unpublished novel *The Kolchak Papers*, this initial film, its sequel **THE NIGHT STRANGLER** (1973, USA, D: Dan Curtis) and the subsequent TV show *Kolchak: The Night Stalker* (1974-75) also inspired Chris Carter's *X-Files* (1993-2002), but the similarities between **THE NIGHT STALKER** and **THE NIGHT FLIER** are quite striking. Darren McGavin as investigative reporter Kolchak, a character very much like Dees, is also skeptical about the existence of vampires as he hunts a serial killer in Las Vegas, but gets more than he bargained for at the realization that Janos Skorzeny (Barry Atwater) is indeed a genuine undead vampire. Dees also doesn't necessarily play by the rules, and acts even more unscrupulously than Kolchak to get his story; kind of like a meaner, even more cynical version of the McGavin character, who's had too many confrontations with the supernatural. Even Dees' boss Merton Morrison is yet another ornery editor a lot like Tony Vincenzo (played by the late, great Simon Oakland [1915-1983] in both the **STALKER** and **STRANGLER** telefilms [see *Monster!* #10 pp.31-40], and also throughout the spinoff 20-episode *Kolchak* series too).

Originally published in *Prime Evil: New Stories by the Masters of Modern Horror* (New American Library, 1988), which also included stories by Clive Barker, Peter Straub, Ramsey Campbell, Whitley Streiber and many others, "The Night Flier" was later reprinted in King's own collection of short stories, *Nightmares and Dreamscapes* (Viking, 1993). The same collection also included "Chattery Teeth", which was later adapted as part of the made-for-TV thriller **QUICKSILVER HIGHWAY** (1997, USA) by director Mick Garris. Barely released theatrically by New Line Cinema in 1998, **THE NIGHT FLIER** made an excellent directorial debut for Mark Pavia, who was recruited by both Rubenstein and King after they saw his 40-minute "zombie love story" short film *Drag*

Four more shots from **THE NIGHT FLIER**, complete with major spoiler (*Oops!* Our [i.e., Mongo's] bad!)

(1993, USA), but for some strange, unexplained reason—if we're to believe the IMDb—he hasn't directed anything between **THE NIGHT FLIER** and his most recent film, **FENDER BENDER** (2016, USA), which is about a serial killer roaming desolate desert highways searching for potential victims. Sound familiar?

In the end, the rather unusual premise and a solid turn from Miguel Ferrer definitely warrants a reappraisal of this first-rate horror film, which, unfortunately, seems to be forgotten by most, which is a real shame.

BASKET CASE 2

Reviewed by Brian Harris

USA, 1990. D: Frank Henenlotter

When last we saw Duane Bradley (Kevin Van Hentenryck) and his deformed, monstrous twin brother Belial, they'd fallen out of a hotel window to their apparent deaths down on the sidewalk below. But not all is as it seems. In other words, it's a sequel and—"miraculously" enough—they're still alive! The twins are hospitalized for their serious injuries and placed under police guard, as they're being held on murder charges due to their killing spree in Pt. 1. Belial has no intention of doing time for his crimes, though, so he uses his mind-control ability to hijack his brother Duane's body in order to escape. Naturally, he leaves more dead bodies in his wake.

Just as Belial and Duane, now fully under Belial's control, leave the hospital, they're unexpectedly greeted by two women in a van. Though initially hesitant to accept their offer of help, Belial agrees after the older woman assures him she knows who they are and that she only wants to help them.

When Duane awakens, he discovers that he's no longer at the hospital, but in the care of "Granny" Ruth (legendary Jazz singer, Annie Ross) and her lovely granddaughter Susan (Heather Rattray). Not only has Granny saved them from a certain double trip to the electric chair, she's also brought Duane and Belial to a safe haven she's created for "unique individuals" (read: *freaks*) away from prying eyes.

Gradually, as Duane heals (he had a few broken bones from his fall, you see), the desire to start a "normal" life—one *without* his brother Belial around—begins taking hold; as does his growing love for Susan. Meanwhile, Belial becomes familiar with the hideous freaks under Granny Ruth's protection...especially one particular she-

Extreme Makeover: In what amounts to just one of the two *Basket Case* sequels' numerous detracting factors, the "new" Belial, often played in heavy prosthetics by his "twin" Van Hentenryck himself—here seen in a shot from **BC2**—looks just-too-gosh-darn relatively *normal* by half when compared to the far creepier and less-recognizably-human original model (see facing page, top)

freak named Eve. With both brothers now safe and in love, nothing can go wrong. Or *can* it?

A sleazy NYC tabloid called *Judge & Jury* is anxious to scoop all the competition as to the whereabouts of the notorious so-called "Times Square Freak Twins", so they send out their best reporter Marcy Elliott (Kathryn Meisle, who hasn't appeared in a monster movie since **BC2**) to pick up the trail—a trail that leads right to Granny Ruth, a.k.a. "Doctor Freak", and her household of unique individuals. Now Marcy, her photographer Arty (Matt Mitler, from **BREEDERS** [1986, USA, D: Tim Kincaid] and a private investigator named Phil (Ted Sorel, from **FROM BEYOND** [1986, USA, D: Stuart Gordon]) know exactly where the Bradley Brothers are hiding, and they're determined to get to them. Unfortunately for their would-be interviewers, however, Granny Ruth, her freaks and the Bradley Bros. intend on getting to the three snoopy outsiders first.

BASKET CASE 2 is, in my opinion, an oddball film. It has all the trappings of an entertaining and twisted little B-movie. There's lots of gross freaks, murder and—Zod help me!—even gross *freak-sex* too. The leads are likable enough and the special effects are glorious. That sounds like gold, right?

However, gone is the gritty, sleazy 42nd Street exploitation horror charm of the first **BASKET CASE** (1982). Instead of icky, gruesome and scary, Henenlotter & Co. here go with clean, wacky and over-the-top. It's the exact opposite of the first in tone, and perhaps that was their intention. Cool. Unfortunately, it *doesn't* work for me.

While Van Hentenryck's Duane is still naïve, kind-hearted, and ultimately likable, he and Belial take a backseat to Annie Ross and her Granny Ruth character. Ross is such a strong presence onscreen, very few of the other actors leave any kind of an impression of their own. The acting quality from the cast varies, but most viewers won't care in the end. This is Granny Ruth's film, and everyone else is along for the ride. That includes the freaks.

Speaking of freaks, it's hard not to admire FX wiz Gabe Bartalos' outrageous creature designs. He did an amazing job and the creatures were certainly fun. However, I wondered what might have been had this film cut out the comedy aspects and if Bartalos had created a much more realistic and scary family of freaks. (Yeah, I'm one of *those* guys!) Most of these freaks were so OTT, it was hard to take moments that were meant to be chilling seriously. Instead of Tod Browning's **FREAKS** (1932, USA), think Alex Winter's **FREAKED** (1993, USA) instead. They were cool,

Top: Belial as he looked in **BASKET CASE** *numero uno*, which is the best of the series by far. **Above:** Japanese "3-D" video store standee for **BASKET CASE 2**

don't get me wrong, and the work put into Belial was impressive, but it all felt so…well, *goofy*. They're more just simpleton monsters than freaks; more "doinky-doinky-doinky" than "dum-dum-duummm".

When boiled down, this is pretty much just a reversal of the first film. In the first, Duane falls in love and Belial ruins it out of jealousy. In this film, it's Duane who does the ruining, both for himself as well as Belial. It really does feel totally unnecessary, but it's here, it's weird—so get used to it, right?! I preferred Belial when he was the antagonist, the nasty, evil side of Duane. Here, they do their best to turn Belial into the protagonist,

Goon Squad: Way-overdone and too-cartoonish/rubbery makeups are another of the *BC* sequels' major minus points. Just for the record, the "freaks" we can most readily identify here are "Frederick the Pinhead" (Sturgis Warner *[rear, second from left]*), plus "Mouse Face" (Deborah Bauman *[front left]*) and him known as "The Man with 27 Noses" (Michael Rogen *[front right]*). Incidentally, Warner's big-headed, lop-eyed pinhead character was modeled after the towering "closet"-monster (played by XL actor Eddie Carmel) seen in **THE BRAIN THAT WOULDN'T DIE** (1962, USA); no less than that film's star/mad scientist Jason "Herb" Evers (1922-2005) guest stars in **BC2**, from which the above group shot was taken

show his emotional side and even elevate him to become the freak group's defender/champion. And as for poor Duane, well, instead he's the one pushed to the dark side this time.

Some find **BC2** funny, but I literally found no worthwhile comedy in this. Not a single laugh out loud moment was to be had, which is probably why I wondered how this would have worked as a straight-up horror film. I mean, if you're going to be a horror comedy, there's gotta be some *comedy*. I suppose I've always expected more than I should from the sequels. People like them, and that's cool.

On the release quality front, man, what a slick, colorful picture. Synapse never disappoint when it comes to their releases. This looked *fantastic* on my HD TV, and the sound was on-point, even through my on-set speakers. I'd say it's a must-own if you love the film or you're a completist. Not a ton of extra material for this film outside of an informative behind-the-scenes featurette from Gabe Bartalos and an interview with one of the freak actors, but I can't see there needing to be more. It's just enough.

BASKET CASE 2 is probably hit-or-miss for some. You either really dig it, or like me, you just *don't*. I *want* to love it, but it's simply not funny, and veers too far from the original. If you've never seen this sequel, give it a roll. If you have and you love it enough, but haven't purchased the Blu-ray release yet, I would highly recommend it.

BASKET CASE 3: THE PROGENY

Reviewed by Brian Harris

USA, 1991. D: Frank Henenlotter

Months after the insane events that unfolded in **BC2**, Duane and Belial are still under the TLC of Granny Ruth, a.k.a. "Doctor Freak". Duane snaps back to reality after his psychotic break, only to discover that Belial refuses to speak to him anymore, choosing to focus on the pregnant Eve instead. That's right: the deformed, murderous little monster without a lower half that was incapable of performing sex acts in **BASKET CASE** (1982)—or *was* he?—was somehow capable of doing so in **BASKET CASE 2**, and has impregnated his grotesque girlfriend for Pt. 3. Congratulations, Duane! You're going to be an uncle!

With Eve pregnant, Susan dead and the gruesome deaths surrounding the *Judge & Jury* investigation still lingering, Granny Ruth decides to pack the entire clan of freaks up and take a trip out to the country to visit Uncle Hal, yet another freak doctor. Uncle Hal isn't the only person she's hoping to see, though: a very special "unique individual" named Little Hal awaits her arrival.

Things begin to look up for the crew, but Duane *still* hasn't shaken his mental instability, and Belial's ongoing refusal to speak to him only worsens it. Convinced that handing himself in is the only way the two can once again be one, he sends the police to retrieve his brother. Bad idea! Instead of capturing Belial, they shoot Eve and kidnap Belial's no less than *twelve* (12!) newborn freaklings.

Now the freaks must take a stand, rescue the beastly babies from the police department, and eliminate the threat to their existence. Unfortunately, Belial is injured during the assault on the precinct, and the sheriff will only agree to hand over the babies as a trade: the kiddies in exchange for their daddy. The trade is agreed upon, but Belial has no intention of

US Blu-ray

allowing his children to be orphans...

If you've seen **BASKET CASE 2**, you know what you'll be getting into with **BC3**. As I mentioned in my review of Pt. 2, the present film also has all the right ingredients to be entertaining, but lacks not only the scares necessary to a horror film, but also the laughs necessary for comedy, too.

BASKET CASE III

Executive Producer: James Glickenhaus; Produced by Edgar Levins
Written and Directed by Frank Henenlotter

US video promo still

71

Ghanaian poster for **BASKET CASE 3** (art by Death Wonder)

Once again, Annie Ross is the dominant force here. Even though it seems as though there's less of her in this sequel, her strong character rules the roost. Van Hentenryck is still just as "Duane" as ever, with the crazy turned-up a few notches more. This aspect was occasionally amusing, but it got old fast. The loopier he gets, the more drama he causes, and though some instances are supposed to be funny, they simply *don't* work. One particular sequence involving the sheriff's B&D+S/M bad girl daughter going full-leather on Duane should have been sexy *and* funny. It just fell flat, like the short-lived tent in my pants. The addition of Little Hal (played by Jim O'Doherty) and his fun quips about pregnancy were entertaining, but we don't get nearly enough of him to keep the laughs rolling. Despite the material being unfunny though, the actors—outside of a few poorer performances—did a solid job.

Returning for the FX is Gabe Bartalos and crew, and, as in the last film, it's all wonderfully weird. The creatures (freaks) seem to have received sculpt touchups and color overhauls since **BC2**, which works well enough (but for me was way too *colorful*). The reds and blues were just out of control! The freaks did indeed become monsters for this second sequel.

Gore? Yes, please! There's all kinds of that as well, and it's killer. The police department segment is

where we see the majority of it, and it's dished-out generously.

I have to say, while I did like the effects work—even though it's still more on the fantastical side than in Pt. 2—the gas-powered, Belial-driven exoskeleton was a true letdown. If you're going to do a psychotic freak in an exoskeleton, you gotta go hard. They did not. While I understand that it's about budget, I don't feel it worked. I cringed as the sheriff attempted to go toe-to-toe with Belial; it wasn't at all convincing. Speed-up the film, give us creative angles, make the machine look strong and fast—do *something*! **ALIENS** (1986, USA/UK, D: James Cameron) this was not. Hell, **RETURN OF THE LIVING DEAD III** (1993, USA, D: Brian Yuzna) this was not. But what can you do? There are times when practical effects fail; this is one of them.

If you're a fan of this film, or a completionist, need I tell you that this is a Synapse release and it's well worth owning? The picture is clean, looks great, and the sound is clear. Some might even say it looks and sounds better than it ought to. *Might*. It's a solid job from Synapse, no doubt about it.

Concerning extras on this disc, there's not much in the way of special features—there's only a trailer, in fact. Frankly, outside of perhaps commenting

Japanese VHS jacket for **BASKET CASE 3**

73

about the freaks' paint-jobs and the construction of Little Hal and the exoskeleton, there just doesn't seem to be *anything* worth knowing about this production. The Henenlotter interview offered in the Gabe Bartalos behind-the-scenes featurette on **BASKET CASE 2** pretty much says everything you'll need to know. They wanted sequels, Henenlotter delivered, the FX people had fun, end of story.

And what of "the progeny" of the title? Were they at least fun? Sure, mini Belials with moving eyes and chomping mouths. They'd make kickass Halloween decorations or work desk buddies. Don't expect much, though.

BASKET CASE 3: THE PROGENY will entertain some, of that I have no doubt in my mind. I wish I could say I'm one of them, but they're just not my cup o' tea. I like creatures, gore and horror comedies, but I don't think they came together in this production, or the last one either, for that matter. They may be prime midnight movies in someone's home, but not *mine*.

GROTESQUE

Reviewed by Eric Messina

USA, 1988. D: Joe Tornatore

This movie-wrapped-in-a-movie has two concurrent storylines running simultaneously. It does get somewhat annoying at times, but stick

with it, and eventually you'll get to the ending, which is fucking incredible and features two "Famous Monsters of Filmland", who set aside time in their busy schedules to appear herein. I was pretty wasted one night and put on **THE SLAYER** (USA, 1982, D: J.S. Cardone), because I've made it my mission to watch everything on the erstwhile "Video Nasty" list, regardless of how boring or terrible they were. (Yes, it's a sickness, I know!) However, YouTube steered me towards this pick instead, and—man—am I *ever* glad it did!

Linda Blair, looking like she's on a *Designing Women*-type sitcom, plays Lisa. She and her non-lesbian gal pal Kathy (Donna Wilkes) venture out to the mountains to visit her father. I know Wilkes as the shrieking Mary Lou Retton-haircutted, piggy-snouted girl from **JAWS 2** (1978, USA, D: Jeannot Szwarc) and as the "Jekyll & Hyde" prostitute from the exploitive Hollywood Blvd. favorite **ANGEL** (1984, USA, D: Robert Vincent O'Neill). Here both actresses are phoning it in, and act more as if they're on a family-friendly sitcom than in a horror flick. Considering this movie is rated "R" and there were tons of opportunities for shower scenes, they really skimped on the nakedness. Then again, Linda Blair was running the production and had full control of what went on, so no sleazy business, unfortunately.

Resembling Ernest Borgnine wearing a John Milius disguise in this movie, Guy Stockwell (who was so incredible in Alejandro Jodorowsky's **SANTA SANGRE** [1989, Italy/Mexico]) here plays the dad, who's a special effects makeup

Dionne Quintuplets, Eat Your Hearts Out! Belial's and Eve's bouncing brood—numbering an even dozen in all—from **BC3**, which was aptly-subtitled **THE PROGENY**; thankfully, however, to date there haven't been any further "new additions" to the *BC* franchise

GROTESQUE

LINDA BLAIR (THE EXORCIST) plays a young woman whose vacation turns into a hellish nightmare when she encounters a band of brutal punkers who get their kicks from murder in GROTESQUE, a frightening horror film soon to be released on videocassette from Media Home Entertainment.

Media Entertainment promo still for the film's US video release

man and horror movie director. Everything seems peachy keen until some punks show up and ruin everyone's party. It seems slightly odd that city slicker-type weirdos would be wandering around the woods of Big Bear Mountain, but that's what happens. These lowlife cretins are the lamest-looking bunch I've ever seen—talk about "punxploitation"! They all incessantly make wisecracks, laugh it up constantly and wear out their welcome within a matter of *seconds*. One of them is played by Robert "**MANIAC COP**" Z'Dar with eye makeup and a goofy Mohawk, but for some reason he just kind of slinks around in the background and hardly gets any dialogue. (One chick actually emits a loud "dolphin" sound— what's up with *that* shit?!) Nels, a second-rate Van Patten brother, is in their crew. I mean, this guy is related to Timothy Van Patten, who played Stegman in **CLASS OF 1984** (1982, USA, D: Mark L. Lester), one of the most *terrifying* punks in film history. That said, the goofball way in which **GROTESQUE**'s poseur punkers behave places them more in league with Zed McGlunk, Bobcat Goldthwait's character from **POLICE ACADEMY 2: THEIR FIRST ASSIGNMENT** (1985, USA, D: Jerry Paris) or that "Randee of the Redwoods" dude from early '80s MTV! I'd imagine about the toughest thing they'd listen to music-wise would be Haircut 100, Big Audio

Dynamite or—maybe, when they're feeling real "edgy"—PIL.

There's a jaw-droppingly shameless plug for Burger King as Blair and Wilkes head on down to the drive-thru, order two sodas, and the cashier (evidently an actual BK employee) looks into the camera as if she's very excited to be in a movie. Every time I get a Whopper, I'll think of this film from now on!

A tertiary punkette (Michelle Bensoussan?) and *faux*-hawked (!) punker Robert Z'Dar (1950-2015)—who had earlier in '88 played the title rogue zombie law enforcement officer of **MANIAC COP**—make a nuisance of themselves in **GROTESQUE**

75

Top: "Bloody Serious" (or perhaps "Seriously Gory"?) – Scandinavian (Danish or Norwegian?) video cover for **GROTESQUE** (art unsigned). **Above:** One of the film's gruesome grotesquerie of images

one puts on the Don Post skull mask featured in **HALLOWEEN III: SEASON OF THE WITCH** (1982, USA, D: Tommy Lee Wallace) and a few other Post masks you might recognize which he finds in Orville's rumpus room. Lurking in the shadows behind a bookcase is the ghoulish sight of a mutated child with superhuman strength. His name is Patrick (played by Robert Apisa), he pulls real goofy faces and looks as if Sloth and Chunk from **THE GOONIES** (1985, USA, D: Richard Donner) got together and fathered a genetic mistake. After he witnesses his surrogate family being butchered, he goes totally ape-shit!

Director Tornatore overly establishes elements such as murders, or policemen walking towards the camera over-and-over on a Hanna Barbera-style loop. However, the surreal way it all pans out convinced me that this filmmaker is worth following and I even checked out another gem called **DEMON KEEPER** (1994, USA). That one gave me the impression that the screenwriter was so impressed by the satanic sorcerer played by Peter Liapis from **GHOULIES** (1984, USA, D: Luca Bercovici) that he took that lameass character and placed him in his own film battling other black magicians.

Tab Hunter does a great job showing up at the last minute to hurl the present film into even further bizarre territory. It's difficult not to give away all the details without revealing any trace of the plot, but I won't. I'll just put it this way: one scene reminded me of Allison Hayes' warped character in **THE HYPNOTIC EYE** (1960, USA, D: George Blair) when she rips her face off! The punkers really get what they deserve during the finale here. The cops predictably pin the blame on the hideous mutant child and claim there's not enough evidence to convict anyone. I only wish this scenario of idiotic cops dropping the ball and letting criminals loose was purely fiction! I liked how, even though it's a story set within an alternate reality, that overdone "twist" ending showing someone waking-up from a nightmare isn't trundled out of mothballs once again. You may think that you've got the ending pegged but—*WHAMMO!*—the rug gets pulled out from under you, and it's totally unpredictable. So be sure to stick around for that!

This film was written by Mikel Angel, who also penned **THE LOVE BUTCHER** (1975, USA, Ds: Don Jones, M. Angel) and **PSYCHIC KILLER** (1975, USA, D: Ray Danton), as well as delving into Blaxploitation early in his career. In fact, both he and Joe Tornatore appeared in Melvin Van Peebles' **SWEET SWEETBACK'S BAADASSSSS SONG** (1971, USA); and you can't get much more street cred than being involved in such an iconic, iconoclastic film as that.

Elsewhere, Stockwell's character Orville Kruger puts on different monster makeups to scare his wife and daughter. In the dead of night, the hooligans break in and slaughter everyone. The way these convicts behave is really irritating, they're either super-horny (but keep their clothes on) or cackling in each other's faces the way Dr. Hibbard from *The Simpsons* laughs all the time at inappropriate times. A couple of these fucktards screw, while

Shout! Factory put this DVD out on a cheapo quadruple feature called the "Vampires, Mummies and Monsters" collection. S!F seem to do that a lot with under-the-radar flicks that I'm fond of, including **CELLAR DWELLER** (1988, USA, D: John Carl Buechler). As for **GROTESQUE**, I highly recommend this film...it's really *out there*!

THE ALIEN DEAD

Reviewed by Christos Mouroukis

USA, 1980. D: Fred Olen Ray

Restoring films for BD releases is a peculiar thing. I am sure that the major studios have teams of professionals who take care of that for them, but I am also sure that not a lot of care goes into a release such as **BATMAN** (1989, USA/UK, D: Tim Burton) because they know that the product will sell itself. Kids who watch major studio product don't read too many reviews, and the product itself is so well-advertised and promptly placed at the top of any listing in all the online retailers that it will sell the minimum copies expected in no time. On the other hand, specialty companies such as Arrow Video and Vinegar Syndrome must and do put a lot of care to their releases, because their audience is reading the reviews (in magazines such as *Monster!* [etc.]) in order to decide what to buy. A film that deserves a good BD remastering—if only for historical reasons—is the one under review, but if you simply cannot wait until then, you'll have to check out the Special Edition DVD that is out there, which is what I did, and it's really good. This is a film that you should avoid seeing on VHS at all costs, because the cinematography wasn't great in the first place, and the downgrading makes it virtually impossible to endure in that format. Speaking of which... A friend of mine recently said to me, "Dude, I remember you going on a VHS hunt twenty years ago, and now only recently hipsters discovered the hobby". To which I replied that, back then *everybody* was renting/buying VHS tapes because it was the only way to see things prior to the advent of the digital age proper. For instance, back in the days before discs, I used to have a videotape of **BIG TROUBLE IN LITTLE CHINA** [1986, USA, D: John Carpenter] which was so worn out that some of the parts had turned to black-and-white. It took me years to discover the true gorgeousness of Dean Cundey's cinematography! So, yes, indeed, what version you see and the quality of your copy are important.

This was Fred Olen Ray's first "official" credit as a director, although **HONEY BRITCHES** (1971,

USA, D: Donn Davison) was expanded by him some in 1986, and **THE BRAIN LEECHES** (1978, USA), which would have been his directorial debut, remained unreleased. As for the present title under

D.I.Y. Zombies Get Busy!
Four shots from **THE ALIEN DEAD**, F.O.
Ray's promising feature directorial debut

review—F.O. Ray also co-penned the screenplay with Martin Nicholas, who can also be seen on-screen playing a doctor herein—you shouldn't be expecting any sort of "lost treasure" by an evolving young artist, although it does rather prove how he was able to execute material efficiently, and that he does, for which he was rewarded with an amazingly prolific and long-running career that spawned many low-budget genre gems ("diamonds in the rough", if you will). **THE ALIEN DEAD** was executive-produced by Henry Kaplan (associate producer of the superior shocker **I DRINK YOUR BLOOD** [1970, USA, D: David E. Durston]) and associate-produced by Shelley Youngren (who also puts in a short "cameo" appearance).

Set in Small Town, Anywhere, U.S.A., this film is about an alien meteor that crashes near said town and turns some of the locals into bloodthirsty flesh-eating zombies. People start going missing and others are getting killed, but at first the authorities, wasting precious time, are convinced that the dead bodies are the work of the nearby swamp's hungry alligators.

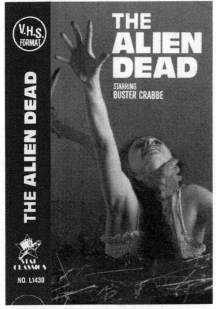

The VHS slipcase of notoriously shoddy discount home video outfit Star Classics' 1989 domestic release ripped-off its cover imagery from a much-more-famous source. This company typically released product duped on the cheapest no-name tapes possible, in either LP ("long-play") or EP a.k.a. SLP ("extended play" or "super-long-play") modes, for shame!

Yes, there are countless generic and establishing shots that last too long and all they actually do is provide standard coverage, and yes, the filmmakers seemed to have never seen how a Molotov Cocktail bomb explodes before, but **IT FELL FROM THE SKY** or **SWAMP OF THE BLOOD LEECHES** (as the film under review has variously been alternately known over the decades since its inception) also has plenty of charms, including its moments of nudity and gore.

Sure, **THE ALIEN DEAD** may be guilty of some lame humor and some stupid kill scenes, but its self-aware intentions for parody are well-served. At its best it is reminiscent of Roger Corman's swamp epics, and during its swamp scenes looks very much like **ZOMBIE LAKE** (*Le lac des morts vivants*, 1981, France/Spain, Ds: "J.A. Laser"/Jean Rollin, Julian de Laserna) and/or **OASIS OF THE ZOMBIES** (*La tumba de los muertos vivientes*, 1982, France/Spain, D: Jesús Franco).

Shot on a mere $12,000 budget on 16mm—which was later blown-up to 35mm for theatrical exhibition—by F.O. Ray (credited hereon simply as Fred Ray), along with Peter Gamba (a TV series editor by trade) and Gary Singer, the film was co-produced by Ray (who also makes a short cameo) and Chuck Sumner (who also has a cameo, but more importantly scored the film's soundtrack), **THE ALIEN DEAD** sometimes resembles like an 8mm student film, but it's better than most of those nonetheless. It stars Buster Crabbe (former Olympic swimming champ and legendary actor in the titular role of **FLASH GORDON** [1936, USA, Ds: Frederick Stephani, Ray Taylor]), and co-stars Mike Bonavia, who was also seen in same director Ray's own **BIOHAZARD** (1985, USA).

I was recently reading Clive Davies' excellent book *Video Spinegrinder: the Movies Most Critics Won't Write About* (Headpress, 2015), and I caught a minor error (which is relevant in this context). On page 17 during his **ALIEN OUTLAW** (1985, USA, D: Phil Smoot) review, Davies writes, "This 16mm production went unreleased anywhere until the recent dvd *[sic]* release (which looks great)". I hate to be correcting well-researched publishers such as Headpress, but **ALIEN OUTLAW** was in fact released back in the day on Greek VHS on the Home Video Center label with box art that is beyond awesome (said item is part of my personal collection). The lesson to be learned here is that pretty much *everything* was released on Greek VHS, including all sorts of weird stuff. One of the many positive things Davies' tome did for me, though, was reminding me to catch up with the film under review, which is definitely worth a look to those in any way

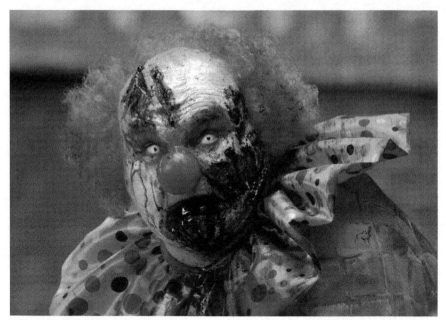
Don't you just *HATE* zombie clowns! But not to worry, this one from **DR:W** doesn't last long

interested in either Fred Ray's canon, or cheapo horror exploitation movies in general.

DEAD RISING: WATCHTOWER

Reviewed by Andy Ross

USA, 2015. D: Zack Lipovsky

It may come as no real surprise, but I reiterate, zombies remain my favorite of the numerous horror archetypes. Over the past five decades, the zombie has played an integral part in horror cinema. From the game-changing **NIGHT OF THE LIVING DEAD** (1968, USA, D: George A Romero) through to the bodice-popping antics of **PRIDE AND PREJUDICE AND ZOMBIES** (2016, USA/UK, D: Burr Steers [see p.50]), the concept of the zombie (i.e., relentless, cannibalistic cadaver) has never been far from the public consciousness. Making the natural transition of such undead creatures from film to the even-more-lucrative field of the video game, the arrival of Capcom's *Resident Evil* series was to welcome the shambling undead into the homes of countless gaming fanatics. Both for participants and for horror fans, the widespread attraction of the zombie-themed console game was by no means surprising. Depositing the player (in either the first- or second-person perspective) into

an unfamiliar environment wherein every dark corner there potentially lurks a hidden menace, the survival aspect of the zombie console game (and the highly personalized challenge it represents) has never grown wearisome. From the clutch of similarly-themed video adventures, *Dead Rising* first appeared on the XBox system in 2006. A survival horror "beat-'em-up", the game was to blend the most addictive elements of the pastime into a particularly frenetic experience. With a relatively light narrative centering on a photo-journalist who finds himself trapped in a shopping mall and forced to fight off wave after wave of zombie attacks, the most amusing aspect of *Dead Rising* was the players' ability to construct increasingly outlandish weaponry. Spawning two sequels and adding PlayStation to its list of compatible systems, *Dead Rising*'s eccentric blend of physical violence/copious viscera was to gain it a faithful and increasingly widespread fan following. On the backs of the (periodically hit-and-miss) game-based footsteps of **STREET FIGHTER** (1994, USA/Japan, D: Steven E. de Souza), **DOOM** (2005, USA/UK/Czech Republic/Germany, D: Andrzej Bartkowiak), **SILENT HILL** (2006, France/Canada/Japan, D: Christophe Gans) and **RESIDENT EVIL** (2002, Germany/UK/France/UK/France/USA, D: Paul W.S. Anderson), **WATCHTOWER**, was released by Legendary Digital media in 2015. Somewhat overshadowed by the still-ongoing output of the Milla Jovovich/Anderson *RE* series pairings, the source-faithful

Tim Carter-penned story was brought vividly to life in **DR:W** by director Zack Lipovsky. As with the game itself, which is an unabashedly tongue-in-cheek affair, the events of the film were likewise set chronologically between parts 2 and 3 of the original video game franchise.

In the fictional quarantined town of East Mission, Oregon, the government-funded F.E.Z.A (Federal Emergency Zombie Agency) are working around the clock to stem the emergence of yet another Zombie outbreak. While they are on the scene relaying news reports of the ongoing crisis back to the studio, keen-to-impress telejournalist Chase Carter (Jesse Metcalfe, from the TV series *Desperate Housewives* [2004-09, USA]) and his camerawoman Jordan Blair (Keegan Connor Tracy, from **FINAL DESTINATION 2** [2003, USA, D: David R. Ellis]) regrettably find themselves in the wrong place at the wrong. With the zombie virus seemingly resistant to the tried-and-tested Zombrex® medication and the containment center steadily losing control of its patients, the pair soon find themselves stuck right in the thick of the action. Upon getting separated from her colleague when his curiosity gets the better of him, Chase's partner Jordan is forced to flee to relative safety behind the quarantine wall, or else wind up zombie nosh. Meanwhile, finding himself well outside the safe zone, Chase joins forces with a female "negative" carrier of the zombie virus (the staunchly-independent Crystal, played by Meghan Ory (from **DARK HOUSE** [USA, 2014, D: Darin Scott]) and a recently-bereaved mother named Maggie (Virginia Madsen, from **THE PROPHECY** [USA, 1995, D: Gregory Widen]). Unable to escape from the city, which is infested with zombies, the trio of comrades-by-circumstance shortly find themselves holed-up in a pawnshop. While the two resourceful women are off gathering supplies and constructing weapons, Chase continues to send up-to-the-minute reports back to his outside connection, TV anchorwoman Susan Collier (Carrie Genzel, from **THE IMAGINARIUM OF DOCTOR PARNASSUS** [2009, UK/France/Canada, D: Terry Gilliam]). Trapped in a city under lockdown and imminently scheduled to be fire-bombed into oblivion by the military, as if the ever-present threat of zombie attack wasn't enough, the emergence of a brutal motorcycle gang led by the deranged Logan (Aleks Paunovic, from the series *iZombie* [2015, USA]) compounds the situation exponentially.

As a film which remains incredibly faithful to its source material, it perhaps comes as little surprise that those unfamiliar with the console game were to find **DEAD RISING: WATCHTOWER** a tad

Top: Director Zach Lipovsky with extra on the set of **DEAD RISING: WATCHTOWER**. **Center:** The third entry in the video game franchise which spawned the cinematic spin-offs. **Above:** In the movie, badass bikers have theirselves a zombie BBQ

confusing. As an aspect of the game that served to make it such an addictive experience in the first place, *Dead Rising*'s disregard for the constraints of reality are what infused the movie adaptation with a dark and yet irrational sense of humor. Inasmuch as zombie-survival horrors go, there's not a lot in **DR:W** that we haven't seen before. For instance, there's the hoary old trope that only direct trauma to the head can stop a zombie dead in its tracks. Similarly, there's the customary inventiveness displayed by the protagonists in the face of seemingly overwhelming odds…every last one of which is out to chomp on their living guts. What sets the film apart from all the competition (placing it very much in the darkly humorous vein of **THE EVIL DEAD** [1981, USA, D: Sam Raimi] and **SHAUN OF THE DEAD** [2004, UK/France, D: Edgar Wright]) is its sick sense of *fun*. Besides ludicrous amounts of blood and gore and some crazy first-person camerawork, the relentless carnage taking place in East Mission is continually interrupted by reportage from the news network, including words of wisdom proffered by guest zombie expert (and vetted survivor of *Dead Rising*'s Willamette Mall outbreak) Frank West (comic actor Rob Riggle, from **THE HANGOVER** [2009, USA, D: Todd Phillips]). Coming across like a hypermasculine hybrid of ex-wrestler-turned-politician Jessie Ventura and crackpot conspiracy theorist Alex Jones, West (whilst opportunistically exploiting his airtime during the ongoing crisis to promote his book, *How I Survived the Zombie Apocalypse*) remains the voice of cold, hard reason. A pivotal second-act addition to the mix, the arrival of General Lyons (Dennis Haysbert, from **JARHEAD** [2005,

USA, D: Sam Mendes]) serves to complicate matters even further. Could it be that the military, pursuing an agenda that directly contrasts the one of F.E.Z.A., are using the outbreak as a means of controlling the general populace…?

Returning to the classical zombie archetype (that of the slow-moving, steadily-decaying monstrosity) as with the game itself, the tension arises not from individual ferocity but rather from the sheer numbers of meandering undead and, fleetingly appearing among the massed zombie ranks, fan favorites the Soska sisters (Jen and Sylvia, from **AMERICAN MARY** [2012, Canada, Ds: Jen & Sylvia Soska]) 2012, Ds: Jen & Sylvia Soska]) each turn in uncredited cameo appearances. Given free rein as the accidental hero, Jessie Metcalfe delivers an initially naïve but progressively more seasoned and resilient performance as Chase, while, as Crystal, Meghan Ory presents a considerable force to be reckoned with. Maintaining ties with past horror masterworks, the inclusion of Virginia Madsen as the melancholy and confused Maggie serves as a timely reminder of her past dalliance with Clive Barker's nefarious **CANDYMAN** (1992, USA, D: Bernard Rose).

A readily-digestible popcorn movie that demands nothing more than a total suspension of your disbelief for close to two hours straight (yes, it's *that* long!), if you like your horrors to be humorous, goriously *[sic!]* gruesome, and rife with walking dead, then **DEAD RISING: WATCHTOWER** should definitely hit your Z-spot.

The first *DR* sequel has already been released.

DR:W's two-fisted heroine Meghan Ory goes Bruce Campbell one better

Boasting the same principal players (as well as—Billy Zane as a mad scientist!), if under a different director, **DEAD RISING: ENDGAME** (2016, USA, D: Pat Williams) gives us more of the same fun-and-funky mix of wry humor, outrageous splatter…and—*of course*—zombies, zombies, zombies!!!

100 MONSTERS
(妖怪百物語 / *Yōkai hyaku monogatari*)

Reviewed by Eric Messina

Japan, 1968. D: Kimiyoshi Yasuda

Back in *Monster!* #24 (p.61), I reviewed the sequel to this film, the same director's **SPOOK WARFARE** (妖怪大戦争 / *Yōkai daisensō*, 1968, Japan), which is the second part of a Daiei Motion Picture Company trilogy that began with the present title; the third and final entry being **JOURNEY WITH GHOST ALONG YOKAIDO ROAD** (東海道お化け道中 / *Tōkaidō obake dōchō*, a.k.a. **ALONG WITH GHOSTS**, 1969, Japan, Ds: Kimiyoshi Yasuda, Yoshiyuki Kuroda). Although I've been viewing them in "staggered" order, so to speak, after that other fun and eye-popping display of monster mayhem I reviewed earlier, I knew it was mandatory to take a look at the other two films as well at some point. Unfortunately, in this Pt. 1, the *yōkai* antics mostly take a backseat to the

dramatic meanderings of the human characters, but there are a few wacky encounters to keep your interest throughout.

100 MONSTERS begins with a wandering villager getting attacked by a one-eyed, bear-like cuddly/fuzzy creature called a *Tsuchikorobi* (土転び / "Earth Roller") that roams the forest and seems more simply intimidating than an actual threat to life and limb. He also makes an appearance in the third sequel as well. I'd be interested in seeing more from this character, as he reminds me of Gossamer, the giant orange guy that always follows Bugs Bunny around in those Peter Lorre haunted castle cartoons, such as *Hair-Raising Hare*. After almost getting clobbered to death, the terrified man returns to his village and begins his spooky tale… A shrill Theremin sounds and the eerie title track begins, which curls up your spine in a satisfying way. Sei Ikeno, whose music is often foreboding, cryptic and unnerving, does the score here, and he also worked on many films in the *Zatoichi* (座頭市 / *Zatōichi*, 1962-73, Japan) series, likewise along with **100 M**'s director Yasuda.

Gohei the caretaker is played by Jun Hamamura, who was in two other spooky Japanese classics: the universally-famous **KWAIDAN** (怪談 / *Kaidan*, 1964, D: Masaki Kobayashi), as well as another film that I recently reviewed in these pages, **UNDER THE BLOSSOMING CHERRY TREES** (桜の森の満開の下 / *Sakura no mori no mankai no shita*, 1975, D: Masahiro Shinoda [see *M!* #25, p.24]).

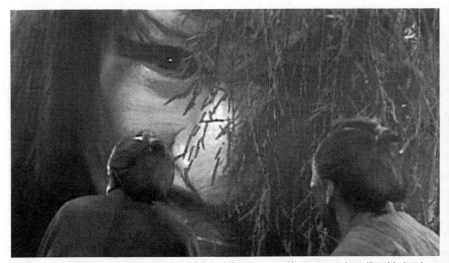

One of the **100 MONSTERS** says *"BOO!"* And if you saw a giant creepy face like this leering at you from out of the bush after dark (or even in broad daylight, for that matter), you'd shriek *"EEEEEKKK!"* just as loudly as these two terrified Japanese gents are

As **100 M**'s plot progresses, some evil landlords move into the territory and threaten to tear down the shrine which was set up to keep all the local folkloric beasties at bay. Once it's been disrupted/defiled, that's a good thing for we the viewers, but totally shitty news for those in the village, because it's about to be invaded by a horde of creepy creatures from hell! (Don't people realize that once a holy place is desecrated it's all downhill from there?!)

The magistrate's immature son Shinkichi, embarrasses his father. As played by one Rookie Shin-ichi in his only known role *[at least according to the IMDb, which, for all its many plusses, is by no means always to be trusted, info-wise – SF]*, the kid's performance rather reminds me of Buddy Hackett doing a bad impression of a stereotypical Asian. What with all of these annoying characters I'm hoping will be devoured and consigned to the stomachs of all the ghastly mythological beings that arrive later, my patience was wearing a little thin for this one. The biggest bone I have to pick with it is that there's too much padding for a Japanese monster movie where all the creatures are prominently featured front and center on the poster art. I was expecting to be wading waist-deep through the fascinating mythos surrounding *yōkai*-mania, but it hardly gets going.

Gohei (Hamamura) ends up mysteriously dead, and everyone in the house spins a few yarns—a *hundred*, to be exact, as per the title—about what went down. Okay, now we're getting somewhere!

The first story begins with two fishermen who are warned by an old monk that the lake in which they plan to fish is accursed; but, of course, they sarcastically chuckle at him and ignorantly continue despite his warnings. These moronic landlubbers are even warned by a disembodied voice not to eat the poisonous fish they have just caught or there will be dire consequences. Things get very Shakespearian, as the wife who cleans the fish is unable to wash the blood from her hands. Not only that, but it turns out she's a *Rokurokubi* (ろくろ首、 轆轤首) a creature whose neck extends into a dangling hose *[Say wha—?! – SF]* and she scares the *sake* out of the two dudes trying to eat their lunch!

A major problem with this film is that there are too many dull samurais yammering on about the monsters, which barely make any appearances. The way it's presented is kind of sleep-inducing, unlike the sequel, which is the best one out of the trilogy, so I'm glad they rectified that oversight later on. Had I not watched the second film and instead started with part one, I doubt I would've decided to venture onward. I'm actually a fan of Japanese cinema and love samurai flicks, but none of the mortal human characters here really

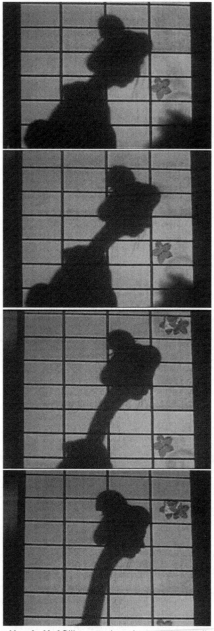

Heads Up! Silhouetted against a paper wall panel, **100 MONSTERS'** *rokurokubi* neck-stretcher does her thing

piqued my interest. After Shinkichi, who is pretty goofy, to say the least, shows up and he paints a *Kasa-obake* (傘おばけ), the cartoonish umbrella creature with a single eyeball and a waggling tongue onto a canvas, it springs to life and even slaps him in the

Top: It's the **100 MONSTERS**...or at least a fraction of 'em! **Center & Above:** Co-ed Tim's very own *Kasa-obake* figure, which he bought at a "flea market" outside a temple during a trip to Japan in 2009. Open the critter up and images of 12 famous *yōkai* can be seen within the pleats of its parasol

face with said extendable oral appendage like a peg-legged, deformed Gene Simmons. No one believes Shinkichi when he tells of this incident, because he acts like such a sub-moronic man-child. It's amusing how he paints the *kasa-obake* all over the walls in different poses, in the style of a stationary flipbook. There are a few moments of sheer lunacy to be had, but ultimately this first movie is pretty uneventful, sad to say. An example of where they dropped the ball happens when one guy gets attacked by a bunch of *regular* umbrellas, not even an army of mutant, one-eyed/legged bouncing ones. Talk about a missed opportunity! I did like the high-pitched sped-up noises the monster umbrella makes, which kind of sound like the one heard in "The Mummy" song by the skeleton pop group Tibia & The Fibulas from the classic stop-motion feature **MAD MONSTER PARTY?** (1967, USA, D: Jules Bass).

During the last 15 minutes of **100 M**, a few of the promised-if-undelivered "hundred" monsters start arriving, but it's not nearly enough and comes as much too little, too late. I hate to complain, because I really liked the sequel a lot. But there were simply too many missed opportunities to ramp-up the frenzied nature of mankind succumbing to the murderous clutches of an army of fiends in this originating series entry for me to excuse; so just consider this first outing as the sampler platter for the smorgasbord that's about to be unleashed later. In the last ten minutes we get a variety of creatures that are more prominently featured in the next film. There's a cool pig guy with a skull on a stick, the round headed Charlie Brown like creep wearing a grassy shirt and a giant flat nosed woman who laughs and laughs incessantly, I know as a five year old that would've freaked the shit out of me. Whenever I heard the *Tales from the Darkside* music as a youngster, it gave me nightmares and I was a total lightweight at the time. All the demonic creatures prance around in unison in a parade of weirdness, where are they going, I'm betting they are gearing up for more screen time in **SPOOK WARFARE** (1968, Japan). I'd say watch these in order so you can appreciate this series as a whole better than I did.

GODZILLA 1985
(ゴジラ / *Gojira* a.k.a. **THE RETURN OF GODZILLA** or **GODZILLA 1984**)

Reviewed by Chris "Doc" Nersinger

Japan, 1984. Ds: Koji Hashimoto, R.J. Kizer

This film—the 16th in the *G* franchise, and the last entry to be produced during the Shōwa period, making it the first entry of the Heisei period—heralded a new era for Godzilla, who'd been absent from the big screen for over nine years by then. The last time the mighty monster had appeared on screen was a decade before back in **TERROR OF MECHAGODZILLA** (メカゴジラの逆襲 / *Mekagojira no gyakushū*, 1975, D: Ishirō Honda). That film's failure at the box-office very nearly sank the franchise for keeps, and by this point many of the adults who had otherwise remained faithful throughout most of Godzilla's onscreen adventures had become alienated from the fold... Godzilla had simply lost his bite as a destructive force of nature by then; having been seemingly unleashed on this Earth via Man's own ignorance as a direct dire consequence of our entering the Atomic Age without properly considering all the huge responsibilities that come with wielding such a vast and possibly catastrophic power.

I myself grew up watching **GODZILLA, KING OF THE MONSTERS** (the English-dubbed alternate American release version famously featuring added insert scenes of future "Perry Mason/Ironside" Raymond Burr [1917-1993]) on late-night TV, and catching a matinee here and there in theaters during the later '60s and early '70s. During that general timeframe, I must have seen **DESTROY ALL MONSTERS** (怪獣総進撃 / *Kaijū sōshingeki*, 1968, D: Ishirō Honda) at least eight times and **GODZILLA VS. THE SMOG MONSTER** (ゴジラ対ヘドラ / *Gojira tai Hedora*, 1971, D: Yoshimitsu Banno) around five times at my local theater the Rivera for a mere buck on the kiddie matinee with my neighborhood gang: David, Mike and Pete, and their sisters Marie and Ginny... We had a *blast*, especially since the Rivera was built back in the day when theaters had balconies, so we got to hang our heads over the balcony railing; from up there, ironically enough, Godzilla loomed even larger, if such a thing is possible. Yes, those were indeed the good old days, filled with popcorn, Milk Duds, Sunkist Fruit Gems, Smarties/Fruit Bombs...and let's not forget loads of crazy *kaijū* monster action!

By the '80s, all that childhood fun and our favorite guy in green seemed to have disappeared, although we periodically read rumors in the monster movie mags that a new Godzilla movie was being proposed. But alas, nothing came of it. Not until years later, that is, long after myself and the ol' gang had stopped hanging out together and all gone our separate ways. News was that there was going to be a new *Godzilla* movie released in the States, starring Raymond Burr once again,

Top: Kids' **100 MONSTERS** trading card of *Dorotabō* (泥田坊). **Above:** New World's US home videotape mag ad for **GODZILLA 1985**

no less! And **GODZILLA 1985** was it. Was I ever excited! However, by the time I was able to catch it beyond its initial theatrical run, **G '85** had already gone first to cable and then to home video, so I watched it on VHS (via the pan-and-scan New World Video release), and, despite what I had read about in some of the reviews in the monster zines, I couldn't help thinking the movie was somehow missing a certain *something*, and that it just didn't have the proper *feel* to it. This was because it wasn't the same version I had read about, and some 20 minutes had been cut from the American version with the Burr scenes edited in. Left on the cutting-room floor along with all the missing footage was the Japanese version's harder, darker edge, which was what I had been waiting for.

Well, for the first time ever, it's finally hit American shores with an earth-shaking roar, and thanks to Kraken Releasing, we have a gorgeous Blu-ray complete with both the dubbed-into-English and Japanese-with-optional-English-subtitles versions. (The latter version is the one I prefer best, and the subs are printed in easy-to-read yellow.) The package also includes the original theatrical trailer, along with ones for both the aforementioned **SMOG MONSTER** as well as **GODZILLA VS. THE SEA MONSTER** (ゴジラ・エビラ・モスラ　南海の大決闘 / *Gojira, Ebira, Mosura nankai no daikettō*, 1966, D: Jun Fukuda). **G '85** makes for amazing viewing in HD with DTS HD audio, and you are going to see and hear the title titan like never before!

The present Big G adventure —a direct sequel to Honda's original "GODZILLA 1954" (ゴジラ / *Gojira*)—opens with a ship lost at sea that encounters, not only a deadly storm, but also what appears to be a very *large* green, scaly creature rising from beneath an volcanic island, plus an overgrown sea louse that drains most of the bodily fluids from all but one crew member—this latter creature has CREEPY written all over it in capital letters! It truly makes for one of the spookiest moments in the film, which boasts a higher special effects budget than usual, especially when it comes to the sets and during Godzilla's ground-stomping, trashing 'n' blasting of city buildings, et cetera…also when he "powers-up" to send debris flying everywhere while the military tries its feeble, futile best to stop him.

It's up to you, oh brave soul, to see whether Godzilla wins, or if mankind prevails to live another day. I'm not telling, but I can highly

If only skyscrapers had legs, they could flee from the city-stomping onslaught of the Big G!

Monster Multi-Tasker: Godzilla herds a fleeing crowd of terrified extras as he blasts away at a weird giant parasitic bug, while actively ignoring the Super-X attack plane buzzing around his head!

recommend you either get on your bike, hop in a car or do whatever it takes to get your butt down to the nearest retail outlet where DVDs/Blu-rays are sold. Either that or let your fingers do the walking and stop by Amazom.com (where it was a bestseller in preorders for over a month prior to its release). It's alternately available via such other dealers as DVD Planet, Deep Discount or FYE.

So for now, this is Doc Nersinger saying with a thunderous roar, "Keep it green!" and I'll see ya at the cinema!

THE FOREST

Reviewed by Christos Mouroukis

USA, 2016. D: Jason Zada

Jess (Natalie Dormer, who you're better off catching in **CAPTAIN AMERICA: THE FIRST AVENGER** [2011, USA, D: Joe Johnston]) is a gloomy/doomy Goth chick with—*what else?!*—dark hair, who often gets into all sorts of trouble (ah, those alternative kids!). Her most recent escapade is a visit to Japan's notorious Aokigahara

Forest (青木ヶ原), a.k.a. The Suicide Forest or Sea of Trees (樹海 / *Jukai*) at the northwest base of Mount Fuji, which is a famous "hangout"—oftentimes quite literally—for those wishing to commit suicide, either alone or in groups. The real-life location has made the news on a number of occasions for that particular reason; mostly in 2010 when no less than 54 people took their own lives therein. As is to be expected from a horror movie called **THE FOREST**, the prodigal Jess goes missing, so the Japanese authorities call her near-identical twin sister Sarah (also played by Ms. Dormer, albeit with blonde hair—oh well!) to break the news.

Although the chances are strong that Jess offed herself in said forest (she has a history of suicide attempts, as Sarah lets us know later), against the advice of her fiancé Rob (Eoin Macken, from **RESIDENT EVIL: THE FINAL CHAPTER** [2016, Germany/Australia/Canada/France, D: Paul W.S. Anderson]), Sarah catches the first flight to Japan, in order to investigate her sis' disappearance on her own. Several locals warn her about the spirits in the forest that feed on visitors' fears and sadness, causing them to see things that aren't actually real, but she nonetheless determines to go find her sister, firmly believing she is still alive, having that special mental connection which twins sometimes share with each other, and hence can instinctively sense when something bad has happened to one another.

At a small local hotel, Sarah is approached by the flirty Aiden (Taylor Kinney, from **ZERO DARK THIRTY** [2012, USA, D: Kathryn Bigelow]), an Australian journalist whose specialty is writing articles about travelling. He expresses interest in doing an article about Sarah's search for her sister, and she agrees (as if indulging in idle small-talk

whilst your sister is missing or worse might be construed as normal behavior!). Aiden too advises Sarah against venturing into the forest alone, but since he can't change her mind, he agrees to accompany her there, along with a local expert named Michi (Yukiyoshi Ozawa, from **THE HIDDEN BLADE** [隠し剣 鬼の爪 / *Kakushi ken: Oni no tsume*, 2004, Japan, D: Yōji Yamada]).

The three finally enter the title heavily-wooded area, and it's not long before they find Jess' things. However, because it's close to nightfall, Michi advises them to return to the hotel, only to have them refuse. Michi has no choice but to leave, but Aiden and Sarah spend the night together in the woods. Scary things happen during the night, most importantly the introduction of Hoshiko (Rina Takasaki, from the same year's **LEVEL UP** [2016, UK, D: Adam Randall]), who is a *yūrei* (a traditional Japanese ghost, about which I'm sure Tim Paxton knows more than I do *[Google or Yahoo are a mere fingertip away, Christos!* ☺ *– SF]*), and claims to have seen Jess. Further creepy occurrences take place, the most beautiful to look at of which is a gorgeous one-shot wherein the female lead ties a rope around some trees and a spirit briefly shows up. But Sarah doesn't have only the paranormal to fight against, as she soon discovers that Aiden has had pictures of her sister in his mobile phone all along! Who is he and what are his real motives? Upon subsequently finding herself stuck down in a basement with him, she will have to fight her fear, sadness, personal issues, demons…and even against reality itself.

Okay, this is more of a "search-and-rescue" film with a few ghosts thrown in, which I believe was mainly done in order to give it "horror movie" cred and ensure it received wider theatrical distribution, because apparently these things seem to be selling tickets these days. But it actually isn't bad at all, mainly due to its scares that come up in unexpected places and moments (which might well have happened unintentionally and purely accidentally, and was not necessarily intended on purpose by director Jason Zada). However, that said, there are many shortcomings to be found in **THE FOREST** as well, especially when too much reliance is placed on mediocre CG effects, when these could easily have been avoided and

Natalie Dormer—and *something else*—in **THE FOREST**

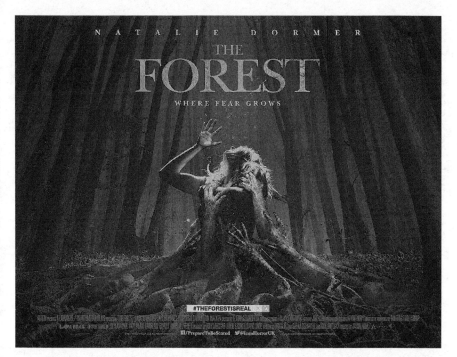

#THEFORESTISREAL

f /PrepareToBeScared   y @IconHorrorUK

done practically instead. For example, female lead Dormer develops an infection on her hand, whose squirmy worms appear to be CGI, for no apparent reason, making us wish that the days of Lucio Fulci and Dario Argento (*et al*) never went away. Another flaw is the lead actress herself, who doesn't seem to want to be here, apparently having been convinced to appear merely because she got a chance to play a dual role. Plus, the screenplay's second act is way too long and boring, but I guess if you are like me and want to see **THE BLAIR WITCH PROJECT** (1999, USA, Ds: Daniel Myrick, Eduardo Sánchez) done without the shaky camera work, this will do just fine! *[I finally stooped to watching TBWP last month for the first time ever, and it made me realize why I had done my best to avoid it for so long! Other than for a few far-between effective moments, talk about* lame*, the supposedly "scary" ending most of all! – SF.]*

This was the first feature-length film to be helmed by director Zada, but he had prior experience making short subjects, as well as penning **THE HOUSES OCTOBER BUILT** (2014, USA, D: Bobby Roe). **THE FOREST** was produced on a $10-million budget by David S. Goyer (executive producer of **GHOST RIDER** [2007, USA/Australia, D: Mark Steven Johnson]), along with David Linde (executive producer of no less than **CROUCHING TIGER, HIDDEN DRAGON** [卧虎藏龙 / *Wo hu cang long*, 2000, Taiwan/Hong Kong/USA/

China D: Ang Lee]) and Tory Metzger (executive producer of **THE ROVER** [2014, Australia/USA, D: David Michôd]). The screenplay was written by Nick Antosca (**THE COTTAGE** [2012, USA, D: Chris Jaymes]), Ben Ketai (**30 DAYS OF NIGHT: DARK DAYS** [2010, USA, D: Ben Ketai]), and Sarah Cornwell.

The present film was briefly mired in controversy ("bad" publicity which helped boost its popularity—at least at the box-office, if not with the critics), and it grossed some $37.6 millions, making it a minor success in terms of ticket sales, although no sequel has been announced as yet. It was executive-produced by Lawrence Bender (no introduction needed), Len Blavatnik and Aviv Giladi (together they also backed **THE BUTLER** [2013, USA, D: Lee Daniels], among other things), and Andrew Pfeffer (line producer of **THE MESSENGERS** [2007, USA, Ds: Danny Pang, Oxide Chun Pang], co-produced by James Ward Byrkit (director of **COHERENCE** [2013, USA/UK]) and Jennifer Semler (**360** [2011, UK/Austria/France/Brazil/USA, D: Fernando Meirelles]), and line-produced by Georgina Pope (**ENTER THE VOID** [2009, France/Germany/Italy/Canada, D: Gaspar Noé] which I recently reviewed over at *Weng's Chop*) and Andjelija Vlaisavljevic (**THE RAVEN** [2012, USA/Spain/Hungary/Serbia, D: James McTeigue]).

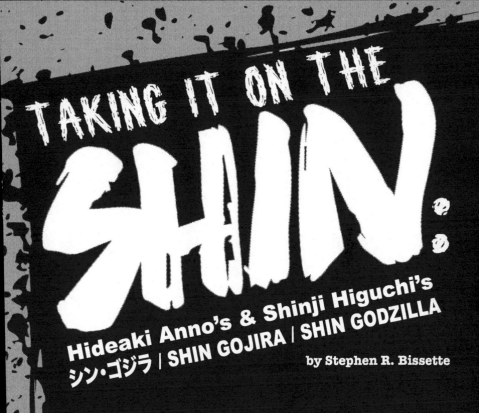

TAKING IT ON THE SHIN

Hideaki Anno's & Shinji Higuchi's シン・ゴジラ / SHIN GOJIRA / SHIN GODZILLA

by Stephen R. Bissette

This regular *Monster!* contributing writer *[Are you ever!* ☺ *– eds.]* fortunately caught Hideaki Anno's and Shinji Higuchi's **SHIN GODZILLA** (シン・ゴジラ / *Shin Gojira*, 2016, Japan) onthe big screen, and I'm mighty glad I did. This is Toho's third revamp (premise: this is the first-ever appearance of you-know-who), and yes, it breaks the rules—it radically revamps Gojira (physically, physiologically, in terms of both his function within the narrative and as a lifeform, as well as in terms of "his" life cycle), and it *tries* to do the same for the *daikaijū-eiga* genre in general. **SHIN GOJIRA** is a "giant monster procedural", paying far too much attention to the kind of bureaucratic boardroom dross that must fascinate Toho business executives (and reportedly was wholly Hideaki Anno's intent and concept), while devoting far too little screen-time to Higuchi's at-times-jaw-droppingly-inspired monster sequences. That said, I've both praise and some constructive criticism to proffer regarding Shinji Higuchi's spectacular special effects and monster set-pieces.

The new Gojira design is compelling, in some ways brilliant; the conceit of Gojira's potential self-evolution culminates in some magnificent images and moments. The penultimate and fully-adult incarnations of Gojira are truly impressive, its body seething with a shimmering magma-like inner fire that seems to be splitting his cooled-igneous-plutonic-rock-like skin/shell, the bristling teeth and tucked, spindly forearms and spidery fingers and massive legs making for a majestic and somewhat demonic *kaijū*. Ah, but those dead eyes—the lidless flat saucer eyes of the amphibious "tadpole" stage (looking for all the world like an *Ultraman* monster-of-the-week!), the nasty wee bullet-eyes of the adult phase—deflates what makes the rest of the creature so fascinating and almost terrifying. These are not the scarily "lifeless" eyes of, say, a shark, but those of a teddy-bear gone wrong. Those eyes, however, are the only real misstep, to my mind, though the writhing, wriggling "tadpole" landed laughs from the audience I saw the film with. Two carefully-timed gore fillips add to the impact—the torrent of rich, red blood gushing from the amphibian "tadpole" Gojira's livid gills, and the splash of blood from the adult Gojira's back as the missile attack from above scores direct hits into the monster's dorsal spines—but nothing here approaches the genuinely horrific imagery that made Shinji Higuchi's two-part **ATTACK ON TITAN**

(進撃の巨人 / *Shingeki no kyojin*, 2015, Japan) features such unexpected nightmare fuel.

Higuchi was a great choice to tackle the shared **SHIN GOJIRA** helm: Higuchi's background in anime and *tokusatsu* included co-founding Daicon Films/Gainax, uncredited special effects assistance on Toho's earlier reboot, **GODZILLA 1985** (ゴジラ / *Gojira*, a.k.a. **RETURN OF GODZILLA, 1984** [see p.84]), direction of the terrific special effects for the innovative Shusuke Kaneko's *Gamera* trilogy, as well as special effects for Kaneko's **GODZILLA, MOTHRA, AND KING GHIDORAH: GIANT MONSTERS ALL-OUT ATTACK** (ゴジラ・モスラ・キングギドラ 大怪獣総攻撃 / *Gojira, Mosura, Kingu Gidora: daikaijū sokogeki*, a.k.a. **GMK**, 2001). Higuchi and Anno had earlier collaborated on Anno's breakthrough anime creation, *Neon Genesis Evangelion* (新世紀エヴァンゲリオン / *Shin seiki Evangerion*, October 1995 to March 1996), for which Higuchi not only scripted as well as assistant-directing, but also handled art direction and storyboard chores too. Higuchi also scored with his special effects work for films like **SAKUYA: SLAYER OF DEMONS** (さくや 妖怪伝 / *Sakuya: yōkaiden*, 2000), **THE PRINCESS BLADE** (修羅雪姫 / *Shurayuki-hime*, a.k.a. **LADY SNOWBLOOD**, 2001), **PISTOL OPERA** (ピストルオペラ / *Pisutoru Opera*, 2001), etc., and directing the boxoffice hits **LORELEI: THE WITCH OF THE PACIFIC OCEAN** (ローレライ / *Rorerai*, 2005) and **SINKING OF JAPAN** (日本沈没 / *Nihon chinbotsu*, 2006), among others. Those are heavy credentials, to be sure, but nothing in **SHIN GOJIRA** comes close to being the game-changer

that Bong Joon-ho's **THE HOST** (괴물 / *Gwoemul*, 2006, South Korea) was a decade ago, and which *may* have inspired—it was a definite predecessor of—Gojira's amphibian-like metamorphosis here.

The **SHIN GOJIRA** hybrid integration of miniatures, rod-puppets, motion-capture CGI and CGI enhancements for **SG** is always impressive and often quite believably staged, but the movie itself is a mixed bag. That duly noted, it's also necessary to tackle the dramatic substance of the film: the human component—which, as always, dominates the running time—that is predominantly Anno's work. **SHIN GOJIRA** is a monster movie recast in the 1960s procedural navel-gazing of Jack Webb (writer/director/star of *Dragnet* [1951-1959/1967-1970], *The D.I.* [1957], etc.), the Otto Preminger of Preminger/Wendell Mayes' adaptation of James Bassett's **IN HARM'S WAY** (1965, USA), or—more to the point—the dogmatic attention to chain-of-command non-dramaturgy that so dramatically paralyzed the Japanese/American Pearl Harbor co-production, Richard Fleischer/Toshio Masuda/Kinji Fukasaku's **TORA! TORA! TORA!** (トラ・トラ・トラ, 1970). More on this momentarily...

I wrote immediately after seeing the film, without having read anything about **SHIN GOJIRA** prior to seeing it for myself, *"Did Toho brass inject novocaine into the cerebellum of the animator/writer/director behind **LOVE & POP** (1998)? I hate to say it, but Hideaki Anno either succumbed to Toho filmmaking-by-committee anti-kinetics (it's as if the entire film traps the audience IN a metaphoric Toho creative committee session, with Hiroki Hasegawa as the surrogate Anno), or he* *thought this functioned as a satire of Japanese government impotence, or of the sorry state of real-world inability of its own governments to cope in any meaningful way with climate change. If so, it fails as cinema, and certainly as a monster movie."*

These kinds of movies have always been, since 1954, in part "mobilization" movies—with ample screen-time expended on the spectacle of military hardware and firepower moving, mobilizing, positioning, all to deliver their payloads at the strategic moment—but **SHIN GOJIRA** is the first to dedicate the same screen spectacle to the mobilization of photocopiers, tables, chairs, meeting rooms, and white-collar personnel. While the real-world Japanese Constitutional dilemma and echoes of the disaster at the Fukushima Daiichi Nuclear Power Plant (福島第一原子力発電所 / *Fukushima Daiichi Genshiryoku Hatsudensho*) following the March 11, 2011 earthquake and tsunami does carry some dramatic (and satiric) weight, the actual film unreels as an increasingly dispiriting and listless affair. Having all this build-up to (I kid you not!) the plan to essentially *freeze an already-immobile kaijū*—well, where it goes in its final half-hour is closer to the heart-transplant operation of **KING KONG LIVES** (1986, USA, D: John Guillermin). Maybe what looks in **SHIN GOJIRA** like insane dental surgery should have added an anal suppository to the "final solution", but one understands the decision to forego such proceedings.

Forget the big fun we had with Shusuke Kaneko's and Kazunori Itō's Heisei period *Gamera* trilogy. What **SHIN GOJIRA** moves toward are, essentially, mock-industrial film tropes—*Oh! Exciting music as we observe corporate chemical plants in operation! Wow!* Happy synchronicity of privatized corporate free-market profiteers harmonized to save Japan!*—that are too po-faced to be funny or energizing; it all becomes increasingly silly, and ultimately tedious. Hiroki Hasegawa, Yutaka Takenouchi, and Satomi Ishihara do what they can with what they're given to work with, and Shinji Higuchi sure as hell delivers one or two extended *kaijū* rampage sequences that are well worth the price of admission (and the long drive getting to the theater!), but Anno's decision to dedicate so much time to protracted, dense-but-banal human activity (and *in*activity), and too little to Gojira—*sigh…*

Per usual, I'd avoided reading or seeing or hearing *anything* about **SHIN GOJIRA** before seeing it for myself, experiencing it *sans* any preconceptions. Afterwards, though, I went digging, curious to know more about the film's production, the co-directors' intentions, and so on. In the comments to my initial October 12, 2016 Facebook review of **SHIN GOJIRA**, Justin Mullis—who is currently a lecturer at the University of North Carolina at Charlotte, where he teaches and writes about topics relating to religion and monsters—shared some information about Anno's intentions. Justin wrote,

Special Envoy for the President of the United States, Kayoko Ann Patterson (Satomi Ishihara), and **SHIN GOJIRA**'s nominal hero, Deputy Chief Cabinet Secretary Rando Yaguchi (Hiroki Hasegawa), both capitalize on their screen time, but Rando is hardly the "fiery rebel" the film seems to want him to come across as, and Ms. Ishihara's struggle with English is at times painful to witness (the actress told interviewer August Ragone, "Sometimes it's so frustrating, I just want to cry")

Prepare yourselves, *Monster!* readers: **SHIN GOJIRA** takes "The Big G" to whole new levels of *daikaijū-eiga* weirdness!

"Enjoyed reading your thoughts Stephen, though I disagree as I enjoyed the movie. ...By all accounts Anno was given complete creative freedom, and $10 million, to make this film and it was his decision to make it a long series of boardroom meetings inspired, principally, by Kihachi Okamoto's WWII drama JAPAN'S LONGEST DAY ('67) which is also three hours worth of boardroom meetings and one of Anno's all-time favorite films. In fact, the only rumors I've heard of studio interference is that Anno's original screenplay treatment was nearly three hours worth of dialogue which Toho pushed back against but which Anno argued he could do by speeding up how fast everyone talked. ...$74.5 million at the box office, not counting receipts outside East Asia, and the highest grossing live-action film in Japan for 2016 plus opening 23% higher than the 2014 Godzilla did in Japan. I would say whatever Anno was thinking was a good idea." [1]

Well, yes. It *was* a good idea, I can see that now. It was a splendid idea.

But...

I can also say, having completely savored a revisit to Kihachi Okamoto's and Shinobu Hashimoto's

158-minute epic **JAPAN'S LONGEST DAY** (日本のいちばん長い日 / *Nihon no ichiban nagai hi*, a.k.a. **THE EMPEROR AND THE GENERAL**, 1967), that my initial impressions of **SHIN GOJIRA** are only confirmed. If only Anno could have come closer to the mark, he would have really had something.

Anyone who loves Toho movies, Japanese cinema, the Showa *Gojira* films, and harbors love and/or affection for **SHIN GOJIRA** owes it to themselves to experience **JAPAN'S LONGEST DAY**. It's a truly great film, with an astonishing cast, pitch-perfection direction, and a historical account of the attempted military coup on the brink of Japan's surrender that's closest, for American viewers, to John Frankenheimer's and Rod Serling's **SEVEN DAYS IN MAY** (1964, from the novel by Fletcher Knebel and Charles W. Bailey II) and the General Jack D. Ripper passages in Stanley Kubrick/Terry Southern/Peter George's **DR. STRANGELOVE** (also 1964), though the points of comparison fall short, even there. There is nothing in **SHIN GOJIRA** that comes close to the emotional engagement and mounting suspense in Okamoto's film—particularly that of the shamed/outraged rebels within the military, who mount an attempted *coup d'état* on multiple fronts: an airfield flying one last desperate kamikaze mission on the orders of the field's malaria-infected commander; a ferocious zealot (played by the great Eisei Amamoto) who leads his ravaged-by-hunger division into Tokyo [!] to assassinate the Prime Minister and council politicians whom he considers cowards and

1 Quoted with permission of Justin Mullis. Justin Mullis has also been a guest on two podcasts about SHIN GOJIRA, which I recommend: go to *http://thefilmfind.tumblr.com/ post/151916035797/bonus-episode-shin-godzilla-with-justin-mullis* -- the podcast in which Justin cites a joint interview he'd read with Anno and Okamoto (when the latter was still alive) in which Anno specifically cited **JAPAN'S LONGEST DAY** as a seminal inspiration and influence.

traitors; and a renegade team of soldiers so intent upon fighting the war to the final breath that they end up butchering their own commander, creating false orders, and seizing the Imperial Palace itself). We go in knowing enough history to know the coup failed, but it doesn't matter, as we are galvanized once the rebellion gains momentum, and its grim conclusions—still shockingly graphic when seen today—as they arrive, are devastating.

If **SHIN GOJIRA** could have mustered even a *fraction* of the intensity of the second and third arcs of **JAPAN'S LONGEST DAY**, it would have been a film to conjure with, among the best of the *Gojira* films _ever_. I see what was being attempted now, clearly, but (unlike **SHIN GOJIRA**) Okamoto's calculated pacing of the first half of the movie—slow, stately, precise in the details of bureaucratic rules-of-order and the individuals involved, all serving their Imperial Majesty with a devotion which Western audiences will have no life experience to draw upon to comprehend— detonates at the 98 minute mark, and everything that follows offers a truly riveting, harrowing account of August 15, 1945. Truth to tell, in terms of contemporary Japanese cinema, Takashi Miike's **AUDITION** (オーディション / *Ōdishon*, 1999) is a closer parallel to **JAPAN'S LONGEST DAY** in terms of the deliberately leisurely pacing, dramatic intent, and, ultimately, knocking the pins out from under the viewer after a slow-burn

build; in every way, **JAPAN'S LONGEST DAY** is superior to **SHIN GOJIRA**.[2]

JAPAN'S LONGEST DAY seriously is a feast for anyone who grew up with Toho movies, particularly Toho's monster movies. Almost *every* key male actor from *every* Showa era Toho monster

2   Also see Don Brown's "One Take on Japanese Cinema: Monsters vs. gangsters vs. (illegal) aliens," The Asahi Shimbun, August 12, 2016 (archived @ *http://www.asahi. com/ajw/articles/AJ201608120006.html*): "...Although Oka-moto's **JAPAN'S LONGEST DAY** has been mentioned as a reference point, the fast-paced, content-heavy style of **SHIN GODZILLA** is more strongly suggestive of the simi-larly relentless 'thesis films' of Nobuhiko Ōbayashi, such as **CASTING BLOSSOMS TO THE SKY** [この空の花 長岡花火物語 / *Kono sora no hana: Nagaoka hanabi monogatari, 2012 – ed.*] and **SEVEN DAYS** (sic) [*i.e.,* **SEVEN WEEKS /** 野のななのか */ No no nanananoka, 2014 – ed*]. However, it only adopts their speed and density, and has no time for the organizational and ideological conflict of **JAPAN'S LONGEST DAY**, nor Obayashi's hypnotic attention-hook-ing rhythms and elegiac humanism that grounds his works in vital emotions and history. Consequently, the film unfolds with the empty bluster of an overcompensating motor-mouth *otaku*, incessantly mumbling mountains of memo-rized factoids to distract a captive audience from his lack of substance..." Brown also notes, "This adheres to the stuffy Japanese cinematic tradition of over-explanatory thrillers that give more attention to men conferring in boardrooms than the calamities occurring outside, such as the original **JAPAN SINKS** (1973 [日本沈没 / *Nippon chinbotsu, a.k.a.* **SUBMERSION OF JAPAN**, D: Shirō Moritani – *ed.*]) and **THE BIG BEE** (2015 [天空の蜂 / *Tenkū no hachi*, D: Yuki-hiko Tsutsumi – *ed.*]), but their obsessive-compulsive ap-proach to labeling and verbal exposition, plus their pater-nalistic extolment of officials and technicians, are amplified to the extreme." True enough.

Boardroom Trauma-Drama: According to multiple sources, **SHIN GOJIRA**'s dramaturgy was shaped in part by Kihachi Okamoto's and Shinobu Hashimoto's 158-minute WW2 epic **JAPAN'S LONGEST DAY** (日本のいちばん長い日 / *Nihon no ichiban nagai hi*, a.k.a. **THE EMPEROR AND THE GENERAL**, 1967), a classic which showcased almost every key Showa era *Godzilla* series male actor at Toho in some of their best performances

movie has a terrific role in **JLD**, and they're mesmerizing onscreen; I particularly loved seeing vet Kurosawa actor—and **THE HUMAN VAPOR** (ガス人間第一号 / *Gasu ningen dai 1 gō*, 1960) himself!—Yoshio Tsuchiya in a primary role, since he loved doing the Toho SF films above all, but was excellent in everything he did for and at Toho. Eisei Amamoto (who played the witch in Senkichi Taniguchi's **THE LOST WORLD OF SINBAD** [大盗賊 / *Dai tozoku*, 1963] and Dr. Who in Ishirō Honda's **KING KONG ESCAPES** [キングコングの逆襲 / *Kingu Kongo no gyakushu*, 1967], etc.) is a real standout as the practically rabid mad-dog captain who is constantly evangelizing, a zealot who leads a brazen attack on the Prime Minister's home(s), then on the council—a single cutaway in his first scene to three close-up shots of his soldiers' barely-wrapped feet, revealing how impoverished and ill-equipped almost all of Japan's foot-soldiers were by 1945, is more tellingly powerful than any single non-monster shot in **SHIN GOJIRA**.

If **JAPAN'S LONGEST DAY** truly was Anno's "role model", I can only say he blew it worse than my first impression of **SHIN GOJIRA** could have fully grasped. Now that I've revisited **JAPAN'S LONGEST DAY** in this context, I commend Anno's best intentions, and I understand completely how the 2016 real-world political climate is reflected in the movie, but the concoction just *doesn't* work. If the intention was to deliberately *undercut* rather than *build* tension, well, mission accomplished, but to *what* end, exactly? With this demonic of a Gojira design, we should be terrified; instead, suspense simply dissipates rather than mounts, evaporating just when the film should be kicking into overdrive. The backdoor plan to freeze an already-immobilized Gojira is executed with risible *mecha*, and in full daylight—despite the "we-must-waken-Gojira-to-deplete-his-energy-again" twist, everything is resolved much too efficiently—leaving us with a statuesque frozen *kaijū* in the final shots. The immobilized Gojira we're left to ponder embodies the dramatic paralysis that derails the final act.

I'll be revisiting **SHIN GOJIRA** once it's legally available on DVD or Blu-ray, but not as often or attentively as I will re-watch **JAPAN'S LONGEST DAY**: Okamoto's masterpiece is highly recommended, truly *essential* viewing, and still available in its OOP DVD.

I *will* revisit **SHIN GOJIRA** someday, and I look forward to doing that.

But I saw what I saw, I experienced what I experienced, and I *wish* it had been a *better* film.

———

Shinji Higuchi's, Mahiro Maeda's and Takayuki Takeya's radical revamp of **SHIN GOJIRA** in its adult phase

SHIN GOJIRA:
SOME OBSERVATIONS ON THE NEW GOJIRA...

by Stephen R. Bissette

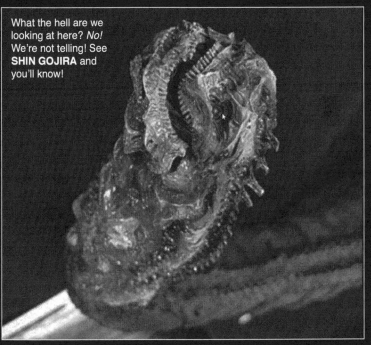

What the hell are we looking at here? *No!* We're not telling! See **SHIN GOJIRA** and you'll know!

The new Gojira that slithers, stalks, and stomps through Hideaki Anno's and Shinji Higuchi's **SHIN GODZILLA** (シン・ゴジラ / *Shin Gojira*, 2016, Japan) is a radical revamp of the most popular of all *daikaijū-eiga* creatures. The prolific anime and effects creator/designer Mahiro Maeda is credited for the innovative look of this new Gojira/Godzilla; Takayuki Takeya constructed the maquette the monster effects creators worked from. Shinji Higuchi's special effects offer a startling blend of traditional and non-traditional *daikaijū-eiga* techniques—an inventive, always imaginative fusion of miniatures, rod-puppets, motion-capture CGI, CGI and CGI enhancements—all to bring to life this new incarnation of the monster that first surfaced back in 1954.

While a recently-released illustrated Japanese "making-of" book (and a single line of dialogue in the film) claims there are *four* life-cycle stages to the new Gojira, we only really see three in the movie itself. Whatever Gojira's earliest stage might have been remains invisible in the film's initial eruption of red-tinged waters; the second stage (the film's first) is the eel-or-salamander-like amphibian seen writhing out of the bay onto land and through canals and city streets. The "salamander"- or "tadpole"-stage Gojira resembles amphibians with partially externalized gills, though not to the extent of a mud-puppy. This young Gojira's gills are slit-like, revealing blood-red gill tissues (presumably heavily veined with oxygenated blood) that echo the "fissure vents" all over the creature's body; the gills, however, are shown to occasionally blossom torrents of blood or a blood-like liquid. This "nymph" form also has lidless, saucer-like eyes, much like those of most fish; however, Higuchi's design and effects team fail to sustain a realistic wet look to the eyes, rendering them listless and lifeless in a way that emphasizes the absurd puppet-like nature of this stage.

While on land, this "nymph" stage matures into a young adult stage, which is first shown as a stegosaur-like quadruped stalking behind crowds of fleeing citizens. Goggle-eyed, mouth lined with budding teeth held idiotically agape, its gills now swollen into sagging pouch-like jowls, forelimbs sprawling out from the sides of its ungainly massive torso, the young adult Gojira looks like some baggy cartoonish New Year's dragon. It is soon revealed to be capable of standing on its hind legs, however. Once erect, its forearms seem more spindly, almost vestigial at this stage, its head more reptilian than fish-like or amphibian-like, despite the still-unblinking saucer eyes. This stage culminates in the Gojira standing erect and becoming temporarily immobile, as if it were either depleted of energy after its first land excursion, or perhaps even entering into a transitional stationary transformative stage in its next growth spurt. The military's mobilized attack force almost launches a missile attack on this "teenage" or "preteen" Gojira—an attack that is halted when a stray human evacuee is spotted in too close proximity to the standing creature—and it's interesting to speculate whether an attack at this stage in the creature's growth might have proven successful. It certainly looks like it's in its most vulnerable stage; Gojira's skin has yet to toughen into the charcoal-like igneous-plutonic-rock look of its adult stage, and there's as yet sufficient of its youthful amphibian form evident to sustain the impression of this still being a formative juvenile being, unable to fully protect itself.

Once the adult-phase Gojira emerges, **SHIN GOJIRA** mounts a series of set-pieces that tease out the potential and capabilities of this new Gojira. While elements of the classical Gojira remain—enough to make this monster still recognizably Gojira: the erect bipedal stance, the profile, the outsized (almost stegosaurian) dorsal spines, the humanoid forelimbs—in other ways, Higuchi's design and effects team have created the first truly 21st-Century Gojira. The penultimate and ultimate full-adult incarnations of Gojira are *magnificent*: the first impression given by the pinpoint eyes and snaggly, bristling teeth is demonic and initially terrifying (the lack of any movement or expression to the lidless eyes, however—a penetrating, unblinking gaze—will either disturb viewers or detract from the initial impression, as the eyes do seem lifeless and too puppet-like to this viewer[1]). The teeth seem to serve no function; though monstrous in and of themselves, we never see Gojira eat anything, and the teeth seem incapable of effectively biting, tearing, or even guiding anything down its throat. Still, it's quite a spectacle, and certainly a fresh take on the venerable Japanese dragon.

---

1 Hideaki Anno said, "Suits are fine, but for this project, I decided to use CGI out of consideration for the film's universe... Making use of CGI's 'inhuman' aspect, I removed any intentions and motives from Godzilla. It is only its gaze looking down at humans that expresses its emotions. That is the same gaze as the first Godzilla's." Anno, interviewed by Atsushi Ohara, in "Evangelion's Hideaki Anno takes Godzilla back to his roots", *The Asahi Shimbun*, August 20, 2016 (archived @ *http://www.asahi.com/ajw/articles/ AJ201608200015.html*)

『ジ・アート・オブ・シン・ゴジラ』ページサンプル

The stegosaurian "young adult" or "teenage" Gojira design, with saucer-like eyes

ページ画像はイメージのため変更される場合があります。

This Gojira's body seems to be illuminated from within by a glowing, magma-like interior furnace—indeed, Gojira's body is described at one point as a biological nuclear furnace, unprecedented in nature—that seems to be fissuring or leeching from the splitting of his almost-black-igneous-plutonic-rock-like skin or exoskeletal shell. This makes Gojira look like a being in constant pain—and one capable of inflicting unimaginable pain, like some sort of hellspawn. In its "preteen" or "teen" interim stage, the risibly tucked, spindly forearms are sticklike and useless-looking, but in the adult stage, these forearms become more formidable, as if the now-spidery fingers flexing at the end of those coiled forearms could be used for snatching or grasping (thought they're never put to use as such). Completing the adult volume and strength are the massive, pillar-like legs, which are rarely seen in real motion—nevertheless, they believably carry the incredible weight of Gojira, their relative immobility avoiding the at-times rubbery "bounce" and flabby appearance of the Showa-era Eiji Tsuburaya Gojira. If redwoods could walk—redwoods burning from within with a fire that never consumes them—they might resemble this Gojira's legs; on the whole, this all makes for a majestically monstrous, often monumentally demonic *kaijū* unlike anything in the Toho series to date.

Throughout these sequences, despite the inexpressive eyes, face, and mouth of this version, Gojira's body language successfully demonstrates the creature's initial astonishment and agonies at each revelatory event, as if his primal biological reaction to the attacks are surprises to Gojira himself, and probably even painful to him. During Higuchi's most galvanizing special effects sequences, Gojira seems to be wrenching his power from within: disgorging smoke, vomiting fire, then unleashing his radioactive breath in excruciating, ejaculatory spasms that give way to the volcanic explosion from inside. These shake the creature like birth contractions, at first; though once unleashed, in each subsequent wielding of his power, Gojira seems more in control, more capable of directing his actions with destructive precision. The same is true of the revelatory release of Gojira's additional abilities: the strafing attack on the creature either creates the spinal fissures that release the nuclear "beams" which fire from his spine, or prompts Gojira into flexing those "muscles" (so to speak) and organs, then directing their rays at his enemies above. The subsequent expansion and expulsion of his nuclear breath—an even more agonizing spasmodic reaction to attack, with Gojira's jaws splitting and almost quartering to allow for a more violent, destructive stream of death from the internal furnaces—also begins as an unexpected,

The Fire Within: Shin Gojira prepares to unleash the first blazing expulsion of the dragon's "death-breath"

even accidental triggering of a previously-unknown bodily function, giving way to real ferocity as Gojira awakens to its potential and cuts loose without restraints.

Then, there's this new Gojira's tail—longer than any ever before, capable of emitting its own destructive "ray", and (in the final shot of the statue-like immobilized adult monster) apparently also its self-reproductive orifice or organ: a sort of ovipositor sprouting thorny fetal or infantile Gojira offspring.

Along with the classical *Gojira* film series, there are a number of cinematic precedents for all that Hideaki Anno and especially Shinji Higuchi and their creative partners have brainstormed, created, and executed for **SHIN GOJIRA**. Aside from a plethora of "models" in nature, one cannot help but think of the stages of development revealed in the Loch Ness Monster's growth (and, during the manufactured rainstorm, shrinking back down to its "tadpole" form again) in George Pal's **THE 7 FACES OF DR. LAO** (1963, USA), thanks to Gene Warren, Wah Chang, and James Danforth's Academy-Award-winning special effects; more recently, the incredible amphibious monster of Bong Joon-ho's **THE HOST** (피물 / *Gwoemul*, 2006, South Korea) also provided a template for the direction Anno, Higuchi and their team's creature's life cycle took. When this adult Gojira's maw opens wider than any previous screen Gojira's, one cannot help but recall the wholly-invented mutant vampires from Guillermo del Toro's **BLADE II** (2002, USA). Given the staggering boxoffice success in Japan of **SHIN GOJIRA**, there are no doubt still more inventive *kaijū* to come!

MYSTERY, MYTH, AND MISDIRECTION:

FILMING THE GUYRA GHOST

by Daniel Best

*Out of the handful of silent films in Australia classified as horror movies, **THE GUYRA GHOST MYSTERY** (1921, scenario [etc.] by John Cosgrove) is the most fascinating in terms of subject matter, casting, filmmaking and screening. This is despite the movie not being seen since 1921 and the story of its conception, making and aftermath being the subject of myth and mystery. That is, until now. The simple fact is that it remains possibly the only commercial movie ever made based upon a real-life haunting that utilized both the actual location and the subjects of the haunting, playing themselves on the big screen. No movie made before had ever attempted to capture a real-life ghost on camera, and no movie since has used real-life locations and people in such a manner. This is the story of both the haunting at Guyra, the aftermath and the long-lost film, **THE GUYRA GHOST MYSTERY**...*

****

The Bowen Family

The Bowen family lived roughly one mile from Guyra in a four-roomed weatherboard cottage that was, as was the fashion of the day, isolated from their neighbors' homes. William Bowen, a second-generation railway ganger, married widow, Catherine Hodder (*née* Shelton) in 1908. Both William Bowen and Catherine Hodder were locals, having been born and grown up in and around the Armidale area, where Guyra was located. When they met, Catherine, born in 1873, was fifteen years older at 35 than the 20-year-old William, who was born in 1888. Catherine had children from her previous marriage to Joseph "Job" Hodder, to whom she was married for twelve years before he passed away in 1905. The children, William John (born 1894) and Mary "May" Catherine (born 1899), weren't very much younger than William Bowen himself. Catherine had another two sons, Victor and Eli, who sadly passed away in infancy. In 1908, Catherine gave birth to her first child with William Bowen, a daughter named Minnie Francis. The pair would go on to have three more children, Mary Ellen (born 1911), Eileen Grace (born 1913) and William John (born 1915).

Minnie and William Bowen

In contemporary accounts, Minnie was described as being somewhat timid and retiring. The two photos that remain of Minnie show her to be tall and thin, with jet black hair. A *Sunday Times* journalist observed at the time of the haunting that she possessed "...peculiar dark, introspective *[eyes]* that never seem to miss any movement in a room. When she speaks to you she never smiles, and seems to look beyond or through you. She has a rather uncanny aptitude for anticipating questions, almost before they are asked".

Scandal hit the quiet family in 1920 when, in August, the Bowens' daughter May gave birth to a son, Clifford, out of wedlock. May refused to tell anyone who the father was, and, due to the ages of both she and William Bowen, people in Armidale might have believed that her stepfather—William, a mere 11 years older than May—was her new son's actual father. May had been a sickly child, plagued by heart problems, and the birth of Clifford placed a heavy strain on her fragile health. She fell ill and ultimately passed away from heart failure in late January, 1921. She was 21 years old, and her passing meant that Clifford would be adopted into the family as William and Catherine's own child, although Minnie would take responsibility for him. May's death clearly hit the family hard; for

GUYRA MYSTERY.

LITTLE GIRL'S STATEMENT.

CLAIRAUDIENT MESSAGES.

GUYRA, Thursday.

What is known as the stone-throwing mystery, which has been puzzling and also terrifying a considerable section of the community since last Friday week, is still far from solved. The mysterious happenings continue nightly at the residence of Mr. William Bowen, a ganger in the employ of the Guyra Shire. Last night, among the large number present, was a gentleman who lives at Uralla, and who endeavoured to solve the mystery by spiritualistic means. Constable Taylor, who was present, relates that a little girl was placed in a room faintly lighted from an adjoining room. Her mother was with her.

An incomplete snippet of a local news report about the incident

Catherine it was her third child that she had now buried. The house was expected to be officially in mourning for the remainder of the year. Adding to the drama was the presence of William "Bill" Hodder and his young family, who had moved into a small cottage adjacent to Bowen house.

The Haunting

The story of what happened in April and May 1921 in Guyra, near Armidale in northeastern New South Wales, is either a textbook case of poltergeist activity or an outright fraud, depending on who or what you believe.

It all began in early April of 1921, when William Bowen appeared in Guyra and told the townspeople of the strange happenings that were going on at his house. Windows had been broken, heavy rocks were landing on the roof and someone—or some*thing*—was knocking on the walls from the

The Bowens' home as it was during the haunting

outside, at all hours of the day and night. All this activity had the effect of constantly keeping the family awake, and neither William nor his stepson Bill Hodder could see or hear anyone about when they'd rush outside to investigate. William then told of the lack of any physical tracks or other signs of any people being present, and that the rocks heaved onto the roof were of such a weight that even he, a strong, well-built man of the land, had a hard time lifting them, let alone heaving them any kind of a distance.

In typical poltergeist activity, such attacks seem to center on young children, in particular prepubescent girls. The Guyra ghost was no exception to this rule, and it was noted that the target appeared to be Minnie Bowen, aged 12. Her windows were broken, stones came through the holes in the window pane and landed on her bed, and the sounds of knocking and banging seemed to follow her around from room to room. The haunting appeared to begin after Minnie told of being chased home by an unknown man, who threw stones at her. As she ran yelling for her father, the man simply vanished. Again, despite William and Bill searching for the perpetrator, no trace was found.

People listened to Bowen's story with a mix of wonder, skepticism and terror. Because the attacks had supposedly started on April Fool's Day, 1921, the accounts gave more than one person reason to pause and ponder if it was all simply one big joke. Spiritualism was still very much in vogue in Australia. Bestselling author Arthur Conan Doyle had even conducted a four-month tour of Australia in 1920-21, where he gave lectures on the afterlife, ghosts and spiritualism. The huge amount of young people who had recently died in Europe during World War One also saw a spike in séances and mediums claiming to have received messages from those recently departed.

Even though the Bowens had never seen any of Conan Doyle's lectures, they were well aware of the phenomena. Books had been written, along with newspaper reports, and each and every country town was familiar with the likes of Fisher's Ghost; that is, if they didn't happen to have their own local variation on that story. All small towns had a resident witch, who usually just turned out to be some elderly spinster or widow, living alone, with a few cats…and ghosts were everywhere. The famous Fox sisters were still in people's minds in Australia, and vaudeville was abounding with magicians and spiritualists alike, some of whom had visited either nearby Armidale or Guyra itself. There was also an equal, if not larger, amount of magicians and hypnotists working the vaudeville circuit who were just as dedicated to debunking the myth of an afterlife and exposing as many frauds as they possibly could. Whatever the cause of the rock-throwing, the town of Guyra was buzzing with the news, and locals eagerly volunteered their time to catch the ghost and/or the culprits responsible.

The stone-throwing continued even when police and volunteers stood guard around the house. The rocks just came in from a further distance, at random, heavier than before, and all from unseen hands. Suggestions for solutions came from many directions. From collecting all the rocks and throwing them onto a large fire (in the hopes of cremating the ghost), to locking up all the local young children, to stationing returned soldiers around the house shooting into the darkness at random, it appeared that everyone knew how to solve the mystery. Other suggestions centered on Minnie herself. It was, even at the beginning, put forward that Minnie was the cause of the activity, that she was engineering a gigantic hoax, that she was throwing rocks and banging the walls, and merely by watching her closely, the activity would stop.

Other disturbing stories began to surface. Newspaper reports claimed that the town was further shocked when an elderly woman, one Mrs. Doran, vanished as she walked over a hill holding two potatoes and telling a local, "I'm taking the spuds to Ould Oireland". The myth has it that, despite an extensive search, no trace of her was ever found. Or so the story went. The truth was a bit less dramatic, and the myth was easily debunked. Doran's body was found at the bottom of a steep incline, with the spuds next to her. She had simply slipped and fallen to her death.

Other events also began to happen as a direct result of the haunting. Some were bordering on farcical, while others were lucky not to have ended with death. One man was reported to have rushed from his house on two successive nights to engage in mortal combat with unseen spooks: one "spook" turned out to be a dog eating food in his pantry, and the other a horse eating his flowers. A policeman, resting in the night while on watch, failed to notice a calf sleeping next to him until it grunted and passed wind, at which point he jumped up, startled, and shot at it; he missed. Another happening stopped just short of tragic results when a young girl, upon finding a loaded revolver that had been placed under the bed "just in case the ghost comes", picked it up and shot herself in the head. After being rushed to the hospital, the girl survived.

GUYRA MYSTERY.

GHOST THEORY COLLAPSED.

SYDNEY, Tuesday.—The Guyra ghost theory has collapsed. No stones have been thrown since Thursday night, and the police believe they have cleared up the mystery. A small girl, Minnie Bowen, admits that she caused some rappings on Saturday night and threw small stones on the roof of the house to frighten her sister-in-law.

Additional details from Guyra show that the police have arrived at the conclusion that the ghost manifestation was worked by five or six persons with the object of getting possession of the house. The police have established the fact that upon several occasions some vigilants furnished realistic effects. Though the police are convinced of the human agency of the affair they have no clue to the perpertrators, and say they hope the thing was fizzled out and that they are done with it.

Top: A contemporaneous statted press photo showing broken and boarded-up windows at the "haunted" Bowen home. **Above:** An undated Australian newspaper item pertaining to the so-called haunting, from the same timeframe

The locals of Guyra closed ranks around the Bowen family. All the available police staked-out the house, as did the townsfolk, with numbers ranging from twenty to eighty people, depending on the night in question. Most of the people surrounding the house were armed and were deployed in a cordon far away from the house so that anyone throwing rocks could not reach the roof. It didn't matter; rocks still hit the roof no matter how many people were present. The bombardment was so severe that the small cottage housing Bill Hodder and his family was totally destroyed, forcing Bill, his wife and children into the main house, thus further crowding the small property.

Not one to believe in ghosts, the local police sergeant, Sergeant Ridge, promptly blamed Minnie herself for all the rock-throwing, the banging and the window smashing, claiming she had given a full confession to all that had happened, the first such confession that would be attributed to her. Doubt was instantly thrown onto this claim, as the rocks were too heavy for Minnie to even lift, let alone actually throw, rocks hit the roof with Minnie

inside, and the knocks followed her around. Adding to the mystery was that those on the outside of the house who heard the knocking believed that it originated from *inside* the house, while those inside were insistent that the knocks and bangs, described at the time as sounding like "a pumpkin in a sugar bag", came from the *outside*. On the 15th of April, a series of events were witnessed by family, friends and policemen alike that would cause even the most skeptical of observers to take pause. In the middle of the haunting, one Mr. Moor, described as a close personal friend of none other than Arthur Conan Doyle with a healthy interest in psychic phenomena himself, visited the Bowens in Guyra to solve the mystery, only to proclaim the haunting as authentic after observing the Bowen family.

Another psychic, Ben Davey, visited from nearby Uralla, and proclaimed that the ghost was an angel announcing the second coming of Christ. After being observed talking to a tree by the railway station and being suspected of using hypnotism and ventriloquism, Davey hurried off to the Bowen household just as the townsfolk were discussing lynching him.

The night of Wednesday, 13th of April, saw a series of events that is still hard to explain, now nearly 100 years later. Minnie, who was described as being "…clever, but backward and at a low standard for her age", and who allegedly had an ability to answer questions before they were asked, was sat in her bedroom, which was brightly lit, and watched all night by a policeman, Constable Taylor, along with Mrs. Bowen, Ben Davey (who had quietly returned) and two neighbors, Alex Hay and Richard Pearson. The neighboring room was full of assorted policemen, family members and locals. Outside an estimated additional 80 townsfolk and policemen, most of whom were armed and ready to shoot, formed a circle around the house. What happened next was attested to by all present, including Constable Taylor, both officially and unofficially.

At 9:00 p.m., a loud knock was heard on the wall of the bedroom. This was followed by two massive thumps which were delivered with such force that the entire house appeared to shake. Everyone noted that Minnie hadn't moved from her bed. Davey suggested to Minnie that she should ask if it was her late stepsister, May, who was the cause of the ruckus. Minnie demurred. "I can't talk to my sister", she replied. "She's dead". Davy coaxed her to speak to the spirit. More bangs were heard so, giving in and crossing herself, Minnie asked, "Is that you, May?"

GUYRA MYSTERY.

STONE THROWING CONTINUES.

GUYRA, Friday.

Despite the reports of the police that the mystery was solved when an admission was recently made by a little girl that she had thrown a few stones, and that since then the incident had closed, there was a recrudescence of stone throwing on Wednesday night. Mr. Fewen reported yesterday morning that the house was struck by a number of stones during the night. The girl was in the house at at the time. He immediately rushed outside with his gun and fired several shots in the direction whence he thought they had come, and there was no further outbreak.

The report of Constable Hardy, in which he refers to a similar stone-throwing incident 15 years ago, was much discussed in town, and old residents deny that any such incident occurred.

Although the little girl told the police that she gave three raps on the wall, this admission does not explain other rappings when she was under close observation. Altogether the residents of Guyra are just as much mystified by these events as they were at the outset. They do not regard the child's confession of having thrown a few little stones as a solution of the matter.

Guyra has had other tragic happenings. An old lady disappeared from her home outside the town at about the time the stone throwing mystery commenced. She has not yet been traced. Then a revolver left handy on a bedroom table in a tradesman's house near the railway station in case the ghost walked in was picked up by a little boy of five years. He evidently thought it was a toy pistol, and fired it. The bullet entered the skull of his sister, aged 6, and, owing to its dangerous position, cannot be removed.

From *The Sydney Morning Herald* (for April 30th, 1921)

The Bowens' original home, much as it stands today

Silence greeted the question, but Minnie looked as if she was listening, crossed herself again and began to cry. It was noted that during the "conversation", Minnie would cock her head and simply say, "All right" or "Very well", as if she was having a perfectly normal conversation, albeit one that was clearly upsetting to her. She then told the room that the answer was *yes*, it was May, and that she now had a message for her mother.

Crossing the room, Minnie sat with her head on Catherine's lap and, still crying, began to talk. "Tell mother I am perfectly happy where I am, and that your prayers when I was sick brought me where I am, and made me happy. Tell mother not to worry, I'll watch and guard over you all". With that the knocking and stone-throwing ceased.

Life began to go back to normal for the Bowens as the following day—and night—saw peace once again fall upon the household. However, the coming Friday brought the most violent outbreak of activity of the entire mystery. That Friday, the Bowens went to work, as per normal, farming their potatoes in the fields close to their property. After the day's work was done, the family came home to find every window in the cottage broken. It wasn't just the windows, though. Heavy wooden shutters that had been placed over them had been removed, smashed and piled-up neatly on the front veranda. The Bowens had spent the day very close to the household, and nobody had been seen walking towards or away from the property, nor had any

sounds of such destruction been heard during the day either. It was noted that noise from the smashing of the windows, at the very least, would have carried to where the Bowens were working, yet they did not hear anything.

This was too much for William Bowen, who promptly packed Minnie off to live with Grandmother Shelton in nearby Glenn Innes. The disturbances in Guyra ceased once she was gone, but a shower of rocks and stones cascaded onto the roof of the Shelton house for two days straight. The newspapers were now gleefully reporting how the ghost had followed Minnie.

This time, police from Sydney moved in to investigate. The head of the investigating team, Constable Hardy, stood on the veranda of the Shelton house and looked into the darkness. As Hardy looked, two heavy rocks flew out of the

Regional Australian newspaper obit, from *The Northern Daily Leader* (for February 4th, 1921)

Minnie Bowen

conveniently explained his nearly being brained by one of the missiles while Minnie was still inside—was the cause of all the stone-throwing and wall-knocking. Catherine Bowen was called for, and she promptly took the chastised and obviously frightened Minnie back to the Guyra household. That was good enough for the police, the media and the public, and all activity thereafter ceased, once and for all.

Those who had witnessed the haunting weren't so easily convinced at the explanation of a hoax. It was noted that Minnie was inside the house when the stones had hit the roof at night, and that her claims she had caused the banging and rapping with a stick or her elbow were ludicrous, as the bangings were delivered with enough force to shake the whole house. Local police also noted that Minnie had been watched very closely and carefully during the activity, and she had not moved when rocks were thrown or bangs heard. Rocks were still being thrown after the Sydney detectives had left the area, placing further doubt on their claims of a hoax. But the people in Guyra, as well as the neighboring towns of Glenn Innes and Armidale, were happy to put the mystery to rest, due to all the adverse attention and ridicule that the controversial saga had brought upon them.

night, barely missing his head and hitting the wall behind him. Hardy stormed back inside and both confronted and threatened Minnie. If she did not confess and cease throwing rocks and banging walls, she would be shipped-off to an asylum. Scared, Minnie confessed that the Guyra haunting was a massive hoax, which she had committed in an effort to scare Bill Hodder's wife, May. Hardy's conclusion was that Minnie, aided by an unknown group of around six other youths—which

Although the official police line was that the disturbances had been carried out by either Minnie or a group of practical jokers, the mystery of the Guyra Ghost still remains. Those in Guyra are reluctant to talk about it, even today, and the Bowen family never spoke about the haunting in public.

The Guyra Ghost On Stage

The ghost was news everywhere, and it wasn't long before people took notice. The first appearance of the Guyra Ghost on stage came when a visiting troupe of colored minstrels—described as "Sixteen of the Finest Looking Niggers in the Country"—sang and danced their way through a routine featuring the ghost at the Inverall Soldiers' Club in early May, 1921. On the other side of Sydney, in competition with the minstrels, was the aptly-named Henry Clay's Bargain Vaudeville Show. Clay began to run a one-act comedy called *The Guyra Ghosts*, in which a bunch of people ran around the stage wearing sheets with eye-holes cut in them, screaming "*Boo!*" and bumping into each other before falling to the floor and "vanishing". Described by some as "screamingly funny", the reviews weren't kind, and the ghosts were quickly squeezed in-between Frank Moran and the singer Bessie Lester as a comedy relief. The one-act show

GUYRA MYSTERY

REMARKABLE DOINGS

BULLHOUNDS BY AERO-PLANE

BLACK TRACKER SUGGESTED

FOOTPRINTS FOUND

POLICE SAY "SPOOK" HAS TWO LEGS

GREAT EXCITEMENT IN COUNTRY DISTRICTS

"KING" TEA BONZER PRIZE COMPETITITION

Regional Australian newspaper headlines, from *The Manning River Times* (for May 5th, 1921)

ran for most of the month of May, 1921 before being retired for good. In Sydney, a roofer named James Muir, cashing-in on the topicality of the case, placed an ad in *The Sun* which pointed out that his brand of roof tiles would have resisted the Guyra Ghost's bombardment with ease.

"The Great Theodore, Master Hypnotist", was also on stage in early May with his own take on the mystery. The Great Theodore, like many others on the vaudeville circuit of the time (*à la* no less than Harry Houdini himself), was dedicated to exposing fake hauntings and spiritualists, and he advertised how he would expose the Guyra Ghost as being a fake by inviting locals up onto the stage where he was appearing, giving readings and making ghosts appear—live onstage.

Another magician, the brilliantly-named "The Incomparable Sloggett", was also dedicated to exposing the Guyra Ghost as a fake. Sloggett (hyped as "The Man Who Could Not Be Hanged"), worked the vaudeville circuit for decades, and had made his name by going from town to town performing the latest attractions of the day. He specialized in the Indian Rope Trick, and liked to show how he could not be hanged, live onstage. He then took to presenting both "The Human Hen" (years before Tod Browning's **FREAKS** in 1932) and how the knocking of the Guyra Ghost was *really* done, live onstage. Sloggett, who also added faux manifestations of ectoplasm, a ghost appearing from within a box of matches, and various objects vanishing and reappearing—*none* of which were reported as having happened at Guyra, I might add—turned the Guyra Ghost into a comedy act which he toured up and down the eastern coast of Australia for the bulk of 1922 to as late as 1925.

The Guyra Ghost On Film

Described as being an impresario along with being an actor and Shakespearian tragic, the bohemian John Cosgrove had been performing on the stage in Australia since the 1880s. Cosgrove was a large man, tipping the scales during various periods of his life at anywhere between 17 to 19 stone (=107-120 kg, or around 236-264½ lbs.), and he was well-known as both a comedy actor and a more-than-capable writer. Cosgrove was also well-known for borrowing money for ambitious stage productions, yet never being in a position to pay it back. This practice, which would continue during *The Guyra Ghost Mystery*'s run, had seen him stuck with the nickname of "The Great Australian

Rural Australian newspaper ad, from *The Bowen Independent* (for July 24th, 1923)

Bite". Cosgrove didn't care, he was having far too much fun, and his overall fun-loving attitude was reportedly too infectious for anyone to get too upset, stay mad at or resist him for long.

Cosgrove had recently been working in New Zealand with film producer/director Frank Beaumont Smith ("One-Shot Beau"), mainly writing comedies, and he was keen to make his own mark in Australian cinema. Upon his return to Australia, Cosgrove found himself enthralled by

Australian newspaper ad, from *The National Advocate* (for July 15th, 1921)

Australian Picture Palace
Liverpool Street, Hyde Park
NOW SHOWING

D.B.O'CONNOR
PRESENTS

A PICTURIZATION OF THE FAMOUS DRAMA

"The FACE AT THE WINDOW"

·IN·

FIVE NERVE THRILLING REELS.

D.B.O'CONNOR FEATURE FILMS
SYDNEY AUSTRALIA.

Supported by "WORTH WHILE," featuring BRYANT WASHBURN
Also comedy "The Merry Models," featuring Ben Turpin

1919 Australian billing for the movie from which **THE GUYRA GHOST MYSTERY** "recycled" its monster mask

all the press reportage about the Guyra Ghost, and he saw an opportunity to create something both unique and profitable. Where other filmmakers expressed a desire to adapt the story and film it, Cosgrove acted first, and in spectacular fashion.

He quickly whipped-up a scenario featuring himself as the fictional Sherlock Doyle *[sic!]*, both in homage to Arthur Conan Doyle, creator of Sherlock Holmes, and also as a parody of the hapless Mr. Moor who had visited Guyra and claimed the haunting as genuine. With his script in hand, he quickly rounded-up a camera and cameraman and made his way to Guyra. Once he reached Armidale, he approached a local film distributor, one Mr. Regan, who was suffering a loss of business due to the hauntings, and obtained the finances he needed by promising that Regan's daughter, Nellie, could appear in the movie. Cosgrove readily agreed. At the time, Cosgrove believed that Minnie Bowen was in Glenn Innes and unavailable for the film. By casting a young girl roughly the same age as Minnie, Cosgrove knew he could promote the film as having all the Bowens in it; after all, outside of two photos that had appeared in *The Sun*, nobody outside of Guyra, or possibly Glenn Innes either, knew what Minnie looked like. Regan assisted him in quickly gathering up a number of locals to reprise their roles of "protecting" the house while "fighting the ghost". With money in hand, Cosgrove gathered his company then walked to the Bowen household.

Upon seeing the Bowens' galvanized iron roof and unable to control his rising glee, Cosgrove promptly picked up and pitched a rather large rock onto it just to hear the noise. As the rock fell off the roof he just knocked on the door, then got ready to introduce himself and announce his intentions to come inside and make a movie.

After answering the door and finding the massive, smiling figure of Cosgrove, complete with a cameraman who was already setting-up his camera, as well as seeing Nellie Regan and a host of locals, Bill Hodder, armed with a rifle that he kept handy, "just in case of a ghost", was incredulous. He was angry at Cosgrove's admission that he had just thrown the latest rock onto the roof, and got ready to shut the door in his face. Cosgrove was nothing if not insistent, and began to turn on the charm. Pointing out that he had travelled all the way from Sydney at great personal expense (ignoring that he'd already obtained funding) with a cameraman and camera, he told Bill he'd not leave the house until he had spoken to the entire family. Bill, now both anxious and nervous, told Cosgrove where he could go and what he could do with himself and his

camera and cameraman, then closed the door on them. Not to be deterred, Cosgrove simply waited. He knocked again. After a few minutes William and Catherine duly led everyone out onto the porch where Cosgrove waited. Cosgrove must have felt a sense of utter delight when Minnie herself came out of the house. She had been brought back from the Shelton house in Glenn Innes by Catherine that very morning. Now, more than ever, Cosgrove wanted this film made! He set about convincing the anxious family that this would be a great way to get their story told properly and, after much persuasion and money changing hands, the Bowens not only allowed him to make the movie at the very house where all the unexplainable phenomena had actually transpired, but also to appear as "themselves" in recreations of scenes that had occurred. As coups go, this was, and remains, one of the most impressive ever recorded in all of ghost cinema!

Cosgrove wasted no time. He began filming that very same day. To portray the ghost itself,

Cosgrove reached out to his professional contacts, borrowing the mask of "Le Loup" from an earlier Australian horror movie, **THE FACE AT THE WINDOW** (1919, Australia, D: Charles Villiers), which was still being shown in cinemas across New South Wales and was also enjoying a second life as a stage play, too. The mask of Le Loup was placed over the head of an unnamed Sydney-based actor whom Cosgrove employed, and who had turned up to the location drunk after drinking what was described as "three pints" on the train journey to Guyra. Capping the costume off was a long, white sheet. Thus, the Guyra Ghost was born for the screen!

The drunken ghost, wearing the costume, ran around the house, peered into windows at the family and, although the movie was a silent one, would frequently moan and yell "*Woooooo!*" and "*Boo!*" Due to Cosgrove using the mask of Le Loup, we now know exactly what the ghost looked like on film, as an excellent still-shot of Le Loup from **THE FACE AT THE WINDOW** remains in existence.

Once the locals saw the sight of the rather large Cosgrove trying to convince the Bowen family to recoil in fright from the sheet-wearing drunkard, who often fell over, they laughed, turned around and walked away. It took the intervention of the police sergeant, whose striking white charger

Cosgrove admired, and who he tried to work into the film, to round up the townsfolk and get them back to the Bowen house. By using trick photography, Cosgrove then filmed William Bowen rushing out of the house and shooting at the ghost with his shotgun; a risky proposition indeed, as Bowen insisted on using live ammunition and expressed a strong desire, more than once, to shoot Cosgrove's "ghost" for real.

Cosgrove then turned his attention to filming at night, with the aid of flaming torches, flashlights and a car's headlamps. He stood behind the lights, out of sight of the camera, and continued to happily pelt rocks at the house. The effect of this, by all accounts, provided some interesting results as night photography was a relatively new concept in Australia and it did appear as if the stones were literally coming out of nowhere. One shot that Cosgrove wanted, but did not succeed in getting, was that of William throwing a stone at the house. "No", William flatly told Cosgrove, "I'm not having it. They'd blame me for the whole thing". Minnie was unable to be convinced to throw any rocks, either. After spending a further day filming the house, inside and out, and the surrounds, including some shots of Nellie Regan holding flowers, Cosgrove finished up, paid people off and left with his cameraman, camera and drunken ghost just as quickly as he had arrived. In total, Cosgrove took three days and two nights to film

The monster terrorizes a cast member (leading lady Agnes Dobson?) in
THE FACE AT THE WINDOW (1919)

the movie from his arrival at the Bowen house to his departure. It was quick, and it was crude, but it was important, as it captured the inside and outside of the Bowen house, the surrounds and, more importantly, the Bowen family themselves, especially Minnie, on camera. And it had all been filmed on the actual site of the haunting, too.

Cosgrove shot an estimated 8000 feet of film at a total cost of £100.00, not an inconsiderable sum for the day. The film was edited-down to 4000 feet for the final release. Wanting to capitalize on his expected good fortune, Cosgrove "bought" another film, **THE HOUSE OF FEAR** (1915, USA, Ds: Arnold Daly, Ashley Miller), and hired Wirth's Hippodrome in Sydney with the view of showing them as a double-feature. With little fanfare and reporting, instead relying on word of mouth and the public's familiarity and interest in the Guyra Ghost, he advertised his film as being based on the real events, featuring Minnie Bowen herself, who had become a household name, and being filmed at the actual location, also strongly suggesting that he captured the actual Guyra ghost on film. He paid for a poster to be made featuring an artist's interpretation of the Guyra Ghost itself. Displaying an amazing lack of basic grammar, the poster proudly proclaimed:

Taken at Guyra on the spot showing the home of the Bowen family showing the actual stone throwing caught by the camera. Most sensational scenes. Flashlight photographs taken revealing most remarkable results at night. The camera was especially designed for night work by Mr A. Moolian and after developing the film it showed unexpected results [sic].

With all of that in mind, Cosgrove, by his own admission, sat back and waited for the profits to roll in.

For the very few who ever saw **THE GUYRA GHOST MYSTERY**, the plot was as simple as it gets. The Bowen family is haunted by a ghost who keeps throwing rocks at the roof and appearing at windows, terrorizing them. The ghost comes inside and scares Catherine and Minnie. William chases the ghost outside and shoots at it, only to find that his bullet goes right through the ghost, leaving it unscathed. The ghost continues popping-up at windows. William enlists the assistance of the townsfolk to fight the ghost, to no avail. For no apparent reason, Nellie Regan arrives and picks some flowers. Psychic detective Sherlock Doyle (played by Cosgrove himself), arrives at the house and takes control of the situation. He witnesses the ghost appearing at windows and convinces

the young Minnie Bowen to tell it to leave, which it does. Roll the credits: Starring John Cosgrove, Nellie Regan and the Bowen Family, scenario by John Cosgrove, produced by John Cosgrove, costumes by John Cosgrove, and so on. Despite

Rural Australian newspaper ads. **Top:** From *The Guyra Argus* (for July 28th, 1921). **Center:** From *The Lithgow Mercury* (for July 25th, 1921). **Above:** From *The NLA News* [sic?] (date unknown)

The terrifying (!) Le Loup mask, as seen in 1919's **THE FACE AT THE WINDOW**

the promises in the ads, however, there were no "unexpected results" when the film was developed. The results hinted at were the stones appearing to come out of nowhere, which was a simple effect.

The profits, much like the Guyra Ghost itself, never materialized. The public, now convinced that the whole affair was a hoax, as evidenced by the widely reported "confession" of Minnie Bowen, didn't bother attending the film. Far from being the horror that it should have been, the public instead found it to be somewhat of a limp comedy. The ads for its release were small, compared to other films of the time, and the movie had the disadvantage of opening, not in the evening, but as a matinee only. The first screening, on Saturday the 25th of June, saw a total of £5.00 taken at the box office— hardly the thousands of pounds that Cosgrove was expecting! Cosgrove knew the movie was a dud when he looked out at the mostly empty theatre that he had rented for the occasion.

Ironically, although Cosgrove and company used the same mask for their own ghost, screenings of **THE FACE AT THE WINDOW** playing cinemas simultaneously, despite the film being three years old and also up for view in its concurrent stage adaptation too, easily outsold **THE GUYRA GHOST MYSTERY**. The latter ran for a further two days, Sunday and Monday, after which time

Cosgrove claimed to have cut his losses and sold the film off to an unknown distributor. It is also possible that Regan, the distributor who had financed the film, staked a claim on it and simply began screening it in lieu of payment for a loan which Cosgrove never had any intention of repaying anyway. Another theory, which comes from Cosgrove himself, is that the only copy of the movie and its rights were sold in an attempt to get Regan off his back. The real fate of the movie is now lost in time, sadly.

No matter if **THE GUYRA GHOST MYSTERY** did or didn't change hands, Cosgrove claimed later to have regretted the move when the film's new owner informed him how he had made over £300.00 from exhibiting just it in Guyra alone, a potential venue which Cosgrove had previously dismissed. Cosgrove had come to the conclusion that the people in Guyra wouldn't wish to view a film of events that they had lived through. The claim of the moving making £300.00 in Guyra alone is a difficult one to believe. While it's true that it was screened in Guyra, it was for one night only. It is possible, however, that the so-called *£300*.00 figure was the total profits from screenings of the movie as it made its way around the New South Wales countryside.

Either Cosgrove, or the new owner, took the movie into regional areas of New South Wales in July, August and September of 1921. Screenings are known to have occurred at Bathurst (15th July), Lithgow (26th July), Guyra (30th July), Penrith (16th August) and Port Macquarie (10th September). It is a distinct possibility that **THE GUYRA GHOST MYSTERY** was shown in more rural towns than can be verified, though. As the film was making its way around the state, it is highly likely that ad-hoc screenings occurred. These screenings might not have necessarily been advertised in the local newspapers, but rather via a poster or handbill placed on the window of the cinema or town hall itself. Word of mouth would have been sufficient to generate interest. The film would have been shown for one evening, then packed-up and taken on to the next town.

The Port Macquarie screening, at Ochs' Pictures in Port Macquarie, where, demonstrating the bizarre nature of the movie overall, it was described as "five reels of laughter" and served as the opening attraction for Charlie Chaplin's *Charlie, The Gang Leader* (1917?). After this final screening, it was shelved…and subsequently lost for all time. All that remains is an image of the movie poster. The movie does not appear to have been screened in any other state other than New South

Wales. Presumably the lack of public interest and the only moderate success of the film in Sydney meant that investing more money to have copies made and get the movie distributed to Adelaide, Hobart, Melbourne, Brisbane and Perth was out of the question.

The other great myth which can be safely debunked is the presence of Minnie Bowen in the film itself. It has been reported that Minnie was not part of the film, as she was in Glenn Innes when it was shot. However, the events of Glenn Innes saw Minnie brought back to Guyra the same morning that Cosgrove arrived at the homestead. Even though Cosgrove had arranged for Nellie Regan to play Minnie Bowen, there was no need, as he now had the real thing on hand.

THE GUYRA GHOST MYSTERY was Cosgrove's only film as producer. He returned to acting and writing for both film and the stage. He continued to write scenarios for silent films, notably **SILKS AND SADDLES** (1921) and **SUNSHINE SALLY** (1922), also acting in these and many other films. He passed away, weighing-in at eighteen stone (114 kg, or roughly 251⅓ lbs.), and quite happy with it, after a run with illness in Sydney on the 11th of August, 1925, at the age of 85. No copy of the film was known to have been found in his effects.

Minnie Bowen went on to marry an Armidale local, Frank Ernest, in 1928. Their only child, Donald, was born the same year, but sadly passed away in 1930. She never spoke publicly about the haunting but, according to her nephew Clifford, whom she raised as her own, and her sister, Ellen, Minnie could make a piano play without touching it and had the ability to move chairs across the room without moving herself. The Bowen family were convinced that Minnie possessed paranormal abilities, but, knowing what she had gone through in 1921, never discussed them in her presence while she was still alive. She passed away in 1988, allegedly due to being decapitated in a car accident, horrifically enough. Her husband, Frank, passed away in 1980, after 52 years of marriage. None of

Another view of the Bowen house in Guyra, this one undated

the Bowens who were present at the household in April 1921 ever spoke in public about the ghost, nor did they speak to any researcher in any detail.

THE GUYRA GHOST MYSTERY, one of the very few Australian silent movies that can truly be classified as a horror film, remains lost. A copy has not been seen since or reported as being seen since its last screening 95 years ago in September of 1921. Regardless of the film's artistic merits (or lack thereof), its importance derives from the simple fact that it was filmed at the authentic site of the alleged haunting, thus giving people an excellent look at the Bowen house and its surrounds, as it appeared in April-May 1921, both inside and out. It would have also given people the opportunity to see Minnie Bowen herself, as she was when the activity took place. With those factors in mind, the loss of the film, as an artefact alone, cannot be quantified.

New South Wales newspaper ad, from *The Truth* (for June 19th, 1921)

This Page: A pair of covers and a title panel from issues of the *Dr. Mortis* comic

CHILLS FROM CHILE
EL SINIESTRO DR. MORTIS AND HIS LOST TV HORRORS

by Martín Núñez

Juan Marino *[center]*, along with some of his *radioteatro* colleagues, look over their *Dr. Mortis* scripts

For North American and European enthusiasts of the macabre, South American horror—excluding now-famous Brazilian horror icon José Mojica Marins, best-known as his alter-ego "Zé do Caixão" *[more informally known to many Anglos as "Coffin Joe" – ed.]*, plus a few Argentinean efforts—seems to be something rare and really obscure; indeed, almost every horror project which emerges from South America (be it made for the big or small screens [etc.]) doesn't get too much attention elsewhere around the globe.

Here's something I should perhaps stress for everyone else in the world outside the United States of America: South America[1] is the subcontinent that runs from Colombia and Venezuela in the north to Chile (my homeland) and Argentina in the South, also including much of the Caribbean Islands, too; Mexico is part of North America[2]; Central America[3] is the region that runs from Guatemala to Panamá. And, as with every region in the world, each one of these separate nations/regions/ territories has its own particular idiosyncrasies andcultural peculiarities, not to mention their own sets of myths and legends *[with some occasional*

---

1   Just for the record, as well as including much of the Caribbean Islands, the American subcontinent encompasses the following nations/territories (etc.): Argentina, Aruba, Bolivia, Brazil, the Caribbean Netherlands, Chile, Colombia, Curaçao, Ecuador, the Falkland Islands (Islas Malvinas), French Guiana, Guyana, Paraguay, Peru, Suriname, Trinidad and Tobago, Uruguay and Venezuela. ~ ed.

2   Also encompassing these countries/regions: Anguilla, Antigua and Barbuda, Bahamas, Barbados, the British Virgin Islands, Canada, the Cayman Islands, the Collectivity of Saint Martin, Costa Rica, Cuba, Dominica, the Dominican

Republic, El Salvador, Greenland, Grenada, Guadeloupe, Haiti, Jamaica, Martinique, Montserrat, Nicaragua, Panama, Puerto Rico, Saint Barthélemy (a.k.a. "St. Barts"), Saint Kitts and Nevis, Saint Lucia, Saint Pierre and Miquelon, Saint Vincent and the Grenadines, Sint Maarten ("St. Maarten"), the Turks and Caicos Islands, the US Minor Outlying Islands and US Virgin Islands, and—last but not least—the USA. ~ ed.

3   Also encompassing Belize, Costa Rica, El Salvador, the Republic of Honduras (la República de Honduras) and Nicaragua. (*There!* You learn something new every day! Okay, geography lesson over!) ~ ed.

crossover, natch – SF.], so anyone who applies the generic catchall of "South America" to the whole continent below the USA's southernmost borders is making a huge mistake, due all the various differences in cultural backgrounds between countries which seem to be so close geographically speaking, yet in some ways are worlds apart.

In what is *actual* South America, natural resources are abundant, but since we've been robbed of them for centuries by profit-hungry outsiders, our economies have been struggling to become—at the very least—decent, solvent ones. However, certain foreign dirty hands have been looting our resources and production, which in large part is why the arts are sometimes the least-important thing for our governments and businessmen to concern themselves with. So, in this context, genre cinema can be considered another expendable victim, "collateral damage", if you will. This unfortunate set of circumstances results in only very minimal amounts of horror fare being produced, or genre production in general, for that matter. But let me tell you something: one of *the* most prolific horror icons came from Chile, and his multimedia career spanned everything from radio plays to comics,

as well as records and a long-lost TV show, all of them being VERY successful in their country of origin, also becoming, with the passage of years, well-known works in some nearby countries, too. Sadly, Dr. Mortis never appeared in a single movie due to the political and economic climate of the 'Sixties and 'Seventies, but this didn't prevent the character's creator, writer Juan Marino Cabello, from enjoying a complete and expansive career within the horror-related sphere, whose canon remains criminally unsung/unknown outside South America, even to this day.

It all started way back in the mid-'Fifties, when Juan Marino created his soon-to-be-legendary Dr. Mortis character as the axis for a long-running radio play that frightened thousands of Chileans out of their wits week after week for over 30 years! Indeed, the character's success was so phenomenal that this radio show was closely followed by an extremely successful monthly comic magazine, launched in the mid-'Sixties, which was further responsible in helping keep Dr. Mortis' monstrous legacy alive for younger generations, especially on into the 1990s.

Above Left: Ad promoting *Dr. Mortis* records. **Top Right:** "A Nice Get-Together with Dr. Mortis"; the fabulous title panel to one of the doctor's tales of terror. **Bottom Right:** Cover to Volume 1 in a 2011 Chilean CD collection of vintage *Mortis* radio episodes (released on the Unlimited S.A. label)

But that's not the whole story. Marino also managed to publish three anthological volumes filled with horror tales, plus a pair of successful vinyl record albums containing exclusive radio plays besides. And, bizarrely, he even released a *Cumbia* record! Titled *Dr. Mortis y sus Zombies Cumbiancheros* (*"Dr. Mortis and his Cumbia Zombies"*), this album of tropical music is, needless to say, virtually impossible to find nowadays.

These above reasons and more are why Dr. Mortis has become so synonymous with horror in Chile, where folks of all ages can still readily identify his characteristically sinister laughter to this day. Yes, if Chilean pop culture has its very own horror legend, it is, no doubt, Juan Marino Cabello and his creepy creation: the Sinister Dr. Mortis!

But what's it all about, you may ask? Since material pertaining to horror and the macabre first caught my attention when I was a kid, luckily enough, the *Dr. Mortis* comic magazines were still cheap and I was able to delve into this whole horror world which, years later, I was able to relate/equate with—let's say—the Warren Publishing empire, because I got into *Creepy* magazine as a direct result after beginning in the horror field by reading *Mortis* magazines.

Years later, when I began delving into "Paul Naschy"/Jacinto Molina Álvarez's world, the puzzle became complete, at least in my mind: you see, Juan Marino Cabello is none other than our local Chilean version of that Spanish genre icon. Not in any sort of "formal" way, because they come from two distinctly different worlds, but their ways of approaching horrific subject matter is quite similar, since both authors share a unique ability to translate classic horror into a personal world in which the macabre and the grotesque can coexist with sexy female characters. Both Juan Marino and Jacinto Molina drank deeply of the "Classic Horror" waters, but each of them was able to shape the elements into fresh new forms thanks to their respective largely dissimilar cultural backgrounds. But what Molina and Marino do have more in common is their mutual love for horror, which manifests itself in every story, script, radio play and/or comic mags (etc.) produced by either artist.

Such Juan Marino comic book titles as "The Man who Challenged Death", "The Cursed Legion", "Black Masses", "Decapitated Maid", "Dr. Mortis' Testament", "Virgins for the Monster" and "Tentacles" (a Lovecraftian tale) give you a good idea of what Marino's world of horror was all about. In Marino's body of work we can appreciate strong influences from other world mythologies, plus the works of E.A. Poe, and—primarily—*huge*

Marino *[second from left]* at the mic on the old *Dr. Mortis* radio show

influences derived from H.P. Lovecraft, which is why so many Marino stories told of cosmic horrors coming to this planet, or ancient monsters emerging from its seas! *[Judging by all appearances, there seems to be more than a little bit of HPL's Nyarlathotep in the doc's makeup – SF.]*

Beginnings

Juan Marino Cabello was born in 1920 in the extremely southerly Chilean city of Punta Arenas, one of the last cities on the continent between the coast of the mainland and the Antarctic waters beyond. It was in this polar region that he developed his love for music, books and movies; according to he himself, it was so cold outside that he spent most of his time reading the classics, as well as some more macabre tales that caught his attention, along with early jazz music too. In this context, when he was only around 20 years old, he pioneered the first ever Chilean radio show which specialized in this musical form, *Jazz en el tiempo* ("Jazz in our Times"). Upon first being aired, this program unleashed Marino's passion for radio so much that he quickly developed still more radio shows, including one dedicated to Chilean folk music and another devoted to Tango; but as a radio pioneer he wanted *more*, so, as he had a day job at a bank, by nights he worked on the aforementioned shows, eventually coming up with a new project that would change Chilean radio forever…

The serialized radio play *El Siniestro Dr. Mortis* was first aired in his home city of Punta Arenas in 1945, whereafter his fame blossomed so quickly that, just a few short months later, Marino relocated to Chile's capital Santiago instead in order to gain access to a wider audience. Listeners got deliciously scared by the program's opening track, which became its trademark: no less than Russian composer Modest Mussorgsky's famous "Night on Bald Mountain", a suitably scary theme which

HISTORIETAS

EN TODOS LOS KIOSCOS DEL PAIS

Mortis comic books (*"historietas"*) ad

can be also heard, amongst many other places, in a segment of Disney's animated classic **FANTASIA** (1940, USA). This track was followed by gales of evil cackling laughter that still give older Chilean people a case of the willies. That introductory laugh was of course Dr. Mortis', and—guess what?—shades of the aforementioned Mojica Marins, alias Zé do Caixão, Dr. Mortis was played

Dr. Mortis creator Juan Marino Cabello, circa the early 2000s

by none other than Juan Marino himself, who, in well-pronounced Spanish, introduced the macabre stories to be heard weekly by literally thousands of Chilean families. These radio plays may well seem exceedingly tame these days—and indeed they are, by comparison to all that's been done in the horror genre since—but they have the great merit of introducing horror in a country which had no other macabre tales to entertain its people with besides their orally-transmitted folkloric ones. So we can properly say that Juan Marino is the true founding father of classical horror in Chile.

While most of the early stories were taken from classic literature (i.e., North American and European ones) he soon began to adapt others into a more local context. Despite the fact that most of the stories adapted were set in foreign lands, they had a universality of experience at their core which triggered an immediate connection within the Chilean locals. In addition, Marino was not afraid to add certain idiosyncratic modifications to the venerable, tried-and-trusted old horror archetypes. As Marino stated in an old interview I was able to conduct with him back in the year 2000, for Chilean audiences the adventures of some guy named "John Smith" can be more interesting than those of someone named "Juan Pérez".

The success of the *ESDM* radio show was so great that, in the mid-'60s, Editorial Zig-Zag, one of the biggest Chilean publishing houses in those days, approached Marino with an offer to translate his horror world into comic magazines that ended up being Dr. Mortis' most-preserved legacy of all, since teen collectors started reading adventures in print when, in the late '80s, the radio show was no more. Now, while the considerable advantage of audio accompaniment was gone, another dimension was added, as fans could at least actually *see* artists' depictions of the various tales as interpreted in the two-dimensional sequential art medium (those of good imaginations could easily add silent sound effects and dialogue in their minds!).

These comics are so full of charm that they have to be seen and read. In terms of draftsmanship, however, the artists were unevenly talented, so the whole thing relied on the scripts, which were penned by Marino himself, of course.

In the comic's first incarnation, Doctor Mortis' character was an omnipresent one whose being was rarely embodied in actual corporeal form, unless it was a necessity; because, basically, Mortis is ethereal Evil Incarnate itself. In order to take on various physical human forms, the character disguised his name *[rather like how Jess Franco did! – SF.]* behind such multiple pseudonyms as "Tiss Morgan", "Dr. M. Ortiz", "Tromsi", "Morgenthys", plus many more besides. Sometimes, other than as a catalytic influence on stories, Mortis stayed right out of the picture while commanding his zombie-like hordes or waking ancient monstrosities, but he often placed hexes through various inanimate objects and some kinds of monsters. To seal the close of the comic's first era, Mortis was captured whilst in his solid human form by an international team of agents and shot off out into deep space enclosed inside a capsule; but—*oh, the horrors!*—without his presence on Earth, death no longer exists, thus driving the world into chaos. As a result, the earthling authorities must out of necessity bring him back so as to preserve the natural (and supernatural?!) order. This launched the "good" (i.e., bad) doctor's second era (his "reincarnation", if you will), in which Mortis was always directly present in human form—complete with devil's horn-like hairdo, devilish goatee and night-black coat—while continuing to terrorize and plague humans to death and beyond.

Mortis Goes to TV

This second era was in the middle of its development when local TV producer Osvaldo Barzelatto, under his company Protab, got in touch with Marino with plans to make the very first Chilean horror TV series ever, for the Canal 13 station.

The birth of Chilean TV was belated due to simple economics, and only became popular thanks to the football *[i.e., "soccer" (sic!) – ed.]* World Cup of 1962, which that year was hosted by Chile, and for which more wealthy families bought television sets in order to watch the games. These sets were still scarce, however. Sometimes there was just a single TV set per an entire block, so half the community would gather in one house to watch the games. Wider local access to television came about when Protab forged a joint deal with North American broadcasting conglomerate ABC in order to bring the first mobile TV equipment to Chile. This assured more and (at least at one time) better contents. It was during this formative "boom" that Chilean TV stations became ever-hungry for new content, which Protab was only too eager to provide.

Marino accepted their offer to adapt his character and stories to the burgeoning new medium, and he began writing the teleplays quickly. Small-screen director and local showbiz personality Germán Becker was contracted to direct the brand new TV horror show, which, I reiterate, was notably the first of its kind in Chile. The year was 1972, and the by then already sizeable Mortis legend consequently increased exponentially.

Shot in some old TV studios in Tarapacá street, the show was an instant success when it was aired—on the same day and in the very same timeslot as the world-famous American teleserial *Dark Shadows*, no less—sometimes scoring even higher ratings than its rough US counterpart.

90% of Dr. Mortis' TV show consisted of original scripts penned by Juan Marino, and for the dramatizations he and Becker shared 50/50 of the production process, with Becker handling all the technical aspects. Mauricio Marino, Juan's son, once told me that Becker and his father used to argue about the art direction a lot, since the director wanted to do everything as cheaply as possible, while Marino struggled to get the show shot on

16.22 Longstreet,
17.12 Dr. Simon Locke. Serie norteamericana.
17.40 Los Picapiedras.
18.10 Ruff y Ready.
18.40 El Correcaminos.
19.05 El Sapo y la Culebra.
19.05 Los Socios. Comedia policial con Don Adams.
19.55 La Gran Jornada.
19.45 Telenoche. Con Pepe Guixé, María Teresa Serrano y Guillermo Parada. El Tiempo.
21.20 El Doctor Mortis. Serie de terror. Realizada en Chile.
21.50 El Sapo y la Culebra.
22.00 Teletrece. Noticias con Pepe Abad.
22.35 Los Atrevidos. Serie canadiense.
23.30 La palabra y cierre.

Contemporaneous newspaper TV program listing

actual locations. Becker on the other hand always preferred to shoot against cheap and unconvincing cardboard theatrical scenography rather than on actual three-dimensional sets. At some point or other, Marino discovered the cellars beneath the show's TV soundstage, and they finally agreed to shoot there instead. The gloomy cellar was full of spider webs, making it an ideal setting whereon to shoot the macabre stories.

But Canal 13, a TV station which was the property of the Universidad Católica de Chile (Catholic University of Chile) was so stingy with the budget that Marino never felt very comfortable, arguing that, being a prime contender against Barnabas Collins, he deserved more resources in order to make a better show. Most unfortunately, however, that dream budget never came... We must consider that TV in Chile was still a half-amateur effort in those days, and that politics were constantly at boiling point at that time, so Dr. Mortis' show provided viewers with a welcome escape from the confrontational sociopolitical climate in which almost every Chilean took part. On the one side people were fighting to keep the democratically-elected government of President Salvador Allende going, while on the other side were the wealthy fascists, who were angered due to the fact that the Unidad Popular (People's Unity) government led by Allende was channeling money back to "common" people and the poor, who needed it

more. In the year 1970, allegedly, authorities suggested Marino should decrease the horror aspect of his comic books, since actual real-life horror was alive in the streets, where militant fascist groups were murdering any civilians, cops and soldiers who swore fealty to the democratic constitution. Marino, who avoided making political statements, took the opportunity to introduce more SF-oriented scripts, many of which were written by his wife Eva Martinic. These weren't the first sci-fi stories to see publication in Chile, but they certainly are the *best* ones.

If the main struggle was in the streets, the studio had one of its own while planning the style of the show: Becker always wanted a naïve approach to horror, but Marino (a fan of Universal classic monsters, and also of Hammer Studios) wanted a more professional look, insisting that *Dr. Mortis* should be more like then-successful British TV series. According to Mauricio Marino Martinic, these creative differences between the creators led to some very interesting debates.

As I said above, extreme right-wing fascist groups were determined to boycott the popular regime, economic blockage being one of their favorite methods, and, much like they are doing in Venezuela these days, they hoarded food, drink, gas, and even materials necessary for production of TV programming. So, producing the show became

Roberto Parada, Ivan Soto, Domingo Tessier, Juan Marino's body and director Germán Becker's head

Actress Sonia
Viveros in gory
makeup!

more and more difficult, leading to a patrimonial tragedy: since the producers had no other tapes to use, the masters got recycled (i.e., re-recorded over) with other content, so this is why we are now certain that *not a single* episode of *Dr. Mortis* was preserved for posterity.

This tragedy has made investigation and reconstruction an impossible thing. I've been investigating this subject for some years now, and every clue leads to another dead-end or deception. Being as how former producer Osvaldo Barzelatto is the only person who might by some chance own a copy of an episode, but, the two times I approached him, this wealthy individual slammed the door on my nose, telling me in a highly threatening manner how he's getting fed up with me bothering him; so,

Article continued on page 124

Dr. MORTIS

DE AQUEL TEMIDO MUNDO DE LOS MUERTOS, HA EMERGIDO UN SER MALÉFICO, ABOMINABLE ENCARNACIÓN O ECTOPLASMACIÓN DEL MAL: EL SINIESTRO DOCTOR MORTIS. ¿QUIÉN ES? ¿UN SER HUMANO? ¿UNA SOMBRA? O SIMPLEMENTE ¿EL COMPENDIO DE LA MALDAD Y LA MUERTE?

REQUIE

LEA LOS MACABROS Y ESCALOFRIANTES EPISODIOS DE FANTASÍA Y TERROR EN "EL SINIESTRO DOCTOR MORTIS".

GHOULISH GALLERY! Above: Title page from a *Dr. Mortis* comic. **Facing Page, Top Left:** Vampire-like, the doctor enfolds a female victim with his billowing cloak. **Top Right:** Title panel to one of the more science-fictional stories written by Marino's wife, Eva Martinic C. **Center:** The shadowy Dr. Mortis puts in an indistinct appearance, backed by his evil minions. **Bottom Left & Right:** A pair of covers for editions of the shock doc's collected stories

LA MUCHACHA IBA A REPLICAR, PERO LA MIRADA DEL HOMBRE LA CONTUVO. VIO LOS OJOS DE FUEGO QUE PARECIAN ABSORVERLA, ATRAVÉNDOLA A UN POZO SIN FONDO...

EL DOCTOR MORTIS
y
LA RESPUESTA DE OTRO MUNDO

¿ES LA MUERTE EL FIN DEL SER HUMANO? EL DR. MORTIS SU PROYECCIONES ALLA DEL TIEMPO?

GUIÓN: EVA MARTINIC M.

¡BUENAS NOCHES, PROFESOR MATTEUS! ¡BUENAS NOCHES, INSPECTOR BRUNER! DEBO CONFESAR QUE NO ESPERABA LA VISITA DE USTEDES... ¡JA...JA...JA!

¡DOCTOR MORTIS!

CELEBRO QUE ME RECONOZCA, MATTEUS...

¡DÉSE PRESO, DOCTOR MORTIS!...

MACABROS RELATOS
DEL SINIESTRO
MORTIS

El Siniestro
doctor
MORTIS
Una historieta de terror y... muerte

Esta revista se terminó de imprimir el XVI-III-MCMLXXI

123

Continued from page 121

without his help, along with Juan Marino's son I've been trying to somehow reconstruct this TV show, but I've managed to come up with very few facts and, not only that, but I'm convinced that there's a *curse* on it!

From my visits to the local library, I can at least tell you that that the premiere episode was aired in October 1972, and the series lasted until April 26, 1973. Because it was a weekly show which ran for somewhere around six months, enough episodes were aired that I'd like to think at least *one* of them survived, although no known collector has managed—at least publicly—to turn up any clue about where to find one, or better yet, some. Not even Mauricio Marino knows of the existence of a single copy of an episode.

Facing Page: Detail of the cover from the first issue ever, signed to this article's author Martín Núñez by *Dr. Mortis* creator Juan Marino himself. **Above:** "Kraken", one of the few lower-budget monotone comics in the series to be released

As the "curse" theory had begun to grow on me, I finally got in touch with Germán Becker, who's now a very old man. Prostrated and almost incapable of speaking in his presence, such was my awe, I managed to get almost no useful info on the show from him, but he did kindly loan me the mere six (6) known photos still in existence from it. In one of them (see p.120), preciously enough, there's Juan Marino dressed-up as Dr. Mortis, but—most unfortunately for posterity!—a young Becker, in the extreme foreground, is unwittingly blocking The Man's face from view with his own head! These photos (presented here for the very first time! *[Excellent stuff, Martín! You rock! – ed.]*) seem to be the only tangible remaining document of the TV show, and, while none of them actually depict scenes taken directly from the show itself, a couple of them do offer us some tantalizing

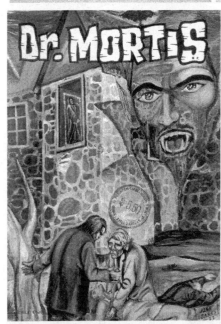

Top Left: Comic page depicting Dr. Mortis himself in the second era. **Top Right:** Another page from the comic. **Above Left:** Cover to *El Siniestro Doctor Mortis*, Year 2, N° 36 (1974); art by Juan Ibañez. **Above Right:** Cover to *El Siniestro Doctor Mortis*, Year 2, N° 6 (1972)

Top Left: Year 1, Nº 53 (1969). **Top Right:** Year 1, Nº 24 (Colombian edition).
Above Left: Year 2, Nº 7 (1972). **Above Right:** Year 1, Nº 5 (Colombian edition)

Top: Juan Marino next to a billboard depicting one of the covers of his comic, *El Siniestro Doctor Mortis*, which was part of "Cartoon Day" at the University of Chile's Faculty of Architecture and Urbanism in November 2003. **Above:** Year 2, N° 11.
Facing Page: Year 2, N° 1 (1972)

"behind-the-scenes" glimpses into its production. Even though I've dug through piles of old magazines and newspapers, I haven't been able to find any other information on the show, since the papers were too busy with politics and TV, magazines weren't produced much in those days, and the precious few there were about cinema/television paid little attention to the local panorama.

Thankfully, however, I've come up with some names of the show's cast members, and I can confirm that many of them came from the original radio plays. This decision was a huge struggle for Marino, since TV executives didn't expect too much from radio actors, but, due to the success of *El Siniestro Doctor Mortis* show, they exceeded all expectations. The cast included some immortal stage-trained thespians like Roberto Parada. Parada was famous for his theatre work, and also for a tragic incident earlier in his career: mere moments before he got onto the stage for a performance, he was informed about his son's death at the hands of military agents under Pinochet's dictatorship, but Parada, being a consummate professional, nonetheless climbed onstage and went "on with the show" until the end of the play.

Another star of the *Dr. Mortis* TV show was the late Sonia Viveros, a young actress who a few years later became one of the most famous soap opera stars in Chile.

The show's second season was planned for the end of 1973, but the tragic civilian/military coup of September 11th not only killed thousands of people, it also killed all cultural activity, and no fiction or politically-slanted local TV shows were allowed, which resulted in a deep cultural void that lasted for several years. Additionally, TV stations suffered intervention from military agents, and any tapes containing "suspicious" material got confiscated and destroyed (in this way, many books and much local music, such as Víctor Jara's work, likewise got destroyed). So that's how fascist politics killed-off the first Chilean TV horror effort, resulting in an irreplaceable loss for our country's legacy. And believe you me, if this show was even *half* as good as the radio play or comic magazines are, we're talking about a major loss for the world's horror patrimony! Because, you have to know, Doctor Mortis is simply one of *the* most important horror-themed cultural phenomena ever to come from South America; one that can be placed alongside no less than Zé do Caixão and/or Narciso Ibáñez Menta's Argentinean work. *[See Les Moore's fascinating bio of señor Ibáñez in* Monster! *#26 (pp.74-81) – ed.]*

Back in 2011, Chilean filmmaker Jorge Olguín (director of the first modern Chilean horror film,

CHILE E$ 10,00

ÁNGEL NEGRO [2000]) announced a new *Doctor Mortis* TV series, and a trailer was even released, but nothing really ever became of it, and (luckily?) the project never saw fruition.

Thankfully, the Mortis radio plays and comics have been reedited and reissued over the years, plus also some local comic artists have continued the saga

by producing new scripts and comic books in an effort to keep Juan Marino's legacy alive. If you understand the Spanish language, do yourself a favor and try to grab a comic and give it a read if ever you find some.

Juan Marino died in June 2007. As for his alter-ego Doctor Mortis, however, he—as well as the unspeakable eternal evil he represents—will *NEVER* die!

Editor's Notes (from SF): There are a number of episodes of the original radio series up for a listen on YouTube. Just key "El Siniestro Dr. Mortis" into the search field there, and take your pick of the links that pop up. If you go to the link entitled "El Siniestro Dr. Mortis – Radioteatro" (@ *https:// www.youtube.com/watch?v=JO4nVJBmdmA&list =PLzs1h02QrBDuFay-_5L5qM3YZtsAqr6FF*), it provides you with links to more than 50 different episodes, averaging-out at about a half-hour apiece, although there are some much longer episodes elsewhere on the site. There are literally scores of links to choose from there, so pickings are easy! Even those (such as myself!) with only the most rudimentary knowledge of Spanish ought to be able to make at least some sense of what's going on in them. Episodes represented there include "*Monstruos*", "*El incubo*", "*Licantropía*", "*El fugitivo de las galaxias*", plus a great many more besides. Also, at the link "Documental del Radioteatro del Dr. Mortis" (@ *https://www. youtube.com/watch?v=x6Op10CAawI*), there's a 45+-minute, Spanish-only documentary (ripped from a Chilean TV showing) about Juan Marino and his best-known creation uploaded at the YT channel named for him. Produced by CNTV

(Consejo Nacional de Televisión) circa 2008, the doc is entitled *El documental el siniestro Dr. Mortis*. Incidentally, while Googling for data on the present subject, I happened across an interesting apparent news item (@ *http://www.loseternautas. com/2012/12/28/mortis-28/*) at a website called Los Eternautas. Dating from December 28th, 2012 and credited to one Yorick Allen, the item (in Spanish), reported that none other than Hollywood blockbuster-maker Guillermo del Toro had announced a possible movie adaptation of *Dr. Mortis*, intended primarily for a Hispanic audience (the item was headed "*Guillermo del Toro concretará película de El Siniestro Dr. Mortis*"). According to the same item, screenwriter Sergio G. Sánchez was hoped to collaborate on a script with del Toro. While this may sound most promising indeed, I wouldn't get my hopes up if I were you. From what I could deduce from some of the skeptical responses at the comments thread at said site, the announcement may have only been a hoax, or possibly simple wishful thinking.

Above Left & Right: "The Memoirs of Doctor Mortis"; covers to two collections of Marino's short stories featuring the "good" (*not!*) doctor

THE *STRANGER THINGS* STUDY & VIEWING GUIDE

by Stephen R. Bissette

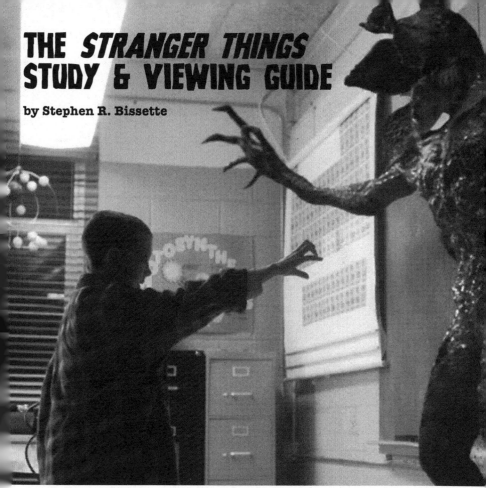

An Apple For The Reacher: Eleven (Millie Bobby Brown) asserts herself in the classroom in the summer of 2016 hit Netflix series *Stranger Things*

Were you among the many who were instantly enraptured by, and addicted to, binge-viewings of Netflix and Matt and Ross Duffer's 2016 original series Stranger Things?

What captured you first: the irresistible cast of child characters/performers; the small-town specificity disrupted by the covert government/paramilitary base's secret experiments; the androgynous telekinetic lass "Eleven" (a.k.a. "El" for short [Millie Bobby Brown]) with the shaved head and odd, intense manner; the plight of the alcoholic single mother whose youngest son mysteriously vanished, only to manifest within the walls of her and her older son's ramshackle home; or was it the whole bundle, wrapped-up in a 1980s-style synth score that recalled an era of SF/horror films which a generation grew up with as staples of cable TV and video-store catalogues?[1]

---

1   Do I *really* have to cite fan postings and favorable reviews? They were *everywhere* this summer! Just go looking, and you'll find 'em in abundance.

"Now I Know My ABC's…": Distraught single mother Joyce (Winona Ryder), her eldest son Jonathan (Charlie Heaton) and his *not*-girlfriend Nancy (Natalia Dyer) sit tight under the Christmas lights while awaiting a message from Will-"Down-Under" (and we *don't* mean Australia!) in *Stranger Things*

Or were you among those befuddled by the phenomenon[2]—put-off by, rather than engaged by and with, its cast of at-times cloying kid actors[3], including the androgynous big-eyed orphan "Eleven", who is capable of moving things telekinetically[4] and making things happen with her mind; its reliance on the overt and ongoing physical, mental, and emotional abuse

2 Tim Lucas (*Throat Sprockets, The Book of Renfield, Mario Bava: All the Colors of the Dark, Video Watchdog*, etc.) wrote in the Video Watchblog, "I keep thinking there must be some underlying sociological reason I'm missing—possibly its ties to Stephen King, whose novels are certainly referenced here (even the title seems to pinion off of King's *Needful Things*), and whose body of work never held the fascination for me that it has for the rest of the world. It can't just be 1980s nostalgia because *Stranger Things* borrows ideas and images from films as recent as **UNDER THE SKIN** and going as far back into the 1960s and '70s as **THESE ARE THE DAMNED** (with its government-sanctioned experiments on children) and **SHIVERS** (with its slug-like parasites vomited down bathroom drains). I could point to nearly every scene in the series and find not just a precedent for it but visual quotations in many. (My favorite was in the last episode, a wink at Joe Dante's **THE HOWLING**.) As I say, I thought it was alright but people had me all but running to my TV set to catch this before the spoilers caught up with me. That's what I don't understand. I can see people getting a kick out of a greatest hits album but not a greatest hits album of cover versions…. Possibly, the way this series has been so warmly embraced may have something to do with its familiar, comfort food values. Set in 1983 and allowed to roll out in a manner consistent with that era (which is to say, without the usual attention-deficit editing that has become the norm for Millennials), it's not really a product of its time, but a straightforward, unpretentious Young Adult novel for television that tells us what we all want to know: that government is not just bad but evil, that family (however screwed-up it may be) is good and always there for us, and that the victors in any situation will hail from the Island of Misfit Toys—like the pre-adolescent Dungeons and Dragons players who are the chief protagonists of this show…." See *Video Watchblog*, "Familiar *Things*," July 22nd, 2016, archived online (@ *http://videowatchdog.blogspot.com/2016/07/familiar-things.html*); quoted with permission.

3 On August 13th, 2016, UK screenwriter and author Stephen Volk (**GOTHIC**, *Ghostwatch, Afterlife, The Parts We Play*, etc.) wrote on Facebook, "Okay I *am* going to give *Stranger Things* more than one episode…. but as a general statement I'm finding American child actors really, really disconcerting... in this series, as well as M. Night *[Shyamalan]*'s **THE VISIT** *[2015, USA]*, as examples, I find them disturbingly over-mature, lacking in any semblance of innocence or inner life, way too knowing and false in their acting, as if 5,000 (adult) acting styles and movies have been downloaded into their heads and they are conscious of the camera in a way that is borderline showing off. I just find it so creepy, like totally self-absorbed grown-ups before their time, it makes me squirm. Please don't tell me that American children are all like this." Mind you, Stephen Volk isn't *per se* against kids or child actors; later on August 13th, in a comment on the same thread, Volk wrote, "Maybe if they don't over-characterize they don't feel they're doing their job. There's something in silence and listening that is much more compelling in a character sometimes than a whole avalanche of ticks and quirks!... Sit them all down and get them to watch **KES** *[1969, UK, D: Ken Loach]*. Then watch it again. And again," adding via personal message to me, "… the small children who perform in **THE VVITCH** *[2015, USA/UK/Canada/Brazil, D: Robert Eggers]* are quite extraordinary!" On August 23rd, 2016, Stephen posted to Facebook: "**MIDNIGHT SPECIAL** *[2016, USA/Greece, D: Jeff Nichols]* is one of the most enjoyable genre films I have seen in a long, long while. Perfectly realised by the writer-director and beautifully acted throughout. … I'll only say it is an old story told in a new way, that I found captivating. More so than say, *Stranger Things*, with which it does bear comparison." **MIDNIGHT SPECIAL** involved a "mutant child" capable of extreme acts of telekinesis and more, played by Jaeden Lieberher. (NB. Stephen Volk granted permission for the appearance here of his Facebook posts/comments.)

4 One of my closest friends, horror novelist and folklorist Joseph A. Citro (*Shadow Child, Guardian Angels, The Gore, The Unseen, Deus-X*, etc.), told me he gave up on watching the series as soon as the little orphan girl was eating in the back room of the diner, and moved the fan blades by concentrating. "I immediately shut it off," he said. (Quoted with permission.)

The Monster Squad: The kids at the heart of *Stranger Things* —Lucas (Caleb McLaughlin), Dustin (Gaten Matarazzo), Mike (Finn Wolfhard) and the orphan Eleven (Millie Bobby Brown)

of that child by a shadowy patriarch (Matthew Modine) that drives the narrative; its initially one-note caricature of a hard-drinking single mom as a showcase for a once-beloved screen actress (Winona Ryder) that rips on her own troubled adult reputation[5]; its painful synth-dominated soundtrack that reminds you of low-budget films you'd rather forget, mixed with top-40 "period" hits to cement its timeframe while manipulating your emotional responses with Pavlovian cynicism; its shamelessly derivative "K-Tel Greatest Hits"-style cannibalization of countless past horror/SF/fantasy riffs, prominent among them the self-evident rebrand of Stephen King motifs (which were, as evidenced by King's own plethora of interviews, his own revamps of venerable 1950s horror/SF literary and movie tropes)?[6]

Me? I was initially straddling both camps.[7] In the end, I wrote this article.
Make of that what you will.

---

5 Artist/activist Annie Murphy (*I Still Live, I Never Promised You A Rose Garden, Part One: My Own Private Idaho* and *Part Two: Ken Death is Dead, The Shirley Jackson Project,* etc.) posted on Facebook on August 2nd, 2016: "SPOILER ALERT: DEBBIE'S DOWNER [*Stranger Things* rant]: Please lord let that be the last time I bingewatch hours of men and boys telling women and girls that they are crazy. I'm overtired of seeing media in which the women's mental health is completely demolished before the men/boys actually believe. It's fiction for fuck's sake, why does that have to be the only element that survives from reality? It's bad modeling. It was brilliant in **THE HAUNTING**, but 50 years later it's just tired.... Don't get me wrong: I love horror, I love nostalgia, I covet the 80s, and I love cheese. I love feminist horror the best and honestly, it is not that hard to pull off—just ask Christopher Pike. But good lord this show could have been much, much better. And shorter. Without the misogynist plot delays or the heavy-handed 80's-product-placement (oh my god!! Remember *Trapper Keepers*??!) it would have been about 3 episodes. I'm gonna go watch **GHOSTBUSTERS** now dammit." Quoted with permission.

6 Kentucky-born artist/musician J.T. Dockery (*Despair Volumes 1-3, Hassle, Spud Crazy,* etc.) wrote, "...It had some fun moments, but it had a lot of problems, both gob-smacking plot holes and some disbelief I couldn't suspend and some of the stereotypes and stock footage, one dimensional characters/character development seemed pure corn starch to me. I will say there seemed to be maybe a solid two hour movie hiding in it, and I was hipped to the fact that it actually was a movie project that got turned into a tv show." Facebook comment, August 2nd, 2016, 3:00 p.m.; quoted with permission.

7 FYI, and whatever it's worth, I posted July 18th, 2016, 9:34 a.m. on Facebook, "Dove into *Stranger Things*; I'm enjoying it, but just that. The sub-Tangerine Dream/sub-[John] Carpenter synth score is obtrusive, as are the interruptive (and oh so typical) overlays of 'here's another song to tell you how you should feel now,' and the narrative is awfully derivative in a piecemeal way ([*Joseph*] Losey's **THE DAMNED/THESE ARE THE DAMNED** via **DEAD KIDS/STRANGE BEHAVIOR** by way of **SUPER 8** by way of **FIRESTARTER** with a shot of "Little Girl Lost" by way of Christopher Garetano's **MONTAUK CHRONICLES** via...). Still, I'm quite enjoying the characters and setup. Solid cast, slickly constructed, very nicely paced and shot, I'm on board for the duration. I'm not in love with this, though; give it time..."

Article continued on page 139 following this handy-dandy episode guide for *Stranger Things*!

ADRIFT IN THE UPSIDE DOWN

An Episode Guide to *Stranger Things*
(Netflix, July 15, 2016)

ATTENTION: SPOILER ALERTS!! If you have not yet seen the series, avoid reading the following. This synopsis serves only to remind those who have seen the series of key plot points. ~SRB

Little Boy Lost: Will Byers (Noah Schnapp) bicycles to meet his fate in the opening episode of *Stranger Things*

Chapter 1: "The Vanishing of Will Byers"

1983, Hawkins, Indiana: A group of boys playing role-playing games—Will Byers (Noah Schnapp) and his friends Mike (Finn Wolfhard), Dustin (Gaten Matarazzo), and Lucas (Caleb McLaughlin)—break for the evening and Will, Dustin, and Lucas bicycle home despite the rain. Will is separated from his pals and gets spooked by *something* unseen that is following him— something that might be from the nearby off-limits Hawkins Laboratory—which stalks him to the shed behind his house...

Next morning, Will's single, alcoholic mother Joyce (Winona Ryder) and his older brother Jonathan (Charlie Heaton) can find no sign of him anywhere. Joyce reports Will as a missing person to local police chief Jim Hopper (David Harbour), but no one will believe her. Meanwhile, an androgynous young girl (Millie Bobby Brown) with a shaved head and garbed in a flimsy hospital gown shows up at the local Benny's Diner, unwilling or unable to speak. Benny feeds her and calls for social workers to rescue her; armed agents show up instead, killing Benny, and the girl—named Eleven—escapes, subsequently running into Will's pals while they are out searching for their missing friend. Waiting at her home for any news of her missing son, Joyce gets a mysterious phone call: through all the static on the line, she distinctly hears what is apparently Will's breathing...

The boys bring Eleven back to Mike's house and hide her there, coaxing her to eat Eggo waffles, which she takes an immediate liking to. Eleven—whom Mike informally dubs "El" for short—tells them that "bad people" are chasing her, and she demonstrates her telekinetic abilities by closing Mike's door without touching it. She recognizes a photo of the missing Will, and cryptically says he's hiding "from a monster". In concealment to avoid discovery by Will's mother, Eleven recalls being imprisoned in a cell out at Hawkins Laboratory. At the same time, Joyce gets another uncanny phone call from Will, corresponding with the lights in her home flashing on and off and the walls seeming to "warp".

Elsewhere in town, Mike's older teenage sister Nancy (Natalia Dyer) is invited by school stud Steven (Joe Keery) to a pool party at his house while his parents are *in absentia*, and Nancy asks her best friend Barb (Shannon Purser) to go with her. While the teens party by the pool, Will's brother Jonathan—searching the woods for his missing brother—watches from the treeline and snaps photos, envious of Steven's proximity to Jonathan's "crush", Nancy. Barb is abandoned at the poolside as the teen couples go upstairs to have sex; left alone, she is taken by the same unseen thing that stalked Will…

Chapter 3: "Holly, Jolly"

We glimpse Barb trapped in an altered version of the swimming pool: it is a dark, tendril-encrusted caricature of our world, from which Barb desperately flees something which is stalking her…

Unable to find her missing friend, Nancy breaks down and tells her mother about the party, and that Barb has gone missing. Downstairs, still hiding in the house, Eleven explores Mike's basement room; as she does, memories of her life in Hawkins Laboratory emerge, where the paternal Dr. Brenner (Matthew Modine) had tested her telekinetic powers. She also recalls using these abilities to kill the men who were guarding and abusing her. Meanwhile, Chief Hopper's investigation of Will's disappearance leads him to Hawkins Laboratory, where he is shown security footage as "proof" that Will was never there, but Hopper notices the lack of rain on the tape—it was raining on the night of Will's disappearance—and rightly suspects Brenner is hiding the truth.

At Joyce's house, she has established tentative contact with the invisible Will by stringing Christmas lights on the living room wall, corresponding to an improvised alphabetical grid she's scrawled onto it; the lights flash "Yes" when she asks Will if he's alive, and "No" when she asks if he's safe. The lights then flash wildly, as if expressing terror, and the very walls seem to stretch; Will is on the run, wherever he is. Outside—the boys, having asked her to lead them to Will—Eleven has led them to Joyce's and Will's home; they grow angry, and she tries to tell them he is there, in a place she calls "the Upside Down". Upon hearing sirens nearby, they rush to the source

Mike (Finn Wolfhard), the walkie-talkie, and Eleven (Millie Bobby Brown), with the tell-tale drop of blood trickling from her nostril...

Eleven, all-suited-up and ready to enter the Upside Down via the sensory-deprivation tank in Hawkins Laboratory

of the sound: a water-filled rock quarry, where the authorities are pulling Will's body out of the icy waters…

Chapter 4: "The Body"

Joyce refuses to believe the body on the slab at the coroner's office is really Will; it lacks an identifying birthmark, so she refuses to cooperate. Trusting Joyce's certainty, Hopper investigates further, finding irregularities in the reported autopsy; that night, he knocks out the guard and probes the boy's body with a knife, finding white stuffing material inside: the body is *fake*!

Meanwhile, Eleven uses the boys' walkie-talkies to locate the missing Will; making the connection, they hear Will softly singing The Clash's "Should I Stay or Should I Go", a song which his brother Jonathan had turned him on to. At the school parking lot, Steve is outraged to find out Jonathan surreptitiously took pictures of the pool party; he smashes Jonathan's camera and rips up the photos. After recovering the pieces, Nancy discovers Jonathan might have snapped a partial image of whatever abducted Barb. When she shares her suspicions with Jonathan, he realizes the same "thing" must have kidnapped his brother, too. The boys have also brought Eleven to school. When Mike is bullied, she uses her abilities to stop the bully and make him publicly piss his pants. However, flexing her powers thus leaves her weak, with a trickle of blood running from her nostril…

Chapter 5: "The Flea and the Acrobat"

Chief Hopper flouts security and makes his way deep into the bowels of Hawkins Laboratory, where he discovers the secret organic "doorway" to the "Upside Down"—only to be seized by Dr. Brenner's henchmen, drugged, then dumped back at his trailer. Upon awakening, he searches his trailer and finds a surveillance "bug", which he destroys. At the news that State Police found Barb's abandoned car at the village train station, Hopper realizes there is a high-level conspiracy going on to hide the fates of the local missing children. He lets Joyce know that her suspicions are correct, and they begin working together.

Eleven reluctantly agrees to lead the boys to Will in the Upside Down, but she deliberately misleads them in order to keep them safe from what lurks there. The boys are livid when they uncover her ruse, and Lucas turns on Mike for defending Eleven. When the conflict escalates, Eleven telekinetically hurls Lucas away from Mike with sufficient violence to knock the former out. Lucas recovers, but Eleven flees.

Nancy and Jonathan search the woods together at twilight, unsure of what they are seeking but hoping to find Barb; they instead find a wounded deer barely clinging to life. As Jonathan prepares to put it out of its misery, something unseen snatches it away. Panicking, the two teens separate, and Nancy shortly finds a slime-encrusted opening in a standing tree trunk. She tentatively looks inside, only to find herself in the Upside Down—with *something else* for company. Jonathan hears Nancy's screams, but he can't actually see her…

Chapter 6: "The Monster"

With the creature in the Upside Down stalking her, Nancy gropes her way back to the gap in the tree, where Jonathan pulls her free in the nick of time. Terrified, she asks him to sleep over at her house; he does so, sleeping on the floor of her room, but Steve shows up and is furious at Jonathan being there. The next day, the conflict between Steve and Jonathan escalates, culminating in a fistfight that results in Jonathan being arrested while Steve and his cronies get away.

Eleven wanders alone into the town of Hawkins, sparking calamity when her hunger drives her into a local supermarket, where she uses her powers to shatter windows as a distraction to escape with an armload of Eggo waffles, which she gobbles down "raw". Elsewhere, the boys are still dealing with the rift between Lucas and Mike; Lucas refuses to make up with Mike and Dustin, and he goes it alone to Hawkins Laboratory while Mike and Dustin search for Eleven. They instead are found by the two school bullies, who are still bearing a grudge. They chase the boys to the quarry, forcing Mike at knife-point to leap off the ledge down into the icy waters far below. However, Eleven intercedes on his behalf, rescuing Mike by telekinetically stopping his fall right in mid-air then lifting him back up to safety before hurling one bully into the air and breaking the other's arm prior to them taking to their heels. Mike and Dustin happily reunite with her, even as Lucas warns them via walkie-talkie to hide: staking-out the Hawkins Laboratory, Lucas watches as Dr. Brenner and his militia pile into their vans and head into town in search of Eleven and the boys.

Elsewhere, Joyce and Hopper have tracked down a woman who had sued Dr. Brenner following her participation in one of his past experiments. She is unable to speak, but her sister can: the woman didn't know she was pregnant at the time Brenner used her as a test subject; Brenner and the authorities claimed she subsequently suffered a miscarriage, but the woman insists that she actually had the baby, which manifested "special abilities" before Brenner abducted the child. Could that child have been Eleven…?

Chapter 7: "The Bathtub"

Dr. Brenner and his militia's vans arrive at Mike's house, but Eleven and the boys elude them. Back at the police station, the parents of the bully with the broken arm seek to file a complaint against Mike and the boys, raving about Eleven and her uncanny "powers". Hopper connects the dots and immediately rounds up Joyce, Jonathan and Nancy, only to find Brenner's agents searching Mike's and

Open Wi-i-i-i-ide! The ravenous Demogorgon monster (suit worn by Mark Steger) from the Upside Down plays cookie-lookie; monster design by Aaron Sims, sculpted by Mike Elizalde's Spectral Motion, animatronic engineered by Mark Setrakian

Nancy's home. Using a walkie-talkie, they contact the boys, who are hiding-out with Eleven at a local scrapyard, even as Brenner's agents arrive in search of them. Hopper, Nancy, and Jonathan rescue the boys, and they all join forces at last to search for Will and Barb.

While recalling Brenner's experiments, Eleven remembers him repeatedly immersing her in an isolation tank filled with water to focus and amplify her powers, enabling her to access the Upside Down. She convinces Hopper and the team that she might be able to locate Will and Barb if they can improvise some sort of sensory-deprivation water tank, which they manage to do in the school gym. She immerses herself while Hopper and Joyce head back to Hawkins Laboratory. They succeed in breaking-in, only to be then captured by Brenner's agents.

The sensory-deprivation pool succeeds, and Eleven enters the Upside Down, only to discover that Barb is dead—her body apparently having been inundated with the creature's slug-like offspring—and that Will is still alive and in hiding, but soon to succumb if he is not rescued. Jonathan and Nancy propose that if they can somehow lure the creature hiding within the Upside Down to enter the earthly realm via Joyce's house, they *might* be able to kill it…

Chapter 8: "The Upside Down"

Back at Hawkins Laboratory, Dr. Brenner has separated Joyce and Hopper. He tries to coerce Joyce into accepting his "help", even as his agents torture Hopper with a Taser. They eventually agree to keep silent about the secret experiments and tell him where the kids are hiding—*if* Brenner will allow them to enter the Upside Down via the lab's organic "doorway" to rescue Will. Once

That Sinking Feeling: Will Byers (Noah Schnapp) faces his uncertain future in the mirror during *Stranger Things'* coda...

inside, Hopper and Joyce explore the dark Upside Down landscape, discovering clutches of eggs and eventually Will himself, alive but incapacitated and unconscious. Hopper removes a nasty tentacle-like obstruction from Will's throat and frantically administers CPR, resuscitating the boy.

Back at Joyce's house, Jonathan and Nancy have rigged an elaborate series of booby-traps, intent upon luring the creature out of the Upside Down into our world with blood, then destroying it with fire. When a repentant Steve unexpectedly shows up, he is forced to go along with the plan as the monster erupts onto the scene. In the melee that follows, the monster gets torched, but it apparently escapes nonetheless, as, upon extinguishing the flames, Jonathan, Nancy and Steve can find no evidence whatsoever of the creature's body.

Back at the school gym, Eleven and the boys witness the arrival of Brenner and his agents, intent upon recapturing Eleven. The boys are corralled and trapped, forcing a drained and weakened Eleven to overexert herself, lashing-out against the armed intruders, killing many in the process. Having severely depleted herself, she faints as Brenner seizes her and his agents capture the boys—but the blood spilled in the conflict attracts the creature from the Upside Down, which does indeed still live. The monster proceeds to savage Brenner and his agents, and the boys find themselves face-to-face with the ravenous creature. Eleven recovers, bidding Mike a fond farewell before mustering enough power to cause herself and the monster to evaporate from our reality.

Coda: Christmas time, one month later. Will is apparently his old self again, reunited with his friends in a role-playing game at Mike's house. Jonathan stops by to pick up Will, pausing to say hello to Nancy and Steve, who are now dating one another. At the police station, Hopper leaves the office Christmas party to drive alone into the woods and place Eggo waffles in a food chest—presumably for Eleven?

Meanwhile, Jonathan and Will join their mother Joyce for Christmas dinner in their partially-repaired home. Will excuses himself to go to the bathroom—where he looks at his wan reflection in the mirror over the sink before before coughing-up a living, slug-like parasite which slithers down the drain, as memories of the Upside Down return...

[End of Season One]

The ultimate in alien terror.

Still The Ultimate! *Stranger Things* wears its shaping (and shape-shifting) influences quite openly; right on its sleeve, in fact. Among the various one-sheet movie posters seen decorating characters' bedroom walls in the show is the now-iconic Drew Struzan poster—that he reportedly painted overnight in a single sitting!—for John Carpenter's **THE THING** (1982), which originally bombed hard theatrically, but is now rightly revered as a classic

****

Whatever side of the camp you found yourself stranded in—happily or unhappily—there's no denying that *Stranger Things* was the among the most unexpected hits of the summer TV season, at a time when Netflix sorely needed some good news.[8]

And whatever side of the camp you set up your site in—willingly or unwillingly—*Monster!* has just the "Study Guide" for you!

It's important to note that The Duffer Brothers immediately acknowledged, with pride, their debt to the pop-cultural roots of *Stranger Things*. As writer Zack Smith noted in July for IndyWeek.com:

"Fans of the era's genre films will spot plenty of visual and narrative homages in Stranger Things, *from the synthesizer-driven score and the Stephen King-style title card to the presence of eighties mainstays Winona Ryder and Matthew Modine in major roles. There are shout-outs to movies such as* **POLTERGEIST**, **THE GOONIES**, **E.T. THE EXTRA-TERRESTRIAL**, *and* **LESS THAN ZERO**, *and to pop-culture touchstones from* X-Men *comics to* Dungeons & Dragons. *'What we responded to when we saw films like that as kids was that they didn't talk down to us, that the stakes were really high,' Ross says by phone from Los Angeles, the day after the last episode of* Stranger Things *is finalized. 'If you read something like* It *or watch that train coming at them in* **STAND BY ME***, you're afraid they could die. The kids felt real, and reminded us of us and our friends.'...*"[9]

If you loved the series, this will inform your second, third, and fourth *Stranger Things* marathon viewings, enrich and deepen the entire viewing experience in ways that might surprise you, and steer you to more to savor until the sequel series to *Stranger Things* hits the streaming venues.[10]

If you loathed the series, this will lend your arguments credence, rekindle your love affairs with the wellsprings you didn't see a need to crudely retread, and provide ammunition for those unavoidable encounters with the pie-eyed devotees of the series.

With the shallow memories of all things "pop" and 21st Century, the buzz surrounding *Stranger Things* only seemed capable of recalling Stephen King's work. Well, sure; part of the appeal of *Stranger Things* is that The Duffer Brothers grew up reading King, watching Joe Dante and Steven Spielberg movies (and there's more of Joe Dante here than Spielberg, to my eye/ear[11]), and were clearly

---

8   See "Cramer shocked that so many Netflix users bailing over a couple extra bucks," July 19th, 2016, archived online (@ http://finance.yahoo.com/news/cramer-shocked-many-netflix-users-151454300.html): "Netflix's price increases scared people away from the streaming service, and the volume of unsubscribes surprised Jim Cramer."

9   Zack Smith, "Two Brothers Funnel Their Nostalgia for Eighties-Era Durham [NC] Summers Into New Netflix Series *Stranger Things*," Indyweek.com (serving Raleigh, Cary, Durham, Chapel Hill, NC), July 20th, 2016, archived online (@ http://www.indyweek.com/indyweek/two-brothers-funnel-their-nostalgia-for-eighties-era-durham-summers-into-new-netflix-series-stranger-things/Content?oid=5051936); quoted with permission of Zack Smith.

10 See "Stranger Things Renewed For Season 2 By Netflix!," July 5th, 2016, archived online (@ http://renewcanceltv.com/stranger-things-renewed-season-2-netflix/)

11 Nice to see Tim Lucas fully agreed on this point; "...it's important to remember that Joe Dante *invented* 1980s Young Adult fantasy in cinema. If you want to see where smart kid protagonists began, the way they still are today (in movies like **TOMORROWLAND** and **GOOSEBUMPS**, for example), you have to go back to **GREMLINS** and **EXPLORERS** and *Eerie, Indiana*...." See Lucas, *Ibid.* (@ http://videowatchdog.blogspot.com/2016/07/famil-

steeped in 1980s genre fare. The Duffer Brothers happily spread their influences all over the kid character's bedroom walls, from Sam Raimi's **EVIL DEAD** to John Carpenter's **THE THING** posters as markers, to the synth score copping from Tangerine Dream and John Carpenter scores of yore. You don't need me to list the Stephen King novels or King-adapted/derived 1980s feature films and TV miniseries, either; those are legion, and readily known and accessed.

But you deserve a wish-list and reference points to enrich your experience post-*Stranger Things*:

Without further ado, as a *Monster!* Public Service, we offer you:

The *Stranger Things* Study/Viewing Guide

1. Joseph Losey/Evan Jones' **THE DAMNED** ([1963, UK] released in the USA in cut form as **THESE ARE THE DAMNED** in 1965) is the original wellspring from which *Stranger Things* flows, where the whole conceit of a secret para-militarized laboratory experimenting on children comes from. **THE DAMNED** is one of the classics of Cold War British science-fiction, starring MacDonald Carey, Shirley Anne Field, Viveca Lindfors, Alexander Knox, and Oliver Reed. Be sure to screen the full-length 95-minute original UK edit of this dark gem, which was misunderstood and reviled by its parent studio, Hammer Films (and its US distributor, Columbia Pictures), severely cut and relegated to a cursory theatrical release two years after its completion. It's available in its excellent original Hammer Films UK version[12] in the US; it's *required* viewing, not to be missed. It is *absolutely essential* that you start with this film!

2. Well, actually, the *real* wellspring from which Jones adapted his **THE DAMNED** screenplay was H.L. Lawrence's novel *The Children of Light* (London: MacDonald and Co., 1960), which is pretty

dear on AbeBooks (*www.abebooks.com*) and elsewhere, *if* you can even find a copy at all. I bought my paperback copy for over $50 some years ago, so I can only imagine it's got to be up in the $75+ range these days. But H.L. Lawrence is the author who *really* laid the bedrock, particularly its being the result of cold, cruel secret government installations and scientific experimentation.[13] Lawrence arguably owed a debt to Theodore Sturgeon's "Baby is Three" (*Galaxy*, October 1952), which Sturgeon expanded to novel form to become the magnificent *More Than Human* (New York: Ballantine Books, 1953).

These two novels are where all telepath/telekinetic/mutant children in our pop culture were born. And yes, Stephen King knows all about all of this: from

13 There's precious little available about Lawrence's seminal novel; see Tim Lucas, "On Reading *The Children of Light*", *Video Watchblog*, September 12th, 2016 (@ http://videowatchdog.blogspot.com/2016/09/on-reading-children-of-light.html)

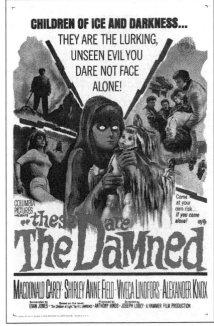

These *Aren't* The Damned! Well, *not* the alien-sired hybrid "damned" of the 1960 MGM hit **VILLAGE OF THE DAMNED**, which Columbia Pictures' publicity department tried like hell to convince potential audiences they were, anyway! (The misleading and lurid 1965 one-sheet poster for **THESE ARE THE DAMNED**, Columbia's abortive American release of the severely-edited Hammer Film **THE DAMNED**)

iar-things.html), quoted with permission.

12 As part of the 2010 Sony Pictures Home Entertainment DVD collection of the Columbia Pictures-distributed Hammer Films from the 1960s, *The Icons of Suspense Collection: Hammer Films*, featuring six of the studio's rarest titles, **STOP ME BEFORE I KILL!, CASH ON DEMAND, THE SNORKEL, MANIAC, NEVER TAKE CANDY FROM A STRANGER**, and **THESE ARE THE DAMNED**. Still available (from https://www.amazon.com/Icons-Suspense-Collection-Snorkel-Stranger/dp/B0034PWPHY/ref=sr_1_1?ie=UTF8&qid=1469012861&sr=8-1&keywords=The+Damned+Joseph+Losey) and other online venues.

Carrie to *Firestarter* and beyond, they're *all* offspring of Sturgeon's "Homo Gestalt".

3. There is another novel that *must* be cited as an essential source for *Stranger Things*: Robert Cormier's *I Am the Cheese* (1977, in both US and UK hardcover and paperback editions from Pantheon Books/Laurel-Leaf Library [US] and Victor Gollancz, Ltd./Fontana Lions [UK]). *I Am the Cheese* was and is a complex, compelling first-person novel in which its young protagonist, orphan Adam Farmer, struggles to make sense of his environment and circumstances while living in a decidedly *odd* facility, which might be a mental hospital (or worse); in doing so, he also juggles fragmentary memories of his former life with his parents and a repressed or buried tragic event. In time, Adam comes to discover the truth about where—and who and what—he is now.

To say anything more would spoil your reading of the novel, but rest assured that *Stranger Things* might not exist without Cormier's game-changing Y/A novel. It is as central to the *ST* narrative (and narrative structure) as *The Children of Light* and **THE DAMNED** are, if in a very different way. Though it starred young *E.T.* co-star Robert MacNaughton as Adam, Robert Jiras' and David Lange's feature film adaptation **I AM THE CHEESE** (1983, USA) never achieved the boxoffice, cable, or home video[14] success of *any* of the Stephen King movie adaptations, but Cormier's novel has remained in print since the late 1970s, also spawning many classroom and library study guide texts. *I Am the Cheese* was and remains one of the essential genre young adult novels; thus, it is a primary source for much that followed, including *Stranger Things*.

4. Somewhat of a precursor to *I Am the Cheese* is the eight-page comic story "The Loathsome" in EC's *Weird Science* #20 (July-August, 1953), story by Al Feldstein, art by Wally Wood. Though the narrative plays out in a very different manner than either of its successors, the setting and situation of the moving Feldstein/Wood story—an orphanage,

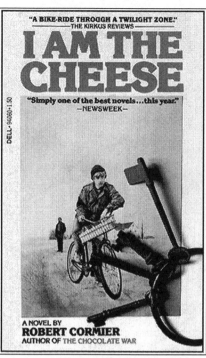

No Cheese Here! Before Y/A heroes like Eleven and her friends ever graced the screen, pioneer "young adult" writers like Robert Cormier blazed the trail for such characters in then-cutting-edge and controversial novels like *I Am The Cheese* ([1977] adapted into a shot-in-Vermont feature film in 1983). *ST*'s Eleven owes a clear debt to Adam, this novel's orphaned male protagonist

Bad Girls: Another precursor to *Stranger Things*' Eleven was the unseen-until-the-penultimate-page orphan mutant-girl drawn by Wally Wood for the classic EC Comics SF tale "The Loathsome", in *Weird Science* #20 (July-August, 1953)

---

14 This might be the toughest of all films listed in this Study Guide to acquire a copy of, though I highly recommend it, and available copies are quite affordable at the time of this writing. **I AM THE CHEESE** was released briefly on VHS in 1984 from Vestron Video (and again in 1994 from Front Row Video; though these may have been bootleg editions), and on DVD in 2007 via First Run Features. Both are long-OOP; used copies may still be available via Amazon (see *https://www.amazon.com/Am-Cheese-VHS-Robert-MacNaughton/dp/6303139663/ref=sr_1_1?s=movies-tv&ie=UTF8&qid=1474244426&sr=1-1&keywords=I+Am+the+Cheese+VHS* and *https://www.amazon.com/I-Am-Cheese-Robert-MacNaughton/dp/B0007YMW32/ref=sr_1_1?s=movies-tv&ie=UTF8&qid=1474244277&sr=1-1&keywords=I+Am+the+Cheese*).

A MOVIE OF MYSTERY, HORROR AND SUSPENSE.

Before *Stranger Things*, There Was...
Bill Condon and Michael Laughlin's delicious set-in-Illinois-but-shot-in-New-Zealand sleeper **DEAD KIDS** (a.k.a. **STRANGE BEHAVIOR**, 1981). All visible on this one-sheet poster are Michael Murphy as the suspicious small-town cop, Dan Shor as the son taking it in the eye for science, Fiona Lewis as the needling nurse, and Louise Fletcher as worried stepmother

an orphan girl with a secret, and the adults' mounting anxiety about her secret and possible escape—certainly suggests key elements of both Cormier's novel and *Stranger Things*:

A doctor sends a deformed mutant child that was the product of her father's exposure to atomic radiation to be brought up in an orphanage. The women of the orphanage dislike her because she displays poor behavior. One day the younger nurse comments to the older one that the girl is behaving herself recently and the older nurse recalls that all children receive a birthday party at ten years old and the girl must figure she is going to get one. The young woman asks if she is going to give the child one and the older woman states that it wouldn't be right to expect the other children to attend, so they'll just skip it in the mutant girl's case. They discover that the girl was spying on them and when she returns to her room she smashes the mirror. She's punished, and that evening the younger nurse

sees the girl on the grounds stuffing notes into tree hollows. She assumes that she must be up to no good and informs the older woman. The following evening they confront the child demanding the note and the girl flees from them. She climbs up a tree branch overhanging the orphanage's spiked wall and loses her grip. As the note slips from the hand of the dying impaled child, the older woman picks it up. It says "To whoever finds this note—I love you."[...][15]

5. Man oh man, has Bill Condon (script) and Michael Laughlin (director)'s made-in-New Zealand, set-in-America SF/horror gem **DEAD KIDS** (a.k.a. **STRANGE BEHAVIOR**, 1981) cast a longer shadow than anyone could have thought remotely possible when that odd, offbeat little jewel of a film popped up in fleeting theatrical release. Most of us (myself included) first caught it on late-night cable broadcasts; however you first experience **STRANGE BEHAVIOR**, I envy you your initial exposure!

It's as if the planned Condon/Laughlin "*Strange*" trilogy was completed by The Duffer Brothers...*seriously!* Condon and Laughlin did get **STRANGE INVADERS** (1983, USA) out, but couldn't mount the funding for the third feature in their planned trilogy. The Duffer Brothers got their title reference spot-on, didn't they?

I mean, seriously, watch **STRANGE BEHAVIOR**—a marvelous Tangerine Dream score enhances the film, the story involves the disappearance/murder of Illinois teen boys, a local cop (Michael Murphy) investigates to discover all the victims are sons of men who investigated the dicey lab/experiments of a long-dead scientist (Arthur Dingham), whose experiments continue on in a secret government lab and the cop's own son (Dan Shor) is the latest lab rat/research subject—look, just *trust* me on this!

Just see—*experience*—**STRANGE BEHAVIOR!**[16]

15 Synopsis quoted from the Grand Comics Database, *Weird Science* #20, "The Loathsome!", archived online (@ *http://www.comics.org/issue/10707/*), which also lists all available reprint editions of the story, and which is highly recommended.

16 Currently available in the US from Severin Films as a 2014 Blu-ray/DVD combo under its original title, **DEAD KIDS** (see *https://www.amazon.com/Dead-Kids-Blu-ray-DVD-Combo/dp/B00I9N56YK/ref=sr_1_1?ie=UTF8&qid=1475496519&sr=8-1&keywords=Dead+Kids+Blu-ray*), or via either the Synapse Films 2008 Special Edition DVD (still at *https://www.amazon.com/Strange-Behavior-Special-Michael-Murphy/dp/B001D5C1N0/ref=sr_1_1?s=movies-tv&ie=UTF8&qid=1474205050&sr=1-1&keywords=strange+behavior*), or as one of the trio of features (the other two are **PATRICK** and **THIRST**) in the 2003 Elite DVD package set The Aussie Horror Collection: *Terror From Down*

PS: The 1998 **DISTURBING BEHAVIOR** knowingly referenced Condon/Laughlin's film, as did that film's director, *The X-Files*' David Nutter; it's also a film well worth seeing in this context, despite what parent studio MGM did to it.[17]

6. Tough to say much without spoilers, but let's face it: *Stranger Things* emulates more than Stephen King. It's like a prequel to *The Mist*, in't it? Or a much better redraft/remake of *Firestarter*.

But where *Stranger Things* goes owes a debt to H.P. Lovecraft's short story "From Beyond" (1920, but first published in 1934)—read the story, it's all there in principal, and yes, Stephen King knows it well— and all other parallel worlds up to and including the Black Lodge and the Red Room (see: *Twin Peaks,* the complete series, and **TWIN PEAKS: FIRE WALK WITH ME**). According to *Twin Peaks* co-creator Mark Frost, that dimensional element central to the series was cribbed/extrapolated from Dion Fortune's 1935 non-fiction book *Psychic Self-Defense*, which is online[18] if you can't find or afford a hard copy.[19] There are countless examples of "secret experiments (sometimes government/military experiments, sometimes isolated renegade scientists) in the Pre-Code horror comics of the 1950s (including EC Comics stories), but I won't get into that here—our Study Guide would swell well beyond *Monster!*'s page-count limits (which I've tested mightily in the past! *[We'll always find room in our pages for whatever you give us, Steve!* ¡Nuestra casa es su casa!* ☺ – SF]*).

In terms of how these dimensional elements unfold in *Stranger Things*, I'd also steer the curious viewer/reader to John A. Keel's books, particularly *Strange Creatures From Time and Space* (Gold Medal Books/Fawcett Books, 1970), which was revised and ex-

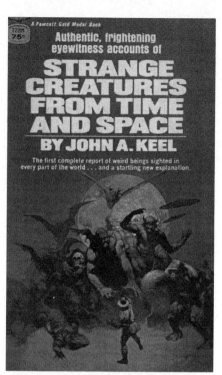

Before *Stranger Things*, There Was... The now-highly-collectible first edition of John A. Keel's seminal volume *Strange Creatures from Time and Space* (1970), which introduced Keel's theories of reported monster sightings as perhaps being attributable to visitors from a parallel dimension; its magnificent cover art was by Frank Frazetta

panded into *The Complete Guide to Mysterious Beings* (Doubleday Books, 1994). Keel expanded upon his views on paranormal events, UFOs, monster sightings, and what he called "ultraterrestrials" in a series of books: *UFOs: Operation Trojan Horse: An Exhaustive Study of Unidentified Flying Objects, Revealing Their Source and the Forces That Control Them* a.k.a. *Why UFOs: Operation Trojan Horse* (G.P. Putnam's Sons and Manor Books, both 1970), *The Mothman Prophecies: An Investigation into the Mysterious American Visits of the Infamous Feathery Garuda* (E.P. Dutton/Saturday Review Press, 1975; Signet Books/New American Library, 1976), and *The Eighth Tower: The Cosmic Forces Behind All Religious, Occult, and UFO Phenomenon* a.k.a. *The Eighth Tower: On Ultraterrestrials and the Superspectrum* (E.P. Dutton/Saturday Review Press, 1975; Signet Books/New American Library, 1977).[20]

Under (still available at *https://www.amazon.com/Aussie-Collection-Patrick-Strange-Behavior/dp/B0000TAYPC/ ref=sr_1_2?s=movies-tv&qid=1474205050&s-r=1-2&keywords=strange+behavior*).

17 **DISTURBING BEHAVIOR**—and what it originally was *meant* to be (recoverable at last thanks to the bonus features)—is still available on DVD and Blu-ray; see *https://www.amazon.com/Disturbing-Behavior-Blu-ray-James-Marsden/dp/B018WQBNEA/ref=s-r_1_2?s=movies-tv&ie=UTF8&qid=1474205323&s-r=1-2&keywords=Disturbing+behavior* for the Blu-ray edition, but the DVD edition may take some searching (be sure to pick up the edition with the extra features to fully appreciate the film with its deleted scenes and alternate ending). Avoid streaming the film, as the theatrical version was severely truncated and tampered with.

18 *http://jacquesricher.com/occult/psychic.pdf*

19 *https://www.amazon.com/s/ref=nb_sb_ss_c_2_19?url=search-alias%3Dstripbooks&field-keywords=dion+fortune+psychic+self+defense&sprefix=Dion+Fortune+Psychi%2Caps%2C190*

20 There are now print-on-demand editions of all these Keel books; they are easily found and purchased in affordable new editions from multiple venues.

And that's *it*. I can't say more without spoiling key elements of *Stranger Things* for folks who haven't yet seen the series.

7. Beyond the John A. Keel speculation that opened this dimensional doorway, I've got to bring your attention to what followed in Keel's footsteps. Along with the so-called Philadelphia Experiment case history—which was a movie John Carpenter wanted to make, but Stewart Raffill [!!!] got to instead[21]—you want to dig into the Montauk case history, specifically the 1992 book *The Montauk Project: Experiments in Time*, by Preston B. Nichols and Peter Moon,[22]and Christopher Garetano's **MONTAUK CHRONICLES** (2015, USA).[23]

In fact, The Duffer Brothers owe a considerable debt to Christopher's film. The series was originally announced in April 2015 under the title *Montauk*; that is indisputably a fact.[24] The Duffer Brothers' pitch reel, it seems, reportedly incorporated/appropriated, *sans* permission, footage *lifted verbatim from* Garetano's **MONTAUK CHRONICLES**—but I'll leave *that* for Christopher to sort out. On July 23rd, 2016, Christopher posted the following open letter on Facebook (and for this, I have retained Christopher's use of capital letters, as in his original post):

I recently read an article, this morning, stating that STRANGER THINGS was only based on MK ULTRA. The article never mentioned that the show was originally called MONTAUK.

This is very strange as the author is well aware of the Montauk Project.

The show was pitched and sold as MONTAUK, not MK ULTRA.

There are blatantly obvious reasons for all of this.

Bottom Line:

The show is good fun. I have no issues with it or ANYONE who is enjoying it. I'm not losing my mind over this at all. I'm fine and inspired as ever.

I'm busy working on my new movie.[25] I've only made a few posts about this on FACEBOOK that took me only a few moments to achieve.

I have my own (network) show that's in production, right now.

I'm not suing anyone. I was in full-support of STRANGER THINGS until I learned of the pitch process that allows VERY-RICH albeit lazy, in the pitch process, people to take the work of others (including independent artists) and use it as part of a proposal to sell a mega-show to a network. It's wrong but it's legal.

The sizzle-reel of my own show also contained scenes from my movie that were combined with work from my co-producers.

It was completely original.

So that's all folks. I think it should simply be illegal to do that.

These folks could afford to shoot a few things and THEN pitch a show.

STRANGER THINGS, was partially inspired by the work that I did with my picture, MONTAUK CHRONICLES. FULL STOP.

OK then, ONWARD and upward!!! Here's to originality, truth, and to the great movies, magazines, websites, and television shows of the near future.

21 Still on DVD, available from *https://www.amazon.com/Philadelphia-Experiment-Michael-Pare/dp/B005FQ2H8W/ref=sr_1_1?s=movies-tv&ie=UTF8&qid=1474206687&sr=1-1&keywords=philadelphia+experiment* —and the SyFy Channel's 2012 remake (on DVD and Blu-ray) is available (@ *https://www.amazon.com/Philadelphia-Experiment-Blu-ray-Nicholas-Lea/dp/B00BWHAP4Q/ref=sr_1_5?s=movies-tv&ie=UTF8&qid=1474206687&sr=1-5&keywords=philadelphia+experiment*). There's also DVD editions of documentaries on the subject: approach at your own risk! See, or *don't* see, the Al Bielek lecture-based documentaries **THE TRUTH ABOUT THE PHILADELPHIA EXPERIMENT: INVISIBILITY, TIME TRAVEL AND MIND CONTROL** (2010, available @ *https://www.amazon.com/Truth-About-Philadelphia-Experiment-Invisibility/dp/B002VRNIJA/ref=sr_1_10?s=movies-tv&ie=UTF8&qid=1474206687&sr=1-10&keywords=philadelphia+experiment*), which is included in the 3-DVD set **THE PHILADELPHIA EXPERIMENT REVEALED: FINAL COUNTDOWN TO DISCLOSURE** (2011, available @ *https://www.amazon.com/Philadelphia-Experiment-Revealed-Countdown-Disclosure/dp/B007I1TGQI/ref=sr_1_11?s=movies-tv&ie=UTF8&qid=1474206687&sr=1-11&keywords=philadelphia+experiment*). Bielek claims to be the sole survivor of the so-called Philadelphia Experiment; Bielek and author/fellow lecturer Preston Nichols link The Philadelphia Experiment with the subsequent Phoenix and Montauk Projects, hence its relevance here.

22 Peter Moon, Preston B. Nichols, and Nina Helms subsequently wrote three more books on the subject: *Montauk Revisited: Adventures in Synchronicity* (1994), *Pyramids of Montauk: Explorations in Consciousness* (1995), and *The Black Sun: Montauk's Nazi-Tibetan Connection* (1997). All are still available via amazon and various online sources.

23 *https://www.amazon.com/Montauk-Chronicles/dp/B00ISGZ65W/ref=sr_1_1?s=movies-tv&ie=UTF8&qid=1469011564&sr=1-1&keywords=montauk+chronicles*

24 See Dana Rose Falcone, "Netflix announces new series *Montauk* arriving in 2016," April 2, 2015, archived online (@ *http://www.ew.com/netflix-orders-montauk-for-2016*)

25 Garetano's new movie will be of instant interest to *Monster!* readers: it's entitled **BIGFOOT** (slated for release later in 2016); the first trailer was posted earlier this year (@ *https://www.youtube.com/watch?v=7nxRmroZH3Q*)

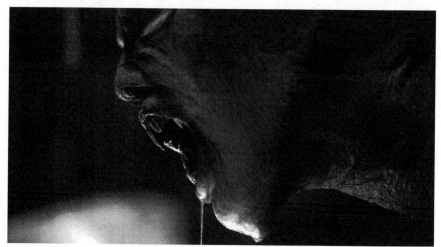

Before *Stranger Things*, There Was... Christopher Garetano's doc **MONTAUK CHRONICLES** (2015, USA), from which the promo "pitch reel" for *Stranger Things* reportedly lifted imagery and sequences in order to sell the Duffer Brothers series. Tut-tut, Duffer Brothers—pay your dues!

Best Wishes,
Christopher Garetano.[26]

While *Stranger Things* takes a very different approach and narrative tack, and they're very different works, there's a major debt there. Maybe it's all worked out for Christopher after all; at the time of this writing, Garetano announced production underway[27] on a related TV series:

In only a few weeks we will begin principal-photography on our MONTAUK CHRONICLES network spin-off show. It's been a long and often an arduous journey making independent movies. The rewards are waiting for those who have the courage, drive, creativity, and conviction to stick to their vision. You must also have and develop a gargantuan sense of patience. Don't ever listen to those who tell you 'you can't.' ...I began shooting MONTAUK CHRONICLES in a suburban basement and now I'm working with a network on a show..."[28]

As to where Christopher was originally coming from, and the links to *Stranger Things*, the Supernatural Research and Analysis Institute's Mark Johnson wrote this past July,

*...most viewers who watch the show [*Stranger Things*] will have no idea that it is based on real events that took place in the United States from the early 1950's, all the way up to the 1970's...and may still be going on today. In 1953, the Central Intelligence Agency officially sanctioned a program known as MK Ultra[29]—an illegal mind control program that performed experiments on unwilling human subjects using mind-altering drugs (especially LSD), sleep deprivation, and torture.[30] President Gerald Ford commissioned an investigation into CIA activities within the United States, MK Ultra was shut down in 1973, and CIA Director Richard Helms ordered all documentation regarding the MK Ultra program destroyed. Yet there is eye-*

---

26 Quoted with permission. For more on Christopher's take on the associative links between THE MONTAUK CHRONICLES and *Stranger Things*, see the July 2016 interview with Christopher archived (@ *http://sarinstitutecom.powweb.com/2016/07/19/stranger-things-mk-ultra-and-the-montauk-project/*)

27 Garetano's own Montauk-based TV series proposal was, in Christopher's words, "in-development long before *Stranger Things* was even in production..."; quoted, with permission, from a personal message to the author, September 19, 2016. The series goes into production as of October 2016.

28 Christopher Garetano, Facebook post, September 15, 2016, 3:30 PM.; quoted with permission. On September 9, 2016, 9:58 PM, Christopher posted, "Our MONTAUK CHRONICLES network-show is now in pre-production and

we're shooting by mid-October." Good luck, Christopher!

29 See *https://en.wikipedia.org/wiki/Project_MKUltra*; this link was "live" in the original online text.

30 Interjecting an SRB footnote here, not part of the original quoted text: The first book I ever found on this subject was John D. Marks' *The Search for the "Manchurian Candidate": The CIA and Mind Control* (Times Books, 1979; WW Norton, 1992), which is recommended; there are now others, too. Primary among the more recent texts are *Mind Wars: Brain Research and National Defense* a.k.a. the revised edition, *Mind Wars: Brain Science and the Military in the 21st Century*, by Jonathan D. Moreno (Dana Press, 2006; Bellevue Literary Press, 2012) and *Mind Wars: A History of Mind Control, Surveillance, and Social Engineering by the Government, Media, and Secret Societies*, by Marie D. Jones and Larry Flaxman (New Pages, 2015).

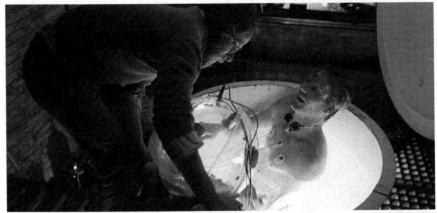

Before *Stranger Things*, There Was... Paddy Chayefsky's and Ken Russell's **ALTERED STATES** (1980, USA). Here, Arthur Rosenberg (Bob Balaban) helps Dr. Eddie Jessup (William Hurt) out of a standing isolation tank during their early experiments in the film

*witness testimony that these clandestine programs continued throughout the 1980's and longer. An excellent documentary on the subject, **THE MONTAUK CHRONICLES**, tells the story of the secret installation in Montauk on Long Island, NY.*[31]

8. Perhaps needless to say—but I'll say it anyway—the entire isolation tank angle was inspired by Dr. John C. Lilly's real-life sensory deprivation tank experiments in the 1950s and 1960s, which in turn inspired the 1963 James Kennaway/Basil Dearden film **THE MIND BENDERS** and, more famously, Paddy Chayefsky's and Ken Russell's mind-bending **ALTERED STATES** (1980), the ultimate "isolation tank" psychedelic film experience. *Essential viewing!*

9. The final text I must bring to your attention predates most of those inspirational sources previously mentioned (except for the Lovecraft short story). Richard Matheson's story "Little Girl Lost" was in many ways *Stranger Things*' Ground Zero of sorts: In a normal suburban home, a little girl disappears in her own bedroom, her voice audible from under her bed, but she isn't there; still, they can hear her, under the bed, behind or between the walls...

It was published in Matheson's second short story anthology *The Shores of Space* (1953), but most experienced it via the March 16th, 1962 *The Twilight Zone* dramatization (I remember it well: it broadcast just two days after my seventh birthday!).[32] It's

where the screenplay of **POLTERGEIST** (both versions, 1982 and 2015) was extrapolated from. Matheson pioneered this whole "parent(s)-lose-child-in-the-walls" template, including the need to scientifically parse-out a rescue from seemingly supernatural events. *Start there*, since everyone else has... whether they know it or not.

And, yes, again; Stephen King knows.

There's more, much more, but this gives you somewhere to go once you've savored—or despised— *Stranger Things*.

I'm on board for whatever The Duffer Brothers do hereafter.[33] May stranger things await us all!

light-Zone-Season-Episodes-Collection/dp/B00C6F61S2/ref=sr_1_1?s=movies-tv&ie=UTF8&qid=1474214201&sr=1-1&keywords=Twilight+Zone+Season+3) or Blu-ray (@ *https://www.amazon.com/Twilight-Zone-Season-Three-Blu-ray/dp/B01KOCLOJE/ref=sr_1_4?s=movies-tv&ie=UTF8&qid=1474214201&sr=1-4&keywords=Twilight+Zone+Season+3)*, or via streaming online.

33 If you want to see what The Duffer Brothers (Matt & Ross) had done *before*, at the time of this writing their original short film *Eater* (2007, based on the short story by Pete Crowther) can still be viewed online (@ *http://www.indiewire.com/2016/08/duffer-brothers-short-film-eater-stranger-things-directors-1201713815/)*; their first feature film, **HIDDEN** (2015, USA), is available via streaming online and at amazon, or via DVD (@ *https://www.amazon.com/Hidden-Alexander-Skarsgård/dp/B014K5F1KO/ref=sr_1_2?s=movies-tv&ie=UTF8&qid=1474205798&sr=1-2&keywords=Hidden)*. They were also the writers/producers of the Fox series *Wayward Pines* (May 14, 2015-July 27, 2016).

31 For a comprehensive overview, see everything the Supernatural Analysis and Research Institute has posted online (@ *http://sarinstitutecom.powweb.com/2016/07/19/stranger-things-mk-ultra-and-the-montauk-project/)*

32 See Season 3 of *The Twilight Zone*, on DVD, still available via Amazon (@ *https://www.amazon.com/Twi-*

GIRLS AND CORPSES

VOLUME 10 Fall

ONLY $8.95

SEX
WITH MAGIC

PENN & TELLER'S FINAL TRICK!

Performed by
LouLou D'vil

GC

www.girlsandcorpses.com

THE ADVENTURES OF

Neutron

THE MASKED MARVEL!

by Steve Fenton

Introduction: A (Monster) Wrestler or *Not* a Wrestler, That is the Question...?

Whether or not all you purists out there consider Neutron to be a bona fide luchador *depends entirely on your personal criteria for what constitutes a Mexican "wrestling movie". Some people don't consider ol' Newt to be of the "masked wrestler" school, while others do. His films contain no scenes of in-the-ring action, although the hero certainly engages in more than his fair share of monster-grappling, as well as coming to grips with even more villains of strictly human physiognomy: these habits combined with his enmasked, incognito persona certainly parallel the obvious elements of the wrestling movie genre.*

Hence, arguing that Neutron isn't a masked wrestler per se just because he never appears in the traditional squared circle of the wrestling ring is a moot point. The very oblongoid frame of the movie screen itself becomes his arena, within which he takes on all comers as fearlessly as any other luchadorean hero might (and indeed should). It's rather like arguing apples and apples anyway. Even several of El Santo's movies contain not a shred of onscreen ring action (e.g., his first two screen appearances, CEREBRO DEL MAL *["Brain of Evil"] and* HOMBRES INFERNALES *["Men from Hell", both 1958], as well as* SANTO CONTRA LOS CAZADORES DE CABEZAS *["Santo vs. The Head-Hunters", 1969], etc.), but are logically enough lumped-in with the rest of the* luchador *genre proper. Nelson Carro's indispensable booklet* El Cine de Luchadores—*put out by the Universidad Nacional Autonoma de México in 1984—lists the Neutrons in its extensive filmography, so that's good enough for me. If they consider him a wrestling star, then they of all people oughta know. Now that we've got that outta the way with, it's on to the initial* Neutron *"trilogy" (which is really just a single serial, when all is said and done). These three features, each formed of a triplet of shorter chapters, as per the norm in Mexico at that time, are the series entries which most pertain to* Monster! *'s "monster movies only" criterion, and I'll be giving them some quite lengthy coverage, often dwelling on the minutiae of their plots, so be forewarned that spoilers are present throughout!*

*[Editor's Note: The bulk of this article consists of a substantially revised/updated version of one which first appeared in issue #4 of my long-defunct Mexcentric fanzine ¡Panicos! *[1993] ~ SF.)*

Above: Future Santonian/Buñuelian alum Claudio Brook has a "bad face day" in **NEUTRON AND THE BLACK MASK**. His hair still looks *great*, though! (Mexican lobby card)

NEUTRON AND THE BLACK MASK

(*Neutrón el Enmascarado Negro* / "Neutron, The Black Mask"; a.k.a. **NEUTRON THE ATOMIC SUPERMAN AND THE BLACK MASK** [actual onscreen US TV title]) Shot in 3 episodes: *El Enmascarado Negro* / "The Black-Masked Man," *Caronte triunfa* / "Caronte Triumphs," & *El invento diabólico* / "The Diabolical Invention"

NEUTRON VS. THE AMAZING DR. CARONTE

(*Neutrón contra el Dr. Caronte* / "Neutron vs. Dr. Caronte; a.k.a. **NEUTRON THE ATOMIC SUPERMAN VS. THE AMAZING DR. CARONTE** [actual onscreen US TV title]) Shot in 3 episodes: *Neutrón contra el doctor Caronte* / "Neutron vs. Dr. Caronte," *El testamento del doctor Caronte* / "The Testament of Dr. Caronte," & *Frente a frente* / Face to Face"

NEUTRON AGAINST THE DEATH ROBOTS

(*Los automatas de la muerte* / "The Robots of Death"; a.k.a. **NEUTRON THE ATOMIC SUPERMAN VS. THE DEATH ROBOTS** [actual onscreen US TV title]) Shot in 3 episodes: *Los automatas de muerte*, *El enano verdugo* / "The Dwarf Executioner," & *La bomba diabólica* / "The Diabolical Bomb"

Mexico, 1960
Estudios America, S.A. / Producciones Corsa, S.A. presentations.
D: Federico Curiel. Prd: Emilio Gómez Muriel. Sto/Scr: Alfredo Ruanova. DP: Fernando Álvarez Garcés Colín. Mus: Enrico/"Enuio" [US version] Cabiati. Ed: Juan Munguia
S: Wolf Ruvinskis, Julio Alemán, Armando Silvestre, Rosita Arenas, Roberto "Beto el Boticario" Ramírez, Rodolfo Landa, Claudio Brook, Grek Martin, Ernesto Finance, Guillermo Álvarez Bianchi, Manuel "Manver" Vergara. Musical artists: David Lama, Trio Los Diamantes / "The Diamond Trio," Los Tres Ases / "The Three Aces," Los Rebeldes del Rock / "The Rockin' Rebels"

While he didn't actually pen any of the scripts for the films themselves, director Federico Curiel holds official credit as the Neutron character's creator; a credit which carried over into the series of *fotonovelas* ("photo-comics") which—beginning late in 1961—subsequently spun-off from the filmic series and continued on into the mid/late '60s; of which, I give more below in our special extended "Sidebar" section on that particular subject (the same section also includes, just for the record, coverage of the three later Neutron movies which came *sans* any legit monster content, more's the pity).

Considering it's the first episode in the initial three-part *Neutrón* serial, NEUTRON AND THE BLACK MASK's introduction could very well be interchangeable with just about any other of the series: the story leaps right into the meat of the matter without much in the way of preamble at all, with Police Inspector Lansing and his trusty assistant Robert discussing the antisocial antics of one diabolical Dr. Caronte and his valiant arch-nemesis, the muscly masked superhero, Neutron—our *hombre* of the hour!

Deep down in his secret subterranean hidey-hole, Doc Caronte and his bow-legged dwarf assistant Nick plot the theft of a powerful neutron bomb

devised by a collective of renowned nuclear physicists. This bomb ("Designed to stop all wars," one scientist self-righteously proclaims [yeah, *right!*]) is stolen from one of its originating creators, Professor Norton. The thief is none other than his weasely soon-to-be-former assistant, Dr. John Walker. This character is portrayed by Claudio Brook (1927-1995), who was later "more prestigiously" seen in Luis Buñuel's THE YOUNG ONE (*La joven*, 1961, Mexico). We however much prefer to remember him for his part here, as well as his other castings in such prime Mexploitation fare as Alfonso Corona Blake's SAMSON IN THE WAX MUSEUM (*Santo en el museo de cera*, 1963), plus two offbeat Juan López Moctezuma-directed horror shockers, DR. TARR'S TORTURE DUNGEON (*La mansión de la locura* / "The Mansion of Madness", 1972) and ALUCARDA (*Alucarda: hija de las tinieblas* / "Alucarda, Daughter of Darkness", 1975), as well as, much later, Guillermo del Toro's revisionist vampire film CRONOS (*Chronos*, 1992).

In *Neutron* #1, the Brook character's senior scientist's soon-to-be-ex-employer is mercilessly gunned down by the treacherous Doc Walker's hired hitman flunky. While mortally wounded, however, with his dying breath the betrayed inventor manages to activate the bomb right in the lab, thus disfiguring Walker with

Dig Those Crazy Helmets! Masked superheroes and malevolent superscience collide in the first *Neutrón* threesome, from whose initial instalment **NEUTRON AND THE BLACK MASK** this is an original Mexican lobby card

151

Self-signed promo postcard (*circa* 1940s) of comic actor/director Federico "Pichirilo" Curiel

searing, scarring neutronic radiation in the resultant (decidedly localized and feebly-focused) "blast".

Jimmy Norton, the son of the murdered doctor (known as "Jaime Yáñez" in the original Mexican

Behold The True Face Of Evil! A candid shot of *Beto el Boticario, sans* his Dr. Caronte mask (photo by "Alex")

version; played by Armando Silvestre [last name subtly modified to "Silvester" on US prints], who provided sturdy heroic mettle in slews of Mexploitation flix) is summoned to the crime scene by Insp. Lansing ("There it is, Robert!" overstates the inspector to his assistant above the residual/vestigial remains of the evaporated scientist. "Now we know what *radon gas* can do!")

Also turning up at the scene are Jimmy's closest *amigos*, Charles "Chuck" Harris (a.k.a. "Carlos Márquez" in the Mex cut; played by *lucha* film superstar Wolf Ruvinskis [1921-1999]) and Martin "Marty" Nelson (originally known as "Mario Núñez"; Julio Alemán [1933-2012], who also played the hero of Curiel's *Nostradamus* vampire saga, amongst other things [by the by, I shall be covering said four-film saga in a future issue of *Monster!*). This fearless clique forms a Three Musketeers-like alliance ("One for all, and all for one!" is the familiar battle-cry heard here). This trio is introduced to Nora (Rosita Arenas, whose first name was for some reason given as "Roslia" on US export prints). Nora is the pretty nightclub singer niece of the duplicitous—if at this point still unsuspected—Dr. Walker (Brook's character, you'll recall). Ever since the murder of Prof. Norton, Nora's guilty uncle has gone into hiding, aided only by his loyal butler, Marco. That very night, Walker—who has been left with permanent severe facial scars due to his recent impromptu "radiation treatment"—attempts (exact motives unclear) to murder his niece Nora, whereafter she flees to the safety of Jimmy's apartment (if not his actual bed!).

To this point, criminal mastermind Dr. Caronte seems to have spent an inordinate amount of his screen-time strolling hand-in-hand (!?) with his diminutive accomplice (catamite?) Nick along mood-lit castle corridors (*hmmmmm...?*). In basic appearance, the Caronte character bears a certain passing resemblance to the famed *luchador* of both film and the real-life wrestling ring, *El Médico Asesino* ("The Killer Doctor" had portrayed none other than the future El Santo's prototypical character Himself in René Cardona, Sr.'s Mexi-wrestling melodrama **EL ENMASCARADO DE PLATA** ["The Man Masked in Silver", 1952], which formed the basis of what later became the iconic Santo as played by his long-time portrayer Rodolfo Guzman Huerta). Despite his no doubt intentional resemblance to *El Médico*, Caronte was actually played by, not a lesser-known real-life masked wrestler but simply a masked actor (i.e., *Beto el Boticario* / "Beto the Apothecary", a.k.a. Roberto Ramírez Garza [1927-2009]). Generally known for playing comedic roles, "Beto" Ramírez plays Caronte herein with little in the way of a sense of humor, but his comic roles are legion. For instance, billed both under his *Beto el Boticario* alias as well as playing a non-masked character known as Beto onscreen, Ramírez had earlier filled a supporting part in director Mauricio de la Serna's musical comedy **CARAS NUEVAS** ("New Faces", 1955); for which Ramírez's present director Federico Curiel (who also acted for a time under the stage-name "*Pichirilo*") also appeared way down in the cast-list.

While Ramírez had gone non-masked in that film just cited, here his Caronte character's fashion choices—clinical white mask, matching surgical smock and latex gloves—partially bring to mind the aforementioned El Médico Asesino's trademark medically-themed costume (interestingly enough, at some point in time, there was also a real-life wrestling duo/sometime trio who billed themselves under the name Los Karontes a.k.a. Los Doctores Karonte [sic!] and dressed in virtually identical medics' duds as their cinematic unofficial namesake). Caronte's costume also recalls the look of the same-named but otherwise unrelated masked mad medico character in René Cardona, Sr.'s classic **DOCTOR OF DOOM** (*Las Luchadoras contra el Médico Asesino* / "The Wrestling Women vs. The Killer Doctor", 1962, Mexico). Confused much?! (If you're not yet, you soon will be…☺)

Anyway, disfigured Doc Walker visits Caronte's "top secret" underground domicile (some of the same expansive Churubusco-Azteca interior sets also saw use by Curiel for his *Nostradamus* serial from the same general time-frame). Here, the majorly megalomaniacal—so what *else* is new!?—Caronte shows off his basement pit-full of what by Episode 3 had become colorfully termed "Death Robots": these are scraggly-haired, facially indistinct, lumbering lunks in baggy boiler suits. At Caronte's constant beck and call, these creatures can be dispatched at a moment's notice to do the doctor's dirty bidding. Walker forges a loose (*verrry* loose) parasitic/symbiotic partnership with the white-masked ultravillain, which we just know is bound to end badly for him, as per the usual hoary trope.

At first, it is implied by the script that Neutron (identity as-yet supposedly unknown [as if we didn't already know it right up front!]) is also a self-serving bad guy out to secure the fiercely coveted and contested formula for the neutronic super-weapon ("'Neutron'—the *same* name as the bomb!" exclaims Jimmy, putting two and two together, displaying uncanny powers of deduction for a beefcake bimbo/hero). Another project scientist, Prof. Wilson, is soon killed off by Caronte's homegrown monster men. These lumpy-faced, scruffy-maned creatures stiff-leg about with

Top to Bottom: That Dr. Caronte can be a right nasty bastard when he wants to be… which is often!; Wolf Ruvinskis strikes a typical Neutronic pose; Ruvinskis, with Jack Taylor; Caronte's pit-full of "Death Robots" get restless

NEUTRON
EL ENMASCARADO NEGRO

Los Inmortales
Wolf

Top: Rosita Arenas just can't make up her mind which hunky hero she wants! **Center:** Hero #1, Wolf Ruvinskis – Neutron personified! **Above:** Hero #2, Armando Silvestre, here seen in Emilio "El Indio" Fernández's **LA RED** (1953, Mexico). *[See p.163 for a shot of Hero #3, Julio Alemán]*

straightened arms and perpetually clenched fists, appearing decidedly too sluggish and ungainly by half to be very intimidating, but there's definitely no denying they're genuine monsters of sorts, so no bitching, all you picky *M!* purists!

Working independently of the police, our triptych of heroes decides to conduct its own unofficial investigation into the rash of murders which has been plaguing the vicinity. They vow to protect the final remaining scientists, Prof. Albert Duval and his esteemed colleague Dr. Abraham Méndez, who have also been targeted by Caronte. The arch-criminal now possesses two components vital in the manufacture of the deadly neutron bomb, and the two doctors have access to the final pieces needed to complete the desired formula. Incidentally, it should perhaps be noted here that, throughout the serial, the number of alleged "required components" fluctuates if not drastically then at least quite subtly (from three to two and back to three again, etc). Whether such discrepancy existed in the original version or was merely a side-defect of slovenly redubbing, I don't know. Either way, similar ever-shifting continuity was by no means uncommon even in the vintage Hollywood cliffhangers from which the *Neutrón* series took so many pointers; chances are, most kids in the audience didn't much care about such relatively minor considerations anyway!

That night, Neutron (moonlighting as a sneaky cat burglar/ninja in "stealth" mode) shows up at Prof. Duval's home to filch the formula. In the resultant confusion, Caronte's monsters converge to abduct Duval from right under police noses. The imprisoned professor is soon thereafter tortured to death—albeit firmly off-screen—by the sadistic Caronte in an attempt to loosen the victim's tongue and secure his portion of the secret formula. This has been stolen for "safekeeping" by the socially-conscious Neutron, who soon reveals his true colors (i.e., whiter 'n' brighter than The Lone Ranger's hat!) and proves to be—*surprise, surprise!*—a staunch good guy after all; this despite his uniformly **black** tastes in superhero accessories.

Meanwhile, Jimmy, Marty and Chuck (remember now: *he's* Neutron [for *now*, anyhow; more on that later...]) determine to ensure that Dr. Méndez, the last surviving boffin not yet in a coffin, does not meet a fate similar to those of his late colleagues on Caronte's hit-list. The despicable Dr. Walker soon makes a second botched bid to murder Nora. Reinforcements are this time provided by Caronte's monsters, which fend-off our brave heroes. Neutron is then soon back on the case investigating the killing of Méndez, and is forced to combat a huddle of Caronte's death robots in passing. On the print

I originally watched way back when (an early '90s VHS videocassette copy from Sinister Cinema), this action sequence culminates with an odd lingering freeze-frame of a shattered window after Neutron has just dove energetically through it to evade the monsters. This "dramatic device" seems to have been a further attempt to mimic the "suspenseful" narrative techniques of Hollywood cliffhangers. Adding to the old world effect, much of the shrill canned "horror movie" music employed by the soundtrack resembles some of the famous stock compositions heard in various Universal Pictures monster classics from the '40s. These familiar strains enhance the serialesque/matinee atmosphere of the current films.

Over 50 minutes into this first instalment, one Prof. Thomas (played by American-born, future Spanish-based actor Jack Taylor under his cryptic Mexican-period alias of "Grek Martin" [although he went

Mexican one-sheet poster for the first Newt adventure (artist's name illegible)

unbilled by any name on US prints]) turns up to assist with police inquiries. Thomas is soon "abducted" in a taxi whose driver turns out to be—*voila!*—none other than Neutron: still wearing his mask, but also decked-out in a peaked cap and spiffy cabbie's uniform (this makes for a presumably unintentionally humorous image). However, so-called "Prof. Thomas" actually turns out to be—*Aha!*—radiation-scarred Dr. Walker hiding beneath a removable latex Jack Taylor mask, no less! In this fashion he cons part of the formula Caronte requires, leaving only one more ingredient now needed to complete the recipe. Here it might be interesting to mention that Claudio Brook, portrayer of Dr. Walker, would

in real-life later beat-out Jack Taylor, portrayer of Prof. Thomas, for a key role in Buñuel's above-noted THE YOUNG ONE, made during that director's fruitful and much-acclaimed Mexican tenure. On original Mexican posters for the first Neutron outing—and presumably for its "sequels" too—Brook was billed seventh, whilst Taylor got eighth billing as "Grek Martin," a name he only used while working in Mexico. According to something he told me when I interviewed him back in the early '90s for a one-off fanzine I did called *Tame*, Taylor also briefly went under the pseudonym of "Grek Rowan"—an obscure, oddball wordplay on "Greek Roman", according to him—during his Mexican phase. But, I digress. I now return you to our highly-convoluted (yet simultaneously simplistic) plot, still-in-progress...

Prof. Thomas, Nora and Martin—the latter disguised as Neutron (bear that in mind)—are kidnapped by Dr. Walker and his servant Marco, only to be saved from Caronte's monsters by the arrival of the *genuine* Neutron. (If you think this is getting complicated, just wait till *later, amigos...*) During the resultant brawl, Walker is killed by a monster, while Thomas and Nora flee with the neutron bomb, hotly pursued by Caronte and his pet *monstruos*. Upon locking themselves in an adjacent alcove and donning handy anti-radiation suits, Neutron, Nora, Martin and Prof. Thomas decide to detonate the deadly explosive device, "killing" (by apparently dissolving) Caronte and his unnatural minions; then escape. At the close of this, Episode 1, all that appears to remain of the evil Doc C is an

155

Mexican poster *[top]* (art unsigned) and the "extended" US TV title card *[above]* for **NEUTRON VS. THE AMAZING DR. CARONTE**

uninhabited, collapsed and smoking white lab-coat, along with a crumpled, vacant mask. Just before the final fade, the true Neutron—as you'll (hopefully) recall is Charlie—unexpectedly exposes himself... (*um*, you get my drift).

****

"The only thing I still regret is that *no one* was able to identify the corpse!"—So goes the ominously-loaded line of dialogue that introduces Episode 2, **NEUTRON VS. THE AMAZING DR. CARONTE** (*Neutrón contra el Dr. Caronte*), for which the boys and Prof. Thomas—after a job believed well-done—are about to celebrate Caronte's recent (supposed) well-deserved demise. However, a fatso hoodlum named Guillermo Lezman—known as "Marchik" in the Mex version—and his

henchman (working for some suspiciously unnamed—but presumably Red—"foreign" power) take up Caronte's interrupted cause of shanghaiing the recipe for the much-sought-after neutron bomb. Incidentally, in a nod to Hollywood *noir*—whose bleak black-and-white, shadowy milieu the present series sometimes also emulates—this corpulent crook seems to have been superficially modeled after Sidney Greenstreet's memorable villainous turns in the *gringo* classics **THE MALTESE FALCON** (1941, D: John Huston) and **THE MASK OF DIMITRIOS** (1944, D: Jean Negulesco).

Again, during a nightclub musical interlude, Nora our heroine (remember her?) is cornered by our three would-be musketeers in an awkward pseudo (*very* pseudo!) *ménage a quatre*. Forced to select her sentimental favorite when figuratively pinioned and collectively propositioned by her trio of adoring suitors, Nora—natch', as she now knows his true ID is Neutron—unhesitatingly selects Charles. Interestingly, star hero Ruvinskis with his sticking-out ears and rather hangdog features (vaguely reminiscent of French superstar Jean-Claude Belmondo's "homely" look) makes the least likely "romantic leading man" of the three. (For those interested in reading more about this immortal figurehead of both Mexican athletics and cinema, check out Les Moore's bio of Ruvinskis, entitled "'El Hombre Lobo' – I *Am* de Wolf-Man!" in *M!* #26 [pp.19-23]. Amongst other notable genre entries, the actor was the star of Fernando Méndez's prototypical Mexi-monster/wrestling flick **LADRÓN DE CADAVERES** [*"The Body Snatcher"*, 1956], which I covered at some length in that same issue.)

Meanwhile, back in the present film, when his private lab is invaded by the fat man's greasy thugs, who are out in search of the formula, Prof. Thomas is rescued by the fortuitous and rousing advent of Neutron (who makes his appearance framed in the window with a *mucho macho* stance and his chest puffed-out with such comical indomitable intensity that you almost expect him to beat on it with his fists and let out a Tarzan-like jungle call).

Later, Lezman is startled by the unexpected reappearance of the (not-so-)"late" Dr. Caronte; now apparently revivified, or else having somehow managed to outright elude death in part one. Caronte warns Lezman to stay out of the race for the bomb secret, but is taken prisoner by the fat man's flunkies. Lezman then—out of frame—briefly unmasks the good doctor ("It's *you*!" he exclaims with some surprise), but we the audience are never made privy to *Beto el Boticario*'s true face, although it was frequently on display in other movies (at around the time that he appeared in the *Neutróns* he would have been around about 30 years old, and had a bit of a combo Mario *"Cantinflas"* Moreno/ Germán *"Tin-Tan"* Valdés look to him [see photo on p.152]. He also found fame as a prestidigitator, whose son followed in his padre's footsteps).

While feeding scraps to the cellar-load of monsters—which, when not in use, are kept corralled-up in a pit beneath a trapdoor, rather like Bela Lugosi's in-house zombies in the above-par Monogram creey-cheapie **BOWERY AT MIDNIGHT** (1942, USA, D: Wallace Fox)—Caronte's in-house killer dwarf Nick is alerted by his master's incoming radio-transmitted distress signal and swiftly waddles over with the death robots in tow to reclaim the unconscious Caronte. (In the aftermath of this incident, Lezman's right-hand man Tony exclaims in a flawless display of chipboard sincerity, "They were horrible monsters, *without faces!* I emptied my gun at them, *and nothing...!*")

Blackmail regarding the future revelation of Caronte's real identity brings about a stalemate between the two villains; a kind of Mexican standoff, if you will. In a power-play, Lezman announces his imminent intention to expose Caronte's face for all the world to see. Resorting to necessarily desperate measures, Caronte—who despite his unabashed criminality is normally a realist follower of the rational ways of science—suddenly takes it upon himself to evoke the darker, supernatural forces of the cosmos; this apparently (?) in order to obtain a replacement body for himself (sure beats more superficial solutions like plastic surgery!).

Incidentally, just why Caronte should be so concerned about maintaining the "secrecy" of his actual facial features is a bit of a puzzler, considering that he *is* the only character running about dressed in the far-from-low-profile garb of a demented apothecary, not to mention the fact that he's masked on top of it, so you wouldn't think that would make him all that difficult to spot, even in a crowd. Hence, for the purposes of police identification, it wouldn't logically seem to matter at all what his actual face looked like... Oh well, such trite concerns are all par for the course, I suppose. If logic and common sense—not to mention the very laws of physics themselves—played too big of a part in such a zany narrative, it would all come tumbling down like a house of cards. What matters is that the details are logical within the context of the milieu in which the players move, and that's all we need.

A fairly disorienting revelatory confession soon exposes—of all people—*JAMES*, the late Dr. Norton's son, as the still-very-much-alive Dr. Caronte! Said James then supposedly commits suicide when the cat's been let out of the bag and/or the beans have been spilled. "For the first time, I am really

confused!" our hero Neutron manfully admits a short spell later: so was I, and so will *you* be! But that's all part of the fun, right? Before dying, "Caronte"/Jimmy makes known his deep love for Nora.

Despite Jimmy slash the so-called Dr. Caronte's assumed death (for the *second* time), somehow the vital "final" (!) component of the bomb formula turns up missing (was that an oxymoron just then?), and blame-shirking buck-passer Lezman blames that

Calling All Death Robots! In this triptych of screen grabs from **NEUTRON VS. THE AMAZING DR. CARONTE**, half-pint henchman Nick the nipper gives his master's ugly-mugged in-house lunkheads the wake-up call, whereupon they lumber off to commit more misdeeds in Dr. Caronte's name

diminutive knee-nipper Nick (whom he addresses as "Ya little *zombie!*" [Hey, pick on someone your own size, ya big bully]). Not surprisingly, Caronte soon reappears in all his former glory—with the triumphant pronouncement "I've returned from the hell to which you tried to send me!"—and then orders Lezman buried alive in the very grave which had been reserved for the white-masked doctor himself. Seems Caronte has succeeded in "reincarnating" himself by fraternizing with the infernal occult arts, therefore dispensing with the need for his old earthly body (Jimmy?) entirely.

There becomes evident more than one small continuity gaffe that jars with episode #1: In Part 2, Nora—whom we can only assume *hadn't* up and eloped, gotten herself hitched and possibly even divorced in the interim between movies—is now inexplicably surnamed "Sanders" (whereas "Walker" had formerly been her maiden name); while the Marty Nelson character is now for some reason identified as "Mark Merrick" in the English dub-job. By episode #3 (that's up next), secondary supporting characters Insp. Lansing and Prof. Méndez—hey, wasn't he a *doctor* before?—instead respectively become surnamed "Lawson" and "Menzies" (simply an Anglicization of that latter's Hispanic name). Prof. Thomas' name remains con-

A super-stylin', dynamic ad graphic for one of the initial Newt three-pack's Anglo versions

stant throughout, but here his player Taylor has even less to do than in the first outing, although the actor, who was then just making a name for himself, probably appreciated the steady paycheck.

More confusion follows when, later on, Nora swears that "Jimmy" (note quotes) has returned to claim her. Caronte bitterly blames Charles a.k.a. Neutron for stealing Nora's love away from him, and instructs his subservient monster men to kill our black-masked main man: but of course, Newt is ready, willing and able to take on all comers! Although Neutron again eludes danger just as expected, Prof. Thomas is recaptured and used as a hostage in order to compel Neutron to compliantly deliver himself over into Caronte's clutches.

In another spot of taxicab deception, Nora is duped by disguised Nick the dwarf and driven to Caronte's lab (though how the heck he manages to keep his foot on the accelerator and still see over the top of the dashboard to drive is anybody's guess!). Here, further flip-flopping identities maximize plot unpredictability when captured "Neutron" is unmasked as playacting *Mark Merrick* (formerly "Marty Nelson")! And, to further confound comprehensibility exponentially, "Dr. Thomas" is really *Caronte* in yet <u>another</u> disguise! You see, here's the scoop: "Caronte" is now the migratory evil spirit of the late, not-so-lamented *Jimmy* ensconced in the host body of *Professor Thomas!* "I've achieved what no one else could do: *the transmutation of the soul!*" declares "composite being" Caronte / Jimmy / Thomas triumphantly.

What with all its convolutions of storyline—which are oftentimes admittedly largely just a facile means of advancing the plot in an "unpredictable" manner—belying its minimalistic sets and characters and "simplistic" (*¿¡Ay caramba!?*) general plot, the initial *Neutron* trilogy unfolds in remarkably complex fashion (never more so than during Pt. II's conclusion: talk about an identity crisis!). Its frequent major lapses in mother logic and incredible stretches of convenient coincidence at times approach the level of grand farce, as this virtually indecipherable plot synopsis will attest (trust me, it makes a lot more sense down here in cold, hard print than it does up on the screen!).

Pushing the baffling "transference of personalities" concept to a sublimely *ludicrous* extreme, veritable composite life-form Caronte / James / Thomas (as now acted by "Grek Martin," a.k.a. Jack Taylor) is about to have Nora and Mark (himself a mock-Neutron [*PHEW!*]) tossed into the embracing ham-fisted arms of the lunkheaded monsters. But, the *real* Caronte (in his signature mask and get-up) bursts in, resulting in the following dialogue exchange between the main interested parties:

"*Grab him! He's an* impostor!" – "*He lies!* He's *an impostor!*" – "*Look at me!* I *am the real Caronte!*" – "*He* lies! I *am Caronte!!*" (Did you catch all that? Good.)

Whoever the hell's who, "Caronte" / Thomas is clonked senseless by a monster, and then the *other* alleged Caronte—whom, due to his seeming sincerity, we were actually starting to believe was the actual genuine article for a second there—subsequently unmasks himself as the real unmasked Neutron, *Charlie!* Here, the supposed authentic Neutron—or might it perhaps really only be *Caronte* trying to make a proper show of it?—rather brutally fells short-stuff Nick with a pile-driven fist to the top of the dwarf's knee-high skull. Come to think of it, such a cowardly bullying action seems as out of character and beneath Neutron's honorable credo as Nick is now beneath him (i.e., laid out cold on the floor). But we certainly wouldn't believe Dr. Caronte could be incapable of such contemptible behavior, even to his own faithful sidekick, especially when his neck was on the line. So draw your own conclusions as to what's what and who's who.

The genuine—take my word for it, *I promise!*— Doc Caronte (cum-James-cum-deceased *mock*

Thomas, a.k.a. Jack Taylor/"Grek Martin"!) makes a frantic break for freedom, only to be battered into (as it later turns out only temporary, of course) oblivion during an energetic climactic punch-up by barefaced Charlie (cum-*mock* Caronte-cum-*real* Neutron). Nora—thankfully *herself*—and Mark (cum-*mock* Neutron [*SHEEEESHH!!*]) are both liberated, as once again Caronte's sinister plans are foiled...and we're left scratching our damn heads.

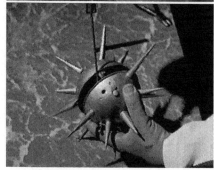

Top to Bottom: The "think-tank" of stolen master scientists' still-living cerebrums, in the brainpan; in **NEUTRON AND THE BLACK MASK**, the treacherous Dr. Walker (Claudio Brook) plots to steal Prof. Norton's superweapon; said weapon, a portable neutron bomb, rather resembles a cross between Sputnik, a naval mine and/or a robotic spiny sea urchin

Land Line: Neutron actually has to get on the blower and dial a number—with his gauntlets on, yet—to make emergency calls!

Hit the rewind button, people. Instant replay. Pay attention now...

"Now, no one will *dare* defy the world again!" proclaims Inspector Lansing, who is clearly an optimist. As **NEUTRON** *numero dos* ends, over our mighty hero's silhouetted brawny physique a narrator then goes on to dramatically intone, "But should anyone dare to, Neutron, The Masked Avenger, always on the side of Justice and Fair Play, will return to prevent it!" (*FIN.*)

And don't you forget it, evildoer!

******

For **NEUTRON AGAINST THE DEATH RO-BOTS** (*Los automatas de la muerte*), the culmination of the Federico Curiel-directed *Neutron* saga, the first line of dubbed script is a tad more optimistic than that which had heralded the start of Part 2:

"The world can breathe freely, its Public Enemy Number One-Plus is *dead*" (that extra plus surely marks Dr. Caronte as one *badass* dude, huh?).

US TV title card for **NEUTRON AGAINST THE DEATH ROBOTS**, bearing the film's extended retitling

While by all appearances he seemed to have been left deceased with some irreversible finality in the previous, central instalment, for this last episode of the three, Jimmy (Silvestre, just to recap for the sake of your reeling recollection) has been successful in making a complete (unexplained and inexplicable) *recovery* from death! A convenient abridged recap of all the main occurrences of Parts 1 & 2 is provided, for all those kids in attendance who might somehow have missed the preceding pair of chapters and were now kneeling on the floor of their folks' rec-room with their eyes glued to the TV screen trying to catch up on what they might have missed. Such is the uniform tone of each film that, as with the Curiel *Nostradamus* films (of which there were four rather than three), if joined randomly in-progress, you're hard put to ascertain just *which* episode you're watching.

Neutron approaches Prof. Thomas (who was essentially seen to be killed outright by the hero at the conclusion of #2) concerning the construction of the neutron bomb. Upon Caronte's surprised reappearance before startled Nick, the "dead" doctor evidently confuses the finale of Part 2 with that of Part 1, explaining:

"I managed to escape before the explosion, but my zombies didn't have the same luck!"

Bear in mind that Caronte—or at least an identical lookalike—was clearly shown to be disintegrated at the end of **NEUTRON VS. THE BLACK MASK** (i.e., Pt. 1)—reduced to a heap of wilted, smoldering lab clothing. I can only surmise that for Part 3, our present episode, the Anglo dubbers wisely elected to avoid all those mind-bendingly chaotic ID switcheroos of Part 2 and simply erased their tracks by offering a fast, pat explanation for Caronte's re-genesism herein (we knew he'd be back anyway; who cares how he got here!); trusting that nobody would notice (or *care*) about all their blatant liberties with continuity. From the Frankenstein Monster to Freddy Krueger *et al*, coherence or logic pertaining to sequel revivals is almost invariably rationalized away with token explanations: all that matters is that the show must go on...

Caronte shows Nick the malevolent munchkin his collection of genetically-created "Death Robots" (hence the title), which are stored in deep-freeze mortuary cabinets in the laboratory. Also, Caronte has kept the bodies of Profs. Wilson, Duval and Menzies (the former Méndez) on ice—body-snatched c/o of that nicker Nick, the nipper—for deployment in some nefarious fermenting scheme.

On the side once again, in spite of the flightily fickle Nora's proclaiming her love for Charles/Neutron in Part 2 (and also the fact that Jimmy was earlier shown to *die*; minor problem, right?), our "late" latter Latin lover here nonetheless returns to woo the indecisive *señorita* ("While there's still a glimmer of a chance, I must keep fighting for your love!" [Oh brother...learn to take a hint, bub!]).

Caronte plans to unite the three preserved cerebrums of the dead docs—"But for that, Nick, I shall need BLOOD! *Lots* of blood!" the evil Caronte explains to his half-pint subordinate. Forthwith, the so-called Death Robots (which, despite that more grandiose tag, are usually referred to by the English-dubbed script simply as "zombies") venture out to harvest this necessary ingredient. Police are left baffled by a string of gruesome blood-draining murders, and with Neutron's invaluable assistance brilliantly deduce that Dr. Caronte is still very much alive (big shock).

This time the plot has a distinct vampiric twist to it, what with the twin wounds found on the victims' necks and the exsanguination of their corpses. Thankfully, the lugubrious-paced monsters are used more extensively throughout this episode, which amounts to perhaps the most fun instalment of the three.

Caronte proposes to combine the purloined cerebral matter of the dead scientific brainiacs into one composite "great brain" that will expedite the arch-villain's megalomaniacal dream of global subjugation. Conversing with this resultant circular aquarium of communal grey matter as if it were a crystal ball (or a magic mirror), Caronte lords it up over his vast (!?) criminal empire, periodically dispatching severely bow-legged (and *castrato*-voiced) Nick the wee knee-nipper out into the field with the zombies to do his dirty deeds.

Another rather glaring continuity blooper is laid bare when it's implied that the identity of Neutron is once again a mystery: although at the end of Part 1, top-lining star Ruvinskis was clearly shown to doff his mask and assume full credit for The Black Mask's superheroic exploits (and we know he wasn't lying!). This latest blunder, like the poorly-explained origins of Caronte's reappearance at the outset of this present chapter, again demonstrate that either the presenters of the US versions (which were released directly to television without any theatrical playoff by Commonwealth United Pictures in 1965)

During **NEUTRON AGAINST THE DEATH ROBOTS,** as seen in the inset of this '70s reissue Mexican lobby card for the film, one of Dr. Caronte's so-called "zombies" poses as the title masked hero for some scenes...though how the hell they managed to lace-down Newt's trademark hood over the monster's XL head to complete the deception remains a mystery!

Which Came First, Neutron Or The Neutron Bomb? In another Mexican lobby card for **NEU-TRON AGAINST THE DEATH ROBOTS**—this one bearing the original earlier alternate border design (artist unknown)—Wolf Ruvinskis poses with the explosive device that took his name

were lazy in keeping track of their story progression, or else they flatly didn't give a *hoot* whether the serial all tied together coherently or not; likely that latter hypothesis mostly holds true. For all I know, the plot errors/omissions may well have been extant even in the original Mexican cuts; errors which might quite honestly have been repeated in the dubbed versions.

Neutron pays Prof. Thomas an unscheduled nocturnal social call. The good doctor suspects him to be either Jimmy, Mark or Charles, but can't decide for sure (you'd think maybe the voice might give the game away; unless we're expected to swallow that Newt fakes an alternate *speech pattern* as well as donning a mask). "I'm just a man who believes in the triumph of Justice, and who goes after it in a rather unorthodox way!" announces Neutron proudly. (No shit, Sherlock.)

Prof. Thomas is targeted yet again for abduction by Caronte, and the monsters move in to make the grab, only to be spectacularly fended-off by Neutron wielding his Handy Dandy anti-death robot flamethrower! (This scene brings to mind Mil/Blue/Santo's deployment of similar incendiary armaments to frazzle **THE MUMMIES OF GUANAJUATO**

[*Las momias de Guanajuato*)], another Curiel epic from 1970). The singed zombies reconvene elsewhere in order to pull a chemical warehouse heist as they gather further materials required by their master necessary to his plans of world domination.

In an amusingly garish scene while the authorities endeavor to follow a zombie's trail back to its home base, the alerted monster promptly yanks off its own *head* and tosses it at police like a volleyball! It then loyally self-destructs by disintegrating on the spot to ensure that our heroes remain ignorant as to the elusive Caronte's "secret" whereabouts. This minor scene brings up still another continuity inconsistency: in both preceding episodes, Neutron had already located Caronte's hideout (which is still at the same location it's always been), so why bother tailing the monster for that reason in the first place?

While possibly emerging as the most entertaining and fast-paced of the three-pack, ironically it is **NEUTRON AGAINST THE DEATH ROBOTS** which seems to boast of the greatest amount of gratuitous musical filler (although to the Mexican movie-going masses in general, the music was merely another vital aspect of the overall entertainment package; a similar state of affairs has of course long existed in India, too). One act which appears within the trilogy is/was (are/were) *Los Rebeldes del Rock*. I am not sure if these are the same guys as the group known as *Los Rockin' Rebeldes* / "The Rockin' Rebels" from roughly the same period, but for what it's worth a band by that latter similar name were included on a vinyl record album entitled *Santo Presents... Mexican Rock and Roll Rumble and Psych-Out South of the Border*, a bootleg compilation of vintage Mexican r'n'r recordings put out (on Santo Records, yet!) *circa* the late-'80s by a *gringo* trash music/movies enthusiast named Mike Lucas. One cut on this album is credited to above-noted Los Rockin' Rebeldes, who give their spirited, rocked-up retake on the traditional Irish (!?) folk song "Danny Boy," albeit performed *en Español* (much in the groove of a late-'50s English rendition released by Conway Twitty).

These musical interludes down at the local nightspot provide backdrop to another uneven plot thread which weaves in and out throughout the duration of all three movies' total running time (which is somewhere around 3½ hours): in Episode #2, Nora openly confessed that, out of her "three musketeers" it is top dog/alpha male Charlie/Neutron—who is actually a *mask*eteer—for whom she feels the most amorous affection (sensible gal). However, by the time of Part 3, once more this fickly flighty broad is shown undecided as to her favorite choice of boyfriend. This means sundry more frivolous wastage of screen-time as she fields romantic advances and innuendos from all three horny heroes; and after how she's been stringing them all along like a kitten toying with balls of yarn, no wonder the poor saps are getting frustrated!

When learned Prof. Thomas (still played by Jack Taylor [remember him?]) is duped by a similarly-attired masked intruder calling himself "Neutron", the easily-fooled police accuse the genuine article of being in complicity with Caronte. Thankfully, it is the only instance of flip-flopped personality this time out: too bad the same couldn't be said for leading lady *señorita* Arenas' interminable "seductive" cabaret numbers, which slow things to a grinding standstill every time. Without this frequent reliance on vacuous tune-slinging and romantic dilly-dallying, the *Neutron* threesome might quite comfortably have been condensed into a single longish instalment of roughly 90 minutes' duration, rather than running for more than twice that long.

Nora's latest gig is thankfully interrupted when the bogus Neutron shows up in her dressing room in the form of a threatening expressionistic shadow and spirits her off to Caronte's lair. Here, the white-

Mexican poster for **NEUTRON AGAINST THE DEATH ROBOTS** (art unsigned)

masked mad medico compels Prof. Thomas to aid him in his "research"; this by threatening to toss the cringing Nora into his chock-full zombie-pit if the reluctant professor refuses to cooperate. "She will make an *excellent* morsel for my monsters!" cries the vile villain.

At long last, the perfected neutron bomb (resembling a spiky miniature Sputnik) is gloated over by the triumphal Caronte, who can now formulate his ultimate plan of global conquest. However, Prof. Thomas tosses a monkey wrench in the works—actually it's more like pouring sugar into the gas-tank—by

Hero #3: A dapper studio publicity photo-portrait of actor Julio Alemán

poisoning the nutrient fluid that feeds Caronte's tri-brain "think-tank" advisory committee, rendering it henceforth inoperable.

The primed neutron bomb is planted in the luggage of an unsuspecting newlywed couple (no, the bride *isn't* the flip-flopping and ever-wishy-washy Nora!), set to go off and destroy the entire city (Mexico City? Presumably on purpose, no specific location is ever mentioned in the Anglo-dubbed print). Naturally, Neutron intercepts the deadly explosive device with only minutes to spare before it is set to detonate. As he hurries the ticking bomb to Prof. Thomas for disarming, Dr. Caronte arrives and a violent scuffle ensues (though why on Earth that mega-genius should want to allow the bomb to explode while he's right there in the room with it is anybody's guess [guess he's not such a genius after all!]). During their climactic fistfight, which extends back home to Caronte's sprawling hideout, the bad doc seeks to coax incorruptible Neutron over to his side for shared global rule. "We would be *invincible*!" tempts the

mad medic. Obediently, Nick—he's the little fella, remember?—causes the whole joint to come crashing down around everybody's ears, while naturally Neutron escapes to fight another day… however, because neither of his final two entries from 1964—**NEUTRON VS. THE MANIAC** (*Neutrón contra el criminal sadico*) and **NEUTRON VS. THE KARATE ASSASSINS** (*Neutrón contra los asesinos del karate*), both directed by Alfredo B. Crevenna—contains monsters of anything other than the mundanely mortal human kind, I shan't be covering them here, but in a supplemental sidebar instead, just to keep things properly segregated.

By the way, as if they're fooling *anybody*, the final scene of the final film of this initial trilogy carefully neglects to reveal the "true" identity of Neutron…as if we didn't already know who he was.

¡¡EL FINITO!!

THE FURTHER ADVENTURES OF

Neutrón

by Steve Fenton

In the interests of completism, I should give at least some coverage hereunder of the remainder of the Neutrón *movie series, the final two of which (as well as an additional nominal if non-Newt entry that was titled as such for its release to US television (not that anyone ever seems to have seen that presumably English-dubbed version, mind you!) don't contain anything that might even be charitably described as monsters, except for those of the more mundane, mortal human variety...including even one bona fide slasher (*Shock! Horror!*), which places the film well outside* Monster! *'s scope. However, within the "bigger picture" context of this expansive Neutron retrospective, it certainly warrants inclusion (that's my story, and I'm sticking to it!).*

Firstly, since the debut of Newt's spinoff series of *fotonovelas* (whose inaugural issue was published late in '61) predated the later, final entries in his filmic franchise, we'll cover things in chronological order and discuss it first before getting into the second, lesser "trilogy" of his movies...

By the time our husky hero of the hour's mag—entitled, simply, *Neutrón,* published by the Editorial Argumentos, S.A. (EDAR) company of Mexico City—debuted in November of 1961, such *fotonovelas* ("photographic comic books", respectively known as *fotoromanzi* [a.k.a. *fumetti*] or *photo-romans* in Italy and France) were far from a novel concept in Mexico; indeed, the long-running and enduringly popular *fotonovela* series entitled *Santo, El Enmascarado de Plata* launched by writer-artist-publisher José G. Cruz (whose debut issue of *Santo* came out in September 1952) had already been going strong for the better part of a decade before *Neutrón*'s came along, and there is no denying that the latter was intent on cashing-in with a similar consumer demographic as the former. Utilizing *fotomontaje* ("photomontage") techniques, both Santo's and Neutron's sepiatone photo-comics—similarly with those of most of their host of imitators, both then and now—typically averaged-out at around 60 pages per issue, were digest-sized, and cheaply

The first issue of N's *fotonovela* (dating from November 1961), which hit Mexican newsstands whilst his initial trilogy of movies (see pp.148-164) was still doing the rounds in theaters south of the border

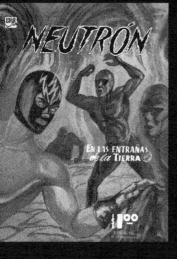

mass-produced; printed on coarse, economical paper stock of a quality only about one notch higher than lowly newsprint. Their labor-intensive, often spartanly grid-like "cut-and-paste" layouts combined photographic cutouts and sometimes heavily-retouched photographs along with, to varying degrees, original artwork elements (typically used for backgrounds and "special props", so to speak), all tied together with hand-lettered and/or typewritten text and word-balloons. Generally, when done well, the whole package made for a decidedly surreal effect indeed. At their best, such magazines cross-pollinated the sequential art format with more "cinematographic" qualities, (somewhat) spanning the not entirely unbridgeable divide between the mediums of comics and movies; offering "the best of both worlds", if you will…or near-as-dammit as can be expected in a static medium without benefit of either moving pictures or sound to enhance their narratives. Not only were these periodicals a whole helluva lot cheaper to produce than movies, but the returns could be quite substantial should any given title happen to become a hit with the paying punters. Many titles—as with *Neutrón*, to some degree—were sold not only on Mexican magazine racks, but might also get exported to other such Latin American nations as Ecuador, Venezuela or Colombia (etc). So these books, as happened with Cruz's *Santo* one, might greatly increase a character's visibility/popularity outside their country of origin if they happened to prove popular. That said, *Neutrón* proved a good deal less phenomenally successful than other titles of its ilk (e.g., as well as El Santo, other top pro wrestlers such as "Blue Demon" [r.n. Alejandro Muñoz Moreno], "Mil Máscaras" [Aaron Rodríguez Arellano], and to a far lesser extent "El Gigante Tinieblas" [Manuel Leal] and numerous others all earned comic books of their own, to varying degrees of success. Monsters and other horrific supernatural elements were mainstays of all of them, and such scenes often enlivened their lurid full-color covers). According to the fine print at the very foot of its credits page, the first printing of the first issue of *Neutrón* numbered some 35,000 copies, but whether or not it went into further printings to meet demand is unknown (at least by me).

Much like Santo's printed pictorial adventures in the early years of his *fotonovela* did, Neutron's also often (I might even go so far as to say predominantly) dealt with more "mundane" subject matter—such as spies, gangsters and other "real world" criminals, etc.—rather than containing monsters or other paranormal/supernatural elements. However, after Santo began tangling more and more with various otherworldly monstrosities on the silver (-masked) screen starting in the early '60s when his fame

This Page Left, Top to Bottom: Issues #6, 8 and 39. While I haven't been able to determine who did their cover art yet, the comics' earliest issues chiefly sported original artwork on their covers. Later issues relied more and more heavily on photographic covers (see central image on the facing page), presumably because they were cheaper

as a movie star finally caught up with his by-then already well-established ring stardom, so too did "his" (i.e., J.G. Cruz's) *fotonovelas* reflect the more fanciful aspects of the caped crusader's cinematic battles with the forces of evil in whatever forms they happened to take. Largely, however, while the print exploits of *Neutrón* did occasionally include such fantastical entities as zombies, mummies and aliens, over the course of the magazine's run (so far as I've been able to deduce, well over 200 issues were published in total; vastly less than Santo's oft-reprinted book ran for), "ordinary" baddies made up the bulk of N's foes, although the stories did often incorporate assorted pulp schlock sci-fi motifs too. Evidently in hopes of having its headliner's mag appeal more to its presumably primarily juvenile male readership by giving them a co-hero they could more directly relate to, more so in the *Neutrón* series' latter stage, the title hero began consorting—purely platonically, you understand!—with a scrawny preteen boy sidekick (portrayed by one Iddar de la Parra), informally dubbed *Neutroncito* ("Little Neutron," natch). This comparatively pint-sized, bare-chested "add-on" character was basically a neutronian cadet/cub scout/apprentice, decked-out in a size "S" version of the real deal's man-sized costume, albeit with his face fully bared (i.e., rather than Newt's trademark full-face mask emblazoned with triple lightning bolts, the kid instead wears a sort of open-faced "balaclava" bearing the same identifying tri-bolt design; this evidently so that readers would better recognize him as one of their "own kind" rather than thinking he was just some midget adult or something [!]). Evidently, said Iddar's brother Manelick de la Parra sometimes also appeared as Neutroncito. Judging by their last name, it seems a distinct possibility that they were either the sons of, or else otherwise related to, EDAR head honcho Guillermo de la Parra. According to Marco Antonio Arzate's son, Tristán Arzate, in an online print interview (*en español* [thanks, Google Translate!]) with (Italian?) *lucha libre* authority Bruno Bernasconi Castelli (a.k.a. "*El Azote Venezolano*") posted in July 2014, Neutroncito was also performed for just a couple of issues by Joselito, the son of José Herrera, who was the magazine's main layout ("*fotomontaje*") guy. Apparently, for a lengthy period between issues #40 and #70 of the mag, the title character was dispensed with entirely in favor of spotlighting his son ("Neutron, Jr."?) instead.

As for the all-important star of the show—or rather, the *fotonovela*—Neutron was portrayed throughout (?) the mag's run by the aforementioned Marco Antonio Arzate, the son of Jesús Sandoval and María Rodríguez García. Born on October 7, 1928 in the scenic Mexican mining pueblo of Angangueo in Michoacán, on May 3, 1942, when he was

This Page Right, Top to Bottom: Issues #45, 72 and 78. As you can see by that bottommost image, Neutron's semi-masked *niño* sidekick Neutroncito—seen sharing cover-space with his adult hero in the center pic—began dominating covers later in the mag's run

but a *chico* of just 12 years young, Marco Antonio relocated—*solitario* (i.e., sans his parents)—from rural México to México City, bent on finding fame and fortune. Rather than getting in with the wrong crowd and becoming an aimless street kid, Arzate instead devoted himself to athletics, in various disciplines of which he excelled and would go on to make a name for himself within.

In addition, Arzate went on to become, amongst other things, a scriptwriter for the Editormex Mexicana publishing outfit (the many magazine titles to which Arzate lent his penhand included *Hermelinda Linda*, *Jornadas Bíblicas*, *Capulinita*, *Cárcel de Mujeres*, *Anicero Verduzco* and *Zor y los Invencibles*). As well as having a passion for writing, Arzate was equally passionate about such "real-

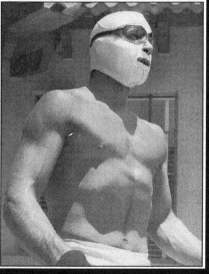

The busy M.A. Arzate also appeared as the title character in Huracán Ramírez movies *[top]*, as well as portraying the title character of *fotonovelas* featuring the *blanco*-clad superhero El Spirito *[above]*

world" physical/athletic pursuits as bodybuilding, wrestling and diving (he was also a skilled player of both racquetball and basketball, plus accomplished in archery too; hence, an all-around sportsman to be reckoned with). It was while he was employed at the Editormex publishing house that he first dipped his toe into appearing as an actor/model in *fotonovelas*; this by appearing in stories featuring the heroic character *Risko el Buceador* ("Risko the Diver"). It was as Neutron in the *fotonovela* of the same name via which Arzate reached a far wider audience and found more lasting recognition, however.

Familiarly to fans of Neutron's cinematic forays, the Dr. Caronte character was reprised as a regular villain of the *fotonovelas*, sporting much the same costume—all-white, in stark contrast to his night-black persona—as was worn by Beto el Boticario in his role as the same character for the first three films. Interestingly enough, in the *fotonovelas* Caronte was largely *also* portrayed by the busy Arzate (who may well have appeared as other characters besides at such times as was necessary [?]). In scenes which required both Neutron and his arch-nemesis Caronte to appear together—such as for their all-important *mano a mano* tussles— the latter's mask/costume were instead donned by Arzate's close personal friend Raúl Martínez (a gig which afforded Martínez the opportunity to find further employment within the *fotonovela* field).

As is so often the case when it comes to trying to sort out who's who within the enigmatic and oftentimes downright confusing world of Mexican *enmascarados*, the mystery, misidentification and misinformation often greatly outweigh the "facts", such as they often are(n't), so I shan't be delving too deeply into such matters here (at least not until some further surefire information shows up). I can say with some surety however—fingers crossed!—that Arzate *did* double for celebrated *luchador enmascarado* Huracán Ramírez on a number of occasions, including in the films **EL MISTERIO DE HURACÁN RAMÍREZ** (1962) and **LA VENGANZA DE HURACÁN RAMÍREZ** (1968 [see *Monster!* #2, p.44]), both of which were directed by the *HR* series' usual director, Joselito Rodríguez. In that former title, Arzate also served double-duty by appearing in his real-life wrestling persona of "Tony Marcus", and in addition portrayed Ramírez the title character while masked in wrestling scenes for both films (as per usual for the *HR* films, "legit" actor David Silva played him in scenes where Ramírez appeared *sans* his trademark mask). Arzate's extensive film work as a stuntman and/ or actor also includes such Mexi-monster classics as Alfonso Corona Blake's sultry *señorita*-stuffed

Bit-player Arzate gets munched by a cave-dwelling *monstruo* in **AVENTURA AL CENTRO DE LA TIERRA** (1964). *[Incidentally, in my coverage of that Mexi-monster* clasico *back in* Monster! *#16, I mistakenly credited fellow* **AACDLT** *cast member Ramón Bugarini (who at times bears somewhat of a resemblance to him) as playing the killer critter's victim during this scene in Arzate's stead. Consider that oversight duly—if belatedly—rectified here! ~ SF]*

shocker **SANTO VS. THE VAMPIRE WOMEN** (*Santo vs. las mujeres vampiro*, 1962) and Alfredo B. Crevenna's fab subterranean monster mash **AVENTURA AL CENTRO DE LA TIERRA** (1964 [see *M!* #16, p.6]), and he even made a brief unbilled appearance in the fifth *N* series entry, **NEUTRON VS. THE KARATE ASSASSINS** (see p.174), though not as the title hero in this instance, needless to say (I like to think that his inclusion in that film was someone's idea of an "in-joke", being as Arzate was then associated with the part of Neutron in the *fotonovela*, while Wolf Ruvinskis was his cinematic counterpart). Arzate's film career also encompassed playing bit parts and doing stunt work in more than one Hollywood "tourist" production which went south-of-the-border for location shooting, including westerns starring John "Duke" Wayne, no less. And not only that, but he even played a Neanderthal in the prehysterical 1981 Ringo Starr/Barbara Bach comedy **CAVEMAN**, too!

As a trained and licensed *luchador*, Arzate also wrestled—*non*-enmasked—professionally for a time (*circa* the early 1950s on into the '60s)

under the ring name "Tony Marcus", an anglicized variation of his given Christian names, Marco Antonio (he was also credited at least once on a billing as "Tonny Markus" *[sic?]*, but perhaps that was just a simple typographical error). According to aforementioned wrestling journalist/blogger Bruno Bernasconi (quote translated from the Spanish), Arzate "is a fundamental part of the history of wrestling, cinema and photomontages" in Mexico.

Marco Antonio Arzate passed away *circa* January 2014, but his legacy survives him. In addition to all his other accomplishments, he can stand proudly shoulder-to-shoulder with the great Wolf Ruvinskis, another all-round action man whose name is equally synonymous with a masked superhero who may not be anywhere near as famous as El Santo was and is, but succeeded in carving himself out a cozy little niche in the annals of Mexploitation monster-wrestling cinema regardless.

—¡*VIVA NEUTRÓN, EL ENMASCARADO NEGRO*!

Early-to-mid-'50s wrestling bills featuring Arzate—billed hereon as "Tony Marcus"—in non-head-lining bouts. (Note popular wrestler *El Médico Asesino*'s prominent billing at the center of the first poster; *Médico*'s look and surgical shtick were a major influence on Dr. Caronte's in both the *Neutrón* films and *fotonovela*. In another bit of related trivia, the last poster features Fernando Osés' name centrally. Amongst many other things, that celebrated *luchador*/actor [etc.] can be seen shar-ing the screen with Wolf Ruvinskis in **NEUTRON VS. THE KARATE ASSASSINS** [see p.174])

Endnotes

The following links were invaluable to me in putting together this piece. Without them, I would have learned virtually doodly-squat about Marco Antonio Arzate's association with the Neutron *fotonovela*! The bulk of the factual data and any and all images directly pertaining to *señor* Arzate were acquired from these sources, which I am duly crediting hereunder.

This fan-made R.I.P. tribute to *señor* Arzate from 2014 was done in the style of a panel from one of his *fotonovelas* as Neutron

"Filmografía de Marco Antonio Arzate 'Neutrón'" (August 24th, 2013), by Bruno Bernasconi Castelli at the Bajo de Capuchas blog (@ *http://bajolascapuchasmx.blogspot.ca/2013/08/filmografia-de-marco-antonio-arzate.html*)

"La Historia Desconocida de Marco Antonio Arzate, el Famoso Neutrón de las Fotonovelas", at the Sensacional de Luchas blog (@ *http://sensacionaldeluchas.blogspot.ca/2014/01/la-historia-desconocida-de-marco.html* and *http://sensacionaldeluchas.blogspot.ca/2014_01_01_archive.html*)

"Revelaciones Sobre los Fotomontajes de Neutrón y Mucho Más…" (July 25th, 2014), by Bruno Bernasconi at his blog De Venezuela Para Mexico y el Mundo (@ *http://elazotevenezolanoelblog.blogspot.ca/2014/07/revelaciones-sobre-los-fotomontajes-de.html*)

NB. Mr. Bernasconi gave acknowledgements for various information and image contributions from Antonio Santillán Franco and Fernando Franco Quiroz (many of whose little-known facts and rare pictures are utilized hereabouts, in the spirit of "spreading the word"). ~SF

And so, to the second and final "trilogy" of Neutron movies…

NEUTRON VS. THE MANIAC

(*Neutrón contra el criminal sádico* / "Neutron vs. The Sadistic Criminal") Shot in 3 episodes; individual titles unknown
Mexico, 1964

NEUTRON VS. THE KARATE ASSASSINS

(*Los asesinos del karate*) Shot in 3 episodes; individual titles unknown
Mexico, 1965

Estudios America, S.A. / Producciones Corsa, S.A. presentations

S: [in **THE MANIAC**] Wolf Ruvinskis, Gina Romand, Rodolfo Landa, Chucho Salinas, Graciela Lara, José Galvéz, Rita Macedo, Rubén Rojo, Guillermo "Lobo Negro" Hernández, Mario Orea, Alberto Mariscal, Nathanael "Frankestein" [sic] León, Antonio Raxel, Julián de Meriche, "The Gay Crooners," Héctor Cabrera

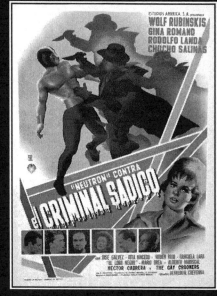

Mexican window card for **NEUTRON VS. THE MANIAC** (art by Leopoldo Mendoza [?])

S: [in **THE KARATE ASSASSINS**] Ruvinskis, Ariadna Welter, Chucho Salinas, Rodoldo Landa, Germán Robles, Carlos López Moctezuma, Fernando Luján, "The Gay Crooners", Imelda Miller
D: Alfredo B. Crevenna. Prd: Emilio Gómez Muriel. Scr: E.G. Muriel, Alfredo Ruanova. Sto: A. Ruanova. DP: Fernando Álvarez. Mus: Antonio Díaz Conde. Songs: Dolores de la Colina, Armando Manzanero, Rodolfo Charles. Ed: Raúl J. Casso. Sets: Arcadi Artis Gener

Four years on from the originating three-film Curiel serial—the series' flagship, if you will—the Neutronic cause was taken up by another prolific and highly competent Mexican B-movie director, namely Alfredo B. Crevenna (who helmed what amounts to one of The Silver-Masked Man's finest non-fantasy actioners, **SANTO CONTRA LOS VILLANOS DEL RING** [*"Santo vs. The Villains of the Ring"*, 1965], which guest-starred the present film's Wolf Ruvinskis in a thinly-veiled—or rather, -*masked*—variation of his established Neutron persona. Likewise of note, Crevenna also directed the interesting shot-in-Haiti, *Vodou*-steeped zombie thriller **SANTO CONTRA LA MAGIA NEGRA** [*"Santo vs. Black Magic"*, 1973], which I did a write-up on back in *Monster!* #23 [p.46]). Of the only two *Neutrón* series entries helmed by that director, the first, **NEUTRON VS. THE MANIAC**, became the most readily accessible (albeit while still remaining

Mexican poster for **NEUTRON VS. THE KARATE ASSASSINS** (art by Leopoldo Mendoza [?])

highly obscure by usual mainstream standards) north of the US/Mexican border; indeed, even way up here in Canada, where I live, albeit only via the erstwhile "modern miracle" of videotape. Under the anglicized title **NEUTRON VS. THE MANIAC**, through Commonwealth United—releasers of the initial trilogy—the film was originally released to '60s US television in English-dubbed form (c/o an outfit called Television Enterprises Corporation); as was—apparently, anyway—the second Crevenna series offering, **LOS ASESINOS DEL KARATE**, renamed **NEUTRON VS. THE KARATE ASSASSINS** (a.k.a. **NEUTRON BATTLES THE KARATE ASSASSINS**).

NEUTRON VS. THE MANIAC was at one time (circa the late-'80s) made available on North American home videocassette by Greg Luce's pioneering video company Sinister Cinema, who then, as now, specialized in PD ("public domain") movie product. Circa 1992, the same version then being offered by SC was released in Canada by Sinister's short-lived Toronto-based "semi-official" offshoot of the company, founded by future made-for-TV *Robocop* sequel(s) director Julian Grant; but their (i.e., his) limited release—which likely numbered in mere hundreds of copies, if even that many—was marred by cheesy and misleading

/ erroneous packaging that conspicuously misidentified it as one of the earlier Neutron vs. Caronte adventures detailed above (see "fine print" on the box cover reproduced hereabouts). That long-forgotten and by now likely nigh on impossible-to-find VHS edition came with unrelated cover art which was a detail lifted from the Mexican poster for Federico Curiel's lame Santo outing **LA MAFIA DEL VICIO** (*"The Vice Mafia"*, 1970).

As for the film itself, much like the preceding Curiel trilogy, a considerable amount of **VS. THE MANIAC**'s running time is taken up by filler (untranslated) song numbers performed in the vernacular on one of the movie's major sets, a swingin' nightclub whereon much of the drama unfolds. Here, we are regaled by the lilting musical stylings of (as quoted in the English-dubbed version) "Oswald, the famous blind pianist!" accompanying twittering vocalist "the one-and-only Margie!" in regular nightly performances. This chanteuse's troubled sister Bertha (named "Berta" in Mex prints; played by Graciela Lara) had approached her seeking escape from a self-destructive, downwardly-mobile lifestyle. But Margie ("Marga" in the original; Gina Romand), using the "tough love" method, turns her sibling away, thinking it the best means of teaching her sis the error of her ways.

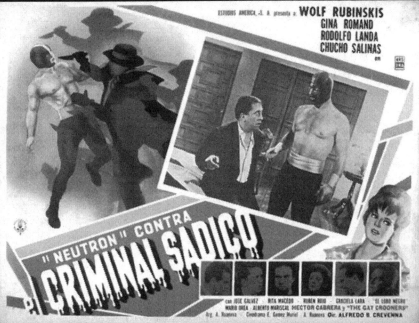

Above: Chucho Salinas *[at left in main inset]* was a frequent fixture as generally none-too-funny "comic relief" in Mexi-Flexis. Here, he mugs it up with Wolf Ruvinskis (shown sporting Neutron's less-memorable "new" costume) in the first of the two A.B. Crevenna outings, **NEUTRON VS. THE MANIAC**; Mexican lobby card (art by Leopoldo Mendoza [?])

When Bertha later strolls home with her sister's optically-handicapped accompanist, she is abducted by a hooded slasher clad in a wide-brimmed hat and flowing cape (that classic **HOUSE OF WAX/** *giallo* conception which recurs so frequently within Mexploitation cinema, as well as in that from other parts of the globe besides). Said sinister figure shortly proceeds to ritualistically film the process of the justifiably terrified Bertha's murder under the blade of a large kitchen knife. This photographing-of-the-victim's-death-throes angle was undoubtedly on loan from Michael Powell's brilliant and disturbing psychological character study, the then-recent **PEEPING TOM** (1960, UK); although it's a foregone conclusion that **NEUTRON VS. THE MANIAC** contains none of the psychological/narrative complexities of that infinitely more famous film, nor any of its innovative technical aspects either.

Left justifiably distraught and guilt-ridden over her failure to come to the aid of her sister in her hour of need—an act which might well have averted Bertha's murder—Margie approaches police Inspector Roberts ([Rodolfo Landa] surnamed "Rivas" in the original Mex print), seeking help. Duly assigned to protect her is Charles "Chuck" Marquand (originally "Carlos Márquez"; Wolf Ruvinskis once again). Chuck soon discovers that Oswald the so-called "sightless" piano-player can in actuality see perfectly well, but maintains his visually-impaired façade so as to nurture his profitable career as a so-called blind musician (what a gimmick!). Contrary to anyone's expectations, he had actually witnessed the late Bertha's abductor with his own eyes, but is afraid that if he comes forward and admits to being able to see, that the scandalous revelation might destroy his career.

In Neutron mode, Charles infiltrates the nearby Los Robles sanatorium, run by one Dr. Van Nielsen, after being directed there by the formerly "blind" musician who had witnessed the hooded killer entering there. Once inside, the willfully trespassing N-guy dukes it out with the hospital's surly, burly head attendant, Gastón (played by chrome-domed vet *luchador* Nathanael [or Notamael] León, better known by his ring-name of "Frankestein" *[sic!]*). When Gastón and other orderlies attempt to unmask Neutron ("Let's take a look at your pretty face!"), our hero makes good his getaway with his secret identity still intact. Upon later returning in the guise of his maskless alter-ego Charles, Newt checks into the clinic for "observation" (oh, he's observing alright!), ostensibly for a therapeutic "rest" so as to unwind.

When Margie goes missing, Neutron gets back in action, while his other personality Charles attempts

to maintain inroads at the sanatorium. Here he meets Dr. Van Nielsen's other resident "guests" / red herrings. These include an eccentric Russian grand-duke, a turbaned Hindu mystic, a neurotic woman who imagines herself to be a world-famous actress; as well as a shell-shocked war veteran and a punch-drunk former wrestling champ named "Tiger" Miller (latter portrayed by real-life wrestler/actor Lobo Negro / "Black Wolf" [r.n. Guillermo Hernández], who appeared in many, many Mexploitation movies, often those involving actual monstrous villains rather than mere human maniacs). In addition to this assortment of stereotyped characters, Charles meets none other than kidnapped Margie (Romand), who has allegedly been admitted as a patient due to her tormented conscience over the recent brutal and senseless slaying of her down-on-her-luck, ne'er-do-well sister. As if brainwashed, she initially fails to recognize Charles, who works toward solving the mystery of the madman in their midst…

The "trashier" comicbookish style of the earlier *Neutron* threesome is by far preferable to the somewhat forced and stilted would-be whodunit/who's-a-red-herring formula of **VS. THE MANIAC**. The goal here—*à la* innumerable old dark house thrillers of the '30s or even older—seems to be to throw suspicion off the real titular maniac and onto the sundry cuckoo inhabitants of Van Nielsen's psychiatric clinic. But because we're already fully cognizant of the fact that the doc's going to be implicated in the homicides somewhere anyway, all this preliminary antiquated audience manipulation with the suspicion-transferal business registers most redundantly indeed.

Once more, dorky "comedy relief" is provided by unfunny funny-man Chucho Salinas as Chucho, Charles's lily-livered wimp-cop partner, who's afraid of his own shadow. Salinas had played a virtually identical role in both René Cardona, Sr.'s **DOCTOR OF DOOM** (*Las luchadoras contra el Médico Asesino*, 1962) and its sequel **THE WRESTLING WOMEN VS. THE AZTEC MUMMY** (*Las luchadoras contra la momia*, 1964). While other *Neutron* series entries are bereft of legit wrestling content, in addition to this later franchise entry's expected musical and comedic padding there is even some token ring action included (albeit without Newt's participation). This *lucha libre* interlude occurs when fallen champion "Tiger" /Lobo attempts unsuccessfully to reclaim his formerly fearsome wrestling reputation, only he's too far gone to make a comeback.

Ultimately, **NEUTRON VS. THE MANIAC** is just too sluggish for its own good, and the clumsily-revealed "twisteroo" ending comes as a bit of a

Wolf as the "new" Newt struggles to maintain a firm hold on an antsy Asian "karate assassin", while seasoned character actor Carlos López Moctezuma keeps our hero covered in a Mexican lobby card for **NEUTRON VS. THE KARATE ASSASSINS** (art by Leopoldo Mendoza [?])

groaner too. Plus there's not a single damn Death Robot in sight, for shame!

****

The *N* saga's fifth episode, **NEUTRON VS. THE KARATE ASSASSINS** (if indeed it ever actually existed under that title), seems to be unavailable in any English-dubbed format at this time (???), although presumably it must have been extant in that form at some point or other. Most fortunately however, it is currently viewable—in untranslated Spanish, natch—as an upload on YouTube, evidently ripped from a Mexican TV airing; so at least it can now be viewed in some form, thankfully enough. Even if your Spanish is as dodgy as mine is, the plot isn't too hard to follow.

Interestingly enough, no less than (uncredited) aforementioned wrestler/stuntman/actor Marco Antonio Arzate Rodríguez—who, concurrently at that time, regularly donned Neutron's mantle and familiar hood in Ruvinskis' stead for the spinoff series of *fotonovelas* which sprang from the character's initial filmic trio discussed elsewhere— appears briefly in **KARATE ASSASSINS'** prologue

sequence, playing one of its titular mute, automaton-like killers, who whack their assigned targets using deadly karate chops which instantly kill their victims stone dead (!). After having been nabbed red-handed (so to speak) and taken into police custody for interrogation as prime suspect in the latest murder, Arzate voluntarily nosedives out a cop-shop window to his death, kamikaze-style, rather than divulge any details to the authorities. Mexi-Flexi big man Gerardo "Gomar the Gorilla" Zepeda also appears elsewhere herein as a *karateka luchador* known as— *what else?!*—Gorilla, who serves as main henchman of the head heavy (played with a limp and a walking cane by Germán "Count Lavud/Duval" Robles). Also appearing as another *karateka* is Mexploitation vet Fernando Osés, who wore many hats in the genre (including those of wrestler, stuntman, actor and writer, if not that latter one here).

After initially being ingloriously "chopped" down to size by them, Wolf subsequently bones-up on his karate and hones his skills before later returning to decimate the karate-choppers in payback; making it personal rather than professional, when he does this he isn't even wearing his Neutron outfit (i.e., crime-fighting uniform). Speaking of which, here as in **VS. THE MANIAC**), Newt's "new" duds are far less distinctive than his original ones. Gone are his way-cool triple-lightning-bolt-streaked black mask and stylized jagged/zigzag "N" belt-buckle, to be replaced by a much plainer single-striped dark grey mask and a cummerbund of metallic-shiny stretch fabric to go with his black tights instead. This less-memorable simplified costume is a lot blander than the original, but it frankly suits the relative blandness of the two belated "sequels" themselves, that—despite a few spurts of gritty rough 'n' tumble action, which mostly comes in fits and starts—are just too dull to compare favorably with the originating trilogy, and might just as well belong to a completely different series, as far as I'm concerned. While Robles gives his usual polished, cultured reading as the villain, his composedly sinister civility is simply no substitute for the more colorfully schlocky, histrionic villainy of Dr. Caronte.

In time for the conclusion, after being unmasked by a triple threat of Robles' goons and collectively treating them to a thorough thrashing for it (including giving 'em a few extra boot-stomps each, just for bad measure!), Wolf—still bare-faced, with mask in hand—mosies on back to parts unknown whence he came, thus putting final and fitting closure on Ruvinskis' contributions to the *N* mythos. The way he just blends back into the scenery and up and vamooses right before the final fade rather reminded me of how Hollywood western legend Randolph Scott's lone gunslinger characters always seemed to do similarly at the ends of the series of seven amazing westerns he both starred in and co-produced (from 1956 to 1960) for director Budd Boetticher. In closing this the fifth and final *Neutron* film, at least Wolf goes out on a memorably enigmatic note, and in this instance perhaps it was for the better that he simply faded away in time for the "FIN" card rather than wore-out his welcome by sticking around too long.

NEUTRON TRAPS
THE INVISIBLE KILLERS

(*El asesino invisible*, a.k.a. *El Enmascarado d'Oro contra el asesino invisible* / "The Gold-Masked Man vs. The Invisible Killer"; a.k.a. [?] "NEUTRON VS. THE INVISIBLE KILLERS")

Mexico, 1964

A Filmadora Panamericana (Azteca), S.A. presentation

S: "El Enmascarado d'Oro" [=Jorge Rivero], Ana Bertha Lepe, Guillermo Murray, Jorge Pons, Carlos Agosti, Miguel Arenas, Adriana Roel, Manuel Garay D: René Cardona, Sr. Prd: Alberto López. DP: Raúl Martínez Soláres. Mus: Sergio Guerrero

This is the alleged "sixth" *N* adventure which had long been believed to exist, even though it wasn't until more recent decades that its existence and specific identity at

This Page: More rare imagery pertaining to Marco Antonio Arzate Rodríguez (1928-2014), Neutron's portrayer in the *fotonovela* which bore his name. **Top:** A posed studio publicity photo-portrait of the actor (circa the early/mid-1960s). **Center:** Arzate's A.N.D.I. actors' organization ID card (dated December 29th, 1969). **Above:** His official *luchador*'s credentials (dated June 7th, 1954) from early in his wrestling career. *[Our sincere thanks go out to Tristán Arzate and Bruno Bernasconi for indirectly providing us with these images, which we (respectfully) reprint without permission here in the spirit of publicity]*

175

long last became certain... if *not* necessarily under the Anglo title given above, however (a "fact" which has yet to be proven conclusively, at least to my satisfaction. By that I mean more than just the IMDb saying so).

Numerous English-language magazines, fanzines and reference books have mentioned this title over the decades. The existence of an actual film—meaning to say, a genuine English-dubbed print, rather than merely an "orphan" title unattached to any actual film—that owns said Anglo retitling seemed unverifiable with any degree of certainty. Sure, by now it's pretty much become "common knowledge" (note quotes) that the film in question was originally known as EL ASESINO INVISIBLE, and has nothing whatsoever to do with the *Neutron* saga proper; it's Anglo title merely being attached

Mexican poster for NEUTRON TRAPS THE INVISIBLE KILLERS (art unsigned)

to it to "cash in" on the legit series entries, which, according to reports, proved quite popular with kiddies during the films' original TV airings during the early/mid-'60s.

Seeing as no original Mexican listing for this film appears in Emilio García Riera's *Historia Documental del Cine Mexicano*, Jorge Ayala's *La Aventura del Cine Mexicano* or Nelson Carro's handy booklet *El Cine de Luchadores*, we must assume that INVISIBLE KILLERS either doesn't exist, period... or else it is possibly a reissue/TV or obscure regional release title for one of the other entries in the series (highly unlikely on all three counts). Walt Lee's groundbreaking early-'70s work *Reference Guide to Fantastic Films* described the plot thusly, if erroneously (at least in relation to the present film): "Invisibility machine kills at great distance". The Winter-Spring 1971 edition of the Broadcast Information Bureau's *TV Feature Film Source Book* (an industrial television syndication catalogue) encapsulated NEUTRON TRAPS THE INVISIBLE KILLERS like so: "Neutron solves the mystery of the unbelievable crimes committed by the invisible killers, utilizing his superior strength

and courage", which at least gets the rudimentary plotline right. So evidently there was a movie released as such somewhere along the line.

Since none of the *Neutron* series was ever released theatrically in the USA or Canada—nor to theatres in Anglo form anywhere else, so far as I know—this severely limits possibilities. A film was released under that INVISIBLE KILLERS title to TV (minus theatrical playoff) by usual Newt distribs Commonwealth United. "We" (i.e., I)—long before the IMDb ever said as much, I might add! ☺—have come to the conclusion that INVISIBLE KILLERS is actually a 1964 René Cardona, Sr. wrestling picture called—you guessed it, *muchachos*—EL ASESINO INVISIBLE (*"The Invisible Killer"*). Perhaps the problem with identification stemmed from it somehow being mistaken for a legit *Neutron* adventure way back, and hence perpetuation of the unverified rumor. While there is a likelihood that Commonwealth may have slapped Neutron's handle on Jorge Rivero's *El Enmascarado d'Oro* / "The Golden-Masked Man" character, I'm willing to go on record right here in cold, hard print that a genuine separate Newt/Ruvinskis film entitled NEUTRON TRAPS THE INVISIBLE KILLERS simply does *not exist*, period. This seems to be borne-out by all the other evidence which has surfaced since I first made this assumption back in the early '90s. (But trust me when I say I'd love to be proven wrong, in this case. After all, considering how relatively few Mexploitation movies ever got dubbed into English—often by K. Gordon Murray & Co. [if, surprisingly enough, not the *Neutron*s]—we need all we can get; although, in this the age of fan-subs, many heretofore-undubbed movies are becoming available with subtitles, which helps alleviate the shortage of English dubs substantially.)

Directed by René Cardona, Sr. (based on a story by his son, René Cardona, Jr.) and starring Jorge Rivero (billed hereon with his surname modified to the more rendly French-sounding "Rive" instead), **INVISIBLE KILLERS** wastes no time getting right down to business.

A mad scientist (Arenas) invents a hi-tech electromagnetic machine which, when set to the correct frequency, can render objects invisible; including living things, as a "guinea pig" (i.e., bunny rabbit) test subject conclusively confirms. Fave Mexploitation heavy Carlos Agosti (best-known to many as Count Frankenhausen in a pair of wonderfully moody B&W vampire flicks directed by Miguel Morayta in 1962-63), serves as the ol' prof's lab assistant, and we just *know* he's up to no good right from first sight of him. Sure enough, the professor winds up "mysteriously" murdered—yep, Agosti done it!—and his erstwhile subordinate thereafter begins misusing the late brainiac's invisibility machine for his own nefarious ends (i.e., committing high-profile robberies, etc). One of the more inventive plot developments—hinting at a potentially more supernatural angle—reveals that only a cat's eyes can see the invisible assassin, and this development factors rather cleverly into the movie's conclusion.

Unlike in any of the other genuine *Neutron* movies, the masked hero herein actually *is* a pro wrestler by day, who—much like a certain El Santo—moonlights as a crime-fighter in his off-hours (lively sequences in the ring include appearances by such famed real-life *luchadores* as "Karloff" Lagarde). While known, as per his handle, for wearing a golden mask, because the film was shot in monochrome, said headgear simply appears silver anyway, so the Santonian similarity becomes all the more obvious, which was no doubt the producers' express intention (although it should be mentioned that Rivero, a bodybuilder, is a good deal more beefily buff than the more "modestly-built" Santo ever was; not that it's the muscles that make the man by any means). While the macho Rivero—a frequent romantic lead in "straight" features (*sans* mask, natch)—who keeps his identifying hood on throughout here, only appeared intermittently in masked wrestling Mexi-Flexis, he notably co-starred with the mighty silver-masked "S"-man himself in a pair of that hero's finest '60s non-monster adventures (the 007-influenced espionage actioners **OPERACIÓN 67** [1967] and **EL TESORO DE MOCTEZUMA** [1968]), both of which were co-directed by the present film's father and son tag-team, the Cardonas.

While we ye *Monster!* eds don't consider the Invisible Man to be a monster per se, the present film does fall a lot closer to this mag's territory than the preceding two true *Neutron* outings do, and for that we can be grateful. Ironically enough, while it's only an "imitation" *Neutron* film—if indeed that Anglo title is to be believed, and it was ever actually even nominally attached to an English dub of the film—**EL ASESINO INVISIBLE** does a far more convincing job of at least partially recapturing the campy pulp sci-fi flavor of Curiel's originating "N"-dude three-pack; although, that said, perhaps a superhero battling a *sight-unseen* and entirely human menace might seem a

bit of a cop-out in terms of visual dynamics. Some slavering, rubber-suited monster would have been far preferable, for sure (but maybe I'm just biased!). Possessing the appropriate level of hyper-masculine intensity and throwing himself all over the shop with a trained stuntman's disregard for the scenery's

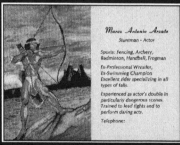

Top: The misleading early '90s Canadian VHS slipcase for **NEUTRON VS. THE MANIAC** (note that mostly-erroneous fine print!) *[Scan c/o The Fentonian Institution]*. **Above:** All-round action man M.A. Arzate's personal printed-in-*Inglés* business card (circa the late 1960s), which he presumably handed out to visiting Hollywood casting directors; the *indio* archer artwork is by he himself. *[Scan c/o Tristán Arzate]*

177

sharp corners, Rivero makes a game go of miming that he's battling a nonexistent adversary, but in the end it all registers a tad limp from a dramatic standpoint. A repeatedly-used gimmick is a revolver (ostensibly held by an invisible hand) floating in mid-air, and a knife flying through the air on a piano wire is also seen. When the invisible assassin climbs into the ring and starts pounding on Rivero and his opponent, it sparks a panic among the arena's spectators without really exciting we the armchair

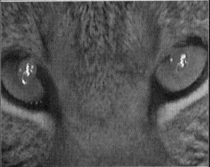

Top: Jorge Rivé *[sic!]* as "The Golden-Masked Man" in the so-called (???) **NEUTRON TRAPS THE INVISIBLE KILLERS. Center:** A feline's eyes espy things mere humans can't see. **Above:** The "invisible killer", disguised in a replica of the hero's costume (note "hollow" mask!)

audience too overmuch. The effects, for what they are—also including footprints "miraculously" appearing where no one appears to be walking—are handled well enough, although wires and other supports are sometimes highly apparent.

After shoving Agosti—now become entirely visible—into a control panel, which electrocutes him, Rivero matter-of-factly rather than triumphantly proclaims, "*¡Este es el fin del asesino invisible!*" (If I need to translate that line of dialogue for you, your *español* is way worse than mine!) But wait… there's a pretty weird and nifty twist ending (hint: "*el* otro *asesino invisible*" [ditto for that line, too!]), although it does make for a quite memorable ending to an otherwise only so-so movie; but then they go and blow it by tacking-on another extraneous and anticlimactic musical number from leading lady Ana Bertha Lepe. Playing "herself", *señorita* Lepe (1934-2013)—best-known to many who care about such things for playing stacked space-babe Gamma in **THE SHIP OF MONSTERS** (*La nave de los monstrous*, 1960, Mexico, D: Rogelio A. González)—here appears as a slinky cabaret singer/ dancer who smokes-up the nightclub stage during several production numbers.

NOTES: Again in reference to the title confusion discussed above, on a similar note, another title which has occasionally been bandied about over the decades in relation to one or another of the *Neutron* series is "NEUTRON AND THE COSMIC BOMB" (it's sometimes attributed as an a.k.a. for **NEUTRON VS. THE MANIAC** [I call hogwash on that!]). We as-yet have not ascertained whether this is a true alternate title for one of the existing five films, but out of all of them the most logical candidate naturally enough falls within the initial Curiel-directed trilogy. A major running plot-thread throughout that saga was Dr. Caronte's aptly-christened "neutron bomb," which might render the title choice somewhat apt. Rather than, as you might expect, using it to destroy Neutron with, Caronte instead threatens Mexico City with destruction by neutronic radiation instead.

In summation, other than for bringing to light this maze of potential misinformation and supposition surrounding the present title under discussion (what's YOUR opinion?), I guess there's not really much more can be said about the *Neutron*s without us really flogging a dead horse more than we've done already, so we'll lay this pesky old nag conclusively to rest…*for now!* ☺

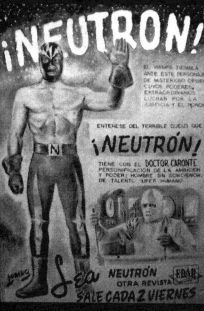

Clockwise, from Top Left: An obscure, unofficial—and decidedly oversized!—Neutron-"inspired" *luchador*, circa the 1970s (identity unknown); Marco Antonio Arzate in a candid shot taken with John Wayne on the set of the shot-in-Mexico western **RIO LOBO** (1970, USA), which co-starred muscleman Jorge Rivero (star of **EL ASESINO INVISIBLE**) in a high-profile part, billed second only to—if in much smaller print than—"The Duke" himself; M.A. Arzate as Neutron re-tangles with Dr. Caronte (whose costume was here possibly worn by Arzate's real-life *amigo* Raúl Martínez) in #95 of the *fotonovela*; and an ad (art by Lozano [?]) for the *Neutrón* mag, again featuring his screen/print nemesis, Dr. Caronte

MONSTERS!

AN ILLUSTRATED MOVIE HISTORY

PART THREE:
THE ATOMIC AGE

WITH THE POPULARITY OF THE CLASSICAL ARCHETYPES ON THE WANE AND THEIR HOUSE OF AND ABBOTT AND COSTELLO MEETS ... SERIES BRINGING THEIR BIG SCREEN DOMINANCE TO AN CLOSE, UNIVERSAL WAS TO SEEK AN ALTERNATIVE AVENUE TO EXPLORE.

WORDS AND PICTURES BY ANDY ROSS

AS A FILM THAT WOULD GIVE RISE TO THE REVENGE OF NATURE SUB-GENRE, THE CREATURE FROM THE BLACK LAGOON (1954) WAS TO VOLUNTEER A REFRESHING ALTERNATIVE TO THE STANDARD UNIVERSAL FARE.

FILMED IN THE FLEDGLING 3-D MEDIUM, AND STARRING RICHARD CARLSON, JULIA ADAMS, AND RICOU BROWNING IN THE UNDERWATER SEQUENCES AS THE CREATURE, THE FILM EXEMPLIFIED THE INCREASINGLY POPULAR 'MONSTER ON THE LOOSE SCENARIO.

GIVING RISE TO SUCH SCIENCE FICTION FEATURES AS TARANTULA (1955),
ATTACK OF THE 50 FOOT WOMAN (1958) AND THEM! (1954) THE POPULARITY
OF THE RAMPAGING CITY SMASHING MONSTER WAS TO REACH ITS PEAK WITH GOJIRA (1954).

RE-TITLED GODZILLA FOR
WESTERN AUDIENCES, THE
GIGANTIC RADIOACTIVE DINSOAUR
WAS TO PROVE A PHENOMENOL
SUCCESS FOR IT'S PRODUCERS,
TOHO STUDIOS.AWARDED THE
TITLE 'THE KING OF THE MONSTERS',
GODZILLA WENT ON TO DOMINATE A
FURTHER 27 FEATURES
FROM THE TOKYO BASED OPERATION.

INSPIRED BY THE ROSWELL INCIDENT OF 1947 AND FEEDING ON THE PUBLIC'S FASCINATION WITH OTHER-WORLDLY BEINGS, THE SCIENCE-FICTION GENRE WAS REALISE A RATHER UNIQUE TAKE ON THE MONSTROUS ARCHETYPE.

SET EITHER IN THE PRESENT DAY, ON A DISTANT PLANET, OR IN THE FAR-FLUNG FUTURE, FIMS SUCH AS THIS ISLAND EARTH, ITI-THE TERROR FROM BEYOND SPACE (1958) AND I MARRIED A MONSTER FROM OUTER SPACE (1958) SOUGHT TO APPEASE THE CURIOSITY OF THE BABY BOOM GENERATION.

WITH THEIR CREATIONS GROWING INCREASINGLY BIZARRE, AND THEIR STORY-LINES EVER MORE OUTLANDISH, THE MONSTER MOVIE OF THE 1950'S WAS TO TRULY EMBRACE THE SPIRIT OF ESCAPISM.

EVER SINCE THE GIANT ROBOT GORT FIRST DESCENDED THE RAMP OF HIS MASTER, KLAATU'S FLYING SAUCER IN THE DAY THE EARTH STOOD STILL (1950) OUR FASCINATION WITH OTHER-WORLDLY BEINGS WAS TO DOMINATE THE ROCK 'N' ROLL YEARS.

BASED ON A STORY BY NIGEL KNEALE AND STARRING BRIAN DONLEVY AS THE NO-NONSENSE PROFESSOR BERNARD QUATERMASS, THE QUATERMASS X-PERIMENT (1955) WAS TO INTRODUCE THE WORK OF HAMMER FILMS TO A MUCH WIDER AUDIENCE.

UNRELENTINGLY AND UTTERLY FRIGHTENING, THE 'IN YOUR FACE' SHOCKS OF THE QUATERMASS X-PERIMENT WAS TO PROVIDE THE BENCH-MARK FOR THE HAMMER HORROR EXPERIENCE.

AN EXPERINCE THAT WAS TO BEGIN IN EARNEST IN 1957...

GONZO FOR GORGONS

MEDUSA IN CINEMA

A snake-locked triple-bill reviewed by Christopher J. Maurer

Avert thine eyes, ladies and gentlemen, for we are here to investigate an accursed creature that slithers out of the ancient mists of myth to turn unwary, fleshy oglers into sightless, stony statuary. She is an archetypal femme fatale with a writhing mass of serpentine hair and but one name only —no, not "Charo", you fools! ...MEDUSA!!

According the Ancient Greek poet Hesiod,[1] Medusa and her two sisters, Stheno and Euryale (collectively known as the Gorgons), were born of a pair of roughneck sea-deities, Ceto, the goddess of whales and sea monsters, and Phorkys (or Phorcys),[2] the god of dangerous waters. Hesiod gives no physical description of Medusa, but refers to her as being different from her sisters, in that she is mortal. According to Hesiod, Medusa was minding her own business getting laid in a meadow by some unnamed, dark-haired stud, when out pops Perseus unexpectedly and chops her head off. No explanation is given for this, either. What makes matters worse is the fact that Medusa was apparently with child at the time—presumably by the same dark-haired stud—and posthumously gave birth to, not just a flying horse (Pegasus) but also to a dude (Chrysaor) with a golden sword besides.

Centuries later, the Roman poet Ovid fleshed-out the Medusa legend in Book IV of his masterwork of classical mythology Metamorphoses. *Therein, Medusa starts out as a real looker, with a lovely head of normal hair. Unfortunately however, Neptune, being the horny old sea salt that he is,*

---

1   Hesiod's *Theogony* (II 270-294)

2   To those who enjoy '80s trash cinema, Medusa might well be described as "*PHORKYS'* [sic] REVENGE"!

These 2 Pages: A reversed detail of the US one-sheet/half-sheet poster art for Hammer's **THE GORGON** (art unsigned)

185

took a liking to her human feminine pulchritude and had his evil way with her in—of all places!—the sacred temple of Minerva, no less. This goddess, being by all accounts a divine virgin, took great umbrage at this skanky desecration of her Sanctum Sanctorum, so she did what any self-respecting irate divinity would do: she cursed the hapless mortal, giving her snakes for hair and a face that only a boulder could love. In Ovid's tale, that bastard Perseus snuck-up on Medusa once again—this time while she and her scalpful o' serpents were sleeping—and with the aid of a mirrored bronze shield (i.e., by gazing at her reflection in it rather than at her figuratively and literally petrifying countenance), he decapitated her, as before. Perseus then weaponized Medusa's head, taking it into battle with him and turning a small army of enemies into instant lawn ornaments, similarly transforming big King Atlas into a mountain, and in the process carelessly dripping venomous gorgon's blood all over the sands of Libya, thus infesting it with deadly snakes from then onward. Ain't mythology so COOL?! Cool indeed.

The Greeks were not alone in their fascination with all things serpentine. Snakes have been powerful symbols of life, death, wisdom, and power in many cultures since time immemorial. The Norsemen have their world-girdling Midgard Serpent, Jormungand (a.k.a. Jörmungandr in Old Norse, meaning "Great Beast"), the Hebrews their mischief-making serpent in the Garden of Eden; the Hindus have their Nagas and Naginis; Haitian Vodouists have the great serpent-spirit Damballah; while the Aztecs had their feathered serpent-god Quetzalcoatl. And as for those Ancient Egyptians, they had more supernatural serpentine deities than Moses could shake a stick at!

Now, on to three different gorgons in film (or rather, two on celluloid and a third on digital video)... The main trouble with portraying a traditional Medusa in a feature-length production stems from the difficulty of building her as a character, be it villainous or

otherwise. Because of her peculiar "affliction", you can't allow her any screen time interacting face-to-face with other actors, for obvious reasons. As a result, it's difficult to develop her motivations through use of dialog, or her emotions through making eye-contact with other characters. Hence, she becomes less of an actual character and more of a gruesome plot device. This is precisely how Medusa is used, albeit to excellent effect, in the Ray Harryhausen stop-motion classic, **CLASH OF THE**

As the poster tagline screamed: *"She Had A Face Only A Mummy Could Love!"* Prudence Hyman lurks with sinister intent amidst the cobweb-slung shadows of **THE GORGON** (1964)

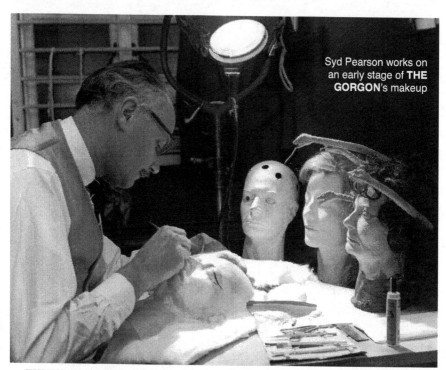

*TITANS (1981, UK/USA, D: Desmond Davis), for instance. The two other titles I will discuss—**THE GORGON** (1964, UK, D: Terence Fisher) and its much more modern SOV homage/spoof, **THE NIGHT OF MEDUSA** (2016, USA, D: Joshua Kennedy)—skirt around this problem of character development through use of a main character who can interact with other actors and make a connection with the audience, yet who transforms into her gorgon form at various points during the film.*

****

A Werewolf in Greek's Clothing?

The action in **THE GORGON** (1964, UK) centers around the accursed village of Vandorf, a fictional Germanic city-state during the early 1900s. In Vandorf, when the full moon rises, people wind up dead. *Aaaaaa-oooooooo!* Werewolf of Vandorf? Sorry, Warren Zevon fans, but no little old ladies get mutilated late at night in this film. Instead, when the victims are brought to the town's taciturn medical examiner, Dr. Namaroff (played by Peter Cushing), their bodies have instead been "gorgo-

nized"—a term they actually use in the movie— which means they've been turned to stone from sheer fright at the sight of something too horrible to behold with the naked eye. The local powers-that-be, including Namaroff and the town's chief of police Inspector Kanof (played by a subdued Patrick Troughton), are covering things up, and the first two deaths in the movie (a local artist and his pregnant lover) are chalked-up as a murder suicide. This does not sit well with Professor Heitz, the artist's father (played by Michael Goodliffe), who attends the bogus inquest and vows to get to the bottom of the mystery. The story builds from there, becoming one of jealousy, death, supernatural possession, metamorphosis...and, of course, rubber snakes!

Visually speaking, the creature's countenance, which includes prosthetic snakes (a collaborative effort between special makeup artists/designers Roy Ashton, Richard Mills and Syd Pearson, with an assist from hairstylist/wigmaker Frieda Steiger), is effectively spine-tingling only while seen at a distance. When the gorgon first appears, materializing out of the shadows in the depths of the haunted Castle Borski, it is a genuinely frightening apparition. That said, however, when viewed in close-up, the wobbly rubber snakes atop the gorgon's head are laughable; but by that point it didn't matter, as I the viewer had already invested myself in the

An early unused makeup concept for **THE GORGON** (1964)

done, but you don't believe in it. Would you believe it? You have to believe in the situations in a film like **THE GORGON**, you can't have it ruined by unbelievable animation of any sort. It's no good you catch the attention of the audience and their imagination and then you can't make them accept it is true.[3]

(Fisher's criticism of stop-motion is much the same as that of modern viewers [myself included] who lament the overuse of CGI effects in today's movies.)

Rubber snakes notwithstanding, I *was* impressed by the makeup effects on the gorgon's victims. A stone finger suddenly breaking off and dropping to the floor was simply done, yet horrifying. Another victim gets a quick glance at the creature, and his transformation to chalky white stone is a slow and painful process. I found this far more dramatic and dreadful (in a *good* way) than the instantaneous "quick-dry cement"-like demises one usually associates with Medusa's "stone dead" victims. As an additional note of interest, James Bernard's haunting musical score also adds greatly to the drama, endowing the movie with a dreamlike quality; parts of it reminding me of the theme intro to the gloomy, gothic soap opera, *Dark Shadows* (1966-71, USA).

All of the actors get the job done quite nicely, including Barbara Shelley and Richard Pasco as the doomed lovers. Peter Cushing plays it close to the vest as the secretive Dr. Namaroff, with Christopher Lee jumping in late in the game as the bluff and imposing Prof. Meister. As the officious police inspector Kanof, fans of classic *Doctor Who* will be pleased to see the second—then-current—incarnation (after the role's originator, William Hartnell) of the good doctor, Patrick Troughton[4] (who was also a Hammer Films regular). I was particularly impressed by Michael Goodliffe's emotionally-charged performance as Professor Heitz, a man who, even in the face of angry villagers, local authorities and supernatural horrors, would still risk his life to uncover the mystery behind his son's death.

My biggest grumble is that the writers[5] tragically bungled their use of Greek mythology to the point where it's less Bulfinch and more *bullcrap!* For

plot and the characters. This investment, coupled with the wild-eyed, malevolent glares given by the creature's actress Prudence Hyman (a former ballet dancer reportedly cast in the mimed role due to her seeming ability to "float" across the screen), allowed me to suspend my disbelief. I was able to turn up a transcript of an excellent interview by Jan Van Genechten with the film's director, Terence Fisher, which appeared in issue #19 of Richard Klemensen's long-running Hammercentric zine *Little Shoppe of Horrors*. In it, Fisher talks about the snakes in **THE GORGON** being moved by wires attached to an ungainly mechanical device. In the same interview, Fisher says they had toyed with the idea of using increasing-and-decreasing amounts of air pressure to move the snakes up and down. My favorite part of the interview wherein the snake-mechanics are discussed is when Fisher's wife suddenly unexpectedly chimes-in to heap praise on Ray Harryhausen's stop-motion animation work, much to Fisher's apparent chagrin:

Mrs. Fisher: What did they use in JASON AND THE ARGONAUTS?
Mr. Fisher: Oh, darling, that...
Mrs. Fisher: That was marvelous*!*
Alan Frank: Actually, it was stop-frame models.
Mrs. Fisher: Was that what it was? It was marvelous.
Mr. Fisher: That's a long and tedious process. We couldn't afford it. And I wouldn't have used it in that film anyway. Because all you do when you see it, is to admire the skill with which it has been

3 Interview reprinted from *Little Shoppe of Horrors #19* (@ users.telenet.be/almaerrante/base/terencefisher.htm)

4 Coincidentally Troughton faced down a stop-motion animated Medusa-like creature four years later in the *Doctor Who* serial "The Mind Robber" (D: David Maloney) ~ *TP*

5 John Gilling wrote the screenplay, based on a story by J. Llewellyn Devine.

the gorgons, they rattle-off the names Tisiphone, Medusa and Megaera. Okay, Medusa is definitely a gorgon, but, as anyone conversant in Classical Mythology (or who at least owns a well-worn copy of the *Dungeons & Dragons* tome *Deities & Demigods!*) knows, Tisiphone and Megaera are actually the names of a completely different batch of mythical sisters—namely, the Furies (a third Fury whose name is *not* dropped in this movie is Alecto, for those keeping score). According to Greek legend, the Furies (a.k.a. Erinyes or Eumenides; which respectively feature prominently in both Euripides' *Orestes* and Aeschylus' tragedy *Oresteia*) are a terrible trio of winged, bestial avengers who, when needed, swoop down out of the heavens to thrash poor deserving mortals with barbed scourges. A movie about them would potentially kick all forms of ass, but that's not what Hammer did here. Instead, they made another tried-and-true Gothic horror movie, complete with haunted castle, insane asylum, brain-in-a-jar, obstreperously Teutonic police chief, and the previously mentioned series of full-moon murders. With all these trappings, this film could easily have been a story of doomed love and lycanthropy, but by '64, when **THE GORGON** was produced and first released, Hammer had already cashed-in on Frankenstein, Dracula, the werewolf and the mummy several times over. Just for a change of pace perhaps, they instead decided to mine the myths of Ancient Greece for their newest villain, rather than beating a dead monster still further. Unfortunately, in so doing they ended up plunking down a Hellenic horror into a gloomy, turn-of-the-19th-century set-piece like a fish out of water, with absolutely no folkloric connections to her surroundings.

Despite this gripe, I enjoyed the film, and would definitely recommend it if you're in the mood for a weird, slow-burning Gothic melodrama. If, however, you are looking for a Medusa closer to the Greek and Roman traditions, you'll have to look elsewhere.

Medusa as Boss Monster!

I had the pleasure of seeing **CLASH OF THE TITANS** in the theater as a nine-year-old lad. The film had many deliciously horrifying scenes for a kid my age. But by far the most chilling was Perseus' encounter with Medusa! The music, the tail-rattle sound effects, the use of shadow and hellish red lighting, combined with the slow, alien, herky-jerky stop-motion movements of Harryhausen's demonic creation, crawling into frame on her hands while dragging her thick, serpentine body behind her, all merged into a waking nightmare of the greatest magnitude.

Top: The moody German A1 poster for **THE GORGON** (art unsigned). **Above:** *Off With Her Head!* Chris Lee takes a swing at Prudence Hyman as the same film's title character

If decidedly loosely in spots, Beverly Cross' screenplay for **CLASH** hews much closer to traditional Greek legends than did **THE GORGON**. Perseus (played by Harry Hamlin), the mortal human son of Zeus (Laurence Olivier), needs to save his beloved Andromeda (Judy Bowker) from being devoured by the monstrous sea beast known as

One of Harryhausen's production sketches for **CLASH OF THE TITANS**

the Kraken. To do so, he must first slay Medusa and use her lopped-off head to *gorgonize* the latter monster—I can't believe I got to use the word "*gorgonize*" twice...no, make that *three* times...in the same article! The film even uses the legend that Medusa's blood has a supernatural bio-potency. The ketchuppy-thick ichor that flows from Medusa's severed neck eats away at Perseus' enchanted shield like hydrochloric acid and, later in the film, mere drops of her falling blood spawn a deadly trio of mammoth-sized scorpions.

The Great Stoneface: CLASH's hideous Medusa in all her glory!

The Medusa character was beautifully sketched-out in charcoal by its creator-from-top-to-bottom Harryhausen, and it's amazing to see that from those preliminary sketches, his vision really made it up on the big screen. Sculptor Janet Stevens took the sketches and prepared the clay sculpt which formed the basis for the creature model used in the film. I'm fascinated by the unsung people who work behind-the-scenes on the movies I love, so I did an internet scrounge on Ms. Stevens. I could find nothing of substance other than the IMDb's references to her also having done sculpting and modeling work for **SUPERMAN** (1978, USA, D: Richard Donner), **STAR WARS: EPISODE V, THE EMPIRE STRIKES BACK** (1980, USA, D: Irvin Kershner), **KING RALPH** (1991, USA, D: David S. Ward), and **ALIEN 3** (1992, USA, D: David Fincher). She had me at **KING RALPH**!

The Gorgon in **CLASH OF THE TITANS** was not Harryhausen's first snake/human hybrid. A highly similar creature appears in 1958's **THE 7TH VOYAGE OF SINBAD**, when a magician combines a servant woman and a cobra into a nightmarish, four-armed, snake-bodied *naga* dancer. This cobra woman seems to have been the physical prototype for his later Medusa; she must have been haunting Harryhausen's dreams for the more than two decades between making the films.

In this film, unlike in **THE GORGON**, Medusa is not really a character at all. Rather she (or rather, her *head*) is merely a plot device: a thing (i.e., prop) which must be acquired by the main character to move the plot proper forward. This observation is by no means a slur against the filmmakers.

In fact, it is precisely how Medusa was used in the old myths by Hesiod and Ovid: as a mere *deus ex machina* within the main story about Perseus Or, in video game parlance, she is a simply a "boss" that needs to be defeated in order for Perseus to get to the next level, where he can kill the "final boss" (i.e., the Kraken). A full review of all the wonders of **CLASH OF THE TITANS** is beyond the scope of this article. Maybe it's what you grew up with, but suffice it to say that Harryhausen's vision of the sneering, rattle-tailed, serpentine she-demon with her deadly bow who slithered across the silver screen way back in '81 will always be the *real* Medusa for me.

Medusa as Agent of Vengeance

Director-producer-writer-actor-editor Joshua Kennedy *[see Troy Howarth's entertaining interview with this talented young "D.I.Y." filmmaker in Monster! #22 (p.80) – ed.]* has created a loving homage to **THE GORGON** in his latest lovingly-made D.I.Y. effort **THE NIGHT OF MEDUSA** (2016, USA). From the first death scene to the final quote ("It has been said that every legend and myth known to mankind is not entirely without its authentic foundation"), attributed to the Victorian English polymath Herbert Spencer,[6] anyone who has seen and enjoyed **THE GORGON** cannot help but derive some level of enjoyment from Kennedy's effort.

A man dies screaming in Central Park under the full moon—or is it just a fleeting nightmare experienced by the newest student at Pace University, Elaine Carlisle (Haley Zega)? You see, Elaine is a mysterious girl from a foreign land (if entirely lacking a foreign accent), who is haunted by dreams—and by a strange, sinister figure in a top hat. Is it the ghost of "Honest" Abe Lincoln, perhaps? Or maybe the Babadook's twice-removed second cousin? You'll have to watch the movie to find out!

THE NIGHT OF MEDUSA is clearly a very low-budget endeavor, but despite the student-film feel, I got sucked into the story and was intrigued by the trials and tribulations of the main character, Elaine, a captivating waif played by the lovely Ms. Zega, who steals the show and keeps it watchable.

If you like your monster movies scary and gory, there is not much to interest you here. This film is more of a slow-burn, just like **THE GORGON**, to which it pays countless respects, peppered with a few moments of comic relief. The snake hair effects had a hinky, CGI look to them, but were apparently done by taking footage of real snakes and somehow superimposing the images onto the actress playing Medusa. As bad as they were, I

Top: Harry Hamlin as Perseus strikes a famous statue's pose in **CLASH OF THE TITANS**; US lobby still. **Above:** If Perseus was her destroyer in **CLASH**, then Ray Harryhausen was every bit her creator

---

6   I couldn't find the primary source for this quote, but Spencer does say something quite similar in his *Principles of Sociology* (1898): "The mythological theory tacitly assumes that some clear division can be made between legend and history; instead of recognizing the truth that in the narratives of events there is a slowly increasing ratio of truth to error". (*Whew!* I suppose we can forgive the filmmakers for not directly quoting Mr. Spencer in this instance.)

preferred Terence Fisher's rubber snakes on strings myself, but maybe I'm just old-fashioned. Kennedy does film some excellent scenes at the Metropolitan Museum of Art, where the main character is enthralled by Antonio Canova's sculpture of "Perseus with the Head of Medusa". I enjoyed his use of classical music throughout the film, which gave the proceedings some much-needed grandeur, and I also enjoyed his subtle nods to many horror movies of the past, including **NOSFERATU** (*Nosferatu, eine Symphonie des Grauens*, 1922, Germany [Weimar Republic], D: F.W. Murnau), **THE CABINET OF DR. CALIGARI** (1920, Germany [Weimar Republic], D: Robert Wiene); and was it

Screen grabs from 2016's **THE NIGHT OF MEDUSA**

just me, or did I hear the manic, raging voice of Martine Beswick from **DR. JEKYLL & SISTER HYDE** (1971, UK, D: Roy Ward Baker) in there somewhere, too?

The present title under discussion is essentially a supernatural revenge flick in the vein of **CARRIE** (1976, USA, D: Brian DePalma). After Elaine suffers the indignities of betrayal and online bullying by her fellow students and roommate (played with bitchy relish by Carmen Vienhage, also seen in two of Kennedy's previous most-recent efforts, **THE VESUVIUS XPERIMENT** [2015] and **SLAVE GIRLS ON THE MOON** [2014, both USA]), the ancient mythological shit hits the 21st Century fan. Elaine discovers who she really is (hint: it's *not* Stheno or Euryale, which only leaves one other option open, gorgon-wise). Soon she lets her herpetological hair down and tears around campus, hell-bent on dishing-up snaky vengeance, served stone-cold...

Sure, **MEDUSA** may be shoe-string, student-filmy, Z-grade, PG-style horror at its cheesiest, and yet, I enjoyed it enough to watch it a second time with the director's commentary, so that's sure saying something. If you have any intention of seeing this movie, though, I strongly recommend you watch **THE GORGON** first, otherwise much of it will zoom right over your head like Pegasus.

NOTES: To name only a few*, for fans of Medusa who can't get enough cheesy "gorgon"zola action, check out the following fantasy films, which I have yet to see, but are on my bucket list, in no particular order: **CLASH OF THE TITANS** (2010, USA/UK, D: Louis Leterrier), the CG-loaded new millennial remake; **7 FACES OF DR. LAO** (1964, USA, D: George Pal), wherein Tony Randall plays multiple fantastic characters, including Medusa; *Voyage of the Unicorn* (2001, USA, D: Philip Spink), a TV miniseries starring Beau Bridges as a mythology professor who travels to magical lands; as well as **PERCY JACKSON & THE OLYMPIANS: THE LIGHTNING THIEF** (2010, USA, D: Chris Columbus), which appears to be chock-full of mythic beings, including Medusa, played by Uma Thurman.

*[And let's not forget the oodles of gorgon-themed movies from other parts of the globe which weren't necessarily directly derived from Greek mythology's Medusa legend: see our following special "GORGONZOLA!" pictorial supplement for some oftentimes wild and exotic titles of interest to those Monster! *readers wishing to broaden their horizons, and whose cinematic borders know no bounds. – SF.]*

GORGONZOLA!
MEDUSÆLLANEA from around the world

Above: A mosaic floor dating from the Roman era; now in the Museum of Sousse, Tunisia

Left: "The Medusa Men from Mars"; *Planet Comics* #41 (March 1946). **Right:** Ghastly gorgons were a recurrent motif of Swiss Symbolist/Art Nouveau painter Carlos Schwabe (1866-1926)

SéLección

TERROR

LOS OJOS DE LA GORGONA
CURTIS GARLAND

1.80 DM / Band 166
Schweiz Fr. 1.90 / Osterr. S 14.—

BASTEI

Neuer Roman

Tony Ballard
Die Horror-S   A.F. Morland

Medusenfluch

Frankreich F 8,00 / Italien L 1800 / Niederlande f 2,25 / Spanien P 150

FOUR SQUARE HORROR   3/-

The Night Side:
Edited by August Derleth
Nineteen masterpieces of the strange and terrible

ALIWAN

KOMIKS MAGASIN

Clockwise, from Top Left: "Eyes of the Gorgon", #201 in the long-running series of pulp horror novels from Spain, c.1970s (art unsigned); "Medusa's Curse", #166 in the 1980s German pulp horror novel series (art unsigned); 1976 Filipino horror *komik*. *[Image courtesy of the Video 48 blogspot]*; and a 1966 British paperback anthology edition (art by Josh Kirby)

Top Left: 2002 volume of artworks by illustrator Christos Achilleos. **Top Right:** 1986 French edition of C.A. Smith stories, including "The Gorgon" (1932). **Above Left:** Anglo export poster for **DEVIL WOMAN** (*She yao jing*, 1970, Hong Kong/Philippines, Ds: "Albert Yu"/Chi-Lien Yu, Felix Villar). **Above Right:** Anglo export poster for that film's sequel, **BRUKA – QUEEN OF EVIL** (蛇妖精 / *Ren tou she*, 1973), which was jointly made by the same pair of countries and directors. Both films starred Rosemarie Gil as Manda, the snake-woman (ad: *"Satan's Sinister Sister!"*). Incidentally, there was another Asian film released in '70—this one entirely Filipino in origin— likewise entitled **DEVIL WOMAN** (D: Jose Flores Sibal), and it *also* featured a gorgon (see p.256)

Clockwise, from Top Left: Asian DVD cover for **THE SNAKE KING'S CHILD** (งูเก็ง
ทอง / *Kuon Puos Keng Kang*, a.k.a. **SNAKER**, 2001, Cambodia/Thailand, D: Fai Sam
Ang); a typically crazed hand-painted Ghanaian poster (artist unknown); cover detail of a
Mexican horror comic, circa the 1970s; and a deceptive German VHS cover (art unsigned)
for Amando de Ossorio's conspicuously gorgon-free **NIGHT OF THE SORCERERS** (*La
noche de los brujos*, 1974, Spain)

Clockwise, from Top Left: *Conan the Barbarian* #134 (May 1982), art by Gil Kane;
Colombian "Bionic Man" comic (September 1979), art unsigned; a collected volume of
comics by Ana Mirallés and Antonio Segura, put out in 1993 by *Heavy Metal* magazine;
and *Auranella* comic #4 ([December 1966] the French edition of Italy's *Uranella* comic),
art by Floriano Bozzi

Left: L.B. Cole's cover art to *Startling Terror Tales* issue #13 (December 1952). **Below:** Panels from the same comic book's title story "...Love from a Gorgon!", by Jay Disbrow. **Above:** The monster mask made for *Kiss of Medusa* (1982, USA), a 16mm student short made at Jersey City State College by Warren F. Disbrow, brother of Jay

Left: L.B. Cole's cover art to *Startling Terror Tales* issue #13 (December 1952). **Below:** Panels from the same comic book's title story "...Love from a Gorgon!", by Jay Disbrow. **Above:** The monster mask made for *Kiss of Medusa* (1982, USA), a 16mm student short made at Jersey City State College by Warren F. Disbrow, brother of Jay

ゴーゴン

Above: Miscellaneous modern Japanese gorgonorrhea! **Top 2 Pics at Right:** Gorgon gals from the Toei TV *tokusatsu* series *Transforming Ninja Storm* (変身忍者嵐, 1972-73). **Pic #3 at Right:** Another Japanese gorgon, circa 1980s (art by Shigeru Mizuki). **Below:** An illustration from *The Yōkai Illustrated Encyclopedia* (妖怪大図鑑, 1966)

Top Left: Tony Randall in gorgonian drag for **THE 7 FACES OF DR. LAO** (1964). **Top Right:** Uma Thurman as a thoroughly modern Medusa in **PERCY JACKSON AND THE OLYMPIANS: THE LIGHTNING THIEF** (2010, USA/Canada/UK, D: Chris Columbus). **Center Left:** Frances Barber in *The StoryTeller: Greek Myths* episode "Perseus and the Gorgon" (1990, USA). **Center Right:** The stop-motion Medusa that threatened Dr. Who with gorgonization in his 1968 serial "The Mind Robber". **Above:** The US company Gorgon Video never actually released any movies with gorgons in, but they sure had an awesome logo!

Clockwise, from Top Left: Japanese horror manga 地獄の顔 / "Hellish Face" (AkeBono Comics, 1973), by author/artist Kazuo Kikuta; Thai poster for **THE LEGEND OF SNAKE** (งูเก็งกอง, Thailand, 2008, D: Komsan Treepong); Thai poster for the Cambodian film **THE SNAKE GIRL** (1980); and a Hong Kong poster for **MAGIC CURSE** (摧花毒降頭 / *Cui hua du jiang tou*, Taiwan, 1975, Ds: Tony Liu Chun-ku, Gwon Yeong-sun, To Man-bo)

Clockwise, from Above: Detail of an illustration by Aubrey Beardsley, from Oscar Wilde's *Salomé* (1907); "Medusa's Kiss", an etching by Wilhelm Kotarbinski (published by Richard Bong, Hanfstaengl, Berlin, c.1890s); a 1934 US fantasy pulp spot illustration by Virgil Finlay; Medusaean imagery has proven enduringly popular with various recording artists over the years, inspiring cover art for many albums; and Perseus raises the slain gorgon's head on high in the world-famous Italian bronze statue sculpted by Benvenuto Cellini in 1545

W. Kotarbinski: „Der Kuss der Medusa".

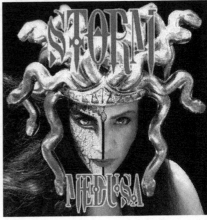

Clockwise, from Top Left: Kara Zor-El has her worst hair day ever in *Supergirl* Volume 1, #8 (November 1973); the September 1950 issue of Mars Ravelo's *Darna* comic, featuring snake-haired villainess Valentina on its cover; the gorgeous gorgon from "Talent for Terror!" in *Adventures into the Unknown* #49 (November 1953) *[Thanks to Carol Tilley for identifying the artist as Ken Landau]*; a vignette by Mahlon Blaine for *Alraune* (1911), by Hanns Heinz Ewers; and *Fantastic Science Fiction Stories* for March 1960 (art by Paul Frame)

THE ALIEN FACTOR's highly-photogenic stop-motion Leemoid beastie says "*Cheeeeese!*" (It was constructed/animated for the film by burgeoning young FX wiz Ernest "Ernie" Farino, who also did other FX work on **TAF** besides)

A FISTFUL OF DOHLER:
BALTIMORE'S B-MOVIE KING!

By Kevin Klemm

Master Monster Maker: Don "D.I.Y." Dohler, in his element

On January 27th, 1976, Donald "Don" Dohler [1946-2006] had a life-changing moment; an epiphany, if you will. It was his 30th birthday, and he was working at one of those jobs that people work just to pay the bills. Don was a creative type, and had been publishing his own D.I.Y. filmmaking zine called Cinemagic since 1972, but it was more a labor of love than a means to support his family.

Don first conceived the idea for Cinemagic in 1964 as a way to introduce homemade D.I.Y. special effects to the budding group of filmmakers who were playing around with their family's 8mm film cameras. It proved to be slightly ahead of its time, and really didn't get off the ground until 1972, when "Super 8" cameras really took-off all across the country. Cinemagic was devoured by a new generation of wannabe filmmakers (myself included), and featured articles on Special Effects Makeup, Stop-Motion Animation, and Optical and Mechanical Effects. Contributors included Dick Smith, Craig Reardon, John Dods, Ernest D. Farino and Ben Burtt. Current Hollywood wunderkind J.J. Abrams got his filmmaking start with the inspiration he found in the pages of Cinemagic.

NUMBER 10   PRICE 25¢

Top: An early Don Dohler zine (from 1961).
Above: DD's 1971 *ProJunior* comic is now
quite the collector's item

But *Cinemagic* wasn't Don's first zine. A huge fan of *Mad* magazine, in 1961 the 15-year-old Don Dohler self-published *Wild*. And just as Mad had a mascot in the form of Alfred E. Neuman, so did *Wild* have ProJunior. Although it only lasted five issues, *Wild* attracted a number of artists (both as contributors and fans) who would grow up to be heavyweights in the Underground Comix

field. Regular contributors to *Wild* included Jay Lynch, Art Spiegelman, and Skip Williamson. In 1971, Kitchen Sink Press produced Don Dohler's *ProJunior*, which featured *Wild*'s mascot in various interpretative strips by 22 of the world's best underground artists—including no less than Robert Crumb.

But let's get back to Don Dohler's epiphany... Here's what he himself had to say about it:

"On my 30th birthday I was working in Washington D.C. in an office. So I was there working and I look up, and there's a guy standing there with a gun to my Aunt's head. I got up and said, 'What the Hell?!' and he pointed it at me. Well, we were getting robbed. So they took us in one of the offices and they made us lay face down on the floor with shotguns at the backs of our heads. And I'm thinking, 'Oh my God; I'm going to have my brains splattered on a rug on my thirtieth birthday, ain't this great!' ...The first thing I'm thinking about is my two kids and my wife, and that's all I can see. You know, you're going along and you think everything is terrific, you know, and here's your life, and you think, 'I'm thirty, I've got another forty or fifty years maybe, plenty of time to do things'. But you think that when you're young, you think you have forever to do things. And all of a sudden—*BOOM!*—here's reality: a guy's holding a sawed-off shotgun to your head and you think 'This guy may just blow my brains out, and that's the end of my life right there' ...And you think about all the things I *DIDN'T* get to do, that I thought I would have plenty of time to do. That was the first thing I thought: 'Damn it, I've been talking about this movie and I want to do a feature film—I'm doing it!'"

So Don quit his job and called-up a film friend in D.C. to say, "I almost got killed today. I'm making a movie".

*That film was **THE ALIEN FACTOR**, and it started the wild ride that would take Don Dohler through almost 30 years and seven features as a director...*

THE ALIEN FACTOR

USA, 1978

Principal photography began in October 1976, just nine months after the robbery incident. Don wrote the script and raised $3,500.00 from friends and family, who each invested $500, and in true D.I.Y. fashion, also enlisted the help of *Cinemagic* contributors and local amateur filmmakers to bring his vision to life. The script follows a sci-

The "Inferbyce," a slithery, man-like cockroach beast from another world—
its sharp claws inject a deadly poison into hapless human victims.
Permission granted for magazine and newspaper reproduction.

Above: The icky insectoid Inferbyce (Larry Schlechter) uglies-up a US lobby still but good

fi film formula straight out of the 1950s (Don's favorite decade), and concerns a spaceship that is transporting creatures from across the solar system to an intergalactic zoo, when something goes wrong and it crashes near a small town in rural Maryland. The monsters escape, and it's up to local law enforcement and a mysterious stranger to stop them before the body count rises...

Don Dohler recruited local actors, TV and radio personalities, as well as friends and neighbors to fill the roles in the film. Some of them, such as George Stover, Dick Dyszel, Anne Frith, and Don Leifert, would go on to become regulars in his future cinematic endeavors.

The shoot was not without its problems. It was in a lot of respects "learn-as-you-go". Key crew members would be unavailable for a particular shooting day, necessitating someone else jumping in to fill the void. Overnight snowstorms would happen, causing continuity problems, etc.—but Don was undeterred, and he put his head down, pushing ever forward.

Two more lobby stills from **TAF**. The first shows the extraterrestrial monster known as a Zagatile (John Cosentino) getting ornery; the second depicts a mummy-like alien

This film utilized every trick in *Cinemagic*, and then some. Full-size monster suits, miniatures, stop-motion animation; you name it. All done practically and in-camera. This was before computers and CGI came along, so you really had to be creative with how you did your special effects.

Hand-painted Ghanaian poster for **THE ALIEN FACTOR** (artist unknown)

THE ALIEN FACTOR was shot on 16mm film, and Don felt it needed to be blown-up to 35mm in order to get any kind of theatrical distribution. So, he hit-up his investors one more time and raised $10,000 for the transfer. Once he had a 35mm print, he held a couple of premiere screenings in the Baltimore area. I attended one of them at the Security Square Mall, and I remember vividly the Zagatile costume "standing watch" over the lobby. But he was having trouble selling the film to distributors. No one seemed interested in this small sci-fi film shot in Baltimore. And then, in 1977, fate stepped in: a "little" Hollywood movie captured the public's imagination, as well as their pocketbooks. That film was **STAR WARS**, and soon TV stations all over the country were looking for sci-fi films to add to their programming schedules. **THE ALIEN FACTOR** was then attached to a group of other like-minded films and sold nationwide in a TV syndication deal. As a result, Don Dohler's first film has probably been seen by more people than all his other ones combined.

FIEND

USA, 1980

When he was unable to pull together funding for a sequel to **THE ALIEN FACTOR**, Don Dohler decided to go the route of a straight-up horror movie. **FIEND** had the smallest budget of any of his films (around $6,000) and so Don had to craft a tale around those budget constraints. Being that he is "D.I.Y." Dohler, Don continued with this film a lifetime habit of shooting in his own house, on his own street (Moray Court) and utilizing his own neighbors as extras in his films.

FIEND opens with a demonic spirit flying through a cemetery searching for a body to reanimate. It picks the grave of Eric Longfellow, who awakes and shakes-off the shackles of earthly death, then rejoins the land of the living. Like a modern day Dorian Gray, Mr. Longfellow constantly needs humans' life-forces in order to stave-off the effects of decomposition. So he moves into a house on a cul-de-sac to teach music, and on the side begins puts his glowing hands around the necks of unsuspecting victims. Sound cheesy? It is, but it's also very effective in creating a really creepy vibe throughout the film. One of the hardest-to-watch scenes comes when Dohler uses his very own young daughter as a victim of the fiend. The scene culminates with the little girl, body covered in a sheet, being loaded into an ambulance, with the Dohlers' real-life neighbors standing outside watching... Dohler regular George Stover plays a "Renfield"-like character to Don Leifert's Longfellow, while—making it a genuine family affair—Dohler's wife, son and brother also make appearances.

I don't remember this film getting any sort of theatrical distribution, though I did see a screening of it once at Balticon, a local Baltimore area sci-fi convention. Once home video became established, **FIEND** first found a niche on Beta/VHS tape, then later on DVD, and it is still widely available today.

NIGHTBEAST
USA, 1982

This is Dohler's most well-known film, and his most awkward... At this point, Don has (somewhat) moved on from utilizing this friends and relatives as investors. This time around, however, he was getting pressure from the money people to add more gore and some nudity to his films. **NIGHTBEAST** may have had the coolest monster to date, but it was basically retreading much the same ground as **THE ALIEN FACTOR** had done.

In this effort, we see another spaceship crash-land in rural Maryland. The same sheriff from **THE ALIEN FACTOR** handles the call as an alien monster goes on a rampage, disintegrating the locals. The monster attacks, blood is shed, guts are pulled out and various townsfolk are vaporized. Dohler had two of the

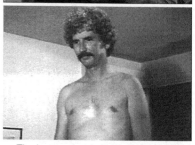

The horror mounts in four shots from **NIGHTBEAST**... In the topmost one, poor Geo. Stover receives a non-affectionate hug from the titular toothy critter. In the bottom two images above, the horrific events reach their screamingly nightmarish crescendo when passable Gabe Kaplan lookalike Tom Griffith doffs his sheriff character's uniform to get touchy-feely with Karin Kardian as his onscreen female deputy (cue shrieking horror movie music here!) *[Kidding! – ☺]*

Top of cover image contains the following text:

NIGHT BEAST

BETA VIDEO CASSETTE

HIS HANDS TEAR THROUGH FLESH AND BONE!

Few people witness the arrival of an alien craft in the dead of the night. The presence of the hostile extra-terrestrial is soon felt by a small American town where mutilated bodies are found. It soon becomes apparent that the creature hungers for flesh and blood and begins to wreak death and destruction to all that stands in its path.

A savage and horrific monster movie right through to the bloody end!!

WARNING

VIPCO's 1980s UK Betamax videotape jacket for one of D.I.Y. Dohler's better-distributed movies

3B's covered (i.e., "blood" and "beast"), but he was having a hard time figuring out how to cover the third one: where to add some T&A (i.e., "breasts"). That is until actor Tom Griffith (Sheriff Jack Cinder) volunteered to do a sex scene with his onscreen female deputy. Don was like a deer caught in the headlights, because the woman playing the deputy was none other than his Aunt's hairdresser! Everything worked out, though; Tom Griffith turned on the charm and talked the actress into getting naked with him. How did the scene turn out? Let's put it this way: imagine you're watching a vintage stag flick from the '70s, and you suddenly realize that the man on the screen with the gray perm and the porn 'stache is your *dad*. That's about how "sexy" this scene plays out!

NIGHTBEAST had a huge budget by "D.I.Y." Dohler standards (around $42,000), but it still suffered from low-budget syndrome. A cool little sidenote is that **NIGHTBEAST** was J.J. Abrams' first feature film credit. He had written to Dohler as a teenager, informing him he was a music composer. So Don wrote him back and asked him to compose some music for **NIGHTBEAST**. And thus the Dohler/Abrams connection was born. It's too bad Don didn't live long enough to see Abrams sci-fi films; I just know he would have been proud!

THE GALAXY INVADER

USA, 1985

This was my own first feature film credit. I was attending film school at UMBC (University of Maryland, Baltimore County), and an old friend of mine, who was in the same film program, approached me about being his camera assistant on the next Don Dohler movie. Don was back to scrambling for money, and bringing my friend Paul Loeschke onboard was a no-brainer. Every Friday, Paul would check out camera and sound equipment under the pretext that he was working on his own student film. We would then shoot **THE GALAXY INVADER** all weekend, then return the equipment to the school on Monday morning. We shot on 16mm film, and when it came time to edit, Paul got Don into the school editing bays to work on his rough cut. As with most Dohler productions, crew members were here one weekend and gone the next. When the sound recordist had to drop out, I was pulled from the camera side of things and took over location sound recording (hence my first film credit!).

THE GALAXY INVADER once again harkens back to Dohler's love of '50s sci-fi. This has more of a "PG" kind of vibe than **NIGHTBEAST**'s harsher "R" rating. In the present film, yet another alien crash-lands to earth, but this time the *humans* are the monsters; kind of like the Don Dohler version of **E.T.**

As in **THE ALIEN FACTOR**, John Cosentino created the monster suit. This time it was worn by Glenn Barnes, Don's half-brother. I remember we had to take special care to hide the zippers after getting Glenn inside the suit. It was so hard to get on and off that Glenn had to stay in it all day. I don't remember how we dealt with bathroom issues, but I do remember Glenn couldn't sit down, so he would take the head off and smoke a cigarette while leaning against something. I wonder if any photos exist of that...

Like most Dohler films, **THE GALAXY INVADER** was far from polished, but we were all incredibly proud to be making this movie. Everyone was treated like a member of the family, and like a family we had each other's backs and pitched-in where needed. Don was also very open to collaboration, and graciously let this green college student suggest shots during filming. Everyone had a great time on set, and I have a lot of fond memories of this shoot. It's funny how this film has developed such a cult following over the years, and I still run into people who see it listed on my IMDb page and tell me how much they love it.

BLOOD MASSACRE
USA, 1991

This film has an interesting story behind it. It's the one that actually caused Don Dohler to throw up his hands in defeat and walk away from making movies! **BLOOD MASSACRE** was written and rushed into production after the funding for what was to be his next feature after **THE GALAXY INVADER**, an unmade horror film entitled "GRAVEYARD", fell through. Wanting to keep up his momentum and thinking the funding problems were only temporary, Don threw together the production of **BLOOD MASSACRE** in the interim. Once again I was onboard this newest production, and for the first time we shot on ¾-inch video instead of 16mm film. This was born out of necessity due to budgetary limitations, and because I was also out of school by this point, we didn't have access to the University's camera equipment if needed.

This first version of **BLOOD MASSACRE** started out with a gang of thugs robbing a video store. The video store was actually owned by one

of my film teachers, Michael Wilson, and Don let me have a little cameo in the scene of a guy stealing videotapes. I don't remember if we had people killed in the video store during the first version, or if that was only in the second...but the gang flees afterwards, only to have their car break down out in the middle of nowhere. They flag down a passing car, take a woman hostage and force her to take them to her house. Once there, they hold the family hostage while they plan their next move. Like the antiheroes in **FROM DUSK TILL DAWN** (1996, USA, D: Robert Rodriguez), our gang find themselves out of the frying pan and into the fire when it's revealed that the seemingly normal family they are holding hostage are actually cannibalistic maniacs!

Top & Above: The title skull-faced alien monster and United Home Video's 1987 domestic VHS cover for the same film

As the film was nearing completion, the backers asked to see a rough cut of what we had completed to date. They were so impressed with what they saw that they asked Don to draw-up another budget, this time to shoot the film on actual 16mm film stock. It was late fall at this point, and another Maryland winter would soon be upon us, so Don shut down production. He wanted to keep me busy, so he offered me the Assistant Director position for "GRAVEYARD" and asked me to break down the script and put together a budget. His hope was that he could go directly into production on "GRAVEYARD" after the film version of **BLOOD MASSACRE** wrapped. However, during this down time, I had some opportunities open up in Los Angeles, so I moved out there before the second version of **BLOOD MASSACRE** began filming.

Once filming resumed, Don had to recast a lot of the roles. People who were available for the first film were unavailable for the second, so Don tweaked the script and shuffled people around. One good thing that came out of this is that George Stover went from being a supporting player to that of the lead. He was now Rizzo, the crazy Vietnam vet and all-round loose cannon. This was quite a departure for George, who is one of the nicest, most mild-mannered guys you'll ever meet. George rose to the occasion, and turned in the best performance of his career.

Things were going smoothly, but that fickle bitch Fate had to rear her ugly head... Right while Don was in the final stages of editing, the money people asked him for the film negative and work print. Don was uneasy, but contractually he had to comply. Besides, he was given assurances that they were only needed to seal a distribution deal, and that they would be returned to him safe and sound. But it never happened... The film and the backers *disappeared*. Don was devastated. He had spent over a year working on two films and had

AF2:TAR's alien kill-beast definitely smiles with its mouth (i.e., teeth), but *never* its eyes

nothing to show for it. Don said at the time, "This is just too aggravating, the Hell with this!" and he walked away from filmmaking for almost 15 years. In 1991, **BLOOD MASSACRE** resurfaced with a small company that specialized in porn films actively shopping it around. The camera negative had been damaged and was now lost, and only the battered work-print survived. In 2005, the rights to the film lapsed and Don was able to get it back. He did some reediting and tried to fix things up, but the film would never be as he had originally intended. "GRAVEYARD", the movie he was hoping to make after **BLOOD MASSACRE**, never got made, and it remains unproduced to this day.

ALIEN FACTOR 2: THE ALIEN RAMPAGE

USA, 2001

Despite its title making it seem like a sequel to his directorial debut, AF2:TAF came about as its own unique beast in Don Dohler's loose "alien" tetralogy. It was Fred Olen Ray who christened the film **ALIEN FACTOR 2**. Don had conceived it as a standalone film, but Ray, who had recently bought-up the rights to **THE ALIEN FACTOR**, felt that by marketing it as a sequel they could take advantage of the built-in name recognition. As you now know, Don Dohler was in a state of hiatus at this time. I'm sure he missed filmmaking, but each film he made took a little bit more out of him. His crew didn't know, but Don *hated* directing. He much preferred to be behind the camera or in the editing room instead. So those in the know were wondering if he would ever direct another feature. But then Don got a call from out of the blue, from lawyer/amateur filmmaker Joel Denning. It seems that Denning had just bought a 16mm camera and a new Mac with the requisite film editing software, and he wanted to show Don what they were capable of. Don left the meeting excited at the prospect of editing a film and seamlessly inserting special effects, and all done from a home computer, yet. It was "D.I.Y." Dohler's dream come true! So he knocked out a script entitled "Alien Rampage".

The basic story concerns a female alien whose ship has "run out of gas", so to speak, so she needs to land on Earth for a fill-up. Naturally, the police and FBI become involved, and when she is captured, this triggers a response from her intergalactic protector still on the ship. Think Gort from **THE DAY THE EARTH STOOD STILL** (1951, USA, D: Robert Wise) crossed with the Predator and

Pumpkinhead. This creature lowers a force-field over the town, trapping everyone inside. He then goes on a laser-tag killing spree, zapping everyone he comes in contact with. Will the townsfolk survive? And where are the trigger-happy rednecks when you need them??!!

This would prove to be Don Dohler's last movie shot on film stock, as well as his last as a director. He did step in and help direct **DEAD HUNT** (2007, USA), but he really was just helping to keep that film on schedule when director Joe Ripple (an actor on **AF2:TAF**) had to miss some shooting days. **DEAD HUNT** doesn't *feel* like a Dohler film, either. He wore a couple different hats on the film: producer, editor, co-director, cameraman; yet it *still* doesn't have that Dohler feel. (It's all yours, Joe Ripple!)

As with most of Don's movies, 50% of the budget goes to film stock and processing (if not more), which doesn't leave much left over for the meat and potatoes of a film. But somehow "D.I.Y." Dohler pulls it all together and puts it up there on the screen, for better or for worse.

Don Dohler died on December 2nd, 2006 after being diagnosed with melanoma, five years after helming **ALIEN FACTOR 2**.

He may not have been the best filmmaker around, but he *loved* movies. And those of us who had the honor and pleasure to know him and work with him, our lives are that much richer because of him. The best lesson I learned from working with Don is to think on my feet. Time is money. If there is a problem on set, think fast, think creatively, and *fix* it. *That* is the legacy of "D.I.Y." Dohler.

[R.I.P., Don! – From the Monster! *Crew]*

Above: The domestic DVD cover for AF2:TAR "borrows" it's central image from the Euro poster art for **HUMANOIDS FROM THE DEEP** (1980, USA)

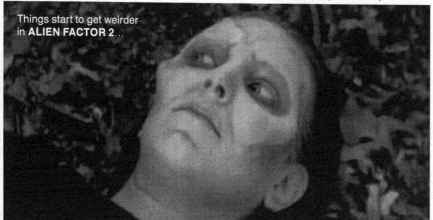

Things start to get weirder in **ALIEN FACTOR 2**...

The Men Themselves: George Stover and Don Dohler *[above]* discuss **THE GALAXY INVADER**'s script between takes

The Monster Itself: The same film's beastie gets a scratchy C/U

GEORGE STOVER:
Baltimore's Most Famous Character Actor
by Kevin Klemm

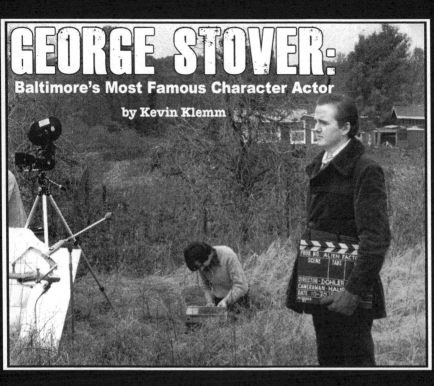

George Stover's early years were spent like a lot of us: watching old sci-fi and horror films on TV and then creating a fanzine to talk about them. *Black Oracle* arrived on the zine scene in 1969, and continued on-and-off until 1978. It featured interviews with such horror icons as Robert Bloch, Forrest J. Ackerman and Peter Cushing. Baltimore area soon-to-be-filmmaker Don Dohler heard about George and his work with *Black Oracle*, and sent him a letter. The two became fast friends, and they went on to work on ten films together over the next 30 years. Although George is most often associated with the films of Don Dohler, he actually got his start with another Baltimore area filmmaker: John Waters.

Stover caught the acting bug in college, acting in various stage productions, local commercials and industrial films, but Baltimore in the early '70s was not exactly a hotbed of feature film production. So George worked a series of regular fulltime jobs, eventually settling into a job with the local DMV (Department of Motor Vehicles), and later with the State of Maryland Insurance Commission, where he stayed until retirement a few years ago. In 1970, John Waters started shooting a series of transgressive feature films, such as **MULTIPLE MANIACS** and **PINK FLAMINGOS** (1972, both USA). But

it was an article on Waters in the *Baltimore Sun* around 1974 that caught George's attention. John, who was shooting his newest feature (**FEMALE TROUBLE**), mentioned therein that it was hard to fill straight-looking character roles in his movies because he typically filled those roles with his friends, and all his friends had long hair—or even *blue* hair!—or generally didn't look like a cop or a school teacher. George figured he had the straight-laced look down pat, so he hit the phonebook to see if he could track down this elusive filmmaker. As it turned out, he was able to get a hold of John Waters' mother, who in turn gave George her son's address. George mailed off a letter of introduction, along with a headshot, and got offered the part of the priest who leads Divine's condemned character to the electric chair. It was his first feature film credit, and since then he has appeared in over 80 more films. In kind of an interesting sidenote, after meeting with John Waters, George realized that he and John had been in the same 8th-grade homeroom class back in the day.

Over the last 42 years, George Stover has been the character actor of choice with local filmmakers. He has played everything under the sun, including doctors, priests, security guards, sheriffs, professors, even the President of the United States himself. As well as playing the kindly grandpa, Stover has also played a murderous psychopath, but in person he is one of the kindest, most unassuming people you could ever hope to meet. But he also has strength and courage in him as well, and it was those two traits which once helped him survive and recover from a terrifying encounter...

It was approaching midnight on February 26th, 2012 when George Stover arrived home to find an armed burglar sitting on the inside stairs as he walked into his house. The burglar, named Bradford Steven Holup, a career criminal with a history of violent crime, first threatened George by firing a shot into a living room chair, then demanded money. George took him to his safe and gave him what he asked for, all the while trying to talk his way out of a very bad situation. But things went south very quickly... After the holdup, Holup wanted to lock George up so he could make his getaway. The only problem was that there were no locks on the bedroom doors. So Holup decided to march George down into the basement and then lock the door. But then at some point while this was happening, he decided he didn't want to leave a witness. As George was walking down the basement stairs, Holup attempted to shoot him in the back of the head. Luckily for George, Holup was a bad shot, and he only grazed his neck. George slumped down on the stairs and Holup, thinking he had killed him, made his escape. Due

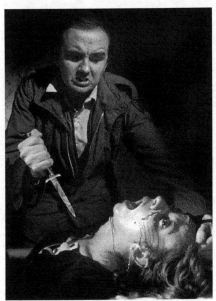

The ordinarily well-mannered Geo. Stover blatantly disregards *M!*'s strict "No Slashers Allowed!" rule in **BLOOD MASSACRE**

to the auto club lock on his victim's steering wheel, Holup was unable to steal George's car, so instead ran off on foot. Since the basement door was left unlocked by the criminal, the wounded George was able to make his way upstairs to a phone and call 911. Holup was caught four hours later, and was eventually sentenced to life in prison without the possibility of parole. George has since recovered, and now, as a retired man of leisure, he has more time to focus on those things he loves: his model trains and his movies.

We reached out to George to see how he's doing and to talk to him specifically about his work with Don Dohler.

M!: In 1978, you acted in Don Dohler's first film, THE ALIEN FACTOR and then went on to appear in every one of his films up until his death in 2006. How did this collaboration come about?

GS: Back in 1972, an article was published about me in one of our Baltimore newspapers, *The Evening Sun*, and the article discussed the fanzine *Black Oracle* that I published. Don Dohler read that article and tracked me down, and we discovered we had a lot in common. He talked about his plans to publish his own zine called *Cinemagic*. Eventually, we got on the subject of making movies, and Don told me that he had made some 8mm silent shorts, but he really wanted to make a full-length science fiction movie with sound. I had already done some plays, and would soon make my movie debut in early 1974 in John Waters' **FEMALE TROUBLE**. I was interested in pursuing acting, and eventually, **THE ALIEN FACTOR** came about, with shooting beginning in late 1976. Filming continued into 1977, and the movie was released in 1978.

Do you have any favorite memories about Don and his films?

Well, just that we got along very well with one another. And there seemed to be camaraderie among cast and crew in those days that I don't always see today. Don saved the best of the bloopers, and would almost always make a blooper reel for each of his movies. They were a hit at the premieres of each film, and now most of these blooper reels turn up on the DVDs. In addition to his filmmaking, Don helped me when I upgraded *Black Oracle* and changed the title to *Cinemacabre*. This was the era before home computers and desktop publishing, and Don was very knowledgeable about the publishing business.

Acting was not your fulltime gig—what was your regular job?

Between the acting, and publishing *Black Oracle* and *Cinemacabre*, and running a mail order videotape business, a lot of people are surprised to learn that I still had a regular job. But acting and publishing and selling VHS tapes just didn't pay the bills! I put in thirty years as an employee of the State of Maryland. Initially, I worked at the Department of Motor Vehicles, and later at the Maryland Insurance Administration. One good thing about this type of government employment was that I could take time off on short notice, and my absence didn't have a great impact on anyone else. So if an audition or an acting gig came along, I could easily take some annual leave. Most of the feature films were shot on weekends, but auditions and acting gigs in local training films or commercials were usually during the work week.

What did your co-workers think of your film work?

For the longest time, no one knew. Then someone was at the library and saw a picture of me in makeup in the book *Filmmakers Guide to Super-8*, and it became known around the office that I was an aspiring thespian. Some people never brought the subject up with me, while others were curious and asked a few questions. However, very few were interested enough to actually sit down and *watch* one of these movies! *[Laughs]* It was then that I learned that a lot of folks just don't appreciate low-budget, independently-made movies! Some people restrict their movie watching to the big-budget Hollywood films with the big stars. But that's okay. Different strokes for different folks.

I worked with you on two films, GALAXY INVADER and the first shoot of BLOOD MASSACRE. One thing that always stuck with me was what a nice down-to-earth guy you are, and how you were game to do anything Don asked of you. In particular, I remember a scene in BLOOD MASSACRE where you were caught in a rope trap. I was one of the guys who pulled the rope to hang you upside-down from a tree. It hurt your ankles and you were upside-down for multiple takes... Was that one of the hardest shoots for you?

During that scene in **BLOOD MASSACRE**, It wasn't easy to be down-to-earth when I was hanging upside-down off the ground! So *YOU* were the guy pulling that rope! *[Laughs]* Yes, that was one of my most difficult shoots! *Ever!!* It was very uncomfortable being upside-down and, as I recall, the shoot lasted all night long until dawn. There was no place to wash up, so I had to drive home with all that sticky blood all over my face. I'm

Right, Top to Bottom: *It's Not The Size That Counts!* Issues #2 (September 1969), #10 (Spring 1977) and #8 (Fall 1974) of Geo. Stover's mighty mini-zine, which, while small in its dimensions loomed large in its quality of contents (depicted cover art, respectively, by Kenneth Hodge, T.J. Johnson and Jim Rehak)

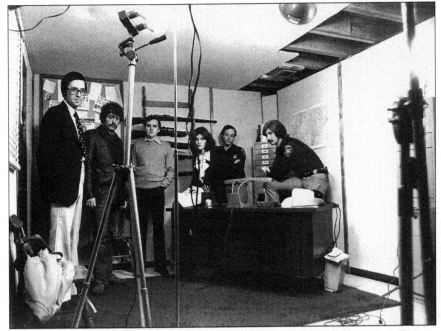

Above: *[from left to right]* Cast members Dick "Count Gore de Vol" Dyszel (Mayor Bert Wicker), Don Leifert (Benjamin Zachary), George Stover (Steven), Mary Mertens (Edie Martin), Richard Geiwitz (Deputy Pete) and Tom Griffith (Sheriff Jack Cinder) congregate on the set of **THE ALIEN FACTOR** (1978)

glad I wasn't stopped by a policeman, or I would certainly have had a *lot* of explaining to do!

Filmmaking has radically changed over the years. The early films you worked on were shot on 16mm film; then came video, now digital HD. The content has also progressed from the "PG" feel of Don Dohler's early work to the gratuitous nudity of a film like VAMPIRE SISTERS. Which do you prefer? Don himself was never comfortable with nudity; he liked to emulate the movies he grew up with. If he were alive, would he still be making films?

As far as technology is concerned, I'm an old film guy. I look back fondly at the days of motion picture film and the noise made by a movie running through a projector. I was saddened when I read that 35mm motion picture cameras were no longer being manufactured, and when I read about movie theaters converting to digital. Granted, film is costlier than digital HD and is harder to edit and more expensive to ship to the theaters, but I kind of miss film. I guess someone like Quentin Tarantino also shares my views, or he wouldn't have released **THE HATEFUL EIGHT** in 70mm in select theaters! And as far as content is concerned, I certainly don't mind gratuitous nudity or gore, especially since those elements are

usually needed to sell a low-budget independent movie. Perhaps I would prefer that a movie not contain such elements…and I wish that they *could* be more like the horror and science fiction movies that I watched while growing up. But it's a different world now, for better or for worse, and if a low-budget independent movie is too tame, it might never get released. Don used the "tame" approach at first, but he finally acquiesced in **NIGHTBEAST** with that nude scene involving the sheriff and his deputy. And **NIGHTBEAST** also has its fair share of gore. Like me, Don grew up when horror and sci-fi movies did not contain nudity or gore. However, he eventually realized that modern audiences like those elements. If he were still alive, I'm sure he would still be making movies, as long as he could raise the money to make them. Instead of getting friends and family to invest directly into one of his projects, he might be raising money on one of those fundraising websites that people use these days!

You were very close with Don. What kind of person was he? How did he touch your life?

Don was a very mild-mannered person, and I never saw him lose his temper. He was very easy to work with and very easy to get along with. He was definitely in the top five as far as people who changed or shaped

218

Top: On the set of **THE GALAXY INVADER** (1985), "D.I.Y." Dohler takes a light-reading while remaining professionally oblivious to the hideous extraterrestrial brute standing mere inches from him. **Above:** The titular intergalactic interloper (Glenn Barnes), with Geo. Stover (holding sphere; no, it's *not* a softball!) and crew members on the set of the same film. **Right:** The late, great Don Dohler (1946-2006) behind the rig during the same film shoot

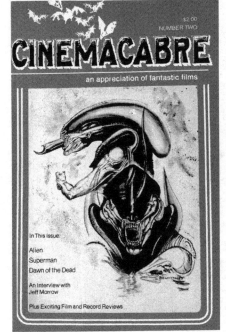

Stover's other horror/monster/fantasy movie zine, this one a digest closer to *Monster!*'s page-size. **Top:** #1, Winter 1975 (art unsigned). **Above:** #2 (art by Bill Levers)

my life, professionally speaking. Don—along with John Waters—allowed me to be in several movies when my prior acting experience had only been in plays. Some of these films have become "cult movies" over the years, and they still seem to have people interested in them. Just to cite one example, **THE ALIEN FACTOR** was recently released on Blu-ray, and all 1,000 copies in the first pressing sold out in a few short weeks. Most of the promotion was on Facebook, and from a few websites that reviewed it….and the only place it was sold was on Amazon.

Don Dohler has passed away, so has fellow actor Don Leifert, and you survived a nearly fatal encounter with a burglar a few years ago. How have these losses and your own brush with death changed you?

Well, these kinds of things make a person realize how temporary and uncertain life really is. One must not take anything for granted, because everything we know and love will not always be around. And if they *are* around, *we* might not be around to enjoy them! One must try to enjoy each day and make the most of our limited time here on Earth.

As you look back over your career, any regrets? Would you do anything differently?

I'm not one to look back and dwell on what I should have done or could have done. If I had my life to live over again, I would probably just end up making the same mistakes, or having the same fears, et cetera as I did the first time around. *[Laughs]* And, just like in the song "My Way"… *"Regrets, I've had a few, but then again, too few to mention…!"*

Lastly, after 42 years in the business and with 84 movies under your belt, any advice for young actors or filmmakers that are just starting out?

Well, one thing I would recommend is to have a backup profession. Don't count on acting or filmmaking to pay all your bills. In my case, I've had a few paying gigs along the way but, unfortunately, never enough such gigs to support myself. Acting has really only been a glorified hobby for me, but luckily I was in some low-budget independent movies that have withstood the test of time, giving me some notoriety that I would never have enjoyed by just doing locally-produced plays. It's always interesting to read what people write on Facebook about these films! Ironically, the paying gigs I've had are the gigs that no one will ever see—outdated training films, or local commercials, or old PBS TV shows. And the cult movies I've been in—which have a *lot* of visibility—are gigs for which I received zero or only very little money!!!

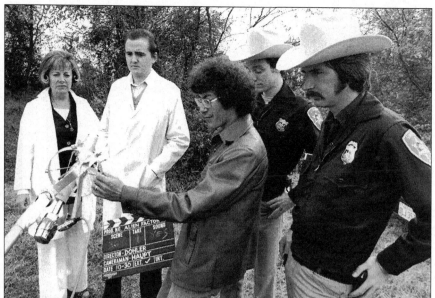

Top: *[from left to right]* Anne Frith (Ruth Sherman, M.D.), George Stover (her on-screen nephew/assistant Steven), director Don Dohler (who also played the bit-part of an ineffectual local yokel "monster hunter" who gets felled by the Inferbyce's pincer in the film), Richard Geiwitz (Deputy Pete) and Tom Griffith (Sheriff Cinder) on the set of **THE ALIEN FACTOR**. **Above:** Another shot from the **TAF** set, showing additional crew members. **Right:** George, with **THE GALAXY INVADER** itself, in promo hype for *MST3K*

WHAT SORT OF MAN READS WORLD OF HORROR?

At work or play, competition is the name of his game. In the working world his future is assured and he's a can — do man, with an eye on the top job. FACT: World of Horror is read by 13 adult males engaged in professional, managerial, or technical occupations and the World of Horror reader has that extra spending power a higher income affords. If you happen to be advertising wise, the magazine to use is World of Horror. FACT: World of Horror is purchased by 2 advertising managers, both earning over £800 per annum. (Source: 1974 Clergymen for Creatures report).

New York. Chicago. London. Tokyo. High Wycombe. Berlin. Paris.

MONSTER MAGAZINES THAT TIME FORGOT:
WORLD OF
HORROR

by John Harrison

Back in *Monster!* #28/29 I took a look at *Shriek!*, a short-lived monster magazine that ran for only four issues between 1965 and 1967, and which was somewhat unique in that it was put together in the UK yet aimed at (and distributed to) the American market. This time around, I'd like to cast my eye over another somewhat forgotten monster magazine that also originated out of England, but had a more traditional publishing network, in that it was produced for the local British horror-loving crowd and was not initially distributed in the US (though it did make it to Australia, as I managed to find several copies of it at local secondhand bookstores when I was a kid).[1]

Published by the Gresham Publishing Group in London, the first issue of *World of Horror* debuted on the stands in 1974, though no month or year of publication is noted anywhere on the cover or interior, a fact which led to both Bob Michelluci's *Collector's Guide to Monster Magazines* (1977, second edition 1988) and Michael W. Pierce's *Monsters Among Us* (1995, second edition 2000) incorrectly giving the magazine a "1972" start date. That presumed '72 date was possibly due to the first issue covering a couple of films from that year—including **DRACULA A.D. 1972** (1972, UK) and **CONQUEST OF THE PLANET OF**

Fangs For The Memory: Seeing this old cover of *WoH* #1 from 1974 again after all these years is enough to make an over-the-hill Monster Kid get a warm, fuzzy feeling inside! (*Sigh...*)

1   Back before I emigrated to Canada with my parents and two kid brothers in 1976 from Swansea, (South) Wales in the UK, I too bought *WoH* as a kid whenever I was lucky enough to find a copy—and happened to have enough pocket money to buy it with, of course. Then in my early teens, I managed to get my hands on several issues of the mag, but I ended up chopping them to pieces and sticking all the cool pictures into scrapbooks, thus ruining the mags! However, about ten years ago while browsing in a Toronto used bookstore, I was lucky enough to score used copies of three different issues, all in virtually mint condition, yet. And they only cost me a mere five bucks (Canuck) a pop, too. Ain't it great when blasts from the past come at such nice prices?! (Just for the record, the issues I scored were #3, #7 and #9, all of whose covers I scanned specially to include with John's article here) ~ SF.

THE APES (1972, USA)—and discussing them as if they were new releases; but the issue also covers later films like the Hammer duo **FRANKENSTEIN AND THE MONSTER FROM HELL** and **CAPTAIN KRONOS, VAMPIRE HUNTER** (both 1974, UK). It's always possible that this first issue was pieced together over a period of time, thus adding to the confusion.

Along with the absence of any publication date, no editorial staff credits are provided anywhere in the first issue of *World of Horror* either, though that

An eye-catching ad from the back pages of *WoH* #5. Amongst numerous other heavily-abridged 8mm home movie reels, *M!* co-ed Steve formerly owned 200-ft. versions of the first and last two pairs of titles shown in the second row of box-tops above, plus a virtually incomprehensible mere 50-ft. reel (just over 2 minutes long!) of the first title in the top row

changed with issue number two, with one Gent Shaw being named as the magazine's editor ("Gent Shaw" turned out to be a pseudonym for Canadian Jim Shier, who is also listed under his real name as the Advertisement Manager).

Published on semi-gloss paper with a substantial amount of color, and in a slightly taller format than most standard monster magazines, *World of Horror* was certainly an eye-catching publication, featuring a nice mixture of *Famous Monsters-*

style nostalgia with the more gruesome modern horror that was becoming prevalent by the early 'Seventies, as well as including some original short fiction and art. Being a British magazine, Hammer Horror naturally has a strong presence within the pages of *World of Horror*, and despite its title it also delved into sci-fi territory on occasion, with cover features devoted to *Star Trek* (in #4) and **BATTLE FOR THE PLANET OF THE APES** (in #5), as well as several articles over the course of the magazine's run about *Doctor Who* and the various creatures that appeared on the long-running series. The magazine at times ventured even further from horror territory with articles on films like Irwin Allen's disaster classic **THE TOWERING INFERNO** (1972, USA).

For their covers, *World of Horror* eschewed the use of any original art and relied instead on bold, full-page photographs, usually featuring a close-up of a character's face—be it Christopher Lee's lightning-charred features from the climax of **THE SCARS OF DRACULA** (1970, UK), Leonard Nimoy's Spock from TV's *Star Trek* (1966-69, USA), or John Huston's stately Lawgiver from **BATTLE FOR THE PLANET OF THE APES** (1973, USA).

Along with the expected range of Hammer and Vincent Price movies, *World of Horror* also covered some more eclectic material, including the Loch Ness Monster and horror cinema from Mexico and Japan, as well as some racier and more adult-oriented titles, like **FLESH FOR FRANKENSTEIN** (*Il mostro è in tavola...barone Frankenstein*, 1973, USA/Italy/France) and the softcore sci-fi spoof **FLESH GORDON** (1974, USA).

My own personal favorite issue of *World of Horror* is #9, its last, mainly because of its cover feature on Sheila Keith, a highly talented Scottish-born actress who was older than the usual "scream queen" and was a memorable presence in a number of British exploitation/horror films directed by Pete Walker, including **HOUSE OF WHIPCORD** (1974), **FRIGHTMARE** (a.k.a. **COVER UP**, 1974) and **HOUSE OF MORTAL SIN** (a.k.a. **THE CONFESSIONAL**, 1976). **FRIGHTMARE** itself had previously been covered in a two-page spread in *WoH* #6, which featured a great cover photo of Vincent Price as Dr. Phibes.

Elsewhere in issue nine we have a six-page article on the first lady of European horror, the enigmatic Barbara Steele, which is nicely illustrated and gives a decent overview of her genre career to that date, though author Gary Farfitt trashes her appearance in Jonathan Demme's then-recent **CAGED HEAT**

Top: As with just about every other '70s horror movie mag, British or otherwise, so it seems, Chris Lee as Drac also graced the cover of *WoH #2*. **Above:** An 'orrible Orc-like Ogron (brutish alien anthropoids seen in the Jon Pertwee-era *Doctor Who* serials "Day of the Daleks" [1972] and "Frontier in Space" [1973]) uglies-up the cover of *WoH #3* just lovely

GIANT COLOUR
DRACULA
PIN-UP INSIDE

Top Left: *WoH* #9's creepy cover girl was (quote) "distaff Karloff" Sheila "**FRIGHTMARE**" Keith, whose first name was conspicuously misspelled as "Shelia" *[sic]* both right on the cover and inside the magazine! **Top Right:** Issue #7's cover bore a photo of a "homemade" skeletal, Death-like figure. **Above Left:** The first issue of a "one-sheet" horror/fantasy mag which folded-out to become a giant-size—and sometimes quite gruesome—wall poster. **Above Right:** A typical page layout from *World of Horror* hyping a then-recent genre theatrical release, this one from Amicus, featuring scream queen Stephanie Beacham and a crawling hand (identified as **CAGED WOMEN** therein [1974, USA]), dismissing it as a role she must have taken purely for the money.

World of Horror certainly didn't take itself too seriously, as evidenced by the occasional "Monster Madness" features, where humorous captions and dialogue balloons were added to full-page B&W stills from various horror flicks (*à la* US publications like the 1966 one-shot *Monster Howls* and Marvel's *Monsters to Laugh With / Monsters Unlimited / Monster Madness* titles). Attempts at a *Mad* magazine-style of satire can also be seen on the back covers of several issues, which feature parodic advertisements asking, *"What Sort of Man Reads World of Horror?"*

Regular or semi-regular columns and features in *World of Horror* included a "Book Corner", the "Scream Scene" news section, a classifieds page where readers could buy, swap and sell their monster goodies, the "Mail Bag" (which, as its masthead, used an altered photo of Harryhausen's Cyclops with a mail-bag slung over its shoulder), and, most interestingly, a fanzine review page, which covered small press/D.I.Y. publications like George Stover's *Black Oracle* (see p.217), Gary Svehla's *Gore Creatures* (later to become known as *Midnight Marquee*) and the lesser-known *Starzine*. Interestingly and amusingly enough, *WoH* #6's fanzine section very prematurely announced that Richard Klemensen's long-running *Little Shoppe of Horrors* had (quote) "at last given up the ghost"— and yet the magazine is still going strong 40 years later in 2016! Another regular *WoH* feature was their "Scream Queens" profile, usually just a single photo of a given actress, which featured names like Valli Kemp (from **DR. PHIBES RISES AGAIN** [1972, UK]), Julie Ege (from **CREATURES THE WORLD FORGOT** [1971, UK]), Marlene Clark (from **THE BEAST MUST DIE** [1974, UK]) and, of course, Ingrid Pitt (from **THE VAMPIRE LOVERS** [1970, UK/USA]).

Advertisements were a big part of any classic monster magazine, and *World of Horror* was no exception. Apart from offering back issues and hawking other titles from the same publisher (like *Mystic* and *Witchcraft*), *WoH* didn't have their own in-house mail order department *à la* Warren's Captain Company or *Castle of Frankenstein*'s back pages, but it did feature advertisements for a number of products offered up by various sellers, including such groovy and gruesome goodies as Christopher Lee Dracula T-shirts and the Hammer *Dracula* LP narrated by Lee (reviewed by myself back in *Monster!* #18 [p.5]), Super 8mm horror home movies (of course), and publications like The

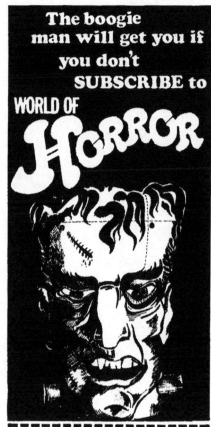

Hey all you Monster Kids, don't forget to renew your subscription to *World of Horror*! (Uh-oh, too late… Make that *40+ years* too late! ☹)

Devil's Prayerbook ("Contains full accounts on the practices of English witches"). The back cover of the debut issue featured a terrific advertisement for horror and black magic paperbacks published by the (in)famous New English Library (NEL).

By the time issue #8 saw print, *World of Horror* was clearly struggling. The interior still had color, but a lot less of it. The semi-gloss paper was replaced by cheaper newsprint on the B&W pages, and the magazine was noticeably a lot slimmer, its page-count down by 14. After the magazine folded with issue #9, editor Jim Shier returned with *Legend Horror Classics*, a publication in the poster magazine format that was popular in the UK during the 1970s (the ultra-gory *Monster Mag* was in a similar vein). Featuring horror comic strips (most of them drawn by Kevin O'Neill) that folded-out and had a large monster photo-portrait poster printed on the reverse, *Legend Horror Classics* enjoyed a decent run of 12 issues, with the last three issues being specials that focused on vampires, werewolves and the Frankenstein monster respectively.

With its nice range of coverage, touches of humor, British flavor and original art and fiction (if of varying quality), *World of Horror* certainly made for a welcome addition to the monster magazine landscape of the early 1970s, and is one well worth seeking out and adding to the collection if you find copies cheap enough (at the time of this writing, several issues were available on eBay at "Buy It Now" prices (between just $5.00 and $10.00 [US] each).

MONSTER! Public Service posting: Title availability of films reviewed or mentioned in this issue of MONSTER!
Information dug up and presented by Steve Fenton and Tim Paxton.

*Thanks to **Dennis Capicik** (as per usual, bless 'im!) and **Les Moore** (who we admittedly do take a bit too much for granted around here, but he's used to it by now [sucker!]) for lending us an always-appreciated assist with compiling the vid info this issue, as well as in the process injecting his own personal critical comments pertaining to the films in question (Les is a BIG Don Dohler fan from way back, hence his quite longish entries about the man's movies printed hereunder, with which we gave him free rein. When he found out we were running some coverage of DD's work this ish, he as good as begged us to let him contribute something on the subject, so we said he was welcome to, with the stipulation that he cover some other of this ish's titles besides, which he did). Incidentally, Monster! would like to encourage other contributors here and now to provide readers with as-reliable-and-up-to-date-as-possible video availability information pertaining to the films they write about within our pages. We're not asking for masses of detail (we can fill in many of the details ourselves, if needs be), just at least a source for whatever copy or edition you happened to watch for review purposes herein, plus any other pertinent data you can think of mentioning and/or interesting trivia.*

100 MONSTERS (1968) *[p.82]* – ADV ad-line: *"A Fantastic World Unlike Anything You Have Ever Seen! A Breathtaking World Inhabited By The Strangest Creatures You Will Ever See! Many Legends, But Only One Message: Heed The Spirits, Or Face Their Wrath!"* As well as this the first instalment, A.D. Vision (ADV) Films/Rubbersuit Pictures' domestic N. American DVD set of Daiei's late '60s *yōkai* trilogy (*"All Three Individual Films In One Complete Collection"*) also includes Pts. 2+3, **SPOOK WARFARE** (妖怪大戦争 / *Yōkai daisensō*, 1968) and **JOURNEY WITH GHOST ALONG YOKAIDO ROAD** (東海道お化け道中 / *Tōkaidō obake dōchō*, a.k.a. **ALONG WITH GHOSTS**, 1969, both Japan), all of which were also released separately by ADV on disc in the early 2000s. In their country of origin, the same titles are also all available both individually and collectively as a set via Daiei Video, but we are unsure at this time whether said releases come with English subtitles. Released in Australia in 2006, the trilogy is also *in esse* from Siren Visual Entertainment / Madman Entertainment.

THE ALIEN DEAD (1980) *[p.77]* – The disreputable Genesis label's cheapo '80s VHS cover-blurb: *"They're Consuming Every Creature In Sight!"* Excerpts from Academy's cover copy: *"The Bodies Are Dead: The Remains Live On... [...] Zombies and ghouls...an army of Alien Dead spreading out like locusts, butchering and devouring everything in their path. You may not have heard of them...but they'll find you!"* Retromedia's Blu-ray tagline: *"They Came From Outer Space To Eat The Living!"* Presented widescreen, said Retromedia Blu is without doubt the best way to view this title that has thus far been released, and shall likely remain so. Alternately known as **IT FELL**

Japanese DVD cover for **100 MONSTERS**

FROM THE SKY and—my personal fave of all its a.k.a.'s—**SWAMP OF THE BLOOD LEECHES**, this first solo feature from F.O. (as in *"FUCK OFF if you don't like it!"*) Ray mines a similar retro/neo-'50s vein as many of Don Dohler's works do, if in a somewhat different manner. Unlike Dohler—evidently simply because he couldn't afford to—Ray typically casts "washed-up" former movie stars prominently in his movies, not just for their name-value, but also because he admires their work personally as a fan as well. And it's a

Top: ADV's stateside DVD set of Daiei's '60s YM trilogy. **Above:** Image Entertainment's 25th Anniversary edition DVD cover (2004)

real treat for old movie buffs that F.O.R. coaxed no less than Olympian gold medalist swimming champ, stuntman and western/sci-fi serial superstar Larry "Buster" Crabbe (1908-1983) out of semi-retirement to appear in a rare role during his twilight years (in '79, the year prior to appearing in the present much lower-profile production, ex-Flash Gordon/Buck Rogers Crabbe—playing an in-joke character named Brigadier Gordon—guest-starred on an episode of TV's *Buck Rogers in the 25th Century* opposite "new Buck" Gil Gerard, which made for a nice nostalgic touch to an otherwise often cheeseball series). Sure, by the time his role in **TAD** rolled around, ol' Buster's acting chops had grown a tad rusty—he was never the greatest of actors technically speaking anyway, primarily being much more of a gung-go/go-for-da-gusto physical action performer—but, being a lifelong athlete, he certainly looks physically robust enough (if a little on the gaunt side), and he musters-up an entertainingly spirited/animated performance as the gruff, no-bullshit sheriff, so we can be thankful that Ray got him to sign on the dotted line for the occasion.

In keeping with its aforementioned catchy **BLOOD LEECHES** a.k.a., which intentionally evokes memories of **ATTACK OF THE GIANT LEECHES** (1959, USA)—known as **DEMONS OF THE SWAMP** in the UK, and whose working title was "ATTACK OF THE BLOOD LEECHES"—the namesake of Crabbe's crusty lawman character in the present film was that earlier one's director, Bernard L. Kowalski (who is also well-known to psychotronic movie freaks'n'geeks for directing another creature feature set in the swamplands, namely his effective man-into-snake shocker **SSSSSSS** [1973, USA], co-starring the great Strother Martin, along with Dirk Benedict and Heather Menzies. Plus, lest we forget, Kowalski's other vital contribution to monster cinema is the Rog & Gene Corman co-production **NIGHT OF THE BLOOD BEAST** [1958, USA], which Yours Truly reviewed back in *Monster!* #17 [p.33]). In addition to name-dropping Kowalski, co-writer/director Ray crams his frequently wittily-written script (jointly penned by Martin Nicholas) with oodles of blatant references to Roger Corman and his films (e.g., Ray Roberts' secondary protagonist "Tom Corman", Mike Bonavia's character "Miller Haze" [= Dick Miller + Jonathan Haze], John Leirier as "Paisley" [after Miller's recurrent in-joke Walter Paisley character], Rich Vogan as "Krelboin" [*(sic)* after Haze's Seymour Krelboyne character in 1960's **THE LITTLE SHOP OF HORRORS**], and Norman Riggins as "Mr. Griffith" [after frequent Corman screenwriter/occasional actor Charles B. Griffith]).

As for the main gist of the storyline, Sheriff Kowalski (Crabbe) has been tasked with keeping the peace in the sleepy southeast US boonies community of Lone Elm. Kowalski suspects that a (quote) "renegade 'gator"—or "renegator", as his smart-aleck deputy (Dennis Underwood) cleverly quips—may be the perpetrator of a spate of killings which leave victims' corpses badly chewed-up and partially devoured. However, city-slicker journalist Tom Corman (Roberts) discredits the rogue alligator theory for the simple reason that the entire local 'gator population has been killed-off and eaten by...*something else*. Yep, you guessed it: *ZOMBIES* are to blame! Although it isn't really dwelled on, the cause of the dead's rising from their watery graves proves to be a radioactive meteorite which had crashed-landed to Earth smack-dab atop a houseboat, whereupon its extraterrestrial radiation had reanimated the corpses of the people aboard who were all killed in the collision (however, none of these potentially costly developments are actually depicted due to the critically low budget, which is otherwise used to wring maximum production values out of minimal funds). Scored with authentic bluegrass/C&W sounds and brimming with convincing rural flavor (e.g., though he only appears in but one scene, "local color" supporting player George Kelsey as crotchety octogenarian swamper Emmet Michaels is a standout character), **TAD** features an onscreen appearance by F.O. Ray himself as a pool-playing redneck with a white cowboy hat.

Despite all appearances in some scenes, while evidently *not* inspired in any way whatsoever by Fulci's **ZOMBIE** (*Zombi 2*, 1979, Italy)—which wasn't first released theatrically in the US until a month after the present film's own premiere—**TAD** was likely influenced in some part by Romero/Argento's **DAWN OF THE DEAD** (*Zombi*, 1978, Italy/USA). An even greater influence still on it seems to have been Ken Wiederhorn's **SHOCK WAVES** (a.k.a. **DEATH CORPS**, 1977, USA), which is especially detectable in shots showing the aquatic zombies (which, needless to say, *aren't* Nazis, as in the Wiederhorn film), bobbing their heads above the water's surface to have a quick look around, before then ducking back out of sight underwater again afterwards. As my learned colleague Christos Mouroukis observes elsewhere in this issue *[see p.78 – ed.]*, some scenes bear a distinct resemblance to—yet actually prefigure—similar ones seen in **ZOMBIE LAKE** (*Le lac des morts vivants*, 1981, France/Spain, Ds: "J.A. Laser"/Jean Rollin, Julian de Laserna); most especially when a purely incidental blonde starlet gets gratuitously topless to go for a semi-skinnydip in the bayou (she shortly doffs her drawers too, albeit with her lower half remaining chastely out-of-frame and underwater the entire time, so no need to get too excited, y'all). Cue the advent of Crabbe's idiotic deputy, who leers at the *au naturel* swimmer while spying on her from out of the undergrowth on the bank with a shit-eating grin on his face. Memorable splatter scenes include a big black dog scavenging among the tangle of guts spilling from a dead man's severed torso, and an old granny getting skewered clear through her abdomen by a pitchfork then getting hoisted in the air like a bale of hay. While staged none-too-convincingly, if nothing else the latter scene deserves mention for its sheer ambitiousness/outrageousness!

For its 'Eighties videocassette release in the Netherlands (as simply **ALIEN DEAD**, in its original English dialogue, w/ Dutch subtitles) by Cannon/Esselte CIC Video—who mistakenly gave the film's year of production/copyright as "1971" in the back cover's fine print—the misleading jacket illustration (a nude photo of what is evidently Laura Gemser [?], of all things!) made it more resemble some softcore porn flick, despite its title.

This VHS release is of indeterminate origin

Much more recently, Retromedia Entertainment issued the film in a domestic Region A Blu-ray edition whose special features include F.O. Ray's "official" directorial debut, the 55-minute B&W feature **THE BRAIN LEECHES** (1978, USA); that film was previously released (in 2004) on both VHS/DVD by Sinister Cinema (ad-line: *"An Odyssey of Terror"*). Incidentally, the **TAD** Blu comes packaged behind lurid "monster-menacing-babe" cover art that originally appeared on AIR Video's domestic jacket for 1987 Beta/VHS release of **BOG** (1978/1983, USA, D: Don Keeslar [see *Monster!* #18, p.19]). Prior to Retro's recent Blu, domestic DVD releases include editions put out by both that same company (in 2003) and by Image Entertainment (as a "25th Anniversary Edition") the following year. In the UK during the '80s, **TAD** was released on Beta/VHS tape by CM Video Productions, bearing an "X" rating on the box, but apparently clocking-in at only 71 minutes, which may mean it was cut (full-length prints reportedly run 74m, although running times on erstwhile video releases sometimes varied quite sharply). During much the same general period (1988-89), it was made available stateside on cassette by infamous no-namers Star Classics in at least two slipcase designs which were completely different from one another. Their '88 release depicted passably-rendered original artwork of a vaguely "EC Comics"-style zombie menacing a pretty girl in a red dress, while Star's subsequent '89 rerelease

Massacre Video's retro "Big Box"
VHS cover

under the same product number (#L1430)—much more notoriously and misleadingly—misused **THE EVIL DEAD** (1981)'s famed cover photo showing a woman being dragged down into a grave by a living corpse's hand clutching at her throat; which, as Tim Paxton will tell you, has been misappropriated for use on more Indian movie posters, lobby cards and VHS/VCD/DVD covers over the years than you can shake a stick at! Star's bogus running time printed on the backs of both these entirely disparate boxes, claimed to be "Approx. 89 min." (which is "only" incorrect by *approximately* 15 minutes!); but then, a generic "90-minute" duration was routinely given on countless video releases of that time, so it wasn't really anything out-of-the-ordinary for total times to be incorrect (either accidentally or intentionally). At various other times domestically during the '80s, the more "reputable" label Academy Home Entertainment (in 1985 [Catalog #1005]) and Genesis Home Video—yet another cut-price and shoddy "sell-through" outfit from rock-bottom—both issued **TAD** on tape; chances are the former's edition was substantially better quality than the latter's, though. I think I may have rented the former version at some point, but can't remember any other details. In the same era, again under the slightly shortened title of **ALIEN DEAD**, it was put out on Anglo (?) VHS tape by a company calling themselves Video Rondo (country of origin indeterminate); their crudely-rendered cover art conspicuously misspelled the star's last name as "Crabe" *[sic!]*. Under that same shorter title, it was also issued on Hispanic VHS (by Cannon/MG Video); once again, that release's precise place of origin (Venezuela? Puerto Rico?) is unknown at this time. ~ **Les Moore**

THE ALIEN FACTOR (1978) *[p.206]* – AVI Video tagline: *"A Galactic Frightmare."* *[Who better to put in his two cents' worth on this issue's clutch of Don Dohler vids than the ever-cost-conscious Les Moore, who chooses his words as economically (if not necessarily always sparingly) as he chooses his movies... Take it away, Les! – ed.]*

This was the film which helped Maryland-born semi-pro (?) actor Don "Ben Zachary" Leifert (1951-2010)—as well as others of his fellow cast members—achieve lasting cult superstardom virtually overnight...okay, maybe not *that* quickly, but nearly 40 years after the fact **TAF**'s players are well-known indeed within "D.I.Y." creature feature circles, and that's surely a damn sight better than being totally forgotten by everybody, right? In an interesting bit of trivia, the name of the small town infested with aliens in **TAF** ("Perry Hill") is highly similar to the one ("Berry Hill") in **MUTILATIONS** (see separate entry below). The plot of an alien spaceship ferrying ferocious extraterrestrial lifeforms from one planet to another which crashes to Earth, so releasing them to run wild on our planet—if in a highly localized regional area—is simple, yet effective, the monster FX are done with enough enthusiasm to allow to overlook their rough edges, and the film is overall difficult to resist (but why ever would you want to?!). It's the best place to start if you want to foster a fondness for Mr. Dohler's works. If you can't get anything out of it, you might just as well give up right there, because you obviously don't (or won't) ever "get" it!

VCI cover blurbs: *"Gripping Sci-Fi Terror From Beyond... The 1950's 'Golden Age of Horror' is brought stunningly up to date in this riveting science fiction thriller!"* The film was released on domestic Betamax/VHS cassette by VCI Home Video/Media Home Entertainment way back in 1984. In the new millennium, it was put out on domestic DVD in a "Super Duper Special Deluxe Edition" by Retromedia as part of their Drive-In Theater line in 2001, then again by them in 2005. The amusing back cover hype to that edition read: *"Alien Monsters Invade Baltimore As A Broken Down Space Ship From Another Galaxy Dumps Its Petting Zoo In Somebody's Backyard!"* Much more recently (in June 2016), Retromedia rereleased **TAF** as a "Limited Edition" Blu-ray numbering a mere 1000 units, each copy individually autographed by actor George Stover; according to what he tells us in the interview with him this ish, all thousand copies sold-out real *fast*, disappearing quicker than hotcakes fresh off the griddle! That 2K HD (1080p) 16x9 widescreen edition's transfer print was scanned directly from Dohler's original 16mm negative (incidentally, evidently at some point [circa the late '70s/early '80s?], the film was released full-length in a 16mm home movie version [label unknown], with sound). In his customer review of the Blu on Amazon, the film's DP Britt McDonough (who originally shot **TAF** on slow-speed, fine-grain Ektachrome reversal film stock using his personal 16mm Bolex SBM camera), "The image quality of this release is light years better than the previous DVD release, which was a bit flat, dark, under-saturated, and very grainy. The images in this Blu-ray are bright, very sharp, and virtually grain-free. Some of the flesh tones are a bit red, and many of the actors are walking around with red noses, but this is because it was very, very cold when we shot the exteriors on this film. [...] I never understood why the older releases looked so bad. Now it looks exactly the way I imagined it when I shot it. [...] Kudos to George Stover, who worked very, very hard to

John Cosentino's 's Zagatile was cover-ghoul on issue #9 (1977) of DD's FX zine

make this happen. If you're a fan of '50s sci-fi, the cinema of Don Dohler, or so-bad-they're-good cult movies, you'll love this!" There are a number of sometimes quite lengthy (i.e., ½-hour+) special features included with Retro's limited Blu edition—which stands as the ultimate/optimal version released to date, and shall probably remain so for many years to come...perhaps even for all time. Bonus features include a commentary track by key cast and crew members; behind-the-scenes footage (6:17); "The Television Years" (38:19); a "Meet the Cast & Crew" featurette (35:22); "**THE ALIEN FACTOR** Reunion" (from 1993 [31:59]); an alternate sequence featuring Ernie Farino's sto-mo Leemoid (2:13), complete with explanatory commentary track; plus a blooper and outtake reel. Both Image Entertainment (in 2004) and Mill Creek Entertainment (in 2011) each alternately issued it on domestic DVD to variable quality levels. Way back in the 1980s, it was issued on domestic N. American videotape (both Betamax and VHS) by Media Home Entertainment. On 1980s Norwegian cassettes, it was known as **SKREKKEN FRA ROMMET**, in its original English dialogue and with Norse hard-subs. There is at least one rip of the entire film on YT, but a better option by far would be scoring yourself a copy of Retro's recent if already-OOP Blu-ray, if you can find one up for grabs. (As of this writing, there were a number of copies of said disc, both used and still-sealed, being offered on eBay, with prices ranging from just a nickel shy of $80.00, all the way up to nearly $170.00; that's in US currency.) ~ **Les Moore**

ALIEN FACTOR 2: THE ALIEN RAMPAGE (2001) *[p.212]* – Retromedia Entertainment's DVD hype: *"It's Happening Again!"* Despite that tagline, this is an in-name-only follow-up to **THE ALIEN FACTOR** (see previous entry above), whose cash-in title was imposed on it by Retro's honcho F.O. Ray for its DVD release by them. In terms of its basic contents, **ALIEN RAMPAGE** perhaps inevitably shares numerous similarities/tropes with DD's other "rampaging-alien-monsters-on-Earth" scenarios. That said, it is totally in keeping with the kind of product which Ray himself has directed over the years (e.g., **BIOHAZARD** [1985, USA; see *Monster!* #20, p.18]), and it looks pretty damn slick by Dohler standards while still retaining that all-important D.I.Y. look and feel.

When a quantity of refined uranium is stolen from a nuclear power plant, the lamming thief does a runner whilst hotly pursued by a pair of federal agents (Patrick Bussink and actor-director Joe Ripple). After they shoot the suspect, she—er, *it*—proves to be what is an evidently female humanoid alien (played mute to eerie effect by LauraLee O'Shell in alternately pale-greenish/bluish facial greasepaint with matching contact lenses). Meanwhile, back at the only-wounded-and-silently-immobile femalien's spacecraft, it known as "The Protector", a monstrous hulking, constantly grinning, big-toothed beast (in actuality a biogenetic cyborg) is automatically unleashed—shades of Klaatu's invincible robotic guardian Gort—and goes on the prowl looking for its missing mastress. While doing so, this endearingly clunky critter ("It must be eight feet tall!") with glowing red eyes begins slaughtering every human being it encounters ("This thing sure is *nasty!*") with its wrist-mounted beam-zapper. The primary setting is Grace Point (*"My*

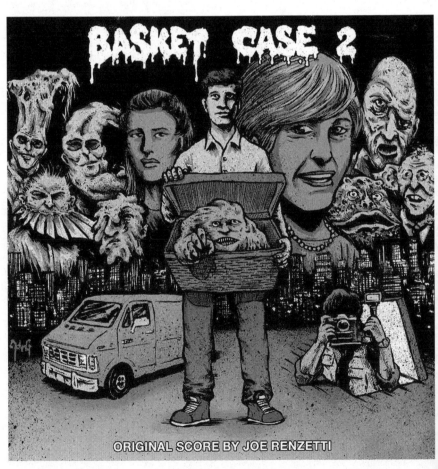

Ship to Shore's limited edition 2016 US vinyl soundtrack album (art by John G.)

God! Are we in redneck hell, or what?!"), a small boondocks burg somewhere in America (evidently the deep south, judging by some of the hillbilly accents heard). This time, in an attempt to keep apace of the more politically correct climate, we get not only a super-bossy black FBI chief (Larry Everett), but also a super-bossy white female sheriff (Donna Sherman), just for good measure. A nighttime human vs. cyborg shootout illuminated by raygun zaps and the muzzle flashes of firearms inevitably recalls a highly similar sequence in **THE GALAXY INVADER** (see separate entry below). As Lisa the heroine, Jaime Kalman gives one of the best performances ever seen in a Dohler flick, it must be said, really getting into her character with conviction. Also in top form giving a likeably naturalistic performance is Geo. Stover, whose character (a uniformed deputy named Mickey) surprisingly actually survives till the end of the movie for once. Doddering around stooped over on a walking cane, long-time DD trouper Anne Frith appears in a couple incidental "comic relief" scenes as Aggie, an unkempt bag lady prone to digging around in dustbins and dumpster-diving (!); it goes without saying that Frith's character winds up getting zapped dead by the beast. Both Richard Ruxton and Glenn Barnes—portrayers of, respectively, one of the human villains and the title creature in afore-cited **THE GALAXY INVADER**—put in reappearances for **AF2:TAR** in supporting roles; the former as a slightly pervy (possible necrophile?) coroner and the latter (who also functioned as the film's sound recordist) as an anonymous bar patron. Do-it-all Dohler's daughter Kim Pfeiffer (*née* Dohler), by this point grown into full adulthood and gotten married, functions as continuity girl as well as playing an extra in a crowd scene. SFX were by DD himself, with miniatures and pyrotechnics by Phil Lister and special makeup by Doug Ulrich (who also wore the cyborg-monster's suit).

Put out on Region 1 DVD in a "Special Deluxe Edition" by Retromedia (@ *www.retromedia. org*) in 2004, it's also been released on disc by them in conjunction with Image Entertainment at some point (?). What was apparently the same version of the film was formerly streamable VOD via Egami on Amazon, but that version is presently (permanently?) unavailable. Its title shortened back to its original form as simply **ALIEN RAMPAGE**, the film has been uploaded with the express permission of its co-executive producer/DP Joel Denning, and is screenable free on YouTube at the official DonDohlerFilms channel (@ *https://www.youtube.com/channel/ UCdPB4a6sZZ6aFy8mZ0wvYvA*), which has also posted very decent uploads of the following

other DD films: **THE ALIEN FACTOR** (see previous entry above), **BLOOD MASSACRE** and **FIEND** (see separate entries below), as well as the backwoods psycho-killer thriller **HARVESTERS** (2001, USA, D: Joe Ripple), on which Don functioned as co-executive producer (as mentioned above, Ripple also plays an acting role in **AF2:TAR**); its co-star Stover was also an associate producer on the production. The present film should not be confused with **METAMORPHOSIS: THE ALIEN FACTOR** (1990, USA, D: Glenn Takakjian), another nominal "sequel" to Dohler's aforementioned **TAF**, whose title always pops up in links (and vice versa) whenever you Google the present film's, so if you weren't paying proper attention it would be easy to mix 'em up (not for me, though; I'm an expert! ☺ *[Me too!* ☺☺ *– SF]*). ~ **Les Moore**

BACKLASH: OBLIVION 2 (1995) *[p.47]* – Full Moon/Pioneer's '90s laserdisc ad-line: *"It's High Noon at the End of the Universe..."* **B:O2** was released on German videocassette by Full Moon/Highlight Fiction under the anglicized title **BADLANDS**; cashing-in on an obvious source, that release's cover design incorporated a fleet of very Millennium Falcon-like spaceships plastered atop a spacey star-field background, with a facial photo-portrait of the lizardy-complexioned evil E.T. Jaggar placed front and center (thereon shown without his late "twin" brother Redeye's "eye-patch", so you can at least tell them apart— although guest vid info co-compiler Les Moore's wiseass remarks in his reviews of the *O* duo and their attendant picture captions about how identical the alien villains look do pretty much still hold true, so don't go getting all nitpicky on us about petty details, okay [that's *our* job! ☺]). The film was also released to German telly under another Anglo title, **GALAXY HUNTER**. (See also our separate **OBLIVION** entry below.)

BASKET CASE 2 (1990) *[p.68]* + **BASKET CASE 3: THE PROGENY** (1991) *[p.70]* – Polygram Video/Medusa Pictures' 1990s UK Beta/ VHS tape tagline for *BC2*: *"We were cut apart AND NOW...we're together again! This time he's not alone."* Tagline for *BC3*: *"It's Time To Build A Bigger Basket!"* – Without doubt two of the best video options open to diehard fans (wherever they may be!) of these the two lesser *BC* sequels are Synapse Films' 2007 Blu-ray editions. Another mighty fine option is Second Sight Films' Region-Free steelbook Blu-ray set *Basket Case: The Trilogy*, which comes with a whole basketful of extras (it has also been released by SS as a Region 2 DVD set). Said extras include: the making-of feature "What's in the Basket?" an overview of

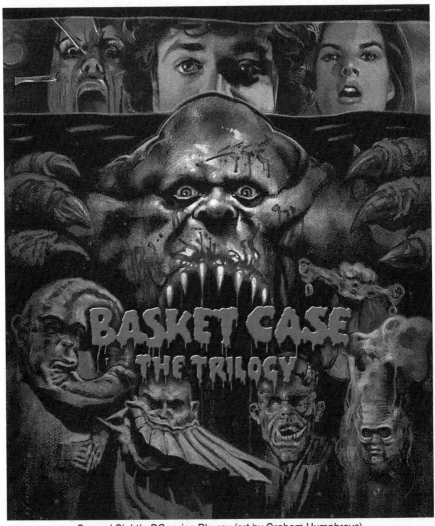

Second Sight's *BC* series Blu-ray (art by Graham Humphreys)

the series' production history, featuring first-hand reminiscences by Henenlotter, along with actors Kevin Van Hentenryck ("Duane"), Beverly Bonner ("Casey") and Annie Ross ("Granny Ruth"), as well as those from producers James Glickenhaus and Edgar Ievins, plus same from writer "Uncle" Bob Martin and makeup effects artists John Caglione, Jr., Kevin Haney and Gabe Bartalos; Henenlotter, Ievins and Bonner also contribute an audio commentary; plus there's the video short "The Hotel Broslin" (2001), and other features besides. As with same director Henenlotter's originator, the vastly superior **BASKET CASE** (1982, USA)—which is a true original, brimming with twisted wit and inventiveness—both follow-

ups have been released in the whole plethora of standard formats (including Beta/VHS, laserdisc, DVD) since their initial releases, which we won't go into here to conserve space, simply because innumerable options are easy enough to come by all over the place, both online and off. For soundtrack buffs, there's composer Joe Renzetti's *BC2* score, coupled with his one for Henenlotter's **FRANKENHOOKER** (1990, USA), which was originally released on vinyl and CD by Silva Screen Records in 1990. Just this past July, the Ship to Shore PhonoCo. record label reissued the two films' scores as LPs (respectively pressed on red-and-black-splotched and opaque purple vinyl) in a limited edition of just 1000 copies (500 of each).

BLOOD MASSACRE (1988/1991) *[p.211]* – Seen wearing a khaki combat jacket throughout and looking a lot more rough'n'ready than in his usual roles, cast top-liner Geo. Stover ("I don't *have* any friends" [no wonder, ya nutjob!]) looks suitably skeezy, sweaty and desperate as Rizzo, a mentally-addled, misanthropic, wound-way-too-tight Vietnam veteran who has an axe—not to mention a switchblade ("Is *that* all you can get-up?!")—to grind with the whole of humanity, but women especially. After conspiring to commit an armed robbery (with homicide) in the big smoke, Stover as Rizzo and his lowlife partners-in-crime hole-up out in the sticks, not realizing that the Parkers, a family of poor country folk whose home they invade and take hostage, are actually a bunch of cannibalistic psychopaths with a hankering for human meat. One by one, the lowlifes fall afoul of the cannibals, who are far more sicko and violent than the common criminals are. Appearing as the matriarch of the cannibal clan is Anne Frith (who had played Stover's auntie, Dr. Ruth, in **THE ALIEN FACTOR** [see separate entry above]; that film's main makeup men, John Cosentino and Larry Schlechter, as well as Dohler himself, perform similar functions here, only in this case there aren't any kooky alien monsters to be had). Splatter scenes include a single-swing'n'slice beheading by sickle, an in-through-the-front-and-out-through-the-back stomach-staking, plus some tastefully restrained (!) gut-munching. In a cute bit self-promotion, a scene at a video store—one of whose counter clerks is played by Don "FIEND" Leifert—includes shots of rental tapes of Dohler flicks (including **NIGHTBEAST** [see separate entry below]) arrayed on the shelves.

It's pretty easy to tell that **BLOOD MASSACRE** was never properly finished, as this fact really shows during some moments of time-filler "freestyle" editing in which random images from elsewhere in the narrative are strung together to form manic montages of rapid-fire imagery, intercut with sundry C/U's of star Stover's psychotically glaring facial features, for no apparent reason other than to reemphasize his character's already well-established mental instability. For **BM**'s unexpected big "ironic" twist/role-reversal during its final act, Stover's slobbering sociopath Rizzo uses jungle guerrilla warfare tactics he picked up in the 'Nam (including explosive booby-traps and other jerry-rigged weaponry) to put paid to the cannibal crazies, next to whose antisocial antics his own appear positively mild by comparison. (*ATTENTION: SPOILER ALERT!) However, in an even stranger twist still that is reminiscent of something straight out of an EC Comics "revenge from beyond the grave" scenario, the family members he has just killed—*surprise, surprise!!*—return to life, tear off their regular human faces to reveal those of ghastly greyish ghouls beneath, then proceed to gleefully slaughter Stover in turn by stabbing him with sharp implements while he dangles suspended ([quote] "well-hung") from a tree upside-down by one of his own accidentally self-activated deadfall/leg-hold snares! Hence, all our expectations that **BM** *isn't* going to be a monster movie are ultimately proven wrong when, in its final minutes, it *does* indeed actually prove to be one after all. And to think that Tim & Steve thought they might have to cut it out of the mag because, neither of them having seen it, they incorrectly assumed it was just a "standard" psycho/slasher shocker! That said, **BM** has been comped in a 6-movie DVD collection containing fare which definitely doesn't appear to fit *Monster!*'s rigorous content criteria: for Pendulum Pictures' box set collectively entitled *Serial Psychos*, **BLOOD MASSACRE** is listed first on the front cover above five other presumably more formulaic serial killer/slasher movies (whose titles, just for the record, are: **THIRTEEN, HIP HOP LOCOS, LAS VEGAS BLOOD BATH, I HATE YOU** and **SLASHER**). ~ Les Moore

CLASH OF THE TITANS (1981) *[p.189]* – Currently available on both Blu-ray and DVD from Warner Home Video. In 2012, Warners also released it in the same two disc formats as a twofer, double-billed as the second feature to the redundant CG-overkill 2010 remake; they subsequently (in 2015) reissued both films as a threesome along with the remake's first sequel thus far, **WRATH OF THE TITANS** (2012, D: Jonathan Liebesman). Care of Warner Bros., it is currently on offer streaming VOD on Amazon as an insta-vid, in HD only (for sale @ $7.99 and $3.99 for rent). During the '80s, it was issued on domestic (and Canadian/Australian, etc.) Betamax/VHS cassettes by MGM/UA Home Video, who also put it out on laserdisc circa the '90s. Its sweeping Laurence Rosenthal score was issued on both vinyl and CD by Columbia/PEG.

DEAD RISING: WATCHTOWER (2015) *[p.79]* – On domestic DVD (but as yet evidently not Blu-ray [?]) from Sony Pictures Home Entertainment, it's also out on Region A/1 Blu/DVD in Canada from No Equal Entertainment, in the same two formats via Animatsu Entertainment in the UK, and on Australian DVD (and Blu?) from Anchor Bay Entertainment. A limited edition of 1000 units only was released on Region B (UK import) steelbook Blu-ray by Platform Entertainment. The film is available to stream VOD over the internet from any number of the usual sources, including

Crackle. Its recent equally entertaining sequel, **DEAD RISING: ENDGAME** (2016, USA, D: Pat Williams), is set for domestic release on disc this coming December 6th.

FIEND (1980) *[p.208]* – Yet another Cinemagic Visual Effects stalwart/standard, which seemed to be all over upper North American vid-store shelves back in the '80s/'90s (but we can only wonder at how many times it ever actually got *rented* by anyone, and how many of its renters genuinely enjoyed it, assuming they even watched the whole thing before taking it back and angrily demanding a refund! Serves 'em right for judging a vid by its cover!). A glowing scarlet ectoplasmic spirit (vaguely lobster-like in shape, but ethereal in substance) floats into Seville County's heavily-populated graveyard, where it first drifts down to hover above then becomes absorbed into the earth covering one of the graves, which "just happens" to be occupied by the cadaver of one Eric Longfellow (who, now newly reanimated, is shortly revealed to be played by frequent Don Dohler casting choice Don Leifert, albeit here initially seen with an all-over red luminescence c/o the cut-price if nonetheless effective optical FX). This simultaneously cheesy and effectively eerie prologue segues into the first kill sequence, wherein Leifert as Longfellow, appearing very zombie-like and decomposed indeed under a thick layer of pallid and peeling latex skin, proceeds to fatally throttle a young woman who had been making-out with her since-temporarily-absent BF upon one of the sepulchers (talk about a sexy spot to smooch!). Having absorbed his first victim's life essence thusly, Longfellow becomes instantly revivified back to his old (i.e., 38ish-to-middleaged self) again, complete with fittingly funereal all-black attire, his head and facial hair heavily-dyed to match (as well as further emphasize his "rejuvenated" appearance); oh yes, and he also keeps a pet cat called Dorian, which is black as opposed to gray. In order to maintain his "boyish" good looks (!), true to trope Longfellow must periodically top-up his own frequently wavering life-force with infusions of those stolen from a constant succession of fresh victims, who expire as a result. Tom Griffith, leading man of both **THE ALIEN FACTOR** and **NIGHTBEAST** (see separate alphabetical entries above and below for both those titles) here fills a tertiary heroic capacity as an incidental bystander who rushes to the rescue of a young woman whom Leifert's Longfellow molests in the woods; for which Griffith's courageously impetuous character promptly gets ingloriously strangulated to death by the eponymous so-called "fiend" (who *is* rather fiendish at that. He even breaks the neck of a prepubescent girl at one point, albeit firmly

off-screen). Cast to more usual type here than he later was for **BLOOD MASSACRE** (see separate entry above), Geo. Stover appears as Longfellow's fawning nebbish/milquetoast associate, Dennis Frye, who not unsurprisingly falls victim to the grip of the undead strangler long before the final reel rolls around. (*ATTENTION: SPOILER ALERT!*) After the evil entity inhabiting Longfellow is forcibly ousted from his body via a combination of supernatural means and a sharp metal implement (i.e., a sword), he becomes a harmless, lifeless withered human husk once again.

I must admit I do rather like the offbeat vibe that the increasingly jowly and puffy-eyelidded, hangdog-featured Leifert gives off here, right down to his stilted, amateur theatre-style line delivery; oh yes, and let's not forget that stylin' post-'70s-style drop-handlebar upper lip-warmer, which is roughly the same size as both his sizeable sideburns combined, with hair to spare. On strength of his broadly-played, sinisterly civil performance herein, I can totally picture the actor playing lead villainous parts in hoary mystery/horror melodramas along similar lines as one of my long-time favorite performers, the long-late-but-still-great—if largely woefully unsung—British actor, Tod Slaughter (1885-1956). While these two actors, born generations and whole continents apart in entirely different centuries from one another, share no real physical resemblance whatsoever, it's a cinch imagining Leifert, with his *"faux*/pseudo-Limey" Maryland accent, hamming it up to the rafters in over-the-top roles like Sweeney Todd, Stephen Hawke, Sir Percival Glyde, or as the skirt-chasing squirrelly Squire Wm. Corder in **MARIA MARTEN, OR THE MURDER IN THE RED BARN** (1935, UK, D: Milton Rosmer)! As for **FIEND**, unlike some DD movies, it actually runs full feature-length at over 90 minutes, which allows the writer-director ample time for establishing mood and character development, and it boasts some of its casts' finest and most naturalistic portrayals of all. And who can forget the unintentionally (?) amusing moment when Longfellow's visiting male neighbor, while awkwardly trying to make small-talk, off-handedly compliments his host's musical instrument ("Nice *organ*!" [Guess you had to be there]). Paul Woznicki's electronica score, while at times a tad overbearing, often adds greatly to the overall eeriness of the proceedings. ~ **Les Moore**

Regarding **FIEND**'s video info, we've allowed Les to take the easy route and simply reprint practically verbatim what we ran about it in conjunction with Michael Hauss' earlier appraisal of the same film back in *Monster! #24* (p.39)... Prism's tagline: *"Super-Strangler Strikes in*

Suburbia!" Under its original title, this decidedly humble horror offering was put out on domestic NTSC Betamax/VHS cassette by the prolific Prism Video back in 1985 (on their packaging the film itself was copyrighted 1983, when in actuality it had been made some three years earlier). Also during the '80s, the Video-Huset A.S (VH) label of Norway put it out in the same tape formats, with its original English dialogue and Norwegian subtitles. Retitled **DEADLY NEIGHBOR** (adline: *"Suburban housewives are his prey... "*) and duped in the dreaded LP ("long-play" [4-hour speed ⊗]) mode, the film was reissued on VHS by Video Communications, Inc. (of Tulsa, Oklahoma) in 1992. F.O. Ray's budget outfit Retromedia later released it on DVD as a so-called "Special Collectors [sic] Edition".

THE FOREST (2016) *[p.87]* – Available on domestic DVD from Gramercy Pictures, as well as from the same distributor to stream VOD as an HD-only Amazon insta-vid (for sale only @ $12.99).

THE GALAXY INVADER (1985) *[p.210]* – United's 1980s home video ad-line: *"It Came From A Galaxy Far, Far Away, An Alien Explorer—It's* [sic] *Mission... TO SURVIVE!"* Opening with an economically fleeting optical effect depicting what appears to be a flaming meteorite ("fireball") entering Earth's atmosphere from out of deep space, this is yet another of "D.I.Y." Dohler's affectionate homages/throwbacks to 'Fifties monster sci-fi flicks. Skullface-masked, woolly-pelted suit worn by Glenn Barnes, the herky-jerky handheld camera P.O.V. of **TGI**'s eponymous extraterrestrial ("...a spaceman from Mars or something") as it prowls around is ominously accompanied by the sounds of heavy breathing on the audio track. Long-time DD trouper/zinehead Geo. Stover here plays the part of JJ Montague, the eldest son in a dysfunctional family of poor white trash country folk who for the large part make the average guest on *Jerry Springer* seem positively demure by comparison. Puffing on a big stogie and sucking on a can of Budweiser under a black cowboy hat while affecting a *faux* "Texan" drawl, Don Leifert (here virtually unrecognizable from his other roles) really gives it his all—stretching his acting talent to its very limit, in fact—as Frank Custer, a fast-talking huckster/entrepreneur ("bum and crook") who hopes to bring the alien in alive and turn a tidy profit by selling it off to the highest bidder. After JJ and his spindly, pot-bellied pa "Paw" (top-billed shameless over-actor Richard Ruxton, seen wearing a custom-ripped, filthy "white" wife-beater throughout) find and make off with its (for wont of a better term) "glowing

power sphere", the creature stuns JJ out cold with a zap to the solar plexus from its cattle-prod/Tazer gizmo, then reclaims its stolen property. Under Custer's command, the Montague menfolk and other local men hunt it by night out in the woods, intent on running the apparent monster to ground then capturing it. The alien responds to their gunfire in self-defense by picking-off the human shooters one at a time with its spark-shooting hi-tech (!) zipgun. However, the humans succeed in overpowering the creature—informally dubbed "the green man"—and take it prisoner. With it now in captivity—if left unattended and only flimsily bound, stupidly enough!—Paw and JJ concoct a scheme to make a killing off its "devastating" ray-pistol ("I bet the Russians'd pay a *million dollars* for this!"). JJ's ma ("Maw") is portrayed by regular Dohler performer Anne Frith (1928-2007), who is about the most level-headed and least-trashy of the Montague clan. Although Frith played various different characters within the Dohler canon, most of them are essentially the *same* character; i.e., sensible, practical and likeably no-nonsense/take-charge women—even her maternal figurehead of a family of cannibalistic creeps in **BLOOD MASSACRE** (see separate entry above)!—and we get the distinct impression that the actress was probably of much the same staunch and sturdy character herself in real-life. Having sprouted a whole lot taller some five years on from **FIEND** (see separate entry above), director Dohler's son Greg (a future real-life photojournalist) has since grown into late adolescence/young adulthood, although his acting hasn't improved much in the interim; Greg's genuine younger sister Kim Dohler (likewise seen in **FIEND**) also gets a part herein as Stover's onscreen baby sis, Annie. Along with fellow DD acting alum Dick Dyszel as conscientious scientist Dr. William Tracy, Greg Dohler endeavors to rescue the stranded intergalactic traveler before the trigger-happy guntards get to him first. (*ATTENTION: SPOILER ALERT!*) It doesn't end well for a substantial number of **TGI**'s supporting cast, including the poor marooned Galaxy Invader itself. Indeed, the closing scenes of "nihilistic excess" (at least by Dohler standards) have an almost (*very* almost)—dare I say—"Peckinpahesque" ring to their tragedy, and the sensitively maudlin music heard behind the closing credits immediately following the downbeat resolution really milks it for poignancy. First issued by them back in 1987, **TGI** was formerly available on domestic Betamax and VHS cassettes via United Home Video; VCI Home Video also put it out on tape. Domestic DVD editions have been released by Synergy Entertainment, Alpha Video Distributors and Mill Creek Entertainment. ~ **Les Moore**

GODZILLA 1984 US Blu-ray

Anchor Bay Entertainment released the alternate US version on both VHS (in 1997) and DVD (in 2003). By far the best way to go for this title domestically is Kraken Releasing's only-recently-released Blu-ray of the original uncut/unedited Japanese version (*sans* the US insert scenes with Raymond Burr), bearing the slightly altered Anglo title of **GODZILLA 1984** (ad-lines: *"For The First Time In North America! The Uncut and Uncensored Original Epic!"*), which comes with both English-dubbed and Japanese audio track options, with optional English soft-subs.

GODZILLA 1985 (1984) *[p.84]* – Kraken's deluxe Blu-ray cover-blurb: *"A New Era In Giant Monster History Begins!"* Originally released stateside back in the mid-'80s on both Beta and VHS tape by New World Video, and later (in 1992) released on tape by Starmaker Video, during the same general period (i.e., late '90s/early '90s), it was released on laserdisc by Image Entertainment.

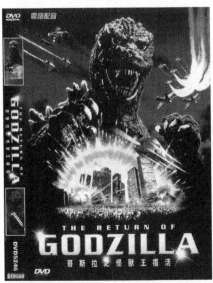

This 2000s Toronto Chinatown bootleg DVD-R c/o the Triads came with English subs and cost a mere 2 bucks Canuck (...no, *of course* I didn't buy one! *[wink]* ~SF

THE GORGON (1964) *[p.187]* – This past September, temporary licensers Mill Creek Entertainment put out this as the bottom half of a "Hammer Films Double Feature" in a pairing with **THE TWO FACES OF DR. JEKYLL** (1960, USA, D: Terence Fisher). While this edition comes with no special features, the transfer prints are apparently more than presentable according to at least one customer review on Amazon. In 2015, Mill Creek also packaged the present film in their 5-film DVD box set entitled *Hammer Films Collection Volume One*, along with the aforementioned **THE TWO FACES OF DR. JEKYLL**, plus the unfairly much-maligned **THE CURSE OF THE MUMMY'S TOMB** (1964, D: Michael Carreras), **TASTE OF FEAR** (under its US release title **SCREAM OF FEAR**, 1961, D: Seth Holt), and the lesser-known/seen thriller **STOP ME BEFORE I KILL!** (1961, D: Val Guest). The present title was formerly extant in a whole plethora of incarnations, including on British Beta/VHS cassette via Columbia Tristar Home Video/Encore Entertainment and in the same tape formats from RCA/Columbia Home Video here in the States. As part of Sony Pictures Home Entertainment's 2008 nice-priced DVD box set *Icons of Horror Collection: Hammer Films*, **THE GORGON** was packaged with all of those previously-cited titles, minus that last-listed one.

GROTESQUE (1988) *[p.74]* – Originally released stateside on Beta/VHS by Media Home Entertainment the year it was produced, if you can't track down a copy of that long-OOP and now rare tape and would like to see it after reading Eric M's fond review here in *M!* #31, there is a passably watchable rip from it uploaded on YouTube at the channel of one Kamis Nascimento, in English but with hard-coded Portuguese subtitles. *Better than nothing!*

THE GUYRA GHOST MYSTERY (1921) *[p.101]* – *Monster!* believes that chances are there's a far greater likelihood of Lon Chaney/ Tod Browning's long-lost Horrorwood shocker

Top Left: *Good Golly Miss Gorgon!* 妖女ゴーゴン – RCA's 1985 Japanese VHS jacket for **THE GORGON** (1964). **Top Right:** Late '80s Japanese VHS jacket for **GROTESQUE**. **Above:** Good Times' 1988 US budget VHS tape was recorded in cheapskate LP mode, to cut costs

This Indian lobby card "reimagines" a detail of **GROTESQUE**'s poster artwork (at right)

LONDON AFTER MIDNIGHT (1927) being rediscovered after all these decades than there are of this currently well-extinct title ever seeing the light of a projector again. Odds are also good (i.e., exceedingly bad) that **THE FACE AT THE WINDOW** (1919, Australia), the even earlier film from which **TGGM** "borrowed" its goofy monster mask, has likewise long since gone the way of

![Mutilations DVD cover]

The alternate flipside to Massacre's 2016 US DVD jacket (see also p.43)

the dodo and the dinos, too. But at least one still from the latter lost horror remains extant (see p.110+112), so that's definitely better than nothing, and it does give us a glint of a glimmer of a glimpse at how **TGGM** *might* have looked, at least in part.

HISSS (2010) *[p.58]* – Venus Video/SplitImage's Telugu VCD version (now OOP) came with optional Hindi, Telugu and English audio (no subs); I have no idea if Venus released a DVD edition as well. The Shemaroo/Venus release of the film came Hindi-dubbed—well, the English sections did, at least—and with English subtitles. Shemaroo released this as both a separate VCD and DVD (complete with a making-of featurette), and also as part of numerous DVD "3-in-1" sets (which don't have subtitles, and neither does the VCD). This version is still in print and easy enough to obtain. ~ **TP**

MUTILATIONS (1986) *[p.41]* – Dialogue quote: *"It was once a* cow. *But now it's* something else. *Something mutilated, mutated... something* half-eaten*!"* Originally released on domestic VHS by Baron Video, a label put together specifically for this film, it's almost impossible to find nowadays, except via going the torrent route, but thanks to the good folks at Massacre Video, it's now become much more easily accessible on both DVD and—just for old times' sake—VHS too. Released earlier this year, Massacre Video have decked out their disc release with all sorts of extras including an audio commentary with director Lawrence Thomas; "Yesterday's Biscuits: a MUTILATIONS Retrospective" is a 40-minute documentary featuring interviews with the director, actress Shelly Reynolds (a.k.a. Shelly Creel) and Norman Hixenbaugh, the "one-man army in the camera crew". Thomas discusses some of his inspirations, including such prototypical alien invasion flicks as Byron Haskin's **THE WAR OF THE WORLDS** (1953) and Fred F. Sears' **EARTH VS. THE FLYING SAUCERS** (1956, both USA); how the film was shot on 16mm and edited on tape, which was a "financial decision", but which worked-out well in the end; the enormous contributions of sound designer Bill Belknap and Edwin L. Robinson's synth score; and the strange connection to the Mormons, which, according to Lawrence was "in no way subversive to the Mormon religion". Other extras include an original local TV interview with Thomas from 1986; bloopers and behind-the-scenes footage; an image gallery with stills, storyboards and more; a DVD-ROM of the original script and trailers for some of Massacre Video's other product. Massacre Video also issued this in a very limited, collectible VHS housed in an oversized clamshell case, which is currently out-of-print. ~ **Dennis Capicik**

I thought the oddly charismatic drawlin' middle-aged bubba in the diner *[Charley Hill, played by Harvey Shell – ed.]* who affectionately pats his trusty sidearm in its hip holster should've been the star of the show! Him and the diner proprietor *[Buck Jenson, played by Bill Buckner – ed.]*, who were among the few cast members to display any real shred of acting talent or personality (it's a cinch picturing them both as 'shine-runners in a hixploitation movie from the '70s! Such as Gus Trikonis' **MOONSHINE COUNTY EXPRESS** [1977, USA], say. *[Speaking of which, check out my good bud Dennis Capicik's review of Code Red's recent Blu-ray of that flick at his fine cult/trash movie blog Unpopped Cinema (@ www. unpoppedcinema.blogspot.ca); howzat for a blatantly opportunistic plug! – SF.]* Unfortunately, both these fellers only appear in two scenes during **MUTILATIONS**. Amusingly and surreally enough, the "kids'" (!) pedantic prof Jim McFarland, played by Al Baker, seems to be existing in a different dimension entirely than the rest of the cast, lost in his own little world; rather like he might have been so intently concentrating on delivering his lines "properly" (note quotes) that he wasn't able to expend extra concentration on ensuring his considerable contributions to the dialogue were properly integrated into the normal flow of reality…whatever little of *that* is to be had in such a right-out-to-lunch concoction as this! Definitely one to watch again…hell, at not much more than an hour long, you can nearly watch it twice in the time it takes to sit through the average Hollywood blockbuster. ~ **Les Moore**

NEUTRON series (1960) *[p.148]* – One of the very first VHS tapes I ever purchased back in the late '80s (after switching from Betamax) was

Japanese DVD jacket for **HISSS**

243

Sinister Cinema's copy of **NEUTRON AGAINST THE DEATH ROBOTS** *[p.160]*, whereafter I also ordered Sinister copies of both **NEUTRON AND THE BLACK MASK** *[p.151]* and **NEUTRON VS. THE AMAZING DR. CARONTE** *[p.156]* too, all of whose masters were struck from scratchy old English-dubbed US TV prints (none of the films received theatrical releases in the US). I haven't been able to determine yet whether Sinister has ever offered the films in DVD-R versions, possibly duped from digitally remastered all-new transfer prints (I think that might be too much to hope for, somehow! But by all means correct me if I'm wrong). As of this writing, there was an upload of what is quite likely a rip of one of Sinister's old VHS tapes of said **AMAZING DR. CARONTE** on YT (@ *https://www.youtube.com/watch?v=5hvY-znpv5Y*), which, unfortunately, appears to be the only Anglicized dub of the three on the site at present. However, there are rips of the original Spanish-language Mexican versions of the entire trilogy thereon at the AyalaVideo CanalTV channel (@ *https://www.youtube.com/channel/UC3EHVub-lWPrB0C_InJniCQ*), which has all sorts of other Mexploitation-related content of interest at it too. The same channel also offers *en español*-only copies of the other 2 films in the legit Newt series, **NEUTRON VS. THE MANIAC** *[p.171]* and **NEUTRON VS. THE KARATE ASSASSINS** *[p.174]* under their original Mexican titles (which are, respectively, **NEUTRÓN CONTRA EL CRIMINAL SADICO** and **NEUTRÓN CONTRA LOS ASESINOS DEL KARATE**), as well as **EL ENMASCARADO DE ORO CONTRA EL ASESINO**, the alternate Mex title of the so-called "sixth" series entry allegedly (?) known in an English-dubbed version as **NEUTRON TRAPS THE INVISIBLE KILLERS** *[p.175]*. As for the *Neutróns*' availability on Mexican disc, the first, last and fifth films are on offer as a budget three-pack ("*3en1*") DVD set as part of the *Colección México en Pantalla* series, in Spanish only. The same company has also released the same and other titles in the *N* series singly/separately on DVD. The dreaded RiffTrax also offer "fucked-around-with" versions of at least one of the films on DVD, but one glance at the utterly HIDEOUS

Sinister's 1980s Neutron tapes

jacket "design" (*GAG!!!*) was enough for me not to give a shit...not that I would have even if it did come with an even quasi-presentable cover. They clearly know next-to-nothing about both *lucha libre* culture and masked wrestling movies in general, judging by the error-filled "hype" on its back cover, which makes the whole dubious thing seem that much more condescending. *Pass!* ~ **SF**

THE NIGHT OF MEDUSA (2016) *[p.191]* – A trailer blurb proudly announces: *"The 10th Film By Joshua Kennedy."* This latest D.I.Y. JK opus is out on disc as part of Alpha Video's ongoing Alpha New Cinema line, double-billed with **SLAVE GIRLS ON THE MOON** (2014, USA); as of this writing (Nov. 12), it was on offer from Alpha (@ *www. oldies.com*) marked-down to a mere $5.95 (from its usual full list price of $9.98). For a preview of other Joshua Kennedy/Gooey Film Productions' goodies, check out the YT channel bearing his name, whose uploads include the promo reel *The Gooey Film Legacy (2010-2016)*, plus trailers for his other fun homemade video features, including **ATTACK OF THE OCTOPUS PEOPLE** (2010), **CURSE OF THE INSECT WOMAN** (2011), **VOYAGE TO THE PLANET OF TEENAGE CAVEWOMEN** (2012) and **THE VESUVIUS XPERIMENT** (2015).

NIGHT OF THE LIVING BABES (1987) *[p.54]* – A rip of this title struck from its original domestic videotape source (the late '80s Beta/ VHS cassette from Magnum Entertainment) was formerly uploaded to YouTube, but since seems to have been taken down—somebody actually bothered to copyright such rot?!—although there are a number of false links to uploads there. Odds art that those who are desperate enough to see it to want to bother going out of their way to track down a copy know better than we do where one might be found. You're on your own on this one, peeps! ☺

NIGHTBEAST (1982) *[p.209]* – Troma Video tagline: *"If You Have The Guts—He Wants Them!!!"* VIPCO's Brit cassette tagline: *"His Hands* [why not the more logical '*Claws*' instead? – ed.] *Tear Through Flesh And Bone!"* Opening much akin to both Don Dohler's **THE ALIEN FACTOR** and **THE GALAXY INVADER** (see separate entries above), the present title depicts a UFO alighting to Earth somewhere in the Maryland wilderness. A direct link to the former of those two titles just cited is provided by two of its same principal cast members, Tom Griffith and Richard Geiwitz (who also served as DP on it and other DD efforts), reprising their earlier roles from **TAF**, namely Sheriff Jack Cinder (sporting

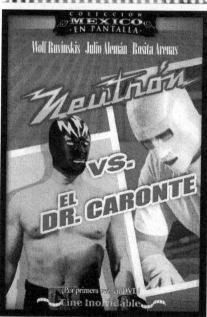

Top: Mexican Neutron DVD 3-in-1 set. **Above:** Mexican DVD cover for **NEUTRON VS. THE AMAZING DR. CARONTE** (in Spanish only)

a "with-it" new spring-curled silver-grey perm for the occasion!) and Deputy Pete (who gets killed-off this time out), respectively. While **TAF** had contained a combination of both malignant—or rather just plain viciously bestial, like animals—and benignant creatures from other worlds and **TGI**'s eponymous alien was benevolent but misunderstood to be malevolent in nature, the **NIGHTBEAST** is an out-and-out *nasty* invasive species, for sure. Vaguely—*very-very* vaguely—**ALIEN**esque, without provocation, it starts zapping local yokels dead with its disintegrator raygun, which turns its targets first into flashily-colored optical FX before then reducing them to blackened human-shaped outlines of cinders. After Shf. Cinder and his posse get pinned-down in a late-night firefight with the alien ("Guns have no effect on that thing!"), it barrages them with enough cheesy optically-printed energy beams to turn a cheapo "Al Bradley"/Alfonso Brescia Italian **STAR WARS** rip-off green with envy. We get loads of pointless gunplay elsewhere too, with plentiful firearms being discharged whose shooters seldom seem to hit what they're at shooting at (at least *attempting* to aim straight might help!).

Don Leifert (who played Ben Zachary in **TAF**) got cast as an "all-new" character named Drago for this go-round, although he doesn't really factor into the main plotline in any major way at all, and is seemingly present just to pad things out to somewhere in the vicinity of full feature length (=80m). A loudmouthed, black-leather-jacketed and decidedly rapey greaseball biker

Troma's 2004 DVD edition

("You little slut!") who rolls up on his *faux* "hog" (i.e., Kawasaki) at right around the half-hour mark, Drago has bad news written all over him right from frame one, and in sour demeanor Leifert's broadly-hammed "bad boy" routine comes across rather like an Americanized poor man's Oliver Reed. More so than Dohler's usual fare, **NIGHTBEAST** concerns itself a lot more with cheesecake (including sexy starlet Eleanor Herman as Dyszel's bimbette secretary/mistress busting-out of a one-piece swimsuit at a pool party), and even some outright flashes of nudity (c/o leading lady Karin Kardian and Monica Neff as Drago's abused ex-moll/punching-bag, who doesn't survive for long after he re-hits town with evil on his mind. In payback for her senseless strangulation, using only his bare hands, her new BF the secondary hero [Dohler newbie Jamie Zemarel] beats Drago half to death without actually going all the way, unfortunately enough). Dick Dyszel, Geo. Stover—neither of whom survive till the final fade—and Anne Frith all also reprise their characters from **TAF** herein, and performances are for the most part a marked improvement over those seen in DD's much-more-amateurish debut feature. Greg (seen wearing a souvenir T-shirt from Montréal, Québec) and Kim, Dohler's early-teenage son and preteen daughter, play a brother and sister whose onscreen Uncle Dave gets slaughtered by the beast out in the woods after dark (it *is* called the "nightbeast", after all), as well as pursuing them back to their family home to graphically shred-up their father and mother right before their eyes, too; the Dohler kids' real-life poppa once again casts himself as a tertiary character. Other incidental bit-parts are filled by Baltimore zine pioneer and long-time (from 1984 to 2004) Fanex convention organizer Gary *"Gore Creatures/Midnight Marquee"* Svehla—blink, and you'll miss him!—here making his one-and-only appearance in a Dohler production along with his brother Dick Svehla (who was also seen as a rifle-packing redneck in DD's above-noted **TGI**).

I have a copy of the All-Region DVD edition that was put out in 2004 by Troma Team Video, which is of perfectly watchable quality, and came with a few funky extras, including: a feature-length commentary by director Don Dohler, behind-the-scenes footage and outtakes/bloopers, plus the film's original theatrical trailer (yes, it actually played in theaters!), as well as "How To Rip an Arm Off", from Lloyd Kaufman's 5-disc documentary DVD box set *Make Your Own Damn Movie!* (2005), and a selection of Troma trailers. *[According to Dennis Capicik, said Troma DVD, now long-OOP, currently commands quite hefty price-tags among collectors – SF.]* The film was originally made available on domestic Beta/VHS cassette by Paragon Video Productions in 1983, and was released in Canada in the same two magnetic oxide tape formats by Premiere Entertainment International (ad-blurb: *"Nothing Can Save You Now..."*). Featuring back cover artwork pinched from Tim Hildebrandt's wicked poster for **THE DEADLY SPAWN** (1983, USA, D: Douglas McKeown), **'BEAST** was once available on Beta/VHS cassettes in the Netherlands on the Video For Pleasure (VFP) label, presented in English, with Dutch *ondertitels* (...no prizes for guessing what those are!). On a related note of trivia, there's—*big surprise!*—even a rock (*ahem*) band calling themselves Nightbeast; but why ever for, who knows. Rather than the screaming, shredding deathcore sounds which might better suit their name, the few brief snippets of their music which I subjected myself to on YouTube (I couldn't stand any more than a few seconds) reminded me of a "heavier" (note quotes) version of Barenaked Ladies. So, needless to say...*UGH!* Certainly *not* what I'd expect a band with such a name to sound like! (I can totally picture a garage punk or psychobilly act called The Nightbeasts, though. Come to think of it, there probably are at least ten or a dozen out there somewhere... and there definitely *is* at least one movie in existence called **NIGHTBEASTS** [2010, USA, D: Wes Sullivan], starring Zach "**GREMLINS**" Galligan versus a pack of monstrous hominids). ~ **Les Moore**

THE NIGHT FLIER (1996) *[p.65]* – Originally made available on both VHS videocassette and DVD by HBO Home Video in 2000, the DVD, quite surprisingly, is a fairly decent 16x9 transfer which retains the film's original 1.85:1 aspect ratio. As expected, extras are rather sparse, including the customary cast and crew bios, some notes on the film and a theatrical trailer. Sadly, this DVD is long out-of-print, but if it does get reissued (which seems a distinct possibility sooner or later, considering the Stephen King connection), hopefully it won't come with the same spoiler-ridden cover art. For those with Region 2 capabilities, **THE NIGHT FLIER** was also released on DVD in the UK in two editions. The first release came in 2002, while the second release, in 2005, was a "director's cut", but we here at *Monster!* are not aware of the differences between these two editions. Unfortunately, like its US counterpart, both UK editions are also out-of-print. ~ **Dennis Capicik**

OBLIVION (1994) *[p.45]* – Artisan Entertainment's 2002 US DVD tagline: *"Cowboys. Aliens... The Frontier Will Never Be The Same."* This movie first showed up stateside on VHS (and presumably Beta) tape via Paramount Home Video in the year it was produced ('94). As well

Top: Domestic US DVD cover. **Above:** A domestic Full Moon triple-DVD set which includes **OBLIVION** Pt. 1 + two other Band schlock sci-fi'ers. Can you identify the sources of all the different ripped-off elements of its cover art?

as Artisan's disc edition from earlier in the new millennium, we've also gotten DVD editions of this seemingly quite enduringly popular sci-fi western schlocker from both Wizard Entertainment (in 2010) and Shout! Factory (in 2011). This the first film in the *O* duo alone has also been made available as part of a domestic Full Moon triple-DVD set which includes a pair of other Charles Band-produced schlock sci-fi'ers: **LASERBLAST** (1978, USA, D: Michael Rae), co-starring Kim Milford and Cheryl "Rainbeaux" Smith (1955-2002) and **BAD CHANNELS** (1992, USA, D: Ted Nicolaou). Full Moon Features are offering **OBLIVION** VOD as an Amazon Instant Video, in the SD format only (@ $2.99 to rent or $9.99 to buy); it's currently also streamable on Hulu too (we're a poet and didn't know it!).

PRIDE AND PREJUDICE AND ZOMBIES (2016) *[p.50]* – Available on domestic Blu-ray/DVD from Sony Pictures Home Entertainment. Dialogue: *"The Four Horsemen have risen from Hell! The Zombie Apocalypse is here!"* (You wish. Talk about overstatements!) If a picture is indeed worth a thousand words, when it comes to motion pictures, sometimes a few sensationalistic words of dialogue can conjure up imagery in our mind's eyes which even many thousands of pictures all strung together could never adequately convey, let alone actually do justice to, and such is the case with that dialogue excerpt just given. I mean, how *could* a movie ever live up to such ostentatious ballyhoo?! Officially known as **P+P+Z** for short, this much-anticipated movie went totally tits-up at the box office, and, quite frankly, it's easy to see why. We can only wonder whether its commercial failure means we won't be seeing any further, hopefully much-more-imaginative "alternate literature/history" vs. monster mash-ups. We sure hope that's not the case, because the possibilities are virtually endless! (Not that, judging by how carefully **P+P+Z** connects the dots and colors between the lines, you'd think there was much wiggle-room to be had.)

Speaking personally, in regards to the film's principal cast—representatives of "The Ruling Class" one and all—I was hoping the zombies were going to chew up and spit out the whole damn lot of these overdressed toffee-nosed gits with their stiffly-starched manners and stiff upper lips! (*"Eat the rich!"* as Motörhead's late, lamented Lemmy once bellowed.) As though relative greenhorn American director Burr Steers—who has absolutely no profile whatsoever within the horror genre, I might add—would have much preferred to direct an episode of *Downton Abbey* or *Poldark* instead, the decidedly schizophrenic narrative spends *waaaayyy*

too much time on stately subterfuge and the petty, self-serving romantic aspirations of its pampered, over-privileged protagonists, who seem far more concerned with their stupid soppy love affairs than the fact that the whole world is going all to hell in a handbasket right under their (snootily turned-up) noses. The central portion really drags for these very reasons, and its distinct shortage of over-the-top zombie action for too-long stretches was probably the likeliest cause of **P+P+Z**'s poor box-office receipts rather than anything else. When an incidental character indirectly informs us—purely in the interests of sparing the producers' the cost of actually depicting it happening in even the smallest way—"All of London's fallen to the zombies," we don't believe it for an instant, because we are shown hardly any scenes at all relating to this supposedly catastrophic event. A supposed massed attack by living dead on Hingham Bridge, the nation's last bastion of defense against the horror horde, is so lamely presented that we barely see a single zombie in amongst the defending redcoat infantrymen. Literally an entire hour goes by—like molasses, I might add—with scarcely a thing of interest occurring. As for Lily James as heroine/#1 Bennet sis Elizabeth ("My courage always rises at every attempt to intimidate me" indeed!), she's real badass when she's having a teary-eyed temper tantrum and first coldcocking then beating on a guy who's too much of a chivalrous simp to smack her back like she deserves, but at times she and her prissily prim'n'proper sisters wield their dainty/girly snickersnees like they'd much rather they were Swiffer sweepers instead (or rather, in keeping with the historical period, feather-dusters). And for such limber young things supposedly well-versed in the Shaolin martial arts (!!), these little women—who pout their lips and flare their nostrils way too much in hopes of appearing more intense—sure move pretty damn *slow* most of the time! But buying their unconvincing combination hyper-feminine/masculine characters is all part of the fantasy, of course. But if you can't properly suspend your disbelief and buy into it all (such as there is to be bought), it comes across as highly self-conscious and clumsily contrived (i.e., a transparent ploy on the producers' part to exploit the trendy "women's emancipation from the stays of *[so-called]* patriarchal oppression" [or whatever; *YAWN!*] angle in hopes of luring more female punters into theaters). Now, if they'd gone whole-hog and given us plentiful scenes showing the prissy sisses giving zombies the beatdown/chopdown and hoofing 'em in the 'nads while dressed in little more than their lacy, blood-spattered skivvies, the action might have registered far, far more entertainingly than it does(n't). However, the filmmakers instead opted to play it coyly chaste, which, despite fitting the repressive Victorian context like a tailor-made whalebone corset, seems exceedingly lameola indeed in this the "Anything-Goes" age. Ironically enough, in their efforts to remain as strictly PC as can be, the makers come across like puritanical post-Victorian prudes themselves, despite laying on lashings of guts and grue (if staying well within the bounds of "acceptable taste" while doing so).

As for the film's more technical aspects, I will say that its period costumery and settings/ locations were all impeccably chosen, even if all the surface glitz and glam does rather register as an obvious attempt to camouflage the film's many shortcomings elsewhere. Again on the minus-side, in some scenes, "multi-printed" CG shots showing hordes of zombies on the rampage are so carelessly thrown together that you can plainly make out the very same extras repeated in triplicate or even quadruplicate right in the same shots together! (This conspicuous fact must have been all the more laughably obvious when viewed on a cinema screen.) The fact that virtually every last principal character of both sexes is such an imperialistic, privileged and pampered pillock/prat makes it difficult—nigh-on *impossible*, in fact— to even give a flying fuck (let alone actually root for) any of these blue-blooded bastards. Simply because there's nothing better to do, poor pacing and lackluster direction only cause you to dislike these stuck-up, hoity-toity toffs all the more; although, to be fair, Matt *"Doctor Who"* Smith does make something more of his wimpy parson character than merely a cliché, unlike most of the rest of his colleagues, who largely play it like they've got broom-handles shoved up their arses right to the colon, and they're trying their hardest to maintain a grip on them so they don't slip out. If done as a cleverly sardonic satire, P+P+Z could have made some pointed commentary on how the aristocracy/monarchy (not just in Britain but everywhere else in the world besides), while safely sequestered away in their reinforced palatial homes with servants and soldiers at their beck and call to cater to their every whim and protect them from harm, continue to thrive and prosper while the "lower" classes they lord it up over as though it's their God-given right to do so go to the dogs all around them (tellingly enough, the zombies are at one point heard referred to by an aristo arsehole as the "common hordes", indicating that working class commoners—as in we, The Great Unwashed, my brethren and sistren—make up the vast bulk of their numbers). That said, a much more truthful title for this might be "PRIDE AND PREJUDICE... OH YEAH, AND THERE'S ZOMBIES TOO", which better expresses the off-handed randomness

SHIN GOJIRA Thai poster

of the titular combination, as what should rightly be one of the main ingredients largely register as little more than an afterthought, tokenly tacked-on simply because zombies are an "in-thing" and it was expected. Definitely more cornball chickflick than gonzo zombie shocker, **P+P+Z** amounts to such a complete waste of potential (I hesitate to say celluloid) that I refuse to spend any more time on it whatsoever, and I certainly won't be watching it ever again. I had such high hopes for it, and really *wanted* to like it, but it turned out to be a real letdown. *Next!* ~ **Les Moore**

SHIN GOJIRA (2016) *[p.91]* – Following its limited US theatrical release, the film has yet to be released on domestic disc.

STRANGER THINGS (2016) *[p.131]* – This smash-hit Netflix series is still streaming thereon, but has yet to be released in disc form.

SUNDOWN – THE VAMPIRE IN RETREAT (1989) *[p.44]* – Vestron/LIVE's original videotape tagline: *"There's Two Kinds Of Folks In The Town Of Purgatory. Vampires. And Lunch."* **S-TVIR** was first released on domestic Beta/ VHS cassette in 1990 by Vestron Video/LIVE Entertainment (back cover blurb: *"They're Mean. They're Ornery. They're Vampires"*), whose box copy misspelled the name of David Carradine's vampiristic villain as Count Margulak *[sic]*, with

サンダウン

〜ボクたち、二度と血は吸いません〜

SUNDOWN 1151

Ascii Pictures' 1992 Japanese videocassette cover for **SUNDOWN**

by Silva Screen ([FILMCD 044] UK, 1990), and gathered together a total of 18 tracks, including such titles as "Mort's Duel in the Sun" (02:02), "Shane in Pursuit" (02:45), "Hell in Purgatory" (03:32) and "Showdown" (02:41). Much more recently, the exact same track list was repeated on BSX Records' ([BSXCD 8923] USA, 2013) CD reissue, which was pressed in a limited edition of just 1000 copies. A single **SUNDOWN** track, "Redemption of the Damned – Finale" (05:43), had also previously appeared on Silva America's *The Essential Vampire Theme Collection* ([SSD 1020] USA, 1993), along with one-track-only selections from 13 other bloodsucker movies, including **THE RETURN OF DRACULA** (1958, USA, D: Paul Landres; music by Gerald Fried), **VAMPIRE CIRCUS** (1972, UK, D: Robert Young; music by David Whitaker), **THIRST** (1979, Australia, D: Rod Hardy; music by Brian May), **VAMP** (1986, USA, D: Richard Wenk), **THE HUNGER** (1983, UK/USA, D: Tony Scott; music by Leo Delibes), and **CHILDREN OF THE NIGHT** (1991, USA, D: Tony Randel; music by Daniel Licht), plus 7 more tracks from as many other films besides.

VEERANA (a.k.a. **THE WILDERNESS**, 1988) *[p.7]* – Retitled **VEERANA: VENGEANCE OF THE VAMPIRE**, this landmark Indian creature feature was issued on domestic twofer DVD (*"Over Five Hours Of Monster Movie Madness"*) by Mondo Macabro in 2009, paired-up with **PURANI HAVELI: MANSION OF EVIL** (1989, Ds: Shyam Ramsay, Tulsi Ramsay), as Volume 2 in MM's much-too-short-lived "Bollywood Horror Collection"; it goes without saying (but we will anyway!) that both films came complete with English subs. Mondo's edition has been long-OOP, and copies now command inflated prices from collectors (e.g., as of this writing, there was a copy on offer at Amazon for $101.99, and another on eBay for $99.99). However, much cheaper, lower-quality copies of **VEERANA** are still readily accessible from India, albeit presented only in the film's native tongue. For instance, it is available as part of a horror quintuplet ("5-in-1") DVD set along with **SAU SAAL BAAD** (1989, D: Mohan Bhakri), **PURANI KABAR** (1998, D: K.I. Sheikh), **BHAYAANAK PANJAA** (1997, D: R. Mittal) and **KABRASTAN** (1988, a.k.a. **KABRISTAN**, D: Mohan Bhakri) on the Priya label (#PDVD-12869), without subtitles of any sort. The same company have released the present film in a number of different DVD/VCD multi-packs, including a single-disc, 3-movie set triple-billed with Shyam & Tulsi Ramsay's **SAAMRI** (1985) and (once again) **SAU SAAL BAAD**. Other combo packs are also available from Priya which include **VEERANA**. (Online retail sources for this

a "g" in place of a "d". Bearing the alternate Anglo title of simply **SUNDOWN** on its cover, the film was released on Japanese videocassette by Ascii (ASCII?) Pictures in 1992. It was released on German video as **SUNDOWN: DER RÜCKZUG DER VAMPIRE**, which is basically a German translation of its original Anglo title. Its (bootleg?) Czech DVD release is entitled **SLUNCE, ÚSVIT A UPÍŘI**, another foreign-language variation of its English title. Likely the optimal edition of this title thus far released is Lions Gate Entertainment's 2008 domestic DVD "Special Edition" (Lionsgate's same [?] transfer print is currently also up for streaming VOD on Amazon, in the HD format only ($3.99 for rental, $9.99 to purchase). The DVD version includes such special features as an audio commentary with both director Anthony Hickox and his DP on **S-TVIR**, Levie Isaacks; "A Vampire Reformed", an interview with star Carradine (who died under much-publicized bizarre circumstances in 2009, the year following the DVD's release); "Memories of Moab", an interview with co-star Bruce Campbell; plus another on-camera interview, this one with M. Emmet Walsh (who plays Mort Bisby in the film), entitled "A True Character". Composer Richard Stone's **S-TVIR** soundtrack (at a total duration of 00:50:17) was issued on CD

title in its original Hindi version [all sans subs] include *www.Induna.com* and *www.webmallindia. com*). At both the Goldmines Telefilms and Goldmines Movies channels on YouTube, there are identical full-length, English-subbed uploads of **VEERANA**, viewable *gratis*; just key the film's title into the search field, and links to those two versions should pop-up right at the top of the list. On a related note, just prior to when we went to press, a copy of the split 6-track 12" vinyl soundtrack LP (which is actually more of an EP) *Laal Paree* b/w *Veerana* (on the Venus label, an Indian subsidiary of CBS Records) was on sale at *eBay.com*; Side A of said disc features a selection of four Nadeem Shravan (lyricist: Anwar Sagar) compositions from director Hannif Chippa/Hanif Chhipa's man-meets-mermaid fantasy **LAAL PAREE** (1988 [whose release date the IMDb gives as 1991]), while Side B features a pair of Bappi Lahiri-composed tracks (with lyrics by Indivar & Anjaan) from **VEERANA**, "Sathi Mere Sathi" and "Dil Ki Dhadkan Kya Kahe".

Mondo Macabro's now-OOP-and-pricy double DVD

UK VHS

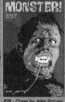

BONUS
GORGON GALLERY

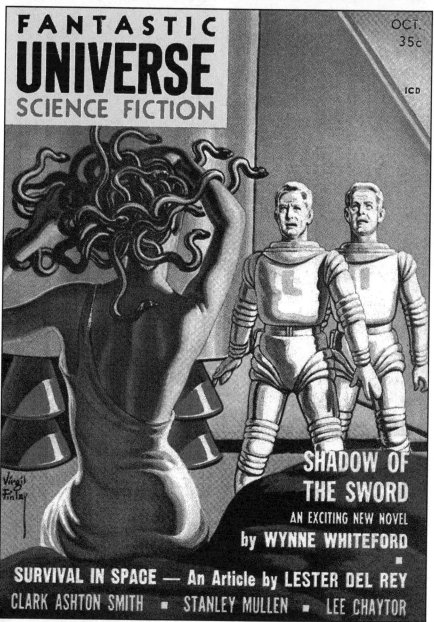

FANTASTIC
UNIVERSE
SCIENCE FICTION

OCT.
35c

ICD

SHADOW OF
THE SWORD
AN EXCITING NEW NOVEL
by WYNNE WHITEFORD

SURVIVAL IN SPACE — An Article by LESTER DEL REY
CLARK ASHTON SMITH ▪ STANLEY MULLEN ▪ LEE CHAYTOR

Virgil Finlay cover art for the Clark Ashton Smith story "Symposium of the Gorgon" (October 1958)

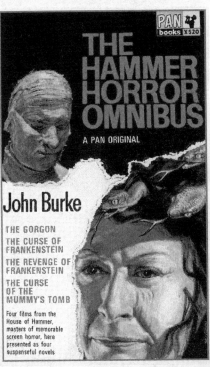

Clockwise, from Top Left: *Thrilling Wonder Stories*, Volume 25 #2 (Winter 1944), art by Rudolph Belarski; 1973 Swedish horror comic; 1st edition paperback anthology (UK, 1966), which included a short adaptation of Hammer's **THE GORGON** (1964 [see p.187]); and a Japanese horror manga from the 1980s (artist unknown)

Clockwise, from Top Left: Anglo Thai
poster for **NAAK** (ปาฏิหารย์รักต่างพันธุ์,
2008, Thailand, D: Teerawat Rujintham);
a 2001 Hong Kong DVD cover; HK VCD
cover (entitled 人蛇大戰之蛇魔轉世) for
the Thai film **DEVIL MEDUSA** (งูเก็งกอง,
1995); the Gorgon (ゴーゴン / *Gorugon*), as depicted by manga artist Gōjin Ishihara; and
a Thai poster for the Khmer film **THE SNAKE MAN** (*Puos Keng Kang / Ngu Keng Kong*,
a.k.a. **THE SNAKE KING'S WIFE**, 1970, Cambodia, D: Tea Lim Koun)

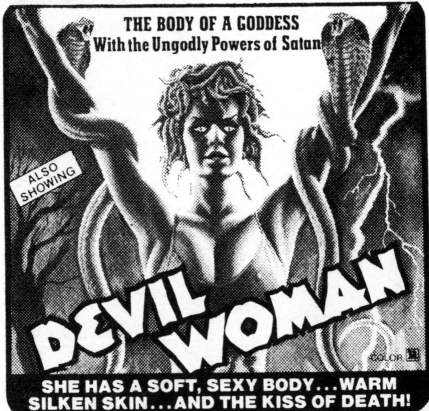

THE BODY OF A GODDESS
With the Ungodly Powers of Satan

ALSO SHOWING

DEVIL WOMAN

COLOR

SHE HAS A SOFT, SEXY BODY...WARM
SILKEN SKIN...AND THE KISS OF DEATH!

Top Left: Gloria Romero as the title character's nemesis Valentina in **LIPAD, DARNA, LIPAD!** (*"Fly, Darna, Fly!"*, Philippines, 1973) *[Image courtesy of the Video 48 blogspot].*
Top Right: Iwa Moto as the same snaky villainess on the 2009 *Darna* TV series. Above: US pressbook ad for **DEVIL WOMAN** (1970, Philippines, D: Jose Flores Sibal)

Top Left: 1904 Italian poster by Basilio Cascella for Dante Alighieri's *Divina Commedia* (1307). **Top Right:** Tandem Books horror anthology paperback edition (UK, 1971). **Above:** A still from **THE SNAKE MAN** (*Puos Keng Kang / Ngu Keng Kong*, a.k.a. **THE SNAKE KING'S WIFE**, 1970, Cambodia)

Left 3 Pics: *"Serve the Gorgon!"* The petrifying alien Abbess from *The Sarah Jane Adventures*' two-parter "Eye of the Gorgon" (S1, Eps 3+4) does her Medusa routine, albeit *sans* snakes. **Top Right:** A typically garish heavy metal album cover on the theme. **Center Right:** Marion Thompson does the snake bit in *Land of the Lost*'s (1976) "Medusa" episode. **Bottom Right:** Kira Clavell as the gorgeous gorgon of the US miniseries *Voyage of the Unicorn* (2001, D: Philip Spink)

Top: *Stone Dead!* The still-alive/active severed gorgon's head-in-a-box from "The Mask of Medusa" segment of the classic special 3-in-1 *Thriller* episode "Trio for Terror" (1961, USA, D: Ida Lupino). **Above:** Natalia Vodianova as the woeful Medusa in Louis Leterrier's 2010 **CLASH OF THE TITANS** reboot

259

Top Left: Damien Hirst's vision of singer Rihanna as Medusa. **Top Right:** A panel by Pete Morisi from his "Mask of Medusa" story in *Weird Terror* #7 (September 1953); **Above Left & Right:** John Buscema's art of Marvel's "scary-hairy" superheroine Medusa and the Jack Kirby-drawn supervillain Gorgon, her foe, with nary a serpent to be seen between the pair of 'em!

... A LIVING PORTRAIT OF HELL ITSELF!

HAAAAAAH!

N-NO!

A panel from the comics adaptation of **THE GORGON** (1964 [see p.187]), in the UK's *House of Hammer* magazine #11 (1978); written by Scott Goodall and rendered by artists Trevor Goring and Manuel Cuyás

ENDNOTE

We're not entirely certain yet what goodies shall be coming your (and our!) way in *Monster!* #32 two months or so from now. But we do know for sure that we'll have Part 1 of Steve Bissette's as-yet-untitled epic 6-part, career-spanning article on/interview with that master D.I.Y. monster moviemaker, Brett Piper himself, which is bound to be a real page-turner!

Meanwhile, Steve Fenton's kicking around the idea that he might do a belated follow-up to the "Terror of the Were-Kitties" reviews/articles he did all the way back in *M!* #'s 9+10; so, those with a jones (himself included!) for movies featuring Asiatic feline monstrosities should prepare themselves for... "Revenge of the Were-Kitties"!

Brett and monstrous pals the rat-thing from **THE DARK SLEEP** (2012) and the carnivorous plant from **TRICLOPS** (2015) *[photo courtesy of brettpiper.com]*

Contents page art: Vince Bonavoglia

Contributors: Eric Messina, Daniel Best, Michael Hauss, Dennis Capicik, John Harrison, Chris "Doc" Nersinger, Christos Mouroukis, Stephen R. Bissette, Kevin Klemm, Andy Ross, Christopher Martinez, Jonathan Clode, Martín Núñez, Kinshuk Gaur, Christopher J. Maurer, Les Moore, Brian Harris, Steve Fenton, and Tim Paxton

Timothy Paxton, Editor, Publisher & Design Demon
Steve Fenton, Editor & Info-wrangler
Tony Strauss, Edit-fiend
Brian Harris, El Publisher de Grand Poobah
Coffee/Whipping-Boy & General Scapegoat/Doormat: "Mongo" McGillicutty

37246835R00157

Made in the USA
Middletown, DE
22 November 2016